THE PUBLIC LIFE OF OUR LORD JESUS CHRIST

AN INTERPRETATION

BY

THE MOST REV. ALBAN GOODIER, S.J.

ARCHBISHOP OF HIERAPOLIS

VOLUME I

ST. PAUL EDITIONS

Mary, Immaculate Queen
of the Universe Center
P. O. Box 40025
Spokane, WA 99202

TO HIS EMINENCE
FRANCIS CARDINAL BOURNE
THIS BOOK IS DEDICATED
IN GRATITUDE
IN ESTEEM
WITH DEEP AFFECTION

Authorized American Edition

Printed in the U.S.A. by the Daughters of St. Paul
50 St. Paul's Ave., Boston, MA 02130

The Daughters of St. Paul are an international congregation of women religious serving the Church with the communications media.

TABLE OF CONTENTS

Volume I

vii

INTRODUCTION

1. Lives of Jesus Christ

SPEAKING generally, there are three main categories under which lives of Christ may be divided. There are the devotional, in which the example of Our Lord, as seen in the Gospels, is made a matter mainly of contemplation, and meditation, and of application to our own lives. Such, for the most part, are the studies and homilies of the early Fathers ; such is the earliest well-known life of Christ, the one attributed to S. Bonaventure ; in more modern times we have many more, De Ponte, S. Jure, and their followers. A second class may be called the scientific ; the class of those who would dwell on the history of Our Lord, on His circumstances and surroundings, and would study the evidences with the eyes of the critic. From the days of Origen and Tatian this class has been well known ; nevertheless it has come mainly into vogue during the last two hundred years. On the Catholic side there have not been wanting numerous writers of this class ; for example Grimm, Veuillot, Fouard, Lesêtre, and last, summing up all his predecessors, Fillion. But a third class has come out of both of these. It has reacted more or less to the first. It sees that Jesus, the Way, the Truth, and the Life, is something more than a subject for mere historical study and scientific research. It accepts all that the historians and scientists have positively to teach, but grows weary of their endless controversy, and of their attention to detail which is neither here nor there. It is in search of the living Christ, as He was yesterday, as He is to-day, and as He will be for ever. Such, perhaps, are the lives by Didon, Meschler, Delatte ; such is the marked tendency of the studies of Christ which pour out from the non-Catholic press in England in our time.

2. The Present Life

In this third class the author of the Life before us would have his attempt to be mainly considered. Often in the

ix

last forty years the author has planned its scope ; still more often he has written separate chapters and then has thrown them away ; only after a visit to the Holy Land in 1925 did the whole picture seem to come together, and to stand out as a consistent whole before him, in a way that encouraged him to face the task he had often before wished to undertake. After that visit, for more than six months, Providence left him free from other engagements, and he was able to complete the work in a first version. For a year it was left almost untouched ; then after that period of maturing it was written entirely again, with the perspective which a year is wont to provide to a writer's work. In the second writing the author's intention was to cut it down ; in matter of fact, while much was eliminated, much more was added and expanded. Writing as he was, with no limitations as to space, more for his own instruction than with a view to publication, he felt that he could be more natural, and more true to the end he had in view, by allowing his pen to run on. Throughout the years during which the two versions were written he had constantly before himself the question : What was Our Lord, as a Man, like ? What is He like to-day ?

3. Hence its Scope

This will explain the limits which the writer has imposed upon himself. Beautiful and instructive as is the story of the early and the hidden Life, teeming with matter for the theologian and the man of prayer, still it did not seem to him to yield much for his purpose, the delineating of the human character of the Man, Christ Jesus ; moreover, to draw from it what it would yield, it seemed to be full of discussions which would hamper him in his main object. It would need to be taken as a study apart, in a way that it has already been taken by a writer such as Lepin. At the other extreme, when we come to the Passion, the story is overwhelming. Though the Passion confirms in every detail the impressions received from the Public Life, still to attempt to draw it out on the same scale as the rest would expand the work to twice its size ; and to do less would be to dwarf the Passion out of all proportion. It, too, must be treated as a thing apart. For the Risen Life, the author has already elsewhere made some attempt at a description ; but the Risen Life again is unique, and must be treated as an episode apart. The present work attempts to follow Our Lord from the day when He first appeared as a full-grown Man by the Jordan, to the last evening before the Passion, that is, to the day before the Last Supper. It is an attempt at a biography, founded on a harmony which has seemed to the author to be most in accordance with the facts as the Gospels give them to us. In that biography the personality of the central Figure has been made to dominate all else. For the rest, the writer has tried to describe the events as they seemed to him to have actually taken place.

4. The Evidence of the Evangelists

Hence in a work of this kind it has not seemed necessary to introduce any discussion concerning the four Evangelists, the authenticity of their work, or the special characteristics of each. These have been examined and proved by writers far more skilled and learned than the author, and he is content to accept their decision, referring readers who would examine these sources to them. On the other hand, when accepting the Gospels, he accepts them wholly and entirely. It seems to him a futile attitude of mind to take a source as authentic, and then, almost entirely from internal evidence, to proceed to whittle it away. For instance, let us take the miracles. Not only do the four Evangelists record them, but they record them as an essential part of their evidence ; so essential, in every case, that if they are eliminated their whole concept of Jesus tumbles to ruins. There is scarcely any miracle which may be cancelled without involving in its fall many other portions of the Gospel ; eliminate them all, and there is virtually nothing left. Far more fair to the facts, even from the point of view of the rationalist historian, does it seem to the author to take the evidence as he finds it, make of it the best he can, put faith in those whom he professes to acknowledge as his only safe guides, build up his picture of Jesus as they have built it up and with the same material. If he accepts some evidence and rejects the rest, this at least he must confess ; that the conclusion he draws, whether true or not, cannot possibly be the picture drawn by the four Evangelists. In the present work the four Gospels have been taken simply as they are given to us ; the question has been simply asked : What is the Jesus of the four Evangelists like ?

5. The Gospel Text

Another problem which presents itself to anyone who would write a Life of Our Lord in English is the question of the text to be used. Again and again he is aware that he is dealing with disputed sentences ; still more often he is painfully alive to the fact that the English version at his hand does not accurately reproduce the original text. Still, if he does not wish to be drawn aside from his main purpose he must pass these problems by. Their discussion may be found elsewhere, far more learned than he can hope to write ; to pause at them would only hinder the narrative, besides making the whole work hopelessly long. Moreover, even when all these passages and single words are put together, their influence on the whole is small. The author, therefore, has been content to take the Douay Version as he finds it, upon it to build his harmony, and to quote from it the verses which he knows will be most familiar to Catholic readers. He has very seldom delayed to discuss a text ; he has seldom substituted a translation of his own. Though this has involved many disadvantages, the missing of illustrative details, the wrong interpretation of words, still he has preferred to cling to the main object in view. He has seen in other works how a life of Christ, thanks to these apparently necessary digressions, has gradually degenerated into a Scripture commentary, and he has feared to be led along the same direction. As with the Evangelists themselves, so with the Douay Version ; for the sake of the main intention he has had in mind, he has accepted it as he has found it.

6. Historical Questions

The same is to be said of many historical and biographical discussions which the biographer of Our Lord must consider. There are many books which the author has not read and, perhaps, ought to have read. Still he hopes that there are few questions which he has not considered and studied, sufficiently at least for his purpose. If at times he seems to pass controverted subjects by, it will not always be because he has not weighed them ; usually he thinks he can claim it is because he has formed his own conclusion, and with that conclusion has moved on to what has seemed to him more important. This applies to the harmony.

In the main he has followed Tischendorf, as many others before him; once or twice, without further comment, he has chosen a different order. It applies, too, to such questions as that of Mary Magdalen. Many scholars, Catholic and non-Catholic, would regard her as several different persons; while acknowledging the strength of their argument the author does not think it is by any means conclusive, and therefore prefers the old tradition. Another instance is the site of the Transfiguration. Whether Mount Thabor is to be accepted as the site or not, the writer thinks that the evidence, both internal and external, is overwhelmingly in its favour; certainly far more so than is the evidence for Mount Hermon, which has of late become more popular with certain writers. In any case, to stop his narrative in order to discuss a conjecture seems to him to be a hindrance to his purpose without sufficient corresponding good.

7. Use of the Old Testament

On the other hand, if the above features are mainly absent from the following pages, others are conspicuous which may seem to call for some explanation. In the first place will be noticed a somewhat elaborate use of the Old Testament. This the author himself was at one time afraid might have been overdone; he was encouraged to retain the passages quoted by at least one critic whose judgement he values. If one would understand the mind of Our Lord as Man, and of the Jews of His time, it is quite essential that the Old Testament should have great prominence. Both He and they thought under its influence, spoke in its phrases, and had it as a background for all their religious experience. All writers are unanimous in recognizing the tremendous place Old Testament prophecy held in the mind of the Jews of His time; but more than that, as we know from many sources, the old books of the Bible were to them the beginning and end of their theology, their moral standards, and even the means of direction in the common things of life. Therefore, for the sake of keeping that atmosphere, it has seemed well at times to give the Old Testament prominence. Moreover, for the modern reader, who may not be too familiar with the Old Testament text, the author has thought that more lavish quotation, instead of mere reference, will help him to correlate better the two together, and to see how much the New depends upon the Old. Without this recognition of dependence many of the sermons of Our Lord lose much of their significance, both in what they teach and in the portrait they reflect of Himself.

8. Repetitions

Another point which has given the writer some anxiety is ·the not infrequent repetition which, on re-reading his work, he easily detects. As the story has gone on he has brought together, in various places, the evidence that has, thus far, been gained ; at times he has paused in his narrative to summarize the personality of Jesus as He has been discovered up to that point. First of all he would confess that this constant summarizing, and contemplation of Our Lord as He gradually revealed Himself, has always had for the author a peculiar fascination ; during the writing of the present work he had often to prevent himself from drawing the portrait as he saw it over and over again. He thought that, perhaps, others might find the same pleasure in the study ; they would not be anxious to hurry on to the end, they would prefer to look at Our Lord as He stood before them, they would therefore welcome these pauses, that they might look back on the course that had been traversed and bring together what had been gained of the knowledge of Jesus in the way. But there is a second consideration. The author does not imagine that there will be many readers who will read this book from beginning to end ; far more, he suspects, will look at it here and there, will perhaps use it as a book of reference, will open it at the scene or event which at the moment they are studying. For such readers the constant use of repetition seems essential ; without it they would miss the very object for which the book has been written, with it they may gain in summary much that has been learned in the pages before. Therefore, at the risk of appearing monotonous, for the sake of the other two classes many of these repetitions and summaries have been retained.

9. The Use of the Imagination

Again in many places it will be noticed that the author has allowed himself to use his own imagination. Nevertheless, in no instance has he done this without attention to the facts, or without some kind of warrantable evidence. In some cases he has been guided by experiences during ten years in the East. For instance, the account of the Marriage Feast at Cana is founded on similar Eastern celebrations which he has attended, descriptions of moving crowds and pilgrimages are taken from like groups through which he has passed, or which have passed his door, many details of daily life are those which may be seen by anyone who lives for any length of time in the East to-day. In other cases, while keeping this experience in mind, especially of up-country villages in India which the ordinary European traveller never sees, he has asked himself how the events described in the Gospels would have been likely to have happened in that setting. Thus the origin and character of the Apostles, as here given, seem to the author something more than merely imaginative ; so also the local self-government in the villages, so common to-day throughout the East, separating one from another almost as if they were little independent kingdoms. On the other hand, to keep his imagination more in check, there is scarcely a single scene in the Life, nor a single journey described, to which he has not given a definite geographical allocation in the country as it is to-day. He would like to say that this alone, the following of Our Lord systematically from place to place, has helped him more than any other material aid to preserve the unity of his work.

10. The Country of Palestine

It is hoped that wherever a geographical explanation seems likely to help the narrative it has been given. Nevertheless, there are certain general remarks which may be made beforehand, and which may be borne in mind. In the first place, the country of Palestine is small ; in area no greater than Wales, but even that comparison may be misleading. During His Public Life there is no record that Our Lord went further south than Jerusalem or the north end of the Dead Sea ; in Samaria, except at Jacob's Well and Sychar, He did no preaching ; consequently, to form a proper estimate, we must divide the area of Wales almost by half. On the other hand, even over so small a country travelling was long and wearisome. It was very narrow, scarcely sixty miles across at its broadest part in Judæa.

Travelling was entirely on foot, and even if with mules or donkeys it went only at a slow pace ; the roads were beaten tracks, unpaved, with boulders often in the way, such as are used to-day by caravans of camels on the hill-sides of Galilee, so uneven that the ordinary English traveller would scarcely recognize them as roads at all. Moreover they led up and down the mountain-sides in great disregard of the traveller's convenience. Excepting the coast of the lake and the plain of Esdraelon, which stretches flat across the country separating Samaria from upper Galilee, the whole of Galilee is mountainous ; one cannot go from one place to another without climbing hills. Going from Galilee to Judæa there is the level road through Peræa along the bank of the Jordan, there is also the hilly road through Samaria ; a journey from Nazareth to Jerusalem on foot, with the encumbrances of those times, would occupy at least three days.

11. The Climate

It is remarkable that in the Gospel narrative little is said of the climate of Palestine which can give any help to the harmonist. At the same time it is clear that this must be taken into account by one who would picture to himself the life that Our Lord and His Apostles led. Roughly speaking there are four seasons ; the rainy season, during the time of the European winter, when the country is under the influence of the western winds ; the hot and dry season, during our summer, when the winds from the east and south across the desert make life for a time almost intolerable ; and the two intermediate seasons, during the first of which Palestine is a garden of flowers, second to no other country in the world. This spring-time, after the rains, was also the time of the harvest ; and this, during the years of which we speak, was a very busy time indeed. Mountains which now are bare rock were then covered with cultivated fields ; the plains from end to end teemed with crops. Though the evidence of exploration seems to show that the people for the most part were very poor, yet there is little sign of general destitution. Only when the rains failed, as they did from time to time, or when the locusts came and devoured the green shoots, was there danger of starvation. But in any case it will be seen at once that for many months in the year the common people had an easy time ; and even in any season, except during the rains, they might have leisure to congregate in the way we find so often described in the Gospels.

12. Conclusion

More than this need scarcely be said by way of Introduction. Other writers have related, at greater length and with far greater learning than the author can claim, the circumstances of Palestine in the time of Jesus Christ ; its government, its religious condition, the divisions of its parties, etc. All that could be done here would be to summarize yet again what has already been written by others before ; if the writer has anything to add that may appear to the purpose, it will be given in its proper place in the book. One only thing he would say, and it is this : In many places he fears he may be wrong, but he can do no better under the circumstances. Sometimes the harmony is more than doubtful, yet he does not at present see how it can be mended. There are scenes which he himself has described in quite different ways, and of these he has chosen what has seemed to him the best. Many places need expansion for clearness ; many parables and addresses of Our Lord need much more development if they are to bear their proper fruit. But he must be content with what he has been able to do ; if some other will come after him and, stimulated by this imperfect study, will produce something more worthy of its subject, the author will account himself more than rewarded.

The author wishes to express his thanks to Messrs. Longmans and Co. for permission to use in this work the material of a sermon published by them in ' Catholic Preachers of To-day ' ; also to Burns Oates and Washbourne Ltd. for a like permission to use much that is contained in ' Jesus Christ, Model of Manhood ', and ' Jesus Christ, Man of Sorrows '.

NOTE. Since one idea runs through the whole of this book, an index seems unnecessary. It is hoped that its absence is adequately supplied by the careful sub-divisions of the chapters and the harmony at the end.

CHAPTER

1

1. The Coming of John the Baptist

IT was the fulness of time. That strange, unruly people had waited long. Jericho, as they passed it on their way to and from the Holy City, had stood there through the centuries, to remind them for ever of that day when Josue had brought their fathers into the land that flowed with milk and honey. They had entered that land, they had spread over it, they had made it their own, and they had all but perished in it. They had established in it the one God who had made them His chosen people, they had built His temple on Moria to be the wonder of the world ; and yet across the valley to the south was the Hill of Scandal, where he who had built the first temple to their one, true God, had built other temples to other gods in the days of his undoing. They had served their God and had forsaken Him ; by Him they had been punished, even to destruction, and yet ever and again the bones of their dead past had been revived. It was a weird tale that they had to recall ; a tale of a stiff-necked people, faithless more often than faithful, nevertheless with a something in it that kept it alive, and united, and conscious of itself as the race that must one day save the world.

The city of David had perished, but another had been built on its site. Solomon's temple had gone, but in its place another had arisen. The very sacred books had been lost but had been found again, and now they were studied as they had never been before. As for their ancient oppressors, Egypt lay buried in its own waste of sand ; the Philistines had sunk in the sea ; Babylon, Assyria, were names that attached themselves to monster ruins ; Antiochus

1

and his Greeks had vanished again as quickly as they had
come. There remained the Romans, the contemptuous,
hated Romans ; but their day would come, they had
sealed their own doom, for had they not violated the Holy
of Holies ? And there were their myrmidons, the creatures
neither Jew nor Roman, Herod and Philip and Lysanias,
whom everybody loathed and felt the shame of obeying ;
surely they had sunk as low as they well could, surely the
dawn was at hand. It had always been so ; always the
Lord had at last remembered mercy ; He would do it
again.

And yet in what could they hope ? They looked at their
Temple, gleaming gold beneath the autumn sun, and it
filled them with pride ; still could they not forget that it
had been built, not by Solomon, not by Esdras, but by the
bloodstained Herod. Because David had been a man of
blood he had been forbidden to build the first temple ;
how much worse had been Herod ! They went into its
courts and worshipped ; yet had they to close their eyes
to much before in His own house they could commune
with their God. They sat at the feet of their teachers and
they came away confused. Their scribes bound them down
to the letter of the Law ; their doctors were divided into
schools and confounded one another ; their very priests
were the puppets of the Roman hand, politic, untrue,
grasping, confined now to a single family, with the old man
Annas as the guiding star of all. The Law had divorced
itself from life ; religion had become a binding bondage ;
men looked with hungry eyes from their city walls towards
the eastern hills as the sun rose beautiful above them, and
longed and longed again that at length there might come
up to them from across the Jordan that other Saviour who
was to bring them light.

That He would come they knew ; they could never doubt
it. Their whole history foretold it ; again and again their
prophets had said it ; above them all the greatest of their
prophets, Isaias. They knew his words by heart ; they
were steeped in his majestic poetry, his language of mystery
they had pondered in their schools. One passage more
than all others they could never forget, so glorious was it,
so absolute, so reassuring. Their king that was to be
would one day come, so it said, and his herald would
announce him.

' Be comforted, be comforted, my people
Saith your God
Speak ye to the heart of Jerusalem
And call to her
For her evil is come to an end
Her iniquity is forgiven
She hath received of the hand of the Lord double
For all her sins.'

Then had the prophet taken his imagery from the grand progresses of the monarchs of old. A runner would go forward to proclaim the king's coming ; mountains would be levelled, valleys would be filled, to make easy his approach.

' The voice of one crying in the wilderness
Prepare ye the way of the Lord
Make straight in the wilderness the paths of your God
Every valley shall be exalted
And every mountain and hill shall be made low
And the crooked shall become straight
And the rough ways plain
And the glory of the Lord shall be revealed
And all flesh together shall see
That the mouth of the Lord hath spoken.'

Along that levelled road would come the herald, telling the imminent presence of the king :

' The voice of one saying : Cry
And I said : What shall I cry ?
All flesh is grass
And all the glory thereof as the flower of the field
The grass is withered and the flower is fallen
But the word of the Lord endureth for ever
Get thee up upon a high mountain
Thou that bringest good tidings to Sion
Lift up thy voice with strength
Thou that bringest good tidings to Jerusalem
Lift it up, fear not
Say to the cities of Juda
Behold your God.'

Last of all, in might and in meekness, would come the monarch himself :

> ' Behold the Lord shall come with strength
> And his arm shall rule
> Behold his reward is with him
> And his work is before him
> He shall feed his flock like a shepherd
> He shall gather together the lambs with his arm
> And shall take them up in his bosom
> And he shall himself carry them that are with young.'
>
> Isaias xl, 1–11.

On words like these men dreamed in and about Jerusalem. At length, in the midst of such a wistful, waiting, hungering world,

> ' The word of the Lord came to John
> The son of Zachary
> In the desert
> And John the Baptist came baptizing and preaching
> In the desert of Judæa
> And into all the country about the Jordan
> Preaching the baptism of penance
> For the remission of sins
> And saying : Do penance
> For the kingdom of heaven is at hand.'

To very many, when he first appeared, John could not have been unknown. There were those who had heard the wonderful things connected with his birth ; his father Zachary and his mother Elizabeth were too prominently placed for that event to be easily forgotten. Moreover, the behaviour of John himself had kept it well before them. From the first he had lived his life aloof :

> ' And the child grew
> And was strengthened in spirit
> And was in the deserts
> Until the day of his manifestation in Israel.'

He had lived in the deserts of Judæa, yet not so far away but that men might find him if they would ; and the fascination of the hermit, the fascination that surrounds all lonely souls, had already drawn men to him.

But now he began to move ; he began to assume a new rôle. Though he clung about the neighbourhood of the city, and still loved the desert places, yet was he often found upon the high roads that passed through them, especially the great main road that led up from the Jordan to Jerusalem. Moreover, his preaching had taken a new turn. Whatever before it had been, now deliberately he proclaimed himself a prophet, a herald of a coming kingdom. He spoke with a new and independent authority ; reverent as he was, he assumed a position of his own. He proclaimed a new beginning, repentance for the past, bringing back religion into life ; he took hold of the old ceremonial of baptism, as a sign of sorrow, and forgiveness, and reform, and gave it a fresh significance.

It is important here to notice the place which John held in the minds of the people ; important because upon it depends much of the action of Jesus in His early public life. While John was prominent on the scene, Jesus bided in the background ; only when John was removed did He come actively forward. The death of John was, it would seem, coincident with the first mission of the twelve Apostles ; the last appeal to the Jews in the temple, before Jesus finally left it, was made in the name of John.

1. One evangelist gives to his birth a prominence greater than he gives to that of Jesus Himself. Much more than half of S. Luke's first chapter is occupied with it ; the story of Our Lord's conception and nativity is more shortly told, and, except for the appearance of the angels to the shepherds, there is less of the wonderful, more of the commonplace, in the whole narration.

2. Three evangelists point to him as the first great fulfilment of Messianic prophecy, while the fourth lifts him to a rank unique among all the prophets. It would be difficult to speak of any man with greater solemnity than this :

> ' There was a man sent from God
> Whose name was John
> This man came for a witness
> To give testimony·of the light
> That all men might believe through him
> He was not the light
> But was to give testimony of the light.'
>
> John i, 6–8.

3. Lastly Jesus Himself speaks of him in terms which raise him above any other man that has lived.

' And when the messengers of John were departed
He began to speak to the multitudes
Concerning John
What went ye out into the desert to see ?
A reed shaken with the wind ?
But what went ye out to see ?
A man clothed in soft garments ?
Behold they that are in costly apparel
And live delicately
Are in the houses of kings
But what went ye out to see ?
A prophet ?
Yea, I say unto you
And more than a prophet
This is he of whom it is written
Behold I send my angel before thy face
Who shall prepare the way before thee
For I say unto you
Among those who are born of women
There is not a greater prophet
Than John the Baptist.'

Matthew xi, 7–11.
Luke i, 24–28.

Nor was this the only occasion ; at another time He
spoke of him as

' A burning and a shining light ',

John v, 35.

and yet again as

' Elias that is to come.'

Matthew xi, 14.

4. To all this must be added the extraordinary reverence
paid to the name of John throughout all this period, which
continued steady and unabated even when the name of
Jesus had waned.   For instance :

i. On this account, though he held him prisoner, Herod
hesitated to execute him :

' Having a mind to put him to death
He feared the people
Because they esteemed him as a prophet.'

Matthew xiv, 5.

ii. While he was in prison his disciples never ceased to
keep him informed of all that was going on in Galilee :

'And John's disciples told him
  Of all these things.'

Luke vii, 18.

iii. They followed his advice in their attitude to Jesus
Himself :

'John the Baptist sent us to see thee saying
  Art thou he that art to come
  Or look we for another ? '

Luke vii, 20.

iv. After he had been put to death his disciples did
honour to his body :

'Which his disciples hearing
They came and took his body
And buried it in a tomb
And came and told Jesus.'

Matthew xiv, 12 ; Mark vi, 29.

v. After his death Herod his murderer lived in constant
fear of him :

'Now at that time Herod the tetrarch
Heard the fame of Jesus
And of all the things that were done by him
And he said to his servants
This is John the Baptist
He is risen from the dead
And therefore
Mighty works shew forth themselves in him
And he was in doubt
Because it was said by some
That John was risen from the dead
But by other some
That Elias hath appeared
And by others
That one of the old prophets was risen again
Which Herod hearing said
John I have beheaded
But who is this
Of whom I hear such things ?
John whom I beheaded
He is risen from the dead
And he sought to see him.'

Matthew xiv, 1, 2 ; Mark vi, 14–16 ; Luke ix, 7–9.

vi. At a much later date his evidence for Jesus is

quoted in Judæa as being more convincing even than miracles :

> ' And he went again beyond Jordan
> Unto that place where John was baptizing first
> And there he abode
> And many resorted to him
> And they said
> John indeed did no sign
> But all things whatsoever John said of this man
> Were true
> And many believed in him.'
>
> John x, 40-42.

vii. On the very last day of His public teaching Jesus is able to confute His enemies by an appeal to the baptism of John :

> ' For all men counted John
> That he was a prophet indeed.'
>
> Matthew xxi, 23-27 ; Mark xi, 27-33 ; Luke xx, 1-8.

viii. Years afterwards, when the Church had spread far abroad, disciples of John are still to be met with who,

> ' Being fervent in spirit
> Spoke and taught diligently
> The things that are of Jesus
> Knowing only the baptism of John.'
>
> Acts xviii, 25.

Though this coming of John need not at first have seemed very remarkable, for others of his kind had from time to time appeared, still there was that about him and his preaching which differentiated him from all the rest. Above all was his method different from that of the spiritual leaders whom the men of Judæa had been wont to follow. These came before them particular in their dress, their fringes and their phylacteries, conforming with exaggerated detail to their interpretation of the Law. He discarded all this ; he would not even heed common convention. He would clothe himself with just that which came first to hand ; he would eat just that which nature placed within his reach in the wilderness, and nothing more.

> ' And the same John
> Had his garments of camel's hair
> And a leathern girdle about his loins
> And his meat was locusts and wild honey.'
>
> Matthew iii, 4.

'He was dressed as Elias of old.'

cf. 4 Kings i, 8.

His preaching, too, was different. Their guides taught them the details of the Law and its minute obligations, placing in their observance the height of sanctity. John never mentioned these ; he broke right through them and dived into the very hearts of men. He appealed to their inner knowledge of themselves, of right and wrong, of good and evil, truth and falsehood. If they would have ceremonial, then let it be such as declared the soul, true acknowledgement of evil done, true reform of life, true preparation for whatever was to come.

Preaching such as this soon began to tell. Travellers up to Jerusalem, merchants from the East, pilgrims coming to the festivals, would look at this strange figure, and listen for a while, and pass by. They might affect to disregard him ; they might call this man but another fanatic revivalist ; they might say the things he taught were of no concern to them ; busy, preoccupied as they were, they might resent the intrusion as unwarranted, vulgar, unseemly. Still would the chance words they heard refuse to leave them ; they had pierced their hearts and their consciences, and would not be quieted. These men went on their way ; they talked among themselves ; they linked this teaching up with the teaching of the Law, and saw that it gave the Law new life. Gradually they came back, bringing others with them ; some only curious to see this new phenomenon ; some in timid hope that here might be a new beginning ; some, who had hungered for long years, seeing already in this sudden revelation a sign that the day of salvation was at hand. They came and they were conquered ; they came to learn and they discovered themselves. From the city they came and from the hill country round about ; they would not return till by an open avowal they had confessed their belief in this man.

' Then went out to him
All the country of Judæa
And all they of Jerusalem
And all the country about Jordan
And they were baptized by him in the river Jordan
Confessing their sins.'

Such a movement could not fail soon to attract those in authority, the guardians of the Law, the doctors in Israel, the men who, first among all, were to recognize and welcome the Messias when He came. They knew the signs, they interpreted the prophets ; when they were fulfilled it would be for them to judge ; in the meantime they were the masters, of Israel and of its Temple. Of course this John, whoever he might prove to be, must never be allowed to interfere with their prerogative. On the other hand so long as there was no sign, and little fear of that, he might be countenanced ; out of such revivals usually grew a greater observance in the Temple. They would go down to him themselves ; they would support the movement by their presence ; by their own submission to this ceremonial of the Baptist they would give it a mark of their approval. In this way at least they would keep a hold upon this new preacher, whom already it might be dangerous to oppose.

But the Baptist was not to be deceived. Not for nothing had he spent his years of preparation in the desert, studying men, learning men as only he can learn them who leads his life apart, sifting the truth from the falsehood of their ways. Not for nothing had he searched the Scriptures, and separated grain from chaff. The specious defence that these people held up before themselves, that they were the children of Abraham, that they were the chosen of God, that they were therefore secure from rejection, must be broken down if the ' way of the Lord ' was to be made straight. Plainly and at once they must be told of their crafty nature, of their blind self-deception, of the emptiness of their claim. If they would rightly inherit their birth-right there must be truth to the core ; there must be a renewal of the inner man, there must be no make-belief, no substitute of outward show for sincerity. The fruits they produced must be from themselves, not from the hollow fulfilment of a hollow Law.

He spoke alike to all, but it was to the Pharisees and scribes mingled with the crowd that his words were specially addressed. Mercilessly he spoke to them ; from the beginning there should be no mistake. After submission of heart, the one great mountain to be levelled before the Lord could come to His own was the hardened refuse piled up and trodden down about the Law.

' And seeing many of the Pharisees and Sadducees
Coming to his baptism
He said to the multitudes .
That came forth to be baptized by him
Ye brood of vipers
Who hath shewed you to flee from the wrath to come ?
Bring forth therefore fruits
Worthy of penance
And think not
Do not begin to say within yourselves
We have Abraham for our father
For I say to you
That God is able of these stones
To raise up children to Abraham
For now the axe is laid to the root of the trees
Every tree therefore that bringeth not forth good fruit
Shall be cut down
And cast into the fire.'

Language such as this was not to be mistaken. From the
outset John threw down the gauntlet, refusing to parley ;
it was a declaration of war with a definite enemy, which
was to end only on Calvary.

The people heard, but the significance of the challenge
passed them by. They were too much concerned with
themselves to take much heed of the Pharisees and Scribes ;
it was enough for them that the Baptist taught the need of
' fruits worthy of penance.' They asked for further light
and guidance. They were a motley crew, for the most part
men of no particular religious reputation ; common men,
tax-collectors bearing an ill name, soldiers restless and
discontented, whose power and position gave them opportunity for every kind of evil, poor folk from the country-side,
not over-burthened with intelligence, still more wanting in
instruction, whose hard lives had closed their hands to
their neighbours and had killed in them the first elements
of love. But they wished to rise to better things ; and here
was one who would teach them how they might do it.
They asked him, and to them John altered his tone ; treated
them tenderly as sheep that had no shepherd ; imposed on
them no burthen heavier than they could bear ; simply, in
language of their own, told them just the duties of their
state of life. In these last words of counsel there is a

gentleness and sympathy of nature which goes far to explain the hold of John upon the people ; it is an anticipation of Him who

> ' Would not crush the broken reed
> And smoking flax would not extinguish.'
> ' And the people asked him saying
> What then shall we do ?
> And he answering said to them
> He that hath two coats
> Let him give to him that hath none
> And he that hath meat
> Let him do in like manner
> And the publicans also came to be baptized
> And said to him
> Master what shall we do ?
> But he said to them
> Do nothing more
> Than that which is appointed unto you
> And the soldiers also asked him saying
> And what shall we do ?
> And he said to them
> Do violence to no man
> Neither calumniate any man
> And be content with your pay.'

Can we now picture to ourselves this first appearance of the Baptist ? He came into a world with an ancient tradition, with a belief, a conviction, that a great future lay before it, yet were both tradition and belief marred by the dross that had gathered round them. He came among men intent upon their own affairs, especially their own political affairs, in consequence suspicious, self-centred, prone to hatred. Religion for them was a rigid, stereotyped substitute form ; against its claims and ever-growing tyranny many had long since begun to chafe, though they could not lay aside the old inheritance, nor rid themselves of its ceremonial, nor reject altogether the hope in the future which it gave. He came at a time when many, eager souls as well as souls that feared, were on the tip-toe of expectation, strained so far that they were in danger of despair. He came and stood in the desert by the river, at the gateway leading into Judæa, on the very spot that was still hallowed by the memory of the prophet Elias, hard upon the main road along which the busy world had to pass ; a weird, uncouth, unkempt, terrible figure, in harmony with his surroundings, of single mind, unflinching, fearing none, a respecter of no person, asking for nothing, to whom the world with its judgements was of no account whatever though he showed that he knew it through and through, all its castes and all its colours. He came the censor of men, the terror of men, the warning to men, yet winning men by his utter sincerity ; telling them plainly the truth about themselves and forcing them to own that he was right ; drawing them by no soft inducements, but by the hard lash of his words, and by the solemn threat of doom that awaited them who would not hear ; distinguishing true heart-conversion from the false conversion of conformity, religion that lived in the soul from that sham thing of mere inheritance and law ; going down into the depths of human nature in his ceaseless search for ' the true Israelite in whom there was no guile ' ; an angel and no man, a fearless voice to which the material world seemed as nothing ; compelling attention, fascinating even those who would have passed him by, making straight the path through the hearts of men ; cleansing, baptizing, pointing to truth of life, but as yet, until all was prepared, saying nothing of that Lord whose coming he was sent to herald, content to foretell only the Kingdom ; John, the focus upon which all the gathered light of the Old Dispensation converged, from which was to radiate the light of the New. All this those felt who now began to ask, concerning themselves : ' What then shall we do ? ' concerning him : ' Who is he ? '—crowds of every kind, publicans, soldiers, citizens from the great towns and country villages, patronizing Pharisees and submissive disciples.

2. The Prophecy of the Messias

The minds of men being what they were, and the tension of the times so great, it was inevitable that questions should be asked concerning John himself. There was the evidence of his early life, and it was confirmed by the evidence of the present ; men had found one in whom they believed, who spoke on his own authority, and not after the manner of the Pharisees and Scribes. The time was at hand ; the Messias, so it was said both by the common folk and by those who ought to know, was due at any moment.

When He came, He might well be expected to be such a one as John. The question was answered by a rumour ; the rumour spread, growing ever more credible as the number grew that favoured it. Was not John the anointed of the Lord, and would he not soon reveal himself ?

This was John's opportunity. Hitherto he had spoken only of the Kingdom and of the preparation for it ; now it was time to announce the King. These simple people had submitted to his baptism, and had thus proved their good-will ; he would take them further and show them that there was a baptism yet to come which would put his own to naught. They had grown in devotion to himself ; he would assure them that to the One who was soon to stand amongst them he was not fit to be a slave. His own baptism was only of dead water ; that which was to come would be of living spirit. His did but wash the outer surface, for the rest was a symbol and no more ; that which was to follow would reach the very soul, would try it as gold is tried in the fire, would be a source of very life, not merely a sign of penance.

He would tell them this, and he would tell it in language such as these simple country people could understand. Up the hill in the distance might be seen some husbandman at work, blowing away with his fan the chaff from his heap of corn, the rich grain purified settling on the floor beneath. It was a happy illustration for his purpose ; it would emphasize each point, the utter purity of the Kingdom, the utter truth of the King, the blessedness of membership, the evil of rejection, the added sanction to the belief in eternal bliss or punishment, which had struggled to the light through the ages.

' And as the people were of opinion
And all were thinking in their hearts of John
That perhaps he might be the Christ
John answered and preached
Saying unto all
I indeed baptize you in water
Unto penance
But he that shall come after me
Is mightier than I
Whose shoes I am not worthy to bear
The latchet of whose shoes
I am not worthy to stoop down and loose

> He shall baptize you with the Holy Ghost
> And with fire
> Whose fan is in his hand
> And he will thoroughly cleanse his floor
> And will gather his wheat into his barn
> But the chaff he will burn
> With unquenchable fire.'

Again let us sum up the impression, for on a clear under-standing of this scene depends much that is to follow. With hearts lost to him these simple folk believed in John ; given such sincerity they could not hold back. With their eyes of longing turned towards the future, to the sun that was to rise above the eastern hills, and with the light of the past shining red behind them, setting over Jerusalem and the mountains of Judæa, they could not but ask themselves whether at last the time had come ; whether this singular man, who proclaimed a new Kingdom to be near, who knew the secret of its membership, were not indeed the Messias ; whether the signs they were to look for were not upon him ; the superhuman vision that made him a safe guide ; the conquering conviction that compelled assent ; the likeness to the prophets of old whose line had long since perished ; the knowledge of hearts, the message of repent-ance, the opening of the way to new life, the insistence on utter truth, the contempt of formalism. Miracles and signs of that kind they did not expect, such things were not in their category ; it was miracle enough that he baptized as with power and spoke as one having authority.

In this spirit they had come to him, and he had received them. Tenderly, gradually he had led them higher, yet never yielding one whit of his sternness. Humbly, without fear of losing hold upon them, he had debased himself before the Light that was to come :

> ' He was not the light
> But was to give testimony of the light.'

Firmly he had repeated to them the need of preparation for its coming. Let there be no mistake ; the Master who is to come is One who will not be deceived. He will see through the outward appearance ; He will not be content with mere form ; He will search the hearts of men, and will have no surface substitute ; He will accept none but the true, the sincere, the genuine ; He will not endure the husks with the grain, but will have that grain purified at whatever cost, even though with His own hand He must waft the husks away. One can feel how and why John puts this utter truth of Jesus above all things else, utterly true Himself, seeking only utter truth in others, whose work in the world would be to ' bear witness to the truth ' and to be believed, as John himself had been believed, on His own authority alone. To a people grown stereotyped in form, to whom a species of self-deception had come to be considered a virtue, this was essentially John's message, and was indeed ' good tidings of great joy '.

The Evangelists one and all imply that, if they would, they could say much more concerning John :

> ' And many other things exhorting
> Did he preach to the people.'

But for the present this must be enough. More will yet follow ; he is too important, his witness is too convincing, to be set aside with this single notice. Still it is sufficient that here he should be set before us, a gaunt figure on the horizon of the yellow-brown desert, the Judæan hills before him with the Holy City beyond, the Dead Sea with its memories of doom on his left down below, the sun rising over the hills of Moab and brightening the sky behind, while he stands between two eras, the link between the old and the new, the summary of the past and the foreshadowing of the future.

3. The Baptism of Jesus

It is at this moment, and in the midst of circumstances such as these, that Jesus at length makes His appearance. There is no great disturbance, neither Nazareth nor Judæa notice it. It is the late season of the year, when the country-side is bare and work in the fields is less pressing. It is on the occasion of some festival, it may have been the feast of Tabernacles in October, when numbers make towards the Holy City. The news concerning John and his baptism has reached as far as Galilee, and a carpenter living at the upper end of Nazareth, with others who have long ' waited for the consolation of Israel,' goes up by the ordinary route that runs alongside the Jordan, crossing the river into Judæa at the ford where John is preaching and baptizing. Like the rest of the band of pilgrims He stops at the ford to listen to the earnest preacher ; like others who have come well-disposed, when the preaching is over, He draws nearer and adjusts His clothing to take the step which is proof of a sinner's submission. He waits till all the rest are baptized, yielding to the eager throng that presses forward, Himself easily unnoticed and pushed aside ; then, the very last in the group of penitents that day, He Himself walks into the water.

This is the simple matter of fact as the evangelists give it to us. There is not, and obviously during the last eighteen years there has not been, the least indication that Jesus of Nazareth is anything more than any of the men standing round Him. Even John on a later occasion declares that at first he did not know Him who He was ; for that even he required a direct revelation from above.

' And John gave testimony saying
I saw the Spirit
Coming down as a dove from heaven
And he remained upon him
And I knew him not
But he who sent me to baptize in water
said to me
He upon whom thou shalt see the spirit descending
He it is
That baptizeth with the Holy Ghost
And I saw
And I gave testimony
That this is the Son of God.'

John i, 32–34.

Still, already before the revelation was given, naturally, instinctively, John stayed his hand ; he hesitated to baptize. Though he knew not all that Jesus was, yet as a relative he knew Him. He knew the story of His birth, so intimately connected with his own, he knew what his own mother had said of Him ; if before he was born he had leaped for joy at His coming, now when they met he could not fail to be stirred. Whoever Jesus was, John knew He was no sinner, and this baptism was not for such as He ; whoever He was, by comparison with Him John himself could scarcely be called clean. Was His coming then a sign that it was time for him to yield, and allow this better man to take his

place ?   He stayed his arm ; he made a sign of protest ;
for a moment he held Jesus back.

> ' But John stayed him saying
> I ought to be baptized by thee
> And comest thou to me ? '

The answer of Jesus confirmed the recognition ; it was
the answer of one man to another whom he knew and who
knew him.   It was also an answer of command ; Jesus did
not hide from John that He understood, and accepted the
honour done to Him.   Though He submits, yet is He the
Master ; it is the same Jesus, acting in precisely the same
way, as the Jesus of eighteen years before in the Temple,
Master of His Mother and Joseph, yet afterwards in all
things ' subject to them '.   Though He stands there in the
stream to be baptized, yet the baptism is not given without
His order ; it is the same Jesus as, three years later, was the
Jesus of Calvary who submitted unto death, yet laid down
His life when and as He chose and in no other way.

Thus though the words He speaks are those of complete
subjection, nevertheless there is in them the authority and
firmness of one who had a mission to fulfil, and who knew
exactly all that it included ; before the Spirit came upon
Him Jesus knew.

> ' And Jesus answering said to him
> Suffer it to be so now
> For so it becomes us to fulfil all justice.'

There was nothing more to be said or done.   Submissively
the meek John baptized the meek, submissive Jesus ;
Jesus had indeed begun at the very beginning.   The crowd,
already baptized, was threading its way homeward ; the
few that remained noticed nothing strange ; it would seem
that what then happened was known alone to John and
Jesus.   He came up out of the water ; for a moment He
stood upon the bank absorbed in prayer ; while He prayed,
with His eyes raised upward, a common attitude as we shall
often see :

> ' Lo !   He saw the heavens opened to him
> And he saw the Spirit of God
> Descending in a bodily shape as a dove
> And coming and remaining upon him
> And behold there came a voice from heaven saying
> This is my beloved Son

In whom I am well pleased
Thou art my beloved Son
In thee I am well pleased.'

When we read separately the three accounts of the
baptism of Jesus, it seems manifest that to each of the
evangelists the chief part of the story is ' the voice from
heaven ' and the witness that it gave.   Next it would seem,
from the mere construction of the sentences, more especially
in the narrative of S. Luke, that the coming of Jesus of His
own accord to be baptized, and the humiliation of the
baptism, are looked upon as preludes to this ;   the first
public act of self-abasement being followed by the first
solemn declaration by the Father, the formal acceptance of
the Sonship of Man, with all its sin to be atoned for, being
rewarded by acknowledgement as the Son of God ;   true
Man, with the consequent burthen, true God, with the
consequent right.

' He hath humbled himself
Therefore hath God exalted him ' ;

this would seem to be the meaning of the mystery, and it is
confirmed in the mystery of the Temptations that follows.

The ' voice from heaven ' compels us to link up this scene
with that other scene later when the same ' voice from heaven '
uttered the same words, the Transfiguration.   As then the
vision and the voice were confined to three, so now are they
confined to one ;   as then they were given to confirm the
three in the faith they had already professed, so now it
would seem they were permitted to confirm and enlighten
the Baptist.   It was the sign that he looked for, henceforth
he knew ;   and it was meet that he should know, both as a
reward for his fidelity and as a guide through what was next
to come.

But for the rest all was darkness.   The people were given
to see nothing ;   they were to discover for themselves by
other signs as time went on, or not at all.   From the beginning to the end Jesus would thrust Himself on no one.   He
would give such signs as, if men chose, they could question
and reject ;   He would come to them as one of themselves
and they should come to Him in response.   He would have
their willing faith only, their spontaneous allegiance only,
the more free, the more their own, the better.   That this
might be engendered and developed He would bide His

time, He would go ever so slowly, He would endure unceasing disappointment, endless misunderstanding ; He would even submit to the failure of many if only in the end He could win true faith and love and trust and glad allegiance from a few. If we forget this feature of the character of Jesus we lose the key to many mysteries.

4. The Temptations in the Desert

JESUS came up from the river, and in a true sense a new spirit was about Him. He had always been Jesus, Son of Man, Son of God ; but hitherto the latter had, as it were, been hidden beneath the first. To many it would always be so, even to the very end ; they would pass Him by, would deal with Him and touch Him, yet would discover in Him just the Son of Man and nothing more. But now, for others to discover if they would, a new thing was shining through the outer surface ; and though from the first His oneness with the Father was perfect, yet can the evangelists find no better way of describing this new thing than by saying that He was

' full of the Holy Ghost.'

He came up from the Jordan, and made His way towards the Holy City. Over against Jericho, to the right as one tramps along that route, rises a range of hills, steep and bare and rugged, one of which is known as the Hill of Temptation. Beyond is desert stretching northward to Samaria ; to the East the Jordan trails through the valley ; Jerusalem and all Judæa to the West ; to the South the high road joins them, winding in and out, and up and down, among rolling hills. It is a lonely region, though so near to the stream of life, where a hermit might long dwell and none but the wild beasts would know or disturb him. As Jesus made His way along the road, the last of the throng that day, something drove Him to turn aside at this spot and seek that quiet shelter. In a sense this was nothing strange. He had loved the mountains from childhood, the mountains that clustered round Nazareth, northward rolling wave upon wave, southward breaking abruptly over Esdraelon ; among those mountains He had long since formed a habit of lonely prayer which was to cling to Him, and to be an abiding relief, for the remainder of His days. It was not

then unnatural that at this moment, when so manifest a
sign had been given, He should turn aside as the sun began
to set, to commune with His Father before He went along
His way.

Nevertheless on this occasion there was something different
from before. The Spirit led Him, the Spirit drove Him;
He was as a man marching to doom. He left the road and
struck across the plain to His right, blindly and onward as if
He had no will of His own. He climbed the mountain side,
He spent the night in prayer; to do so was no new thing.
But in the morning, when the day again dawned over the
hills beyond Jordan, and Jericho below became astir, the
Spirit that had led Him kept Him on the mountain side,
and He knew it was His task to stay. There He remained
the next day and the next, and the next; for forty days and
nights, six long weeks, He waited and waited, praying
always, increasingly weary, patiently abiding the time of
His Father's will. The beasts of the desert became used to
Him; of Him they were not afraid; even to them He was
'only Jesus', and as a child He could lead them. Yet
alongside of them as He lay down at nights He endured
the humiliation of the outcast, more than the child at
Bethlehem, more than the leper in the lane who might not
live with other men. There He remained, eating nothing
all the time, hungry, growing ever more emaciated, already
'a worm and no man'; one who had met Him might well
have supposed that He was an outcast leper like the rest.

And yet this Man had been proclaimed the Son of God!
The voice from heaven had said it, the Baptist had confirmed
it; for one at least it was essential that he should know
whether this were literally true. 'If he were the Son of
God!' For the 'Prince of this world' it was important
to make more certain what this title signified. True, there
were already indications. His Mother, immaculate from
the first, was a sign; since the making of Eve there had
never been a woman like her. The story of His birth and
nativity were signs, above all the significance of His name.
Much since then had happened which had made him more
than suspicious; not least the fact that while he could enter
into the souls of other men and tempt them from within,
to the heart of this Man he could gain no access whatever.

Still, to one who willed not to believe, none of these signs
were final; he would try others of which the prophets had

spoken. First there was the sign of bread. The sign of Melchisedech, the sign of Moses, the sign of David, the sign of Elias, Priest, Prophet, and King alike had foreshadowed it ; Elias after forty days of fasting had shown when it might be. He would venture, he would try Him. Before the wasted and hungry figure the tempter suddenly appeared. With deference he accosted Him, as one who wished to know more ; the word had been spoken by the Jordan river, and he would have it confirmed. It was said that He was the Son of God. A sign of the Son of God, so the Sacred Books declared, would be in His command over bread ; let Him show that sign and he would be satisfied. He took up a handful of stones and said :

' If thou be the Son of God
Command that these stones be made bread.'

Jesus looked and listened ; listened unmoved to the tempter Satan ; He who knew what was in man knew what was in him, and nevertheless endured him. Satan had appealed to a well-known sign, the sign of Moses in the desert ; He would answer him by the interpretation of that sign given by Moses himself. In his death-address the patriarch had warned the people gathered round him against their too material dealing with their God. God would help them in their needs, as He had always helped them ; but the greatest need of all was that His will should be done. Hence when he spoke of the bread Moses had said :

' He humbled thee
And suffered thee to hunger
And fed thee with manna
Which thou knewest not
Neither did thy fathers know
That he might make thee know
That man doth not live by bread only
But by every word
That proceedeth out of the mouth of the Lord
Doth man live.'

Deuteronomy viii, 3.

' And Jesus answered him and said
It is written
That not in bread alone doth man live
But in every word
That proceedeth from the mouth of God.'

Satan had appealed to an act of Moses, Jesus answered by appealing to the lesson that Moses drew from that act. It was enough for the present, and for such a one as Satan. Yet the time would come when He would go further ; when in very deed He would fulfil the prophecy, and be known to all the world by the sign of bread.

The tempter had been silenced by an appeal to Scripture ; to Scripture, then, would he himself next go. He brought Jesus up to Jerusalem or he carried Him there, it matters not which. He placed Him on the pinnacle that stood at the south-east corner of the Temple. Outside the walls, on either side, the valley of Kedron and the valley of Hinnom sank almost sheer down. In his first onset he had come when the natural need for food might have been supposed likely to strengthen the temptation ; now he would appeal to another and a nobler craving, the desire to become known to men. This he would encourage by a quotation from Scripture. He would urge it as a prophecy to be fulfilled ; if Jesus were indeed the Son of God, He would hold nothing of more account than the fulfilment of the prophets.

> ' Then the devil took him up
> And brought him into the holy city of Jerusalem
> And set him upon the pinnacle of the temple
> And said to him
> If thou be the Son of God
> Cast thyself down from hence
> For it is written
> That he hath given his angels charge over thee
> That they keep thee
> And that in their hands they shall bear thee up
> Lest perhaps thou dash thy foot
> Against a stone.'

The tempter had quoted Scripture ; he had gone to the Psalmist.

> ' Because thou hast made the Lord thy refuge
> Even the most high thy habitation
> There shall no evil befall thee
> Neither shall any plague come nigh thy dwelling
> For he shall give his angels charge over thee

To keep thee in all thy ways
They shall bear thee up in their hands
Lest perhaps thou dash thy foot
Against a stone.'

Psalm xci, 9–12.

To us the passage might seem scarcely one of prophecy. Yet not on that account need the temptation have appeared to the tempter less cogent. On the contrary, the air was full of what may be called prophetic imagination ; in the schools prophecy was looked for everywhere. To discover a prophetic allusion where before it had not been noticed was a sign of a deep and diligent student of the Scriptures. When then the tempter chose this sentence from the Psalmist, he might well suppose that this Jesus would be impressed.

But he received a fitting answer. In the first encounter he had been shown the spiritual sense of a material symbol ; now, instead of this superficial reading of a text, he was taught the spirit that underlay all the service of God. Before, Jesus had quoted the words of Moses ; He quoted him again, as the true interpretation of the Law.

' Thou shalt fear the Lord thy God
And serve him
And shalt swear by his name
Ye shall not go after other gods
Of the gods of the people which are about you
For the Lord thy God
Is a jealous God among you
Lest the anger of the Lord thy God
Be kindled against thee
And destroy thee from off the face of the earth
Ye shall not tempt the Lord your God
As ye tempted him in Massah.'

Deuteronomy vi, 13–16.

' And Jesus answering said to him
It is written
Thou shalt not tempt the Lord thy God.'

It was enough. Whether Jesus were the Son of God or not, by signs at least He would not reveal Himself at the tempter's bidding. The tempter must try another method.

Among all the prophecies of old none rang louder than the prophecy of the Kingship of the coming Son of God.

It was repeated and repeated ; it was typified in David and others after him ; the royal line of David had been preserved because from that line the King of the future was to come.   At the moment all Israel could think of the Messias in scarcely any other terms ; the Priest and the Prophet, almost the Sonship of God itself, had become overshadowed by the glamour of the King.   Now this Man, be He whatever else, was certainly of the house of David. Before He was born it had been said of Him :

> ' He shall be great
> And shall be called the Son of the Most High
> And the Lord shall give unto him
> The throne of David his father
> And he shall reign in the house of David for ever
> And of his kingdom there shall be no end.'
>
> Luke i, 31–32.

After His birth an angel had announced Him as—

> ' A saviour
> Who is Christ the Lord
> In the city of David.'
>
> Luke ii, 12.

An old man in the temple had called Him—

> ' A light to the revelation of the Gentiles
> And the glory of thy people Israel.'
>
> Luke ii, 32.

From afar kings had come and had enquired after Him :

> ' Where is he
> That is born king of the Jews ?
> For we have seen his star in the east
> And we are come to adore him.'
>
> Matthew ii, 2.

If, then, this Man were the Son of God, He was, or some day He would be, a King ; and a King, not only of a petty Judæa as the little Judæans imagined, but of a kingdom that would have no bounds, that would reach to the ends of the earth.   If on the other hand He were not the Son of God, but were only another false claimant to the title, then all the more would He be enamoured of the name, and would yearn to possess its glory.   On this ground, then, would the tempter next try Him.   At present in a sense Satan ruled the world, and the kingdom belonged to him ; he would tamper with that half-truth to good effect. The perfect liar does not tell open and apparent lies ; his proficiency consists in the use he can make of the truth ; and Satan, the arch-liar, can tell the truth to his purpose as well as any other angel.

He again came to Jesus in the desert. He carried **Him** into a high mountain, it matters not how or where. There at last he revealed himself in his true colours ; he **was** transfigured before Him : Lucifer, King of Light. The mighty monarch lifted the veil ; the whole world revolved about their feet ; distance was destroyed to their gaze ; past, present, and future went in procession before them. Kingdom followed kingdom in all its panoply ; it was a wild orgy of triumphant pride for the ' Prince of the powers of this world.'

> ' Again the devil took him up
> Into a very high mountain
> And showed him all the kingdoms of the world
> In a moment of time
> And the glory of them.'

It was all his own, it should not be lost without a mighty battle. And yet the prophecies said it would be ; nay more, if this Man were the Son of God, then this Man would one day be his conqueror. Would it not be well to come to terms betimes ? Could not the prophecies be peacefully fulfilled ? Might He not be given the Kingdom even now, and yet the honour of Satan abide ? All things were possible ; and to be worshipped by Him whom he himself had long since declined to worship—what a triumph might not that be ! And how worth the sacrifice of all the rest ! It was more than a temptation ; it was a bold throw of the dice ; Satan meant what he said, and heightened the temptation by showing that he meant it, as in the full assumption of his dignity he pronounced the words :

> ' To thee will I give all this power
> And all the glory of them
> For to me they are delivered
> And to whom I will I give them
> If therefore thou falling down
> Wilt adore before me
> All shall be thine.'

Yes, it was more than a temptation ; it was at once an

offer and a challenge. Do this, it seemed to say, and all
may yet be well between us ; refuse, and it will be war to
the death. And as such did Jesus take it ; He answered
by declaring war.

> ' And Jesus answering said to him
> Begone Satan
> For it is written
> The Lord thy God shalt thou adore
> And him only shalt thou serve.'

He had not gone far for His words ; He had done no
more than quote the text which has already been cited.
Nevertheless in those very words were contained the whole
essence of Judaism, of the Jewish revelation, in contrast
with the welter of paganism around it. They were the
hall-mark of the true Kingdom, as contrasted with the
kingdom that had just been offered to Him, ' of the powers
of darkness ' ; at the end, when the battle was almost over,
and the issue was now clear, He did but refine this down
as summing up the whole fruit of His conquest.

> ' Father the hour is come
> Glorify thy Son
> That thy Son may glorify thee
> As thou hast given him power over all flesh
> That he may give eternal life
> To all whom thou hast given him
> Now this is eternal life
> That they may know thee
> The only true God
> And Jesus Christ
> Whom thou hast sent
> I have glorified thee on the earth
> I have finished the work
> Which thou gavest me to do.'
>
> John xvii, 2–6.

But that was not yet. For the moment Satan had been
worsted, but perhaps he had learnt all he had cared to
know. Whoever this Jesus was it was clear He was a power
with whom he would have to reckon. He left Him, but in
no confusion ; he left Him, but, as the evangelist carefully
tells us, only ' for a time '. He had other weapons at his
disposal and he would use them, even till that last night
when would come

'Your hour
And the power of darkness.'

Luke xxii, 53.

Meanwhile Jesus Himself was at peace. He could ask His Father, and His Father would give Him legions of angels to help Him in His work ; but that would not be His way. He had not become an angel, He had become Man ; and man should be His helper. Still, because of His humiliation He should not be deserted ; He who had submitted to this buffeting of the spirit of evil, should be visited by the spirits of good. As at the beginning in Bethlehem, as at the end in the Garden, so now in His first desolation,

'Behold angels came
And ministered to him.'

5. The Witness of John the Baptist

Two months had now passed by since Jesus had come to be baptized. During all that time John had waited, looking for a further sign ; meanwhile up in Jerusalem the talk was growing rife. Already John had warned his hearers that they should not mistake him, that they should not count him for more than he claimed to be ; but that sort of warning did not carry far. The Scribes and Pharisees had shown him respect ; men continued to talk ; the more vulgar and more easily affected were growing in enthusiasm ; they were quoting the prophets, raking up old local traditions, and applying them to him. Some were asking whether he were not the Christ that was to come ; others claimed that at least he was Elias returned, seeing that it was from the very spot where he preached that Elias had been carried to heaven in the chariot of fire (4 Kings ii) ; others again, clinging more to the present, would maintain that he was a prophet, independent and inspired as the prophets of old, that the age of the prophets was returning. The talk was persistent, was threatening ; it was time the authorities, the oracles of the Law, took more notice of this man and his pretended mission.

Yet what could they do ? To condemn him unquestioned was unwise ; to persecute and silence him might be dangerous. Besides, as they had owned from the beginning, there might be something in all this gossip. Were he indeed a prophet, or Elias, above all were he Christ Himself, they would need to be careful before they passed sentence. There must be some kind of formal enquiry ; they would send trustworthy men to the Jordan to cross-examine him ; whether he were all men said of him or not, they would judge him from his own mouth. Thus while Jesus in the desert but a few miles away was being tested by Satan the Tempter, John His witness was being questioned by the priests of Judæa ; the time would come when the two powers would combine, and would test their victim with terrible effect.

The court of enquiry came down, priests and levites, all of the sect of the Pharisees, sticklers for the Law, hard interpreters of the Scripture, suspicious of any innovation that was not of their own making, tolerating none but their own ceremonial, men not likely to let slip any single advantage. They came in all their authority ; they stood about the Baptist and watched him. When he paused they came forward ; they let him see that this meeting was more than a casual affair, as they put their question,

'Who art thou ? '

And John understood. They meant more than the question conveyed. Deepest in their hearts, what made them anxious above all things, was the doubt whether or not he might indeed be the Messias.

Of that anxiety he would at once relieve them ; on that point at least they could set their minds at ease.

'And he confessed
And did not deny
And he confessed
I am not the Christ.'

The main point was thus quickly settled. Next was the question raised among the people ; at least to them, official judges from the Temple, he would be bound to give an answer.

'And they asked him
What then ?
Art thou Elias ? '

They were not disappointed ; again he could reassure them ; they had a right to question him and he had a duty to reply.

'And he said
I am not.'

Still there was a further question. Once on a time Moses had spoken of a prophet that was to come ; whether or not he had meant the Messias was a question disputed in the schools. He had said :

> ' The Lord thy God will raise up to thee
> A prophet from the midst of thee
> Of thy brethren
> Like unto me
> Unto him shall ye hearken ' ;

and again :

> ' I will raise them up a prophet
> From among their brethren
> Like unto thee
> And will put my words in his mouth
> And he shall speak unto them
> All that I shall command him
> And it shall come to pass
> That whosoever will not hearken unto my words
> Which he shall speak in my name
> I will require it of him.'
>
> Deuteronomy xviii, 15, 18, 19.

This man might be that prophet ; if he were, then again, from the warning of Moses himself, they would need to receive him carefully. So again they asked him :

> ' Art thou the prophet ? '

and again they received the emphatic and laconic answer :

> ' No.'

After that there was little that need trouble them. They had learnt nothing ; they had only satisfied themselves on the points that gave anxiety to their masters in Jerusalem ; the rest could matter very little. Still it would be well to learn something positive. John had said who he was not, could he be induced to say who he claimed to be ?

> ' Then they said to him
> Who art thou ?
> That we may give an answer to them that sent us.'

The question was contemptuous enough. For their part, they seemed to say, they cared not who he was ; their business was official, their enquiry was official, and no more. And as such John treated them ; he gave them the answer he had given when he had first formally begun his preaching, and until they asked for more he would give them nothing else.

> ' He said
> I am the voice of one crying in the wilderness
> Make straight the way of the Lord
> As the prophet Isaias said.'

It was the same answer, and yet in the last sentence there seemed to be a note of rebuke. Of course, that was not to be permitted to affect such men as these. They were ' of the Pharisees ', and were above such hints ; they were priests and Levites, and needed not to be told what the prophets said. Still they could not but retaliate. They would feign a counter-attack ; if he hinted a rebuke to them they would openly rebuke him. It is a common method of falsehood.

> ' And they asked him and said to him
> Why then dost thou baptize
> If thou be not Christ
> Nor Elias
> Nor the prophet ? '

The fourth title they ignored, the only one which John had claimed :

> ' The voice of one crying in the desert.'

And in like manner John ignored their question. By what authority he baptized he would not tell them, for he had already told them what sufficed. He would call attention only to the nature of his baptism, which was feeble enough in itself. He would argue no more about himself ; instead, with these men, whose duty and office it was to hear, he would seize the opportunity to proclaim Him for whom he himself had come. They had pretended to be seeking the Messias ; he would tell them He was at hand.

> ' John answered them saying
> I baptize in water
> But there hath stood one in the midst of you
> Whom you know not
> The same is he that shall come after me
> Who is preferred before me
> The latchet of whose shoe
> I am not worthy to loose.'

We are told the exact spot where this cross-examination

and this momentous declaration were made ; Bethania across the Jordan, as distinguished from the better-known Bethania higher up the road at the foot of Olivet. We are even given a hint as to the day. In other words it would seem that the evangelist, John, who tells the story, was a witness of the scene ; and it would seem that he looks upon it as one of the landmarks in the revelation of the Son of God. And indeed it was ; there at the gate of Judæa the King was formally announced to the leaders of the Jews in solemn conclave ; there from the first, had they wished it, they might have found and known their Messias.

6. The First Disciples

It was now two months, as we have said, since Jesus had appeared by the Jordan, during all which time John had patiently waited for the next sign that was to guide him. He had gone on preaching as before, but with even more assurance ; now that the Lord had definitely appeared he was able to speak of His presence with greater emphasis. As for the rest he was content to wait ; he had already waited long, and had learnt to abide the moment of God.

At length one day, the day after the examination by the priests and Levites, Jesus again was seen, walking towards him on the other side of the Jordan, the side of Jerusalem and Jericho.

<blockquote>
' The next day
John saw Jesus coming to him.'
</blockquote>

There was nothing at all about Him to distinguish Him from any other man, as there had been nothing to distinguish Him during all these eighteen years. He walked down the bank of the river as He had walked down the streets of Nazareth, so like others that after thirty years not a neighbour had discovered in Him anything of note. He came down the river-side as one might who took a walk, apparently with no special aim, occupied with His own thoughts, interfering with, intruding Himself on, no one ; so that, had John not observed Him, He might have passed by and none would have noticed. Such is His first appearance when He opens His campaign.

But John recognized Him, and could not let Him so pass by. He was there to be the witness to Him, and he knew the time was come to declare Him. He must point Him out to those around him ; yet to do so he chose a singular description. Hitherto he had spoken of Him in terms that inspired awe and fear—'the Lord', 'the wrath to come', 'the axe laid to the root', 'the mightier than I whose shoes I am not worthy to bear', 'whose fan is in his hand', who 'will burn the chaff with unquenchable fire'. Now on a sudden all is changed. He harks back to that lamb of Moses, whose blood was shed for the redemption of his people. As he spoke, there would have been some in whom the words he used must have awakened memories, not least that prophecy of Isaias, that the future Messias would one day be led

> ' As a lamb to the slaughter
> Not opening his mouth.'

John knew that the announcement he made, concerning such a man as he pointed out, would be wellnigh incredible to any who heard him. He had spoken of the Messias as a great King to come, for whom the valleys were to be filled up and the crooked ways made straight ; he had spoken of himself as the forerunner of all this pomp and greatness ; how then could it be that the countryman across the river, from His dress evidently a Galilæan, from His manner no one in particular, should be the King for whom they were looking and longing ? Even to John himself the paradox had been overwhelming ; even he at first had failed to recognize Him in this garb ; with all his knowledge and interior perception he had needed a divine revelation to enable him to understand. All the more, then, must he emphasize the fact ; that man, even that seemingly plain man who passed by them, was in very truth the Lamb of God, was all that the prophet Isaias included in the term ' Son of God ' ; impossible as it seemed, nevertheless he had it on the same authority as he had his own commission to baptize.

> ' And he saith
> Behold the Lamb of God
> Behold him who taketh away
> The sin of the world
> This is he of whom I said
> After me cometh a man
> Who is preferred before me
> Because he was before me

And I knew him not
But that he may be made manifest in Israel
Therefore am I come
Baptizing in water
And John gave testimony saying
I saw the Spirit
Coming as a dove from heaven
And he remained upon him
And I knew him not
But he who sent me to baptize in water
Said to me
He upon whom thou shalt see the Spirit descending
He it is
That baptizeth with the Holy Ghost
And I saw
And I gave testimony
That this is the Son of God.'

At times the words read almost as if John had spoken them in self-defence, to justify his own bold action. Incredible as it seemed, over this man and no other the signs had appeared ; and he had obeyed the signs, he had listened to the voice of faith instead of to the voice of human reason, let the consequences be what they might.

Jesus passed on His way down the river-side, and the shrubs and willows soon hid Him from sight. He had given to John no sign of recognition ; He had made no effort to be known. As before, as everywhere, He would intrude Himself on no one ; before He began He would wait for man to make the first advance. The next day He would come again, and again and again if need be ; in the end, if only out of curiosity, someone would take notice of the Baptist's repeated witness. And as for John, he too would wait in patience. What more he should do was not made manifest to him ; he was to be a witness and no more, and with that for the present he would be content.

But the very next day the change came. It was well on in the afternoon, when the sun was still high overhead and the road was quiet. John was at the ford, but was resting ; with him were a few followers, members of a chosen group which had gathered round the Baptist and which, as disciples from a master, had begun to receive from him a special training. To this group John had already given lessons in prayer ; he had taught it the practice of penance ; he had prepared it that its members, should the need come, might go forth and preach and baptize. As of old the prophet Elias had built up a school of prophets, so did John lay the foundations of a school that should carry on his work until the Messias definitely appeared.

While, then, these were seated beside the river, the same figure came walking towards them on the other side ; the figure of a working man, remarkable in nothing, save perhaps that He was deeply occupied with His own thoughts. Again John looked up at Him, watching Him intently but doing nothing more ; again he uttered the same words :

' Behold the Lamb of God.'

This time he did not speak in vain. Two men of the group,—they were both from Galilee, which would imply that they had already definitely thrown in their lot with John,—could not but be struck by the repetition of their master's words. Whoever He was, whatever His appearance, the Man that walked down the opposite bank was in John's mind someone of importance. It was the afternoon, there was nothing to detain them ; they would follow this Man and see what they could discover about Him.

They let Him go forward ; then they crossed the river, and walked down the narrow path behind Him ; unknown to themselves the first followers of Christ. They followed Him in silence till the very distance betrayed them. The way they were going was no ordinary route ; it led nowhere in particular ; no one would go along that path but for a purpose ; hitherto He had always gone that way alone. Obviously, therefore, they were tracking Him ; clearly He was justified in speaking to them. He slackened His pace ; He let them come nearer ; as a stranger who speaks to a stranger in a lonely place, the loneliness making them companions, He turned about and accosted them.

' And Jesus turning
And seeing them following Him
Saith to them
What seek you ? '

Such are the first words that Jesus spoke to men at the beginning of His mission. They are a key to all that followed after ; they might be taken as the motto of His life. In various forms as the months roll on they are

repeated, till that last time when they are spoken in Geth-
semani ; after He had died and risen they are again almost
the first words with which His risen life begins. Jesus came
to men that He might be found by men, but He would be
found only by those who sought Him. He would speak
and He would act in such a way that only those who had
eyes to see would see, only those who had ears to hear would
understand. He would call them, when they came He
would welcome them, but the searching question is never
long silent. ' What seek you ? '—' Do you believe ? '—
' Whom do you say that I am ? '—The eagerness of the
appeal grows stronger and stronger as His public life moves
on.

At first the two men were taken aback. This stranger
had caught them unawares. There was an independence
in His manner which commanded respect, making them
ashamed that they had seemed to pry into His secrets ; at
the same time there was a friendliness which invited their
companionship. They stood close in front of Him ; their
answer was the spontaneous expression of their thoughts,
unpremeditated :

'Rabbi',

they said, which proved that already they knew He was
more than themselves ;

' Where dwellest thou ? '

The answer gladdened their hearts. It was a word of
welcome, an offer of friendship, an expression of willingness
to share with them what He had to share.

' Come and see ',

He said ; the first use of that wonderful invitation which
was so often to be repeated afterwards.

We see the three walking down the path through the
jungle growth along the river bank ; forming now one
group, Jesus in the middle, the men on either side, giving
themselves away to Him in answer to His questions, by the
end of that walk seeming to have known Him all their lives.
At first they had spoken with reserve and caution ; soon
they had become so much at home that they had forgotten
the stranger in whose company they were ; His presence
stirred their hearts and their tongues. He drew them
on and they did not notice it ; He was one with themselves and they were eager to tell Him whatever came

into their minds. He was a man to be trusted at first sight.

At a bend of the river in the middle of the thicket was a little thatched hut made of wood. It had a wide open doorway but no windows ; the roof, coming down further in front, and resting on two poles, made a kind of verandah, keeping off the midday sun ; the floor was just the beaten ground. Here Jesus stood still. This was where He lived ; if His companions would rest with Him awhile He would gladly entertain them. They could not refuse even if they would ; gladly they would be His guests ; they sat down on the ground, with the evening sun behind them while He brought from His store food and water. Did their minds, steeped in prophetic symbol, go back to that scene when their father Abraham entertained two guests in his tent ? Later, when He was indeed the Master, and sent the disciples two and two to preach His Gospel, did they recollect this first occasion when He had welcomed them in twos ? And later still, when on a certain road as it were by chance He joined Himself to two others and

> ' they knew him in the breaking of bread ',

did they recall that first day when they too had first known Him, eating His bread in His cottage by the Jordan ?

> ' They came
> And saw where he abode
> And stayed with him that day.'

This is all we are told of that eventful meeting, but the very silence is eloquent. What passed between them we do not know ; in spite of his fondness for recording conversations on similar occasions it would seem that on this occasion John has nothing to tell. All we know is, and we can see the influence growing insensibly upon them, that as the hours passed by, and the sun sank behind the hills of Judæa, they found it increasingly difficult to leave Him. When at last they did leave, and retraced their steps to their little camp beside the Jordan ford, they conversed with one another on the way, and wondered at the manner in which their hearts had been warmed by this Man who had spoken to them ; and they had become convinced, they knew not how or why, that indeed John was right, and this was truly the Lamb of God, whatever that might mean.

' And Andrew
The brother of Simon Peter
was one of the two
Who had heard of John
And followed him.'

It comes to us with some little surprise that apparently
the chief disciples of John the Baptist were in great part
Galilæans. John was in every sense a Judæan ; the crowds
that came to his baptism at the Jordan ford must have been
mainly from Judæa. Galilæans with others will have
passed over on their way to and from the Holy City, but
this alone will scarcely explain the prominence of the
fishermen of Galilee among the followers of the Baptist.
This has led one biographer at least to place the scenes of
the Baptism and all that followed after higher up the river,
at the crossing, or near it, in Galilee itself. But there are
other reasons, intrinsic and extrinsic to the Gospel narrative,
which seem to justify the local tradition, indeed to make it
necessary. Still this need not concern us. Be the explanation what it may, it was two of these Galilæans who had
heard the words of John and followed Jesus ; of these one
was Andrew, who had a younger brother, a fisherman like
himself, called Simon. Not unnaturally, as soon as he was
able, since both were believers in the Baptist, Andrew
sought out his brother, a man more decided and enthusiastic
than himself, and told him of their experience of that day.

' He first findeth his brother Simon
And said to him
We have found the Messias.'

At such short notice, on such slight evidence, this was a
bold statement to make ; what, in the minds of Andrew
and Simon at that time, could it have implied ? One
conjectures not much ; a hope long-lingering, seeking to
find expression, the wish to believe confirming the discovery
of the day before ; in Simon, confidence in his elder
brother's judgement inducing him at least to go and
examine for himself.

So they went together, these two, from their encampment
near the ford, down the same track that Andrew and the
other had gone, in and out among the tiny trees and brush-
wood, till they came again to the little hut where this
stranger from Nazareth had made His abode. He was

alone as before ; as before, as they were often enough to find Him later, He was seemingly occupied with His own thoughts, a hermit rather than a man of action ; nevertheless, when the two appeared, it was as if He had expected them. Before Andrew could introduce his brother, Jesus by a gesture silenced him. For a time, till both were awed by the long delay, He gazed steadily into the eyes of Simon. At last with solemn emphasis, yet with a ring of encouragement, even of friendship and of welcome, He said :

'Thou art Simon the son of Jona
Thou shalt be called Cephas.'

Thus from the beginning did Jesus show that He knew whom He would choose.

To Simon himself this act of recognition was disconcerting enough. He had come, with that independence of judgement that made at once the strength and weakness of his character, to sift the matter for himself, to make up his own mind about the Man whom his brother had called the Messias. Before he had been able to put a single question, almost before he had had the time to take in the outward form of this carpenter of Nazareth, the Man had shown that He already knew him through and through ; that not he, Simon, was to be the judge, but that already the other was the Judge and Master of Simon. The memory of that sudden conquest could not be forgotten ; when the prophecy came true it was recalled ; then more than ever Simon understood the care that had always shielded him ; and all he owed to Jesus drew from him an ever-growing torrent of love.

It was now some three months since Jesus had been away from Galilee and it was time for Him to return. The rains were wellnigh over, the country-side was gleaming green and bright with flowers as perhaps only Palestine can show them. The season was agreeable for the three days' walk across Judæa, and Samaria, and Esdraelon. A few preparations were needed, some food to be bought in the bazaar, a pot and material for cooking, perhaps a sandal to be mended or some article of clothing to be patched. To make His arrangements Jesus goes into the nearest village. He stops at this shop-front and that, open on the street, providing Himself with what He needs. As with other purchasers about Him there is no waste of words, the business is just done and He moves on.

As He passed again down the lane to His hut by the river-side, He came upon a young man who eyed Him carefully. This man's name was Philip ; he, too, came from Bethsaida, the home of Andrew and Simon. He had heard these brothers discussing with each other the discovery they had made. Their words had stirred him ; simple, believing, trustful as he was he had longed to know more of the Man whom they called Jesus. On the other hand his nature was against him. He was humble and retiring, he thought himself but one of the crowd. Andrew and Simon, after all, in Bethsaida were not unimportant and therefore might well be noticed ; but for himself, who was he ? Of so little account that to be considered at all did not so much as occur to him.

Silently, then, this plain youth, Philip, stood gazing at Jesus as He passed ; he could at least look on Him if he could do no more. But what was this ? As Philip looked at Jesus, Jesus in turn lifted up His head and looked at him. Their eyes met ; they were the glad eyes of a friend meeting a friend ; as the day before by a single word He had shown Simon that He knew him, so now, by only a glance, He showed Philip that he too was known and understood. They were friends at the instant, wherever that friendship was to lead ; Jesus just said

‘ Follow me ’,

and the meekest of the future twelve apostles was won.

But as is not uncommon with meek and gentle people, Philip could not contain himself for joy. Like Mary after the Annunciation, who must needs hurry away and carry her glad tidings to one whom she looked upon as greater than herself, so now Philip, full of his wonderful adventure, could not but bear the news to one who in many ways was his superior. Philip was from Bethsaida, a little fishing village, Nathanael was from Cana, a busy town upon the high road of traffic, where men saw life in many forms. Philip was by nature docile and made little of his own opinion ; Nathanael was cautious and discriminating. Nevertheless, in this camp where all were ‘ seekers after the redemption of Israel ’, between these two a mutual esteem had sprung up, the weaker leaning upon the stronger, the stronger yielding to the weaker more than he knew.

Upon Nathanael, then, as he took his rest beneath the

shadow of a fig-tree, Philip broke in and poured out his message in a torrent. Andrew had told Simon that the Messias had been found. Philip must go further ; his mind had been working since he had heard the name and had analysed the meaning of the term. Andrew had said nothing more, to him the discovery was enough ; Philip must say what he knew of this Man, if only to prove how utterly he had been conquered.

> ' Philip findeth Nathanael
> And saith to him
> We have found him
> Of whom Moses in the law
> And the prophets did write
> Jesus
> The son of Joseph
> of Nazareth.'

With childlike breathlessness Philip poured out his tale ; with becoming condescension Nathanael listened and bore with him. That Philip and his friends from Bethsaida had discovered the Messias, well, that might or might not be ; that the Messias was Jesus Bar-Joseph of Nazareth, here was trifling not to be endured. He came from Cana, a few miles only from Nazareth, and therefore he knew something of the place ; Philip was from the Lake, a long way off, and no doubt could not know the significance of his words. Of Nazareth ! Why Nazareth was next to nowhere, flung up on a hill-side where nobody went, and where nobody lived who was able to live elsewhere ; a forlorn place, with not a single interest about it, whose inhabitants in consequence, narrow and obstinate and ignorant and gross, were notorious for their boorish stupidity and fanatical discontent. Nathanael could only pity Philip, and warn him against this enthusiasm utterly misplaced.

> ' Can anything of good come from Nazareth ? '

he asked, and thought that alone would be enough.

But for once Philip was not to be so easily silenced. Nazarene or not, Jesus was all he had said ; let Nathanael but meet Him and he was sure he would discover for himself. He would not argue, he would only hold on.

> ' Come and see ',

was his urgent appeal, and his confidence won the day. To humour his young friend, Nathanael allowed himself to be dragged along, down the path which was now becoming more frequented, to the little hut at the bend of the river. Outside the door, under the overhanging roof, Jesus of Nazareth was seated in the midst of a group of men ; among them was one of those who had first followed Him, whose name was John. With affected indifference, as if he were no more than a chance passer-by, Nathanael of Cana came within hearing. Jesus looked at him ; then, with a smile as of recognition, He turned to the companions about Him and said :

> ' Behold an Israelite indeed
> In whom there is no guile.'

Nathanael was taken by surprise. Like the two who had first followed Jesus, like Simon who had followed his brother, he too had come with caution intending to judge for himself ; before he could begin his investigation he found himself summed up and judged. The sentence passed upon him was kindly enough ; still whether or not he should take it in good part he could not at once decide. He looked a little coldly at this Nazarene. He knew no Nazarene himself, and he was not sure that he cared that a Nazarene should know him. So with a touch of resentment in his voice, he raised his head and asked :

> ' Whence knowest thou me ? '

But Jesus was not to be so easily set aside. Through all the outward affectation and prejudice He had read Nathanael's heart. After all he thought of Nazareth only as every other of his kind thought of it ; why the Nazarenes themselves had no opinion of one another, as later He was to learn to His cost. He would treat Nathanael in another way. Simon He had won by a word of recognition and a hint as to what he would one day be ; Nathanael had been struck in that he had been recognized, he should now be awed still more.

> ' Jesus answered and said to him
> Before that Philip called thee
> When thou wast under the fig tree
> I saw thee.'

Good Nathanael was overwhelmed. Not only had he been summed up at sight ; here was one who could see at a distance. At once he was carried to another plane of vision ; all idea of the Nazarene vanished. The others had been conquered by less evidence than this; they had proclaimed Jesus the Messias; he could do no less. Nay, he would do more. Quickly his thoughts recalled two titles the name of the Messias implied; he would give this Man those titles, it would be some atonement for his rude behaviour. The 'true Israelite in whom there was no guile' was the essence of good manners.

'Nathanael answered him and said
Rabbi
Thou art the Son of God
Thou art the King of Israel.'

Whatever the words might mean, and Nathanael could not have known, to use them of Jesus was indeed an *amende honorable*, and as such Jesus accepted them. But He would not stop there; in faith and love and hope it would never be His custom to be satisfied. When men took what He gave of these He would always give more, when they gave of these to Him He would always ask for more; in giving and receiving He would never be content. Nathanael had surrendered so much; he should be given in return an assurance.

'Jesus answered and said to him
Because I said unto thee
I saw thee under the fig tree
Thou believest
Greater than these things shalt thou see.'

Then, even as He spoke, His face seemed to lighten and His eyes to enkindle. The men around Him saw a sight the like of which they were often to see again, and which when they saw it held them speechless. Though this Man from Nazareth changed not a whit, yet for a moment it seemed as if another soul than His was looking through His eyes, into a world other than that in which they were living; and as if the words that came from His lips belonged to that other world, by ears such as theirs scarcely to be understood. What He said was all true, and they knew in their hearts that it was true, because He saw it and told them what He saw; but what it meant they did not know, they scarcely cared to know. It was the first of many such visions of faith. They looked at Him as He rose among them, and their firm belief in Him was only the more strengthened as the words He spoke were more mysterious.

> ' And he saith to them
> Amen, Amen, I say to you
> You shall see the heaven opened
> And the angels of God
> Ascending and descending
> Upon the Son of Man.'

They did not understand ; nevertheless the imagery could not but recall a like scene described in the Written Word.

' But Jacob, being departed from Bersabee, went on to Haran, and when he was come to a certain place and would rest in it after sunset, he took of the stones that lay there, and putting under his head slept in the same place. And he saw in his sleep a ladder standing upon the earth, and the top thereof touching heaven ; the Angels also of God ascending and descending by it, and the Lord leaning upon the ladder, saying to him : I am the Lord God of Abraham thy father, and the God of Isaac. The land wherein thou sleepest I will give to thee and to thy seed, and thy seed shall be as the dust of the earth. Thou shalt spread abroad to the west and to the east and to the north and to the south, and in thee and thy seed all the tribes of the earth shall be blessed. And I will be thy keeper whithersoever thou goest, and will bring thee back into this land ; neither will I leave thee till I shall have accomplished all that I have said.'

Genesis xxviii, 10–15.

It was the well-known vision of their father Jacob. They remembered how of all his visions this was the one that had touched him most deeply. To it he had most often appealed ; and they knew that in some way, in and by the Man before them, they would see the prophecy fulfilled.

3

7. The Feast at Cana

T HINGS had thus moved quickly during these few days. The Baptist had done his duty well. He had delivered his message fearlessly to all the world, he had won great numbers to his baptism. From these he had selected some whom he had trained apart in prayer and deeper understanding. Out of these again a few had been chosen to whom the more intimate revelation might be made. To them, so prepared, the Lamb of God had been shown ; incredible as the demonstration seemed, they had listened to John and followed, and to their own great surprise they had found it hard to tear themselves away. Thereafter conquest had succeeded conquest. Strong men like Simon and Nathanael had yielded to the fascination, as well as men more pliable like Philip. In this Nazarene's company there reigned a strange sense of contentment, a sense of security under the guidance of one who Himself was safe, a sense of union among themselves because He was their common leader, a sense that a goal had been reached, that the main work of life had been done, that whatever was to follow would only be the issue of the vital present fact before them, the discovery of this Man and His friendship.

With these impressions fresh upon them it is not hard to understand the ease with which the first company of Jesus' disciples was formed. They had been prepared by John ; at his bidding they had passed over to Jesus. They were all Galilæans and must soon return to their homes ; when Jesus made as if He would go into Galilee it was but fitting that they should go with Him.

To Galilee there were two main roads ; one up the Jordan valley through Peræa, along the river bank till it comes near the Sea of Tiberias, the other across Judæa and Samaria and the valley of Esdraelon, rising thence among the western hills towards Cana. Travellers to Capharnaum and Bethsaida, and the cities on the eastern side of Galilee, would naturally take the first route ; Carmel and the coasts of Tyre and Sidon, Nazareth, Cana, and indeed all to the west of Thabor, would be more easily reached by the second. This road has many windings ; once it gets clear of the Judæan upland plain, it twists and turns round the hills of Samaria, diving down along a curve into deep valleys, rising again over high ridges, seldom a straight line till the plain of Esdraelon is gained, which breaks suddenly on the traveller as he comes through the range of Little Hermon. On foot from the crossing of the Jordan in Judæa to Esdraelon the journey would take at least two days ; across the valley and over the mountains into Cana it would require another.

Along this second route Jesus returned. It led to Cana ; there if He chose He could take a branch road westward which ran along a mountain-side, and then over a ridge into Nazareth. His disciples came with Him ; already, it seems, they had given themselves this name. At Cana, if need be, they could leave Him and in six hours more could be at Tiberias to the east.

But there was another reason for going first to Cana. A wedding feast was to be held there, at which His Mother would be present ; if He wished to meet her He would find her there. The news of His coming, with a band of Galilæan companions, soon reached the ears of the master of the feast ; for the sake of the Mother the Son also was invited, for the sake of Jesus His companions.

In this way for the first time we are introduced to the Mother of Jesus. For thirty years she had waited, keeping to herself the secret of the King. Like others of her kind she had lived her village life in Nazareth—' His Mother, do we not know her ? '—taking her place among kindred and friends and neighbours, waiting for the manifestation which she knew must one day come. During all these years her boy had given no sign. She had watched Him as He grew, in age, and grace, and wisdom, visible to her Mother's eyes though others noticed nothing. She had pondered in her heart the wonderful things that had been, the monotony that was, the warnings of the prophets who had looked into the future. Much she had interpreted, much she had not understood ; only now at the end, when for these long three months He had left her, she had divined that the hour of change was at hand. How it would come about she did not know ; only this she knew, that as at the beginning He had not begun without her, as at the end she would still be there, so in some way at the moment of His first appearance she would have her part to play.

The marriage feast went on ; everywhere in the East, with the poorest as well as with the rich, this is a very great affair. With all alike, to the lookers-on, by far the most important function is the entertainment of the guests. Let them be as many as possible; let them be regaled as freely as circumstances will allow ; as much as may be the impression must be given of an open and lavish, even of a reckless hand. The guests would crowd every corner of the place ; special and more honoured friends in the hall where the bridegroom presided ; the rest where they could, in other rooms, on open verandahs, most in the open space around the house.

In such an open space, hard by the servants' quarters, stood Mary and her Son with His companions ; that they were not among the guests of honour is manifestly clear. As they stood there, chiefly looking on, enjoying the enjoyment of others, in a lowly place where the servants mostly congregated, a murmur of trouble reached their ears. The bridegroom himself knew nothing of it ; even the steward, the master of the revels, did not know ; only the poor waiters and servants were unhappy, for to them it belonged to see that every guest had his fill. The wine was failing ; there would soon not be enough to go round ; what were they to do ?

What induced the Mother of Jesus to seize this strange occasion we can never hope to know ; still less what later induced her to encourage others with such confidence that they could not disobey. But we may conjecture ; without a revelation no man can do more. She saw these serving-men in trouble ; with her woman's sympathy, with her own exceeding woman's sympathy, she easily interpreted what was its source. She was sorry for them ; she wished something could be done to help them ; scarcely meaning more than to express her feeling in words, not dreaming that anything would come of it, she pointed to them and said, as any woman would, to her Son by her side :

' They have no wine.'

But what is this ? Jesus seems to take her words seriously.

He seems to behave as if in some way what she had said concerned Him. He does not suffer the remark to pass by, as might have been expected. He dwells upon it, He seems almost to resent it, by His manner He shows that He is wavering over some decision He is about to make ; but a little more and He will yield, whatever the decision may be.

'And Jesus saith to her
Woman
What is that to me and to thee ?
My hour is not yet come.'

To Mary's ears the meaning of the words could not be mistaken. Her woman's sympathy had drawn from her a remark of kindliness ; the affection of her Son had chosen to interpret it as something more. He had taken her statement as a request. That He could grant the request if He would she knew, that the time for such requests to be granted had come she had also guessed ; could it be that this was to her a hint that now, if she so chose, He would begin ? True, as He said, the hour had not yet sounded ; nevertheless if He meant to wait yet longer, why had He said anything at all ? No, His words were not resentful ; rather they were an encouragement to urge the petition ; with all their seeming hardness they betrayed a heart within that was only too anxious to be beaten. Many times hereafter shall we find Him making as if He would not hear an appeal ; and if others could interpret His manner and words aright, much more certainly could His Mother. He was pausing ; He was looking to her to set to the world an example of faith and confidence. She would be brave ; by her courage she would inspire the others ; with an assurance that could not be resisted that valiant little Handmaid of the Lord who once had said :

'Be it done to me according to thy word',
now turned to the waiters and bade them :
'Whatever he shall say to you
Do ye.'

The rest of the story moves quickly. We notice in Jesus the same power of command that we have already seen, that in moments of crisis we shall often see again, so that at His bidding even strangers will do that which at first seems idle and futile. For what servant, to humour a mere onlooker, would himself first fill a vessel full of water and

then present it to his master for wine ?   We notice, too, the
same precision and assurance which give certainty to those
who obey Him ;   because He says it, it is right—this
unaccountable conviction is in the atmosphere of all His
words.

' Now there were set there six waterpots of stone
According to the manner of the purifying of the Jews
Containing two or three measures apiece
Jesus saith to them
Fill the waterpots with water
And they filled them up to the brim
And Jesus saith to them
Draw out now
And carry to the chief steward of the feast
And they carried it
And when the chief steward had tasted
The water made wine
And knew not whence it was
But the waiters knew
Who had drawn the water
The chief steward called the bridegroom
And saith to him
Every man at first setteth forth good wine
And when men have well drunk
Then that which is worse
But thou hast kept the good wine until now.'

The evangelist concludes his narrative with the significant
remark :

' This beginning of signs
Did Jesus in Cana of Galilee
And manifested his glory
And his disciples believed in him.'

And indeed for more reasons than one it is an event which
could hardly be spared.   Only a week or two before one
who had wished to put Him to the test had bid Him turn
a stone into bread, and He had refused ;   now at a woman's
half-suggestion He had turned whole gallons of water into
wine.   Was this only a coincidence ?   Was it significant of
nothing ?   Or was this beginning of signs a warning to
Satan of the prophecy :

' I will set enmities
Between thee and the woman

And thy seed and her seed
She shall crush thy head ' ?

Again, let it be noticed how solitary and alone this miracle stands in the early months of our Lord's public life. There had been none before ; after it none other is recorded until, many months later, He again made His appearance in Cana. When Jesus said :

' My hour is not yet come ',

it would seem that He meant what He said, and that the time for miracles was not yet. Nevertheless on this occasion He forestalled the time ; on this insignificant occasion, in a matter so insignificant that the like is not found in the whole of the rest of the Gospel narrative ; so insignificant that three evangelists have not thought it worth while to record. And He did it at the simple word of His Mother. The miracle at Cana is no more nor less than a public declaration, made at the moment of His parting from her, of the power she would still have over Him. For thirty years He had been subject to her ; He had obeyed her slightest wish ; of that our human reason leaves us in no doubt. He would continue to obey, to the end of time He would continue to obey.

Lastly there is the nature of the miracle itself ; the changing of water into wine, of one substance into another. For the training of men, especially for the training of His own, it was well that He should begin betimes. The day would come when He would use this power with awful effect, so awful as to make it the crowning act of all human faith ; when He would change, not merely water into wine, but wine into something much more precious. It was but according to His forethought and consideration for weak men that this first act of power should be a shadow and a sign of that which was to follow.

' And his disciples believed in him.'

What did they believe ? More than once John sums up a situation with these words, and each time we are driven to ask the same question. All we can answer is that another step in faith had been made. They had begun by faith in John ; on the evidence of John they had put faith in a stranger whom he had given to them as ' the Lamb of God '. They had followed this stranger ; they had submitted to His fascination and had come away satisfied that He was the Messias. The discovery had stirred enthusiasm, the knowledge of Him had enkindled love ; and they had welcomed Him in the fuller sense as

> ' He of whom Moses in the Law
> And the prophets spoke.'

They had come around Him and He had given them proof that He had power to read their lives and their hearts ; they had responded by calling Him still further,

> ' Son of God
> King of Israel.'

In the strength of that attraction they had come with Him into Galilee. As their reward, in confirmation of that faith and that trust, He had done this thing before their eyes and gladdened them, and they knew that their faith was not misplaced.

Jesus left Cana, but He did not turn west, as might have been expected, towards Nazareth. The spring-time was now well advanced, and the country-side was smiling, clad in green. It would soon be the Pasch, and then He would be going to Jerusalem. He had now friends about Him who lived along the bank of the lake that stretched out before Capharnaum ; men who had thrown in their lot with Him, even in so short a time, men to whom He must one day make a return, pressed down and flowing over. As they had come with Him, He would now go with them ; and His Mother and His kinsmen, Simon and Jude and James and others, they too elected to go with Him.

8. The First Cleansing of the Temple

The Pasch was drawing near and pilgrims from Galilee and further north began to gather on the side of the lake of Tiberias. They gathered there that they might go together, along the route which crosses the river below the lake, then runs down the Jordan valley, crosses again below Jericho, and finally leads through Bethania and over Olivet into the Holy City. In general, but especially at this time of the year, it was the better route to take. The other passing through Samaria was liable to provide trouble ; for Samaritans, with their rival institution on Mount Garizim, had no kind feelings for Jews on their way to the Temple.

It was a strange assembly that went on its way ; everyone was loaded, with food, with materials for cooking, with children ; the men went ahead, their staffs in their hands, the women lumbered after as best they might.   They might be weary, but they never said a word ; instead, they tramped along almost as if they would hurry faster.   For shelter at night there was no need to fear ; it was the best season of the year, and they could sleep by the roadside on the open plain.

Arrived near Jerusalem they would encamp in groups, some on the slope of Olivet over against the city, some on the more even plain to the north ; some, it may be, would have friends within the city walls, and at this time of the year every house was open.   There would be others about them from other places, speaking other tongues, particularly Greek, wearing other dress, but all equally intent upon the central festival that made them one.   They would pitch their camps, and then at once would make for the Temple area ; the Golden Gate, looking out over the valley of Kedron, was thronged.

In such a company, and under such circumstances, Jesus made His way to Jerusalem ; when the time came, He entered through the Golden Gate among the rest. Often before He had been there ; He had seen what He had seen and said nothing ; now the Spirit was upon Him and He was changed.   As He passed beneath the arch, and came into the Court of the Gentiles, the open space before the steps that led up to the Holy Place, a busy scene lay before Him.   It was more than one might see in the bazaar of the city, with its jostling crowds, but nevertheless with its shops and streets arranged in order.   Here was a bedlam of confusion ; the clamour of men mingled with the cries of animals, the bleating of sheep and goats, the bellowing of oxen.   Their owners drove them to and fro, now shouting their wares to the passers-by, now, when they had sold them, moving to the places of sacrifice ; all was noise, and filth, and disorder, an anxious scramble for the pilgrims who passed through.   In corners, under arches, seated against the walls and pillars, were sellers of turtle-doves, huddled in their wicker cages ; at the gates, with their hard faces, and their watchful, impassive eyes, before their little tables sat the changers of money.

Jesus had scanned this scene before and had passed it by ; but this time all was different.   From that moment at the Jordan when He had commanded John to baptize Him, the power of His authority, when He chose to exercise it, none could resist.   One by one the first disciples had felt it, Andrew and John at the first meeting, Simon and Nathanael when they came within His gaze, Philip by the roadside.   At Cana the serving-men had yielded to it ; even Satan in the desert had found one whom he was compelled to obey.   So it was on this occasion.   As He came from under the archway of the Golden Gate, indignation seemed to hold His whole body.   His firm face set harder, His eyes looked unflinching before Him, His hands reached towards some bits of binding-cord lying on the ground beside Him.   With His fingers, rapidly, nervously, He knotted them into a whip.   As He did so the traffickers about Him stood still.   They eyed Him with growing anxiety, they began to step back and to leave a space about Him, as one whom they had reason to fear.

Then on a sudden He began to move.   Stretching out His arms on either side, as if He would let nothing pass behind Him, with His tiny whip of knotted string in His right hand He began to press forward.   He did not need to strike ; in front of Him the frightened crowd yielded.   Men, sheep, and cattle broke and fled ; those nearer crushed on those beyond, imparting to them their panic.   Soon the whole court was in confusion ; soon the stream of men found outlets by the gates at the further end which led down into the city.   As He went along He looked on the money-changers by the gate ; with His foot He overturned their tables, the little piles of coin fell jingling to the ground, and were lost in the filth spread about.   At the corners where the poorer people sat upon their stools, anxious for their doves, He stood still for a moment.   To these He was more gentle ; they were less to blame, they were more ignorant than others, the nature of their trade gave them more excuse.   He did not scatter them ; He did not break open their baskets and let the doves free.   More tenderly, but none the less firmly, He said to them :

' Take these things hence
And make not the house of my Father
A house of traffic.'

While the dealers and their beasts fled before Him, those behind, the pilgrims that were entering through the Golden

Gate, stood still in amazement. By the single movement of this Man they saw the whole courtyard tossing in confusion ; before His glance they beheld these hard-souled barterers cringing with fear. As He advanced they followed after ; like a band of souls rescued from bondage they pressed on where their Deliverer led. Foremost among them were the men of Galilee who had come across Kedron with Him. They looked at Him and then at each other ; one to another they whispered that this was yet a further sign, a further proof of the Messias, and of the work that He had come to do. Had not the Baptist said that His wand would be in His hand and that He would thoroughly purge His floor ? With the instinct of Jews their minds sought in the Scripture for a confirmation. At length one recalled the words of the Psalmist :

'And his disciples remembered that it was written
  The zeal of thy house hath eaten me up.'

But there were other onlookers who were in very different mood. On the marble steps that led up to the Holy of Holies, over against the Golden Gate by which the pilgrims entered, stood priests and Levites, Pharisees and Scribes, servants and other hangers-on ; men who could stand upon the platform above and look down on all beneath them, verily the masters in Israel. They beheld the confusion in the court below, not the usual confusion of trafficking but what seemed like a stampede ; the stream of men and animals rolling tumultuously by, to be lost through the gates behind them. They knew that this break in the trading of the day would mean a heavy loss, both to themselves and to the Temple. They looked for the cause of the commotion, and saw beyond the crowd nothing but a working man from the north country, with not a mark of office about Him, no fringes, no phylactery, no scroll, whose single uplifted hand all seemed to fear. They were indignant, they were speechless with astonishment ; both at the sight of the Man who, unauthorized, caused this unseemly disturbance, and with the cowardly herd that fled so easily before Him. Such a panic and for such a tiny cause ! It was too contemptible. But worse, it was an infringement of their prerogative. Who was this Man who so took upon Himself authority within the Temple precincts ? Were not they, and only they, the masters ? They

must put an end to this ; they must resist Him ; the Man
was a fanatic, and for such a Man, after such a crime, the
only place was prison.

Nevertheless as He drew nearer their tone of indignation
changed. In spite of their high authority, when His gaze
met theirs, the firmness of His eye subdued them. As it
had been with others, so was it now with them ; no words
were needed, they knew at once that they were in the
presence of One greater than themselves. They might
resent the discovery, they might struggle to shake off the
thraldom, but for the moment they could not. Later,
when He was gone, they might recover, and treat this
episode as if it had never been ; but to the end the memory
of that day could not be forgotten. Jesus of Nazareth,
contemn Him as they might, was henceforth a Man to be
feared, a danger to be watched ; that He might be more
they would not permit themselves to think.

And as their minds were conquered by His presence, so
did their words take on another tone. They had prepared
to vent their wrath upon Him ; to crush Him with all the
authority of their office ; when He came near they could
do no more than whimper. They had intended to command,
they ended in a feeble protest ; if indeed it could be called
so much as that. He looked at them as firmly as He had
looked at the others ; alone as He was, with his whip-cord
in His hand, at the foot of those sacred steps while they
stood above them, those very steps where long ago an old
man had held Him in His arms and blessed Him, He was
the Master of them all. He stood still while they lost
themselves in frenzy ; silent He stood while they shouted
out their fear, listened unmoved until at last the feeble
remonstrance was spoken :

> ' The Jews therefore answered and said to him
>   What sign dost thou show unto us
>   Seeing thou dost these things ? '

He might well have passed them by unheeded. For a
sign He might have pointed to the panic-stricken crowd
before Him ; was not that sign enough ? But these men
were the officials of the Temple ; whatever in themselves
they were, they were the lawful guardians of the Law and
had a claim to be answered. He would give them their
answer, one which they might or might not understand,

one which they could twist into any sense they pleased, but which nevertheless would be worthy both of them, and of Himself, and of this occasion, this first solemn entry of the Heir into His Father's house. There was ambiguity in the words He used, so that deaf ears might not hear them ; but in His manner there was that which interpreted their meaning, for those who had eyes to see. Firmly, solemnly, with a gesture that centred on Himself, He replied to these His judges, on this His first trial.

' Jesus answered and said to them
Destroy this temple
And in three days I will raise it up.'

They were momentous words, perhaps the most moment-ous that He spoke in all His life. Men would never forget them ; they would discuss them among themselves. Friends would treat them with reverence ; they would wait for the future to explain their mystery ; when the end came they would understand.

' He spoke of the temple of his body
When therefore he was risen again from the dead
His disciples remembered
That He had said this
And they believed the scripture
And the word that Jesus had said.'

Enemies on the other hand would take them in many ways ; as a challenge, as an act of defiance, as a blasphemy, as anything but that which they more than suspected that they meant. They would let the words rankle in their minds until their very shape was altered ; then, when the time came, they would be flung back at Him to complete His doom.

' This man said
I am able to destroy the temple of God
And after three days to rebuild it.'
Matthew xxvi, 61.

' We heard him say
I will destroy this temple
Made with hands
And within three days I will build another
Not made with hands.'
Mark xiv, 58.

'Vah, thou that destroyest the temple of God
And in three days dost rebuild it
Save thy own self
If thou be the Son of God
Come down from the cross.'
Matthew xxvii, 40 ; Mark xv, 29, 30.

So would the words be twisted and perverted ; and yet all the time, beneath the affected scandal, and the raucous clamour, and the bitterness of hatred, they would know that what they said was not the truth. When all was over conscience would accuse them, conscience would not let the true interpretation die. Then, when lying could do no more, the truth would out ; they would confess that they had known all these years what He had meant.

'And the next day
Which followed the day of preparation
The chief priests and the Pharisees
Came together to Pilate saying :
Sir, we have remembered
That that seducer said
While he was yet alive
After three days I will rise again
Command therefore the sepulchre to be guarded
Until the third day
Lest perhaps his disciples come
And steal him away
And say to the people
He is risen from the dead
And the last error shall be worse than the first.'
Matthew xxvii, 62–64.

Worse than the first ! But what was the first ? The error of their own stupendous and continued lie. O Scribes and Pharisees, of whatever generation, if only you would not lie !

For a moment after the words had been uttered, while behind the Temple in the distance the din began to die away, round the steps there was a silence as of dread. Words terrific had been spoken ; what they portended some guessed ; men knew not what to say. But the spell must be broken, and a voice was found to break it. One in the crew would have done with mystery. He would call a

spade a spade ; he would take the words in their baldest
sense and make a mockery of them.

> ' The Jews then said
> Six and forty years was this temple in building
> And wilt thou raise it up
> In three days ? '

Jesus listened to the scorn and answered nothing. For
that day His work was done. He had come into His Father's
house, He had declared Himself, and the rulers in Israel
knew it.

S. John concludes this narrative with one of those
mysterious parentheses peculiar to himself. It seems to
imply so much that we hesitate ; it ends on a jarring note
which makes us wonder all the more.

> ' Now when he was at Jerusalem
> At the pasch
> Upon the festival day
> Many believed in his name
> Seeing his signs which he did
> But Jesus did not trust himself unto them
> For that he knew all men
> And because he needed not
> That any should give testimony of men
> For he knew what was in man.'

At the same time it would be unwise to make too much
of this passage. A few weeks before Jesus had been staying
by the bank of the Jordan ; there, except to a very few,
and they were mostly Galilæans, He had been entirely
unknown. In Jerusalem the most that could have been
said of Him thus far was that He had been specially noticed
by the Baptist. Since that time He had been far away in
Galilee, and little had been seen of Him there ; nothing at
all that could have caused much stir in the metropolis.
Now, like and along with so many others, He had come up
for the Pasch. On entering the Temple court He had done
this wonderful thing ; the priests, knowing better what it
meant, understanding better the meaning of the Baptist,
had challenged Him for ' a sign '. In the bazaars and in
private among themselves He had set men talking ; when
He passed down the narrow streets He could not but be
watched. No doubt, when spoken to He would respond ;
but there is no evidence that as yet He had begun to preach.

In His manner there would appear that same authority and sureness which had already conquered others ; but there is no evidence of miracles, any more than at the Jordan dwelling. Thinking men would piece it all together, the witness of the Baptist, the confirmation of the first disciples, possibly the story of what had been done at Cana, the proof of overlordship in the Temple when men had let Him have His way, the challenge to the priests and Scribes, the abiding, serene certainty and strength behind it all ; and they would easily and willingly conclude that, whoever else He was, He was genuine, He was one on whom they could rely. If John had made so much of Him, all that had followed had confirmed his declaration. When the evangelist says :

> ' Many believed in his name
> Seeing his signs which he did ',

it may be doubted whether he means more than this. Not a miracle is recorded. When in like contexts S. John speaks of ' signs ' he does not seem to mean miracles as such. Later throughout his Gospel he implies that miracles in Jerusalem, except perhaps at the very end, were only one or two, none were performed on this occasion.

All this seems to be confirmed by the remark which follows. Never, either during this first visit or at any other time, was Jesus at home in Jerusalem ; and if in other places

> ' He could not do many miracles
> Because of their unbelief ',

no less would this seem to be true here. In Jerusalem more than anywhere else was He consistently and from the first ignored, opposed, repudiated, rejected, hated. In Jerusalem His life was never safe ; and when John speaks of Jesus as he does in this place, he means, perhaps, that His words should be taken, not of this paschal season only but of all His visits to Jerusalem ; that from the first He knew—indeed He had just declared it—what in the end Jerusalem would do to Him, and that from the first He treated it accordingly.

9. Nicodemus

In all the four Gospels, but especially in the Gospel of S. John, there are passages which, to one who would trace the growth of the revelation of Jesus and His teaching, present, it would seem, insuperable difficulty. They usually stand alone, disconnected from what has gone before or what comes after. They imply that much has been said and done of which we know nothing ; one might surmise they have been inserted as afterthoughts, after the first draft has been written. They are convincing proof that none of the evangelists, not all the four put together, have any intention of telling the whole story. At times they loom up so much apart from their surroundings that one is tempted to wonder whether, as they are presented to us, they are inserted in their proper place.

Such a passage is that which, so early in the Gospel of S. John, describes to us the meeting by night between Jesus and the Pharisee Nicodemus. Had it come later, we are tempted to say, it might have been less difficult. We might then have better understood what were meant by the ' signs ' which had so affected the Pharisee, and we might have been less surprised at the depth of the teaching of our Lord, thus early in His life, when nothing seems to have preceded it. On the other hand, by a paradox so often discovered in S. John, it is evident that the scene must have taken place thus early, indeed at the time where it is here set down. Nicodemus is too prominent later not to have been a student of Jesus from the first.

> ' And there was a man of the Pharisees
> Named Nicodemus
> A ruler of the Jews
> This man came to Jesus by night
> And said to him
> Rabbi
> We know that thou art come a teacher from God
> For no man can do these signs
> Which thou dost
> Unless God be with him.'

Nicodemus, one of the Pharisaic caste, one of those to whom the letter of the Law was very dear, but yet who was not content with the teaching of his day ; who felt that underneath the letter must be something more real, more alive, more hopeful, more human as well as more divine, than the hard, iron-bound interpretation of his school ; a ruler among the Jews, respected for his judgement and sagacity, for we find later that others followed him, not too much led by others, as leaders often are ; weak and yielding, it may be, but with the weakness of a man who was strong ; acquiescing in convention, though he knew there was something wrong ; acquiescing till he found something better, on the look-out for that better thing which his judgement, his very loyalty to the Law, told him must be somewhere ; weak chiefly because he did not know better, but strong to enquire when others would have left things aside ; when lights shone, however dim, strong to stand for justice, even when in its defence he stood alone ; strong in fidelity to the end, and at the end, with the simple courage of conviction, facing the contempt of caste ; such was the man as we know him.

During these days he had heard of Jesus and had seen Him. He was one of those to whom the message of the Baptist had not been given in vain. Without any doubt there were signs, and they all centred round this Man ; the message of the coming of the King, the searching of hearts that had accompanied it, the strong words of John concerning Jesus at the Jordan ; and now these had been followed by His single-handed cleansing of the Temple, by His easy conquest and silencing of the doctors of the Law, by His confident prophecy of the future, whatever that prophecy might mean, by the plain sincerity that shone in His every word and action, by His sheer disregard of Himself at the same time that He assumed for Himself a place unique, by the way He won the people, apparently by His mere presence stirring admiration and raising high ideals in everyone who gave Him a hearing.

No, these things could not be disregarded. Friends of Nicodemus agreed with him ; whatever they might in the end conclude, here was One who deserved to be studied. He might not be the Messias, but at least He was of the line of the Baptist, and the Baptist was akin to the prophets of old. He would probe the matter deeper ; he would search out Jesus and judge. But it must be in secret ; it must not be known that a Pharisee had so acknowledged Him. He would go to Him by night ; he would pay Him his respects as a teacher ; when they met he would see for himself which way the conversation turned.

We can see the two together,—it is still not difficult to find Jesus alone,—in the blackness of the Eastern night with a single lamp on the ground between them ; on the face of the One, as the light shines upon it from below, certainty and peace and authority and kindly welcome, for these are expressed in the words that follow ; on the other, as he draws nearer, and his eyes drink in the vision given to him, fascination and confidence in the truth of words which, nevertheless, he does not understand, covering anxiety and questioning. It is with Nicodemus as it has been with the rest of the men of goodwill who have come near. He has come to judge and he finds himself being judged ; whatever before he may have conjectured, when he comes into the presence of this Man he knows, and gladly knows, that he has met his Master. At first sight he is conquered, and like others before him he owns it.

' Rabbi ', he says,
' We know
That thou art come a teacher from God.'

' The Lamb of God.'
' The Messias.'
'He of whom Moses in the law
And the prophets did write.'
' The son of God
The King of Israel.'
The Worker of the wonder at Cana.
The Lord of the temple.

And now, and that from the mouth of a Pharisee and ruler in Israel :

' Rabbi
A teacher from God.'

Already, before the hour of manifestation has rightly come, long before the period of miracles, upon the minds of those about Him the impression has sunk very deep. So strong, so true, so sure is the personality of this Man that to meet Him with an honest heart is to be won by Him.

So had it been with Nicodemus. But Nicodemus was of quite another type from those who had hitherto been found in Jesus' company ; on this very account has S. John thought it well to record this memorable meeting. He was a Pharisee ; he was a ruler of the Jews ; his knowledge of the Law, his training in the schools, his power to recognize the signs, were far above anything of theirs. To such a man Jesus would speak in language very different from that which He had hitherto employed.

> ' In him was light
> And the light was the life of men
> And the light shineth in the darkness
> And the darkness did not comprehend it.'

In many ways and under many forms S. John teaches this as the real message of Jesus. To him He is much more than a teacher ; He is a creator of a new being. Men do not merely learn from Him something ; they are transformed by Him into something very different from that which they were before ; and to discover this is needful to none more than to those who hope to reach the truth of God by mere learning. Hence with Nicodemus, who had come to Him learned in the Law, who had hoped by his learning to test the learning of Jesus, who had already called Him ' a teacher from God ', Jesus cuts straight across the path of learning and seems to fling it to the winds. Not light but life is what Nicodemus needs ; with His very first words Jesus shocks him into a rude awakening.

> ' Jesus answered and said to him
> Amen amen I say to thee
> Unless a man be born again
> He cannot see the kingdom of God.'

Words like these were more, and were meant to be more, than the Pharisee could at once understand. That their sense was mystical he knew ; long training in the schools had prepared his mind for that ; nevertheless, until the key to the mystery was given to him, he knew that alone he could not hope to fathom it. ' Born again ? ' What could the words mean ? Could he discover ? He would provoke the Master ; he would take the words literally ; he would treat them as implying something absurd. Perhaps that would draw from the Rabbi some kind of explanation.

> ' Nicodemus saith to him
> How can a man be born again
> When he is old ?
> Can he enter a second time
> Into his mother's womb
> And be born again ? '

The question bordered on the insolent, but it was a cry of ignorance as well. Ignorance is often insolent, above all that ignorance which has satisfied itself that it knows ; and with ignorance, however insolent it might be, Jesus was always long-suffering. Proofs of this we shall see again and again, till Calvary, upon it, and after ; on that note, when their turn came to speak, the apostles made their first appeal, alike in Jerusalem and in Athens.

Hence with Nicodemus Jesus would be very patient. He would treat him as a Pharisee, yet also He would treat him as a child. He would take his half-sneering question as if it were a child's remark, yet at the same time He would assume Nicodemus' learning in the Law. Man was much more than body ; the Kingdom was much more than a material Kingdom ; as one learned in the Law well knew. There was a world beyond this world, a vision beyond the vision of this world, an understanding that included and absorbed and reduced to nothing the understanding of things material, a fuller life that so far transcended the crawling thing that men comprehended by the word as to make it appear living death, a life free as the wind, invisible as the wind, which came and wrapped itself about the bodies of men and no man knew whence or whither. Men breathed it, men lived by it, but of it men knew little ; so was it with that other life. The Spirit of God Himself was in it ; let man but breathe and absorb that Spirit and he would be transformed ; then he would see into another world, then he would come into the Kingdom. The words of Jesus to Nicodemus are the foundation of all true mysticism.

'Jesus answered
Amen amen I say to thee
Unless a man be born again
Of water and the Holy Ghost
He cannot enter into the kingdom of God
That which is born of the flesh
Is flesh
And that which is born of the spirit
Is spirit
Wonder not that I said to thee
You must be born again
The wind breatheth where it will
And thou hearest its voice
But thou knowest not whence it cometh
And whither it goeth
So is everyone that is born of the spirit.'

The words were a challenge to the rationalizing mind of Nicodemus and his school. The axe was laid to the root ; Jesus was mercifully merciless, tenderly fearless, clear and emphatic, laying down His doctrine with a certainty that disdained all proof but His own word. He knew, He spoke as one who knew ; and to hear Him with ears that would hear excluded doubt. So would He teach from now to the end.

Nicodemus listened. It was no new thing to him to dwell upon the thought of the Kingdom of God, transcending all the kingdoms of this world ; the sacred books were steeped in this ideal, his own people throughout the centuries, since Abraham, Isaac, and Jacob, had sustained themselves with the knowledge of the kingdom of their God which no misfortune or reverse would ever be able to destroy. But that admission to this kingdom, to citizenship within it, should require a rebirth,—this was indeed a new doctrine. Though he may not have had that earthly view of a political kingdom which prevailed among the common herd, still had he David and Solomon before him. He could not forget the privilege of his race ; he had never dreamt of any fulfilment of prophecy that could be divorced from birth as a Jew. Born again ? For the rest of men he could understand it, but for a son of Abraham was he not already regenerate ?

Still his second question was more humble than the first. He had believed, and faith was growing ; he had seen the dawn, and light was coming to him. There is hesitation but with hope, self-defence but with submission, in the mind of the man who now speaks.

' Nicodemus answered and said to him
How can these things be done ? '

But Jesus will have no doubting. Man, however he may assert it, does not live by reason ; reason of itself does not go far, and that is usually along an endless curve. Man lives upon authority, he believes because he is told ; reason may guide him to the light, but the light itself reason does not give him.

' Not on bread alone doth man live
But on every word that cometh from the mouth of God.'

So had Jesus said to a more subtle reasoner than any Pharisee ; what then should He say to Nicodemus ? Here was a dispenser of light, a ' master in Israel ', yet was he himself groping in darkness. Jesus would seize the moment ; He would convince this man of his need ; thus He would convince him of the need of his people. He would pour out His light in dazzling abundance, so that for the time he might even be blinded ; yet on a future day, the day of all days, it would enable him to see where others would wander in the dark. At this moment He would only test his faith. He would assert without possibility of mistake His own prerogative ; He would claim the allegiance of all men ; in language the full significance of which Nicodemus would only grasp on Calvary, He would give him a pledge in a prophecy. If man would come into the Kingdom he must be born again ; he must be born again by breathing the life of the Spirit, that cared no more for Jew than for Gentile. This life He, Jesus, He alone, would give him. For He alone knew, He alone had seen ; like the serpent lifted up by Moses in the desert He too would one day be lifted up, and in the sight of Him all would be clear.

> ' Jesus answered and said to him
> Art thou master in Israel
> And knowest not these things ?
> Amen amen I say to thee
> That we speak what we know
> And we testify what we have seen
> And you receive not our testimony
> If I have spoken to you earthly things
> And you believe not
> How will you believe
> If I shall speak to you heavenly things ?
> And no man hath ascended into heaven
> But he that descended from heaven
> The Son of Man
> Who is in heaven
> And as Moses lifted up the serpent in the desert
> So must the Son of Man be lifted up
> That whosoever believeth in him
> May not perish
> But may have everlasting life.'

At this point, as after the scene in the Temple, as else-where we shall see the same, S. John drops into a reverie of his own. Through the perspective of close on sixty years he looks back on the scene he has described ; and here again one feels the sense of sadness, almost of indignation, at the way His Master had been rejected, particularly in Judæa, particularly by the lords of the Temple in Jerusalem.

> ' He came unto his own
> And his own received him not
> But as many as received him
> He gave them power
> To become sons of God
> To them that believe in his name.'

In his introduction he had written this as a kind of general thesis. The cry occurs many times in various forms throughout his work ; it is the cry of a lover who loved from the beginning to the end, restless and hurt that the One he knew and loved had been so little appreciated, restless that on this account the whole race of man had lost and was still losing so much.

> ' For God so loved the world
> As to give his only begotten Son
> That whosoever believeth in him
> May not perish
> But may have life everlasting
> For God sent not his Son into the world
> To judge the world
> But that the world may be saved by him
> He that believeth in him is not judged
> But he that doth not believe is already judged
> Because he believeth not
> In the name of the only begotten Son of God :
> And this is the judgement
> Because the light is come into the world
> And men loved darkness
> Rather than the light
> Because their works were evil
> For everyone that doth evil
> Hateth the light
> That his works may not be reproved
> But he that doth truth
> Cometh to the light
> That his works may be made manifest
> Because they are done in God.'

It is well to compare with this passage another outburst

of S. John in his first Epistle, which may almost be called a corollary to the present. In the one he laments the failure of men to see, in the other he speaks to those who have seen and have received. From both we gain some idea of what Jesus was to John, the ground on which his understanding of Jesus was built, what were the Light and the Life of which he never tires of speaking, both reflected in a new power of loving, the very power of the heart of Jesus Himself imparted to us. Thus, through divine love overflowing into human lives, even in the material order did John see the regeneration of the world in Jesus Christ.

' Dearly beloved
Let us love one another
For charity is of God
And everyone that loveth is born of God
And knoweth God
He that loveth not
Knoweth not God
For God is charity
By this
Hath the charity of God appeared to us
Because God hath sent his only begotten Son
Into the world
That we may live by him
In this is charity
Not as though we had loved God
But because he hath first loved us
And sent his Son
To be a propitiation for our sins
My dearest
If God hath so loved us
We also ought to love one another.'

1 John iv, 7–11.

4

10. Further Witness of John the Baptist

THE months were passing by. Jesus had left Galilee for Jerusalem at the Pasch ; it is evident that He stayed there some time, and that by some at least He was noticed. Still, as has been said, though both the Evangelist and Nicodemus speak of the ' signs ' He manifested there, we have no record of a single miracle. Indeed the silence of the disciples of the Baptist in the scene immediately following, coupled with the more marked silence of Jerusalem itself later on, is an eloquent witness that the hour for miracles was not yet come. He was still waiting, still using the same evidences which had won to Him the first disciples by the Jordan. He would still let men find Him of their own accord, give themselves to Him of their own accord ; later would be time for more compelling arguments.

We are not told that Jesus returned to Galilee ; instead we are told that He

'Came into the land of Judæa
And there he abode with them
And baptized.'

Later S. John is more precise and tells us that
' Jesus himself did not baptize
But his disciples.'

Again we are informed that
' John also was baptizing
In Ennon near Salim
Because there was much water there.'

In other words, after the revelation of Jesus, John the Baptist began to move up the river towards Galilee, and by this time had taken up his station just where Samaria touches at its northernmost the tetrarchy of Herod. Following his lead,—it is important to notice how Jesus follows the lead of John, as if He were Himself no more than a disciple,—Jesus comes down from Jerusalem to the crossing of the Jordan, and there begins to carry on the work which John had been doing. Like John, He has a special group of disciples about Him ; like John He preaches to the people as they pass, that they should prepare for the Kingdom that was to come ; like him, He trains His followers in the work of baptizing ; He is unlike him only in this, that He Himself does not baptize.

This cannot have been a matter of merely a few days or even weeks. S. John expressly tells us that He ' there took up His abode ', perhaps in the same hut where His first disciples found Him. The spring passed into the hot summer ; the mountain-sides changed again from green to arid brown ; the clouds of late October began to gather ; such a length of time seems necessary to justify the words of the Evangelist. Since the Baptism almost a year had slipped by, and this was all He had done ; so little that three Evangelists give it no record at all.

Meanwhile on the border of Galilee the Baptist was continuing his work. The land and people of Judæa he had surrendered ; he was now preparing the men of Galilee for the grace which was soon to be theirs. There would come to him, besides, some from Peræa and Decapolis on the east, some from Samaria on the south-west ;

' They came and were baptized ',

a yet more mixed gathering than that which we have seen at the crossing on the road to Jericho.

As the movement grew, there grew alongside the bickerings and controversies inevitable to all such movements. The disciples of John did their work as he told them, at times it might seem with more zeal than prudence,—very probably making more of the ceremonial than did the Baptist himself. Critical Jews standing by would find fault, with the disciples if not with their master, would question this and that, would contrast this baptism with the approved purifications according to the Law, would hint at Samaritan infiltrations and the heresy of Mount Garizim, would look with suspicion at unbelievers from Decapolis and beyond, and scent out some doubtful imitation of their rites, in various forms they would put to the disciples of John conundrums they could not answer. And these disciples in their turn, especially the men from Galilee, impetuous, enthusiastic, but ignorant and wanting in judgement, would make their replies according to their lights, would flounder and would be laughed at, would be roused to indignation and display of temper, knowing they were right and yet unable to solve the problems put to them. All this sordid human element gathered round the Baptist and his teaching as John the Evangelist shows us.

> ' And there arose a question
> Between some of John's disciples and the Jews
> Concerning justification.'

But soon there arose another trouble which affected them much more deeply. During these months some among them had gone up and down to Jerusalem ; at the crossing of the ford they had noticed how the Man from Nazareth had taken up His station there. As the season advanced they were impressed by the crowds that gathered round Him, many more than now came to John, more even than came to him in the first days a year ago. They noticed, too, that many went to Him, led by the words of John himself ; some were now fast followers of Jesus who once had been wholly devoted to the Baptist.

This was surely not to be endured. It was all very well that some months ago their master had spoken of this Man in quite extraordinary terms. Since then, besides, he had mentioned Him, always with deference and respect, and in terms that had induced not a few to leave John and go after Him. Still it could never be allowed that their own leader, obviously a prophet and a saint, should be superseded by this Man, no less obviously of the common sort. Had not John from the beginning been specially chosen by God ? Of this Man's origin they knew nothing. Were not the parents of John quite specially favoured people—Zachary the priest, and Elizabeth, blessed in old age ? But this Man's parents—His father, who was he ? His mother everybody knew. Had not John's life from the beginning been a life of sanctity, in the desert, far from the ways of men ? This Man had always lived in Nazareth, like any other Nazarene, utterly undistinguished, utterly unknown.

So these followers of John argued among themselves, and by every argument were brought to the same conclusion. The disciple must not be allowed to supersede the master ; Jesus was John's disciple ; if then He was to baptize, He must do it under John's direction. John could not be aware of this rival lower down the river ; he must be told.

> ' And they came to John and said to him
> Rabbi
> He that was with thee beyond the Jordan
> To whom thou gavest testimony
> Behold he baptizeth
> And all men come to him.'

John took their complaint with patience. Poor men, they knew no better ; it was only natural that their devotedness to himself should blind them to Him who was more excellent. More than that ; if to see through that humble exterior he himself had needed the revelation of the Holy Spirit, how could it be that these poor disciples should recognize Him ? How could they do so unless it was told to them, and that not once only but again and again ? For what was he there but to tell them ? And for what was Jesus biding there but that He might be pointed out ? What He might do in the future to reveal Himself John did not know ; for the present it was clear that He was content to stand by the river and allow Himself to be discovered by whomsoever followed John's guidance. A year had almost been completed, and yet this was all. John had received no further inspiration ; he must carry on his work, the same work,

> ' Not the light
> But to give testimony of the light '

until it pleased God to show him more.

Faithfully, then, he would seize this occasion to repeat his lesson. With regard to himself and his own mission, he had but to repeat what he had already said ; as for Jesus, and the way He was being received, he would show them the lightness of his heart, even its merriment and joy, for all the coat of camel's hair that covered it. From its strangeness, coming from his lips, the metaphor he used must have astonished his disciples and gone home.

> ' John answered and said
> A man cannot receive anything
> Unless it be given him from heaven
> You yourselves do bear me witness
> That I said that I am not the Christ

But that I am sent before him
He that hath the bride is the bridegroom
But the friend of the bridegroom
Who standeth and heareth him
Rejoiceth with joy
Because of the bridegroom's voice
This my joy therefore is fulfilled
He must increase
But I must decrease.'

In a former place we have noticed the thundering voice of John softening into sympathy with the poor and lowly ; now we hear it rising to glad song in sympathy with the progress of One who was superseding him. It is another trait in the character of this great man ; great as he is he can forget himself, and alike bend down to the lowest and pay joyful homage to the highest.

Here again the aged Evangelist pauses to make reflexions of his own. He had himself listened to the Baptist in those far-off days, and had since been saddened to think how few had understood. Even when their master had been put to death, many had preserved his memory, and had gone on baptizing in his name, and nothing more. Later he had followed Jesus, and from his lips had learned with the help of God to fathom a little of His teaching. Now in his old age he looked back, and saw with dimmed eyes how many there were to whom that teaching had no meaning, no significance whatever. He had watched the church of Jesus Christ grow around him, and yet so many had failed ; failed because they had missed the one thing essential, the recognition of Him as He was ; instead had substituted ideals of their own, founded on philosophy, founded on the synthesis of all that seemed best in their generation, but not founded on Him and His love. All this we must bear in mind when we read the old man's reflexions. They are not bitter, they are not reflexions of despair, they are only sad realizations of the perversity of human nature, which refuses to see what is for its peace.

' He that cometh from above
Is above all
He that is of the earth
Of the earth he is
And of the earth he speaketh

He that cometh from heaven
Is above all
And what he hath seen and heard
That he testifieth
And no man receiveth his testimony
He that receiveth his testimony
Hath set to his seal
That God is true
For he whom God has sent
Speaketh the words of God
For God doth not give the spirit by measure
The Father loveth the Son
And he hath given all things into his hand
He that believeth in the Son
Hath everlasting life
But he that believeth not the Son
Shall not see life
But the wrath of God abideth on him.'

Once more the reflexion finds an echo in the whole of the Evangelist's first Epistle. Its strength is overwhelming ; it almost makes ' us of little faith ' wonder for ourselves ; so absorbed is this ' disciple whom he loved ' in the personality of the Son of God, and all His significance to men.

' If we receive the testimony of men
The testimony of God is greater
For this is the testimony of God
Which is greater
Because he hath testified by his Son
He that believeth in the Son of God
Hath the testimony of God in himself
He that believeth not the Son
Maketh him a liar
Because he believeth not in the testimony
Which God hath testified of his Son
And this is the testimony
That God hath given to us eternal life
And this life is in his Son
He that hath the Son
Hath life
He that hath not the Son
Hath not life.'

11. Jesus goes to Galilee.

And now we have come to the first great turning point
in the public life of Jesus. Already a year or most of a year
has passed and He has done, apparently, almost nothing.
The miracle at the Cana marriage feast has been witnessed
by a few ; that others who did not witness it should have
accepted it unquestioned would under the circumstances be
much to expect. So far as we know the miracle stood alone ;
neither His friends nor His enemies mention any others,
though occasions for mentioning them are many. The
only other event that had stood out as important was the
cleansing of the Temple at the Pasch ; but that, too, by
this time had been all but forgotten, and the Temple courts
were as busy as before. Jesus seemed to be letting time slip
by ; He was almost passive, doing nothing, saying little ;
He stood by the Jordan, preaching at times very much as
John had preached before Him, looking on while His
disciples baptized.

There He remained as long as John was in the field.
He would not eclipse him ; He would allow him the whole
sphere of influence ; from John, while he was there, more
than from Himself, men should learn who He was and
through John come to acknowledge Him. No miracles,
no overwhelming, compelling manifestation ; He would
have men come of their own accord, relying on John as
their chief witness ; when they came, however tentatively,
then He would draw them nearer Himself, then He would
let them taste and see enough to make them recognize Him.
So has it always been.

But now a new thing occurred. At first John had
appeared in the desert land of Judæa, later he had crossed
the Jordan and come into the territory of the tetrarch
Herod. As in Judæa he had not feared to call the Pharisees
a ' brood of vipers ', so in Peræa, and even more in Galilee,
when the occasion called for it, he did not hesitate to
denounce the evil doings of its overlord. For among those
evil deeds was one that was notorious, one that especially
shocked the Jewish mind, for which, had Herod been a
loyal Jew, death by stoning was the penalty. He had
appropriated to himself and married Herodias, the daughter
of one half-brother, and the wife of another, Herod Philip.
Such a crime, shamelessly, defiantly public, such a scandal,

lowering the whole moral tone of his people, was an ill preparation for the coming of the Messias, and if to the humbler classes John must preach repentance and cleanness of heart, no less must he preach it to the highest.

It would seem that somewhere John had openly faced the tyrant, and had charged him with his crime.

> ' For John said to Herod
> It is not lawful for thee
> To have thy brother's wife.'

This must have been in the cooler season, when Herod and his court were in the plain. It may have probably occurred when the cortège crossed the ford in Galilee, on its way to Herod's favourite Magdala. There John could have spoken more safely ; there he was revered by the people ; to have made him a prisoner in their midst would have aroused their indignation, and might have provoked violence in attempts to release him. Hence we can understand why Josephus calls John a centre of sedition. But when the months grew warmer, and the court migrated once more to Herod's hill station at Machærus, then retaliation was more possible ; for Machærus was far away from Galilee, perched high above the Dead Sea, built there that wickedness might hold its revels all the more lawlessly, remote from the eyes of men.

At all events it was while Herod and his courtiers were staying at this mountain place that one day he gave orders for John to be taken. As he describes the event the Evangelist dwells with special horror on the fact that not only was he made prisoner but that he was bound ; as if, for one such as John, that were an indignity utterly uncalled for and unbecoming.

> ' For Herod the tetrarch himself
> Had sent and apprehended John
> And added this above all
> And bound him
> And shut him up in prison.'

Without ado he was spirited away to Machærus ; Herod and Herodias would keep him there under their own eye, where escape or liberation from without was wellnigh impossible.

Thus was the voice of John silenced. But his spirit remained, and disciples trained by him continued along

the Jordan bank the work of preparation. Close by them
for a little longer Jesus still kept His abóde. In itself there
appeared no reason why the imprisonment of John should
alter His plan. Herod did not fear or discountenance the
religious movement or the ceremonial ; such things meant
nothing to him.

But soon there was added another cause for caution. It
was now close upon a year since the suspicions of the
Pharisees in Jerusalem had been roused against John and
they had sent down men to test him ; petty annoyances
had followed and had helped to drive the Baptist further
up the river. Now against Jesus the same suspicions had
awakened, and promised to be still more active. Long
since it had reached the ears of the Pharisees that this new
Baptizer was even more successful than John. They could
not forget, besides, the affront He had offered them in their
own sacred domain, that day when He had defied them in
the Temple. Since that day, and now yet more since
John's capture, the talk among the people had been that
this Man was John's successor. John, it was said, had
pointed Him out as the one who was to come after him,
and was to be greater than himself. In the Temple He had
shown this tendency ; it was defiant, it was revolutionary ;
was there not reason to suspect that His teaching by the
Jordan would be equally tainted ?

So they argued and concluded. They did not act at
once ; they would be more circumspect, and at the same
time more thorough, than they had been on the former
occasion ; the imprisonment of John encouraged them to
hope that they might manœuvre a like fate for Jesus. The
news soon reached His ears ; He had friends about to warn
Him ; it was time for Him to move. John was silenced,
and his witness would never again be heard ; Jesus must
now reveal Himself in what way the Father might appoint.
Judæa had been given the first hearing both of the voice
of the Baptist and of His own ; He had knocked first at its
door, He had waited on its step, and the door had been
closed in His face. He must go back to Galilee whence
He had come ; Galilee the lowly must be made the chosen
of the chosen. There for a time at least He would be able
to act with greater liberty ; from Galilee He could still
carry on His appeal to the rulers of the Holy City. To such
disciples as elected to go with Him He gave His instructions ;

He gathered together His belongings and prepared to depart. He went, says one Evangelist,

'In the power of the spirit ' ;

all let us see that with this journey into Galilee the campaign proper had begun. Hence it is that another, as if to preface all that was to follow, tells us that He

'Came into Galilee
Preaching the kingdom of God and saying
The time is accomplished
And the kingdom of God is at hand
Repent
And believe the gospel
And the fame of him went out
Through the whole country
And he was magnified by all.'

But months were to pass before that was wholly fulfilled. Now, at the close of the year, when the air was cool and the rains were threatening, He started on His journey once more, of some three days, from the Judæan banks of the Jordan, through the north of Judæa into Samaria, then across the valley of Esdraelon and over the mountain ridge to Cana.

12. John the Baptist in Prison

Meanwhile in his prison vault beneath the fortress-palace of Machærus John the Baptist languished. He was not entirely confined to solitude, for his disciples continued to visit him ; had his captor Herod had his own way, John might soon have been released. For Herod was a strange mixture, the meeting of many muddy streams. With such an origin, and such an upbringing, we can scarcely do other than pity him, glad to discover in him any spark of human feeling that remained. In his pursuit of self-indulgence there was no depth to which he would not go. Nevertheless, up to this point at least, he had not lost all sense of what was decent ; that was a doom yet to come. He could still dream dreams, he could conjure up ghosts, conscience was not wholly dead ; with his shrewd judgement of men he could detect a saint when he met one. He was incapable of love, for a vicious life had killed it, instead he was a slave of infatuation. By doing violence to himself he could ignore a prophet's threat, but he could not resist a woman's sneer.

And at his elbow stood Herodias ; she who in her turn could hate but could not love. She had reached that degree of shamelessness when the opinions of men mattered little ; that she might rule, the queen of a court, honour could be flung to the winds. She knew her gifts and her powers and could use them to perfection, above all when there was a question of revenge. She would sin as she pleased and parade it before the eyes of men, but woe to that man who dared to give her sin its name. At whatever cost men should pay her homage and flattery, hollow and insincere though she knew it to be. To silence her contempt for herself she would have about her only thought-killing noise and confusion, remorse should be made reckless by intoxicating dance. John she had made an enemy because of his condemnation, but she hated him more because of what he was ; by her wiles and fascinations she could not hope to conquer him, then she would bring him down by other means. How they met we are not told ; but the arrow had been deliberately shot, and the wound had festered in her heart, and one day soldiers had come to the Jordan and before the eyes of all had bound John and taken him away, and men knew the terror of a woman's hate too well to utter a protest.

Yet, that done, Herod, so far her tool, had refused to go further. It was part of his pleasure-seeking nature to avoid all trouble ; thus much he had done to satisfy her, to do more would disturb the country.

> ' For Herod feared the people
> Because they esteemed him as a prophet.'

Besides, as Herod well knew, John was a good man and a strong one, and the mere sight of him made one like Herod pause. He had visited him in prison ; he had found him apparently indifferent to his lot. He had spoken with him and had been moved to respect for his victim, to unrest about himself, to a consciousness that if he would allow him that man would deliver him from the hell that ever burnt within his soul ; many a time he had avoided an evil deed and done a good one because of the haunting memory of John. No, whatever else he yielded to Herodias, this man's life he would not yield to her.

> ' He feared John
> Knowing him to be a just and holy man

And kept him
And when he heard him did many things
And he heard him willingly.'

13. The Woman of Samaria

About half-way through Samaria the high road swerves
northward round the foot of a range of mountains, running
alongside of them down an open valley till it slips westward
through a cleft into Sichem.   The district about is full of
memories of the Old Testament ; above all it is the land
of Jacob and Joseph.   Here Jacob had first settled after
his return from Mesopotamia.

' And Jacob came to Socoth
Where having built a house
And pitched tents
He called the name of the place Socoth
That is Tents
And he passed over to Salem
A city of the Sichemites
Which is in the land of Chanaan
After he returned from Mesopotamia in Syria
And he dwelt by the town
And he bought that part of the field
Of the children of Hemor
The father of Sichem
For a hundred lambs
And raising an altar there
He invoked upon it the most mighty God of Israel.'
Genesis xxxiii, 17–20.

All this country, from the Jordan to the sea, in the days
of the division had fallen to the children of the two sons
of Joseph, Ephraim and Manasses ; fulfilling the promise
of Jacob, to them had been given the heart of the Promised
Land.

' And he said to Joseph his son
Behold I die
And God will be with you
And will bring you back into the land of your fathers
I give thee a portion above thy brethren
Which I took out of the hand of the Amorrhite
With my sword and bow.'
Genesis xlviii, 21, 22.

Here, when at length the land was finally conquered by Josue, they brought the bones of Joseph from Egypt and buried them.

' And the bones of Joseph
Which the children of Israel had taken out of Egypt
They buried in Sichem
In that part of the field
Which Jacob had bought of the sons of Hemor
The father of Sichem
For a hundred young ewes
And it was in the possession of the sons of Joseph.'

Josue xxiv, 32.

As the high road glides into the valley it has immediately on its left Mount Garizim, sloping steadily and evenly upward, the sacred mountain of the Samaritans, where to this day the people of the neighbourhood offer sacrifice. On the right, several hundred yards lower down the valley, is a very deep well, the Well of Jacob. Higher up the valley, perhaps half a mile, the square white houses of Sichar are in sight, lying like a snake asleep along the base of the mountain ridge by which the high road winds. Sichem is not yet visible; it is behind the mountains on the left.

Travellers on foot from Jericho might have reached this spot in a day and a half; scarcely less. It would then be well on in the afternoon of the second day of their journey that Jesus and His company rounded the bend that disclosed the long valley before them and, naturally enough, chose the well, the only place where water was available, as a halting place. They were all weary, but He was more tired than the rest. Does this imply that His more delicate nature felt these journeyings more than the rougher fishermen of the lakeside? Or was it that on account of His extra watchings He had endured more than they? At all events He must stay where He was while they went forward to the village to see what food they could find; He would wait till their return.

So, a little way from the high road, on the low stone which encircled the well, Jesus sat alone. He had nothing with which He could reach down and draw up the water; He must abide till someone came. He was in a strange land. In spite of the early traditions it was a land of heresy;

the very mountain in front of Him, as He looked up from the well across the road, stood for rivalry and faction, and bitter opposition to the people of Judæa and Jerusalem. Yet these Samaritans knew no better ; they had been born into this faction and there in ignorance they had remained. They had their arguments to support them, their claim of descent from Jacob and Joseph, their record of the rites of Josue performed on this spot as the centre of the Land of Promise. He would understand ; He would pity them and not condemn them. He would give Himself to them, if they would have Him, as well as to any others ; if they would have Him He would bring them back to union upon a higher and a wider plane.

Presently, with her water-pot upon her head, a woman from the village came down the road. It was mid-afternoon ; women usually came to the well for water in the morning and evening, and then they came in chattering groups, the children with them noisier and busier than they. This woman came alone, at an hour that was less usual ; this of itself might give some indication of her character and, if so, might warn a stranger to treat her with caution. But whoever and whatever she was, she would come to the well and go on with her drawing of water as if nobody were there. In the East a woman does not look at a man ; and in a case like this, since the Man was obviously a Jew and no Samaritan, there could be no possible intercourse between the two.

She hooked on the vessel to the rope that hung coiled above the well and turned the windlass, all as if no one else were there. She brought it back to the surface ; as she prepared to go, what was her surprise to hear this Man, this Jew, speak to her ! It was true it was only a natural, an ordinary request He had to make ; still even such a request a Jew would hardly proffer to a Samaritan. Simply He asked her :

> ' Jesus saith to her
> Give me to drink.'

We can see her at first standing astonished at these very simple words. Next we can see her automatically serving out the water and giving Him what He asked for. And we can see Him, the weariness of His face changing into life, that strange something again coming over Him which always held those who had eyes to see, stretching out His hand to receive, from this woman, the first gift recorded in His public life. He had nothing more, it seemed, to say ; only by His manner He had encouraged her, and had made it easy for her to speak.

At length, as He handed back to her the vessel from which He had drunk, she did speak ; asking the question that was uppermost in her thoughts.

> ' Then that Samaritan woman saith to him
> How dost thou
> Being a Jew
> Ask of me to drink
> Who am a Samaritan woman ? '

To her it was a double problem, a double condescension, a double violation of convention ; and she was not yet sure how she should take it.

But she had no cause to fear. We look at this narrative of Jesus and the Woman of Samaria ; we compare it with that which has preceded it, of Jesus and the Pharisee Nicodemus ; and we ask whether S. John had not something particular in his mind when he set these cases close together. In the one Jesus deals with the most eminent in the land, a Pharisee and a ruler in Israel, a man endowed with gifts above the common ; in the other He speaks to a religious outcast and a woman, who shows at every turn the drab dulness of her heart and soul and mind. In the one He meets the scholar on his own plane, then lifts him beyond himself till he is lost in mystery ; in the other, as so often, as always when He turns to the poor and ignorant, He picks up the woman's words and deeds, and by means of them raises her to knowledge of salvation. In the one new birth, to new life, to be found in Himself ; in the other living water, giving new life, in and from Himself ; both alike, high and low, are led towards the same goal.

Thus far between the two there is a certain parallelism, but here on a sudden it ends. What came to Nicodemus from his interview we do not know. We only know that later, on grounds of common justice, he spoke up for Jesus in the councils of the great ; we know that at the end, when the body of Jesus was abandoned, he was one of the two who did it honour. We know that afterwards he was with those who believed and followed. But we do not

know that in any special manner Jesus revealed Himself to
him ; He left him still to find his way.

Not so was it with this woman, sinful though she was and
outcast, upon whom in righteous indignation Nicodemus
would never have cast his eyes, much less would he have
spoken with her. If with the Pharisee Jesus was a
Pharisee, with the Samaritan He is a Samaritan ; so much
does He lay aside that the woman cannot believe her eyes
or ears. Almost playfully He led her on, into realms far
beyond her understanding ; yet was it all in keeping with
the manner of the time, and made her know that He who
spoke to her was something more than common.

> ' Jesus answered and said to her
> If thou didst know the gift of God
> And who he is that saith to thee
> Give me to drink
> Thou perhaps wouldst have asked of him
> And he would have given thee
> Living water.'

Clearly this is language that could have had little meaning
to the woman who stood before Him ; even to better-
trained minds it is language full of mystery. Still is it of
a piece with all that has gone before ; it is of a piece with
all that will come after. It is the language of the hungry
heart that craved to be known, of the thirsty heart that
craved to be satisfied with the devotion of mankind, simply
that in return it might give to man, to every man, no
matter what his status, ' the gift of God ', ' the living water '.

> ' If any man thirst
> Let him come to me and drink.'

It is the refrain of the whole of S. John's Gospel and
Epistles, and is echoed by the saints in all ages.

> ' Thou hast made us, O Lord, for thyself
> And our hearts shall find no rest
> Till they rest in thee.'

And this, with a kind of restless lavishness, did Jesus pour
out on all, even on those who from their very nature seemed
incapable of receiving it ; for such did that poor woman
seem to be to whom at this moment He was speaking.
Water to her was water and no more, and the only water
of which she reckoned anything was the water in the well
beside them. He would give her living water ! Would

He then sink another well ? But that might be a doubtful boon, for it might take away due reverence from the well of their father Jacob.

<blockquote>

' The woman saith to him

Sir

Thou hast nothing wherewith to draw

And the well is deep

From whence then hast thou living water ?

Art thou greater than our father Jacob

Who gave us the well

And drank thereof

Himself and his children and his cattle ? '

</blockquote>

Jesus had patience with her. She was dull, she was material, her vision was confined to the cooped-up valley in which she lived, her understanding could grasp the plain elements of life and no more ; yet had she carried herself at least a little distance. As she spoke she argued with herself, first, that He could not mean the water from the well ; secondly, that He meant some other kind of water ; lastly, that He claimed in some way to have powers greater than Jacob. It seemed to her preposterous, but she did not at once despise it ; the fascination of Jesus was already upon her. She was content to put her doubt in the shape of a question.

Again He answered her, drawing her on yet further, giving her ever more and more though He knew she would not understand a word, as already she had utterly failed to understand. Some day she would realize, and then would recall this conversation for posterity to ponder.

<blockquote>

' Jesus answered and said to her

Whosoever drinketh of this water

Shall thirst again

But he that will drink

Of the water that I will give him

Shall not thirst for ever

For the water that I will give him

Shall become in him a fountain of water

Springing up into life everlasting.'

</blockquote>

From this description one might have supposed that even a dull, material mind would have grasped the meaning of the water of which He spoke. ' Shall not thirst for ever ' ; ' A fountain of water within him ' ; ' Into life everlasting ' ;

surely the words were significant enough. Yet not so to this poor woman. Of the next life she had little idea ; of that ' life everlasting ', partaken of even in this life, she had no idea whatsoever. Even if by nature she might have conceived it, the life she had led and was leading had utterly crushed it out of her soul.

Nevertheless, all was not hopeless. She could frame no conception of what He meant, but she could believe that He meant something. She could express herself only in terms of her own experience, but in doing this she could show that at least she believed so far as she knew how to believe. Thus, ignorant as she was and with her vision all askew, she went further than Nicodemus. Crude as was her act of faith, it was still of the same nature as that of the first disciples. It was akin to that of the criminal who was one day to win His friendship on the Cross.

> ' The woman saith to him
> Sir
> Give me this water
> That I may not thirst
> Nor come hither to draw.'

Jesus had secured what He wanted, faith in Himself according to the woman's lights ; since the beginning of their conversation she had gone far. But now, that she might go further, and that the faith she already had might be confirmed, her eyes must be opened, and she must be made to turn them in upon herself. He would use the same means as before. As He had done with Simon Peter, as He had done with Nathanael, reading their lives and their hearts and thereby compelling awe and recognition, so He would do with this woman. He would let her see that nothing was hidden from His eyes. Stranger as He was, He knew the secret of her life ; though He was so friendly to her He was not deceived. With quiet eyes He looked at her ; His manner was easy and familiar ; He gave no sign of complaint ; He spoke as if He sought merely another to share in their conversation.

> ' Jesus saith to her
> Go call thy husband
> And come hither.'

The poor woman was taken completely off her guard. She had not looked for this sudden change. By this time she knew that she was dealing with one far superior to herself; twice already she had called Him ' Sir '. Yet was He also one of whom she need not be afraid. But on that very account, even at the cost of a little concealment—it is the way with every one of us,—she valued this stranger's good opinion of her. She would tell Him no lie; she would answer what was simply true, even though the inference she hoped He would draw would be false. She was not bound to give herself away; though her fellow-villagers might know all about her, and might so contemn her that she was compelled to live her life apart, to come to draw water all alone while other women came in one another's company, still at least with a stranger she might be allowed to hold up her head a little.

Quickly then, with an instinct for self-preservation, regret in the tone of her voice, tears threatening in her eyes, looking into a world that might have been but no longer could be for her, thinking to hide in what she said the shame that clouded her heart, with a little bravery, a little defiance,

> ' The woman answered and said
> I have no husband.'

There was a pause. As He did not speak she turned to see what impression her seemingly triumphant words had made. She found Him looking at her. The same kindly patience was still upon His face, but now there was something else. By His look He seemed to show her that He knew more than she had said; He seemed to be full of pity and compassion. She had told Him a half-truth, but He was not angry with her; she had told Him a half-truth, and already she was angry with herself.

Then slowly came the answer. In what follows we have a perfect illustration of a feature of Jesus which is easily left unnoticed. Who does not know the difficulty of sin to speak the truth about itself? Nor only of sin as such; when human nature pulls against us, when human respect paralyses us, when our own sense of independence clamours that we should hide that which would demean us in the eyes of others, when the wound is inflamed and shrinks from being touched, when for a long time we have shut our eyes and have refused to look at that of which we are ashamed till at last we have almost forgotten it, when after much internal training and practice we have found a means,

a formula, to defend ourselves, to justify ourselves, to tell
ourselves that we need not trouble any more, who does not
know the ease with which, by means of a half-truth, we can
just cajole ourselves into a false sense of righteousness, and
then assume that attitude to others, by this time scarcely
conscious that it is untrue ?

Jesus knew all this ; ' He knew what was in man ', and
in this matter more than in any other He always had pity.
Invariably He thought the best. He took the writhing
human creature, and ignored the evil, and from the good
it said and endeavoured to think of itself led it on to better.
In this sense among many others He made Himself the
light shining in the darkness, the light that was the life
of men. We see it in many examples ; in Simon and
Nathanael at the outset, in Nicodemus, in Levi, in the
Woman who was a sinner yet could not speak a single
word, in the Adulteress whom He would not condemn, in
the Rich Young Man whom He looked upon and loved,
in many a sinner whom He healed, and was content to bid
them sin no more, ignoring all the past ; in Judas, in Pilate,
in the Jews who brought Him to His death, in the Thief
upon the Cross, in Thomas, in Peter again at the end. He
sums up His own great soul towards the timid, tentative,
shrinking, paralysed, almost speechless sinner in the story of
the Prodigal, above all in the never-to-be-forgotten sentence :

' And when he was yet a great way off
His father saw him
And was moved with compassion
And running to him
Fell upon his neck
And kissed him.'

With His own disciples it seems to make Him stretch
truth itself to its furthest limit when, at the moment at
which they were all about to leave Him, He says :

' You are they
Who have stood with me in my temptations.'

Let human nature, poor self-depending human nature,
He seems to say, only do what it can, however feeble,
however short of the whole truth ; let it come and stand
before Him and give Him the power to act. He will understand, He will do the rest, He will see the good effort and
will ignore the deception ; while it is yet a great way off

He will discover it, and will be moved with compassion, and running to it will fall upon its neck and kiss it. Such is the all-comprehending, all-compassionate character of Jesus Christ, not as imagination pictures it, but as the cold fact of Scripture gives it to us.

And such He was on this occasion. In her anxiety to preserve what little shred was left of her good name, the Samaritan had said that which she hoped would deceive Him, would make Him think better of her than she was. The words were barely true, but that was all ; a stranger who heard them, had he known the whole truth, might well have been indignant. Not so with Jesus ; He took that bare truth as if it were enough and built upon it. He would treat her as if she could do no more, the rest He would do for her ; poor prodigal, she yet belonged to Him. All this is contained in the confession He now made for her :

> ' Jesus said to her
> Thou hast said well
> I have no husband
> For thou hast had five husbands
> And he whom thou now hast
> Is not thy husband
> This thou hast said truly.'

Such words, spoken under such circumstances, might well have ended the interview. Let another have said them, and they might well have become a stinging taunt ; let another have heard them, and their very truth might have driven her away in shame. The proof they contained that her ruse had failed ought to have silenced her. And yet it was not so, as it never is with Him ; no man of goodwill flies from Jesus Christ, no matter what He may say. The woman stood still in astonishment. Her tears should now have flowed, as later did the tears of another sinner in like case, but they were dried. In shame, as she had feared, she should have sunk into the ground, but instead she rejoiced that He knew. She should have fled away to hide herself ; instead, though He had bidden her to go, she could not obey His bidding.

Womanlike, she stayed ; womanlike, with that self-defending laugh which covers shame, she braved the situation ; womanlike, she turned the conversation, from herself to Him ; womanlike, she started on a new discussion ;

womanlike, she argued, not with argument, but with a fact that she deemed unanswerable.

'The woman saith to him
Sir
I perceive that thou art a prophet
Our fathers adored on this mountain
And you say
That at Jerusalem is the place
Where men must adore.'

In the first sentence there was acknowledgement that He had spoken the full truth ; it was enough for Him as an act of contrition. Underneath, it may well have been, was a broken heart ; but it had long been broken, and dragged in the mud, and had become a hardened thing, and sorrow could now express itself only in this dull thud. But there was more behind it. This Samaritan who, a few minutes before, was surprised, almost scandalized, that a Jew should speak to her, now owns this same Jew for a prophet ; it was another step in the conquest. When then she continued her defence, we can see the wistful look in her eyes. This man was more than ordinary men. From the first He had won her respect ; now He had won her reverence ; but a little more and He would win her love and devotion. But for love there must be agreement, and Jews and Samaritans could never agree. As her heart drew the nearer to His, she felt all the more the mountain that was in the way ; no less than the Mount Garizim, that loomed up before them across the high road. Could that mountain be removed ? She did not see how ; yet this prophet might remove it for her, and then she would be able to belong to Him.

Some such thought lay behind the woman's words, longing for an answer. And it came ; in that grand way by which Jesus transcends controversy, lifting it to a higher plane on which rivalry is lost. As He had done with Nicodemus, even though what He said might have little meaning for the woman, yet to confirm her in her new-born faith, and confidence, and love,

'Jesus saith to her
Woman believe me.
That the hour cometh
When neither on this mountain

Nor in Jerusalem
You shall adore the Father
You adore that which you know not
We adore that which we know
For salvation is of the Jews
But the hour cometh
And now is
When the true adorers
Shall adore the Father
In spirit and in truth
For the Father also seeketh such to adore him
God is a spirit
And they that adore him
Must adore him in spirit and in truth.'

The more we weigh these words the more we are amazed at the divine condescension. ' The poor have the gospel preached to them '. A doctrine so sublime given to, thrown away upon, a poor woman, ignorant, dull, stupid, a Samaritan, a heretic ! The sceptic may well be sceptical, and ask himself whether this is Jesus who speaks, or John who has added something from his own maturer thoughts.

And yet in fact how often is the same condescension seen ! The simple child that has come to Him and found Him, and now knows Him better than any teacher could have taught him ; the sinner repentant, who has crawled leper-like towards Him, and his eyes have been opened, and in a moment he has understood what years of study would have failed to discover ; the thoughtless creature of its day, with vision obscured by fascination of trifles,—on a sudden the trifles have gone, and the great things have been seen, and all has been changed ; last of all, most important of all, the poor, unlettered peasant, the household drudge, to whom this life brings only what is drab, yet whose heart and soul have understanding which have humbled theologians and saints. The Woman at the Well has had many successors, and Jesus has spoken to them as they have drawn the water, and they all unknowing have learnt.

No, however little understood, the words were not wasted on this woman. On a richer soil they might have been wasted ; poured out on this poor thirsting creature they were drunk in. Again, as was always His way, He had answered by giving more than had been asked. The

controversy between Jew and Samaritan was ignored.
Time would solve that problem by destroying its foundations ; more important than all controversy was the basis
of all truth. ' Adore ? ' What did men mean by the word ?
A series of forms, a routine of external sacrifices, a ritual
without a soul, whose life had been throttled by the bonds
tied about it. The very object of adoration had been
forgotten. Men did not know the God whom they adored ;
these men of Samaria had confused Him with the pagan
gods about them. As for the Jews, this at least could be
said for them ; in the midst of their surroundings, and in
spite of their broken past, they had preserved intact the
worship of the one, true God. Moreover, be they whatever
they might be because of misguidance, still must the
Scriptures be fulfilled ; from them must come the Saviour
of the world.

Let then the controversy cease. Garizim ? Jerusalem ?
The God of all the world would soon, even now, offer
Himself to all men everywhere to be adored ; and the secret
of the adoration would be, not in external sacrifices, but
in the inmost places of the heart. To know Him within,
to commune with Him within, to fall down and adore Him
with the full recognition of personally knowing and personally being known, without any intervening substitutes, or
conventions, or devices, this was of the new revelation, of
the salvation whose hour was at hand. The God of the
heart, to be worshipped by the human heart, inside the
human heart, the One real to the other, the other entirely
open to the One, with all the intervening world, and all its
interests, and all its forms, vanished like a shadow between
the embrace of the two,—this was the foundation that
must be restored, without which no true religion was
possible. We hear in this emphasis of Jesus but a confirmation of the teaching of the Baptist, carried now into the
midst of heretical Samaria. We shall hear it again, expressed in many ways ; we shall hear it given to the Twelve
themselves almost as a final warning, when He will bid them

' Beware of the leaven of the Pharisees
Which is hypocrisy.'

All this to the woman who heard it was mystery. Jesus
seemed to be speaking, not to her, but to the heart of the
land around Him, to the mountain with its altar of sacrifice

which stood up before Him. Still through the mystery she discerned one truth ; the figure of the Messias, of Him who was to come and restore all things. She caught at this further point of contact ; she swerved aside from that which she could not fathom to that which she knew. He had spoken of the hour being imminent ; what that meant all the world knew, even the people of Samaria. She would cling to that and leave the matter there ; thus far she could show Him that she believed.

> ' The woman saith to him
> I know that the Messias cometh
> Who is called the Christ
> Therefore when he is come
> He will teach us all things.'

Could her confession of faith have gone further ? She had already owned Him for a prophet ; not understanding she had listened to Him while He spoke. She now declared her belief in the Messias that was to come, and, when He came, her readiness to receive Him. There was in her that sense of weariness which is common among those who are ' without a shepherd ', that impatience with religious bickerings, that sense of doubt and despondency, that contentment to leave things alone, that trust that somehow at the end the Lord will put all things right.

Then indeed did Jesus show His wonderful condescension. He had waited for this moment ; carefully He had led her on, from a mere cup of water to a promise of the living water which it was His alone to give ; from the life to the canker of death which killed all further understanding ; from death to confession and revival ; from revival to acknow- ledgement of Himself as true ; from this to a blinding vision of the light ; from the blinding vision to an act of faith in the Messias, if ever she came to know Him. This was farther than He had hitherto reached with anyone ; He would reward it in a way unique. She would still not under- stand ; she would not believe her own ears ; for the time it would not so much as occur to her that the words she heard could be literally true. But in the after years, when all was over and He was gone, perhaps she would recall the day when she had met Him, and humbly thank God that she alone in those early years had heard from His own lips the declaration of His identity.

'Jesus saith to her
I am he
Who am speaking with thee.'

The hungry heart craving to be known ! As at Cana
love had compelled it to anticipate its hour, and that for
people, as it might seem to us, utterly undeserving, so now
love compelled it to reveal itself before its time, and that
to one whom none but Jesus would have thought worthy
of such a revelation. So explicit a statement we shall not
hear again till He stands before His judges on His trial.

But even as He spoke the disciples appeared on the scene.

'And immediately the disciples came.'

That they were few in number is clear. Not more than two
or three could have been needed to seek for food in the
bazaar at Sichar ; had there been more some would have
remained with the Master at the well. Now they had done
their business and had returned. As they had come down
the road they had seen Him in conversation with a woman,
and that woman a Samaritan, and they had looked at one
another and wondered.

'And they wondered
That he talked with the woman.'

Surely a strange thing for their Prophet to be doing.
For a moment their wondering was akin to doubt ; a good
Jew would never do such a thing.

'This man if he were a prophet
Would surely know.'

Questions arose in their minds ; they read them in each
other's eyes ; they said nothing but they were uneasy.
Could He have wanted anything which they had forgotten,
that should compel Him to speak to this creature ? Could
there be some other explanation ? Already their esteem
and love for Him made them look for some excuse, but it
must be confessed that they were shocked ; so shocked that
they dared not speak to Him about it.

'Yet no man said
What seekest thou ?
Why talkest thou with her ? '

They came to the well in silence, bringing with them the
food they had bought ; grain, baked bread, vegetables,

a little fruit. Of the woman they took no notice whatsoever ;
she might not have been there. And she in her turn understood. Half ashamed, as if she had been caught doing that
which even she should not be doing—she who had been
listening to the beating heart of Jesus Christ !—she picked
up her belongings ; but in her hurry left her water-pot
behind, and made off. It had been a strange adventure,
nothing of the kind had ever happened in her colourless
life before. Stranger still, it had left her happy, very happy,
with happiness of a kind she had never known was possible.
Of the disciples and their rough ways she thought nothing ;
that was to be expected. Much that He had said vanished
from her mind, how could she hope to remember it ? She
would only repeat to herself again and again that He had
read her secret soul, had told her the things she had dreamt
no man would ever know. He had disclosed the skeleton
in her cupboard ; that should have made her restless, yet
somehow it had not done so. On the contrary she was glad,
glad as she had never been before, and her gladness would
not be contained. Like a happy child, she could not keep
from running up the lane. Like Mary who ran to Elizabeth
to relieve her happy heart, she too must run and share her
joy with someone, no matter at what cost to her.

Breathless she came into the village ; all in a torrent she
poured out her tale, to the men at their counters in the
bazaar, to the men squatted in groups on the ground, to the
men seated on the stone bench at the street corner. Dull,
down-trodden woman as she was, nevertheless like so many
such she was a woman of character, and whether they
would or not, when she cared, men had to look and listen.
Soon the whole place was active. They all knew her ;
everyone knew everyone in Sichar, particularly one like
her. Usually she was little more than a source of ribald
joke among them, but this time she was different. She was
alive with a life quite new ; she was on fire, she was certain.
She had seen something and was changed, there was the
evident ring of truth in her cry as she recklessly called, first
to one group and then to another

'Come
And see a man
Who has told me all things
Whatsoever I have done
Is not he the Christ ? '

Thus was that poor woman, that poor, sinful, heretical, Samaritan woman, chosen to be the first apostle of Christ Jesus in this world.

And the poor folk about her listened. Excitements in Sichar were few enough and far between ; whether wnat the woman said were true or only nonsense, it would be worth while to go up the road and see. There was an abundance of time for anything in Sichar, and a stranger was always something to stare at, much more one who had so broken all convention and had so set a woman's tongue wagging.

> ' They went therefore out of the city
> And came unto him.'

Meanwhile the disciples had found their Master absorbed in thought, distracted ; He seemed not to have noticed their coming. Of late a new phase had been passing over Him ; since the capture of John He had been different. Up to that event, while they had been with Him by the Jordan, He had been their leader, preaching like John to the passers-by, instructing apart their special little group, then suffering them to baptize while He stood aside or wandered away to pray. But since the loss of John, a few days, at most weeks ago, He had shown unwonted energy ; and with it, so it seemed to them, reactions of weariness and abstraction which they could not understand. This was one of those moments. They must rouse Him. There was still some way to go that day and He must eat. They opened out their parcels ; they laid out the food on the stone wall where He sat ; then

> ' They prayed him
> Rabbi
> Eat.'

He awoke from His distraction. His eyes turned away from Mount Garizim where they had been resting to the fond disciples by His side. He was grateful for what they had done and He showed it ; at the same time, tired and hungry as they knew Him to be, He betrayed no desire to begin. Instead, with that in His voice which destroyed any suspicion of rebuke, He said :

> ' I have meat to eat
> Which you know not.'

A short time before He had spoken to the woman of
water, and she had been able to understand no more than
the water of the well ; now He spoke to the disciples of
meat and even they, in spite of their six months' training,
could get no further than the common food which lay on
the ledge before them. What could He mean ? He had
food of which they knew nothing ? Had then another been
before them, and given Him all He needed ?

> ' The disciples therefore said to one another
> Hath any man brought him to eat ? '

Jesus knew what they were saying. Poor men ! Before
even they could get a glimmering of the meat He would
one day give them, they had yet a long way to go. Still
already He had begun to prepare them. Satan had guessed
something in the desert ; at Cana He had shown them
what He would do, by changing one thing to another ;
now they should have a lesson, one of very, very many, in
the right understanding of His words. He turned to them
where they whispered to one another ; the old look of fire
came on Him, that look which already they had learnt to
interpret. Then He spoke.

> ' Jesus saith to them
> My meat is
> To do the will of him that sent me.'

Twice already, under circumstances very different from
this, has Jesus defined this one and only principle of all His
life. He has said it to His Mother, His good angel :

> ' Did you not know
> That I must be about my Father's business ? '

He has said it to the bad angel, the Tempter :

> ' Not on bread alone doth man live
> But on every word
> That cometh from the mouth of God.'

Now He says it to those whom He is choosing apart to
follow Him. Even the following of Him, the founding of
the Kingdom, the saving of souls, the highest sanctity, the
gaining of heaven, are what they are just in so far as they
are the fulfilment of the Father's will, the perfecting of His
work, and no further. It is an obvious truism, yet will it
take years to learn. He has come into the world to teach
it ; again and again He will repeat it ; the disciples will

learn it in theory, but before it will appear in practice the
time will be long.

Then He looked across the valley, already bursting into
green as the rainy season had begun to set in. Soon will
come the sun, and then the harvest time will not be far off.
For one who had lived all His life among the hills and dales
of Galilee this is suggestive enough ; it was common ground
for Him and the Galilæans around Him. With this then
He continues :

' Do not you say
There are yet four months
And then the harvest cometh ?
Behold I say to you
Lift up your eyes
And see the countries
For they are white for the harvest
And he that reapeth receiveth wages
And gathereth fruit unto life everlasting
That both he that soweth
And he that reapeth
May rejoice together
For in this is the saying true
That it is one man that soweth
And it is another that reapeth
I have sent you
To reap that in which you did not labour
Others have laboured
And you have entered into their labours.'

It was the statesmanlike vision of the Master. In nothing
is greatness more manifest than in the contentment to do
great things the fruit of which oneself will never see ; to
write a book, it may be, which only posterity will understand, to lay the foundations of a work which others will
later build up, to begin life in a cave and end it on a cross
that all the world may later be conquered. This truth He
takes and makes it spiritual, striking at the root of vain
ambition. If in this world some sow and others reap, much
more will it be so in the vineyard of the Lord. Nor can we
reap the fruit of our own labours ; what we gather is
chiefly the result of the toil of others. While we reap the
harvest of their sowing, let us be content to sow in our turn
that others who come after us may have their gathering.

It was not to be supposed that these men understood the purport of His words ; they who could think of meat in only one crude sense were still untrained for higher things. As it had been with the Samaritan, so it was with them. He was content to sow seed in them which would bear fruit in due season ; even as He spoke He was giving in practice an example of the lesson that He taught. When He had ended He returned to Himself. He took the food they gave Him ; again a characteristic, seen already by the bank of the Jordan, seen at Cana, seen in the Temple court, and to be seen often hereafter ; the sublimity of Jesus the Master alongside of the meekness and need of support of Jesus the Son of Man.

While they were thus eating, groups of men came up the road from Sichar. They stood at a distance looking on in silence, some of them squatting on the ground ; to sit and stare at a stranger was no discourtesy with them. While they sat the meal was ended ; He had nothing to say. And yet in His manner, more than in any words He might speak, was the real secret of His fascination ; lowly yet with dignity, familiar yet stirring reverence, saying nothing yet making men crave to know Him, showing no concern yet provoking love, the equal yet the Master of them all, giving no proofs yet compelling faith and confidence ; it was always the same, it is still the same, it will always be the same, for those who will open their eyes and see. In all learning worth the name there comes a point where the brain of man seems to fail. He can argue and prove no further ; for the rest either he sees or he does not. Those who do not see may pass by, and ignore, and be satisfied with their blindness ; and those who see can only pity them, unable to tell them what they know. Such, but to an intense degree, is it with the knowledge of Jesus ; with those who have seen Him, and read Him, and known Him, and with those who have not, and have not wished to know. And often those who have known Him best are among the poor and ignorant.

' They came and they saw.'

Of another set of men this has already been said, and it was added :

' And they stayed with him all that day.'

Of these poor men from Sichar we are told :

' They desired
That he would tarry with them.'

His route led Him down the valley northward. Sichar
would scarcely have been the place where He would
ordinarily have halted; a better rest would have been
found at Sichem, a few miles further on. They started on
their way, Jesus and His companions, and the noisy villagers
around them. He said little, perhaps nothing, but there
was no need for Him to speak; the men talked to one
another, after their rough manner, loudly for Him to hear,
looking at Him while they chattered, as if that somehow
gave Him a part in their conversation.

And He bore with them, as He always bore with people
of their kind. He let them use this common ruse; by the
time they reached the straggling row of houses by which
the high road ran they had come to look upon Him as one
of themselves. And He in His turn had begun to claim
them, the first flock gathered to His fold. He knew their
need and their inarticulate craving better than they knew
it; He pitied them and cared. His companions might
wish to push on to Sichem before nightfall, but as they
were many a time after to discover, they were to be sacrificed
for the multitude. They must stay at Sichar for the night.

Next day it was the same, and again the next. He had
left Judæa all eagerness to get to Galilee; now He seemed
not to care how long He dallied by the way. The men of
Sichar found Him a hut, and He was satisfied. They gathered
at His door and He made Himself one with them all. They
talked with one another and He took His part with them,
first hearing and asking these wise men questions, these
wiseacre pundits of Sichar; then leading them on, as He
had led on Nathanael, and Nicodemus, and the woman,
to heights that were beyond them, yet of which they saw
enough to help them to believe.

And they went away and talked among themselves.
Wisely they put their heads together and agreed that it
was as He said, though what that was they did not know;
they had been to Him, they had learned Him for themselves,
He was all that the woman had declared and more. Their
village pride was humoured; when next the woman passed
their way they could give her message their approval;
nay, they could let her understand that they saw more than

she. It was all very human ; that keen psychologist
S. John seems scarcely able to restrain his good-natured
humour as he records the results of these two days. In two
short days these men of Sichar had fathomed all the mystery
of Jesus.

> ' And he abode there two days
> And many more believed in him
> Because of his own word
> And they said to the woman
> We now believe
> Not for thy saying
> For we ourselves have heard him
> And know
> That this is indeed the Saviour of the world.'

Dear men of Sichar, may God reward you ! Though
they knew not what they said, though the revelation was
of flesh and blood rather than from the Father who was
in heaven, still had they proved themselves men of goodwill.
Jesus will never forget it. Other men may say what they
may of Samaria and the Samaritans, the Samaritans
themselves may do Him unkindness, but He will always
store up in grateful memory this welcome of the men of
Sichar, and by word and deed will repay it.

5

14. The Second Miracle at Cana

JESUS gave these men of Sichar two whole days ; then
He had to go. Galilee lay before Him, the country
which above every other was to be the witness of His
manifestation. He set out, but He knew beforehand what
would come. Apart from all else, these Galilæans were a
peculiar people ; earnest and enthusiastic, with a great
idea of themselves such as belongs to littleness of outlook,
prone to extremes especially in matters of religion, devoted
for the moment but their devotion, at a single set-back,
liable quickly to cool ; among themselves jealous and
divided, insular, self-centred, sensitive because aware of their
shortcomings, inclined to contempt of their betters, as is
common with people who are obstinate and dull. Out of
Galilee they were well known ; they were looked upon as
odd, and in their oddness dangerous. In Jerusalem their
accent was a joke ; country-folk, lacking in behaviour,
their self-contented independence somewhat tiresome.

He knew all this ; for eighteen long years since His boyhood
He had endured them ; as sometimes in a country village
of our own one will find a youth, born out of due time and
place, enduring as a doom the life around him. But added
to all this there was a further disadvantage. If He knew
them they also knew Him or thought they did, especially in
His own village, Nazareth. They had long since taken His
measure, and it would be hard to make them change ;
familiarity with Him had already bred a species of contempt.
There was an old proverb, particularly applicable to
Galilee, still more particularly to the present case :

> ' A prophet hath no honour
> In his own country.'

Nevertheless for the time being there was something in
His favour. Some of them in the last paschal season had
been with Him in Jerusalem. They had witnessed His

conquest at the Temple, and the way the very authorities had been cowed; they had heard the Baptist, and had seen the movement in Judæa, first to John and then still more to Jesus. Whatever the merits of the case, they had been rather proud of their fellow-Galilæan; He gave them a sense of superiority over the more polished, somewhat contemptuous, and therefore exasperating people of Judæa. Of course what they had seen, on their return was told throughout Galilee, and lost nothing in the telling. The talk had been given time to spread; the story of the wine at the marriage feast at Cana had got abroad; He who could do that, and with a simple glance of His eye could scatter a whole market-place and subdue the very Scribes and Pharisees, could do other things as well. Altogether this Jesus, though He was only from Nazareth, was a man to be noticed.

Hence when He came up out of Samaria and passed over into Galilee the eyes of many were upon Him. As He moved from town to town along the road He was given a noisy welcome; by the time He had reached the hill country beyond Esdraelon the report of His coming had gone on before. At Cana again He rested; He seemed unwilling as yet to return to Nazareth, He still seemed to be waiting before the real work began. Meanwhile, as was to be expected, the news had spread to the shores of the Lake of Galilee. His first companions lived there; He Himself had been there, and had shown for the district a special predilection. The people in the neighbourhood were easily aroused; that in the bazaar He should be much discussed was inevitable.

In this way His name soon reached the ears of the local authorities. Now the Romans, and those who ruled under the Romans from whatever part they came, were a stratum above the Jews whom they governed, and knew it; more educated, at least on the standards of this world, better instructed, possessed of more of the good things of life, more refined in manners, living on a higher, more costly, more luxurious level, born and trained to be masters and command, with an outlook on and knowledge of the Empire which reached far beyond the hills and plains of Galilee and Judæa. Here to-day, and to-morrow back in Rome, or Greece, or Asia Minor, they could afford to live aloof from their Jewish subjects, a ruling caste; indeed it was expected of them. Some of them, secure in their position, could ignore their surroundings ; others would deal hardly with this turbulent people, considering that only by sternness and force could they be kept in order. But there would be some who would be condescendingly benevolent ; would realize that after all these Jews were human beings like themselves, would have an interest in them and study them, their peculiar ways, their ancient history, above all their religious traditions, and spirit, and practice, and teaching, which made them so strikingly a race apart.

Such a man was in authority at Capharnaum ; a βασιλικος, St John calls him, and no one seems able to tell us what this means. He was a man of faith, though he had little or none that could be formulated ; his own native education had had little of that kind to give him. He had watched the Jews about him and had been struck by their practical possession of that which he utterly lacked and yet longed for, and in spite of all their waywardness he revered them for it. He had studied the details of their teaching ; he had wondered with some awe at their unflinching belief in a Messias. He had heard of this man Jesus who had recently appeared and of the wonderful things that were being said of Him. He had put two and two together, more accurately and more significantly than even a wise Jew might have done, and had come to certain conclusions. The Jews were looking for a Messias, and all seemed to show that they were justified in their expectation. The Messias, whoever He might be, would be a messenger from God, and would therefore bring with Him certain divine credentials. This Man, if all were true that was said of Him, had given proof of powers above the powers of men ; if He had these He would have others. He would test them ; like Simon, like Nathanael, like Nicodemus, but on a wholly different plane, on a plane that appealed to the Gentile mind more than to the mind of the Jew, he would try Him and judge for himself.

The occasion for the visit was imminent ; indeed it had hastened his conclusion. He had an only son, a mere boy, who had contracted one of the obstinate fevers of the country. It had persisted ; do what they would the physicians could not bring the fever down, and the boy was wasting away ; even now the father had been warned that he might die at any moment. Just then he had come to know that

Jesus had returned into Galilee and was at Cana, barely
thirty miles away. It occurred to him, first as an extravagance, then it seemed by no means so absurd, to go to
this Man and tell Him of his trouble. That Jesus could
heal his son if He so chose he felt sure, at least if He were
what men declared Him to be. In any case, whether he
succeeded in his request or not, he would have had the
opportunity to judge of this Man for himself.

The decision once taken it was acted on ; there was no
time to waste. With a bodyguard he took horse and set
out for Cana, and reached the town in the late afternoon.
His coming raised a stir in the little place, all the more
when it got abroad for what end he had come. Such a
man would have little difficulty in finding where Jesus
abode ; the townsfolk were only too proud to show their
Galilæan—they had already forgotten that He was from
Nazareth—to this government official.

They soon were introduced to one another. At first the
ruler lost nothing of his dignity ; he was born to command,
and sum men up, and to treat them as from a higher plane.
He came in to Jesus ; with becoming politeness, but with
dignified reserve, he addressed Him. Being no Jew, he
pretended to no claim upon Jesus ; he would state the
object of his visit, and leave it to Him to decide. He came
from Capharnaum, and was a high official there ; he had
a son who was sick, indeed was at the point of death. He
had been told that Jesus was the Messias, and he was
inclined to believe it ; if He were, then no doubt He would
give proof of it by use of some power from God. Perhaps
He would like to use the present opportunity ; perhaps
He would condescend to come down to Capharnaum
with him and his escort, and see what He could do for
the boy.

Jesus looked at this man, and His heart was glad ; though
he was no Israelite yet was he ' a man in whom there was
no guile '. His reason and goodwill had brought him far,
had brought him even to the feet of Jesus ; for that alone
he should not go unrewarded. It was the fourth type of
His converts ; first some venturesome Galilæan fishermen,
then an equally venturesome Pharisee, thirdly a heretic
woman, and now this foreigner, venturing like the rest.
And as with the others, so should it be with him ; the timid
step of faith should be welcomed, it should be encouraged

till it grew firm ; no man should ever come to Him of his own accord but should go away knowing and believing far more than he had ever conceived.

But here again it was the old story. Like Simon, and Nathanael, and Nicodemus, and the villagers of Sichar, the man had come to judge Him according to his own human standards, to test Him by a material test ; faith in Him was not yet, though its shadow was there, and that before all else must be evoked. Jesus would draw him on ; He would give him light ; in a different way, suited to this special case, as He had done with Simon and the others, He would show Himself to be the Master, and thereby through humility win this man to faith. He looked at him ; with those convincing eyes that went through every soul of goodwill He read him. His old authority came over Him, and

> ' Jesus said to him
> Unless you see signs and wonders
> You believe not.'

It was a revelation. At once this Gentile knew ; the words were a proof that this Man was all He was said to be, that He accepted the insinuation, that what was asked of Him He both could do and would. Goodwill had again been enlightened and had responded ; he was another of those who had been conquered by a look and a word, added to the line of Andrew, and Simon, and Philip, and Nathanael, and Nicodemus, and the Woman of Samaria. He no longer wished to deal with Jesus as with an equal ; he was a supplicant at His feet, humbly entreating from one in whom he now believed, and whom believing he trusted.

> ' The ruler saith to him
> Lord ',

the title at once betrays his change of attitude,

> ' Come down
> Before that my son die.'

It was enough. Such an appeal was a confession of faith, all the more worthy because of the man who made it, founded on so little human evidence. It could not but be heard. And yet not quite as the ruler would have wished. The hour for miracles was still not yet ; for the moment it was wise that no stir should be made. Instead, seeing faith so deep, He would give it further grace, He would

make it deeper still.   With assurance once more, with that
strength of certainty which to ears that heard compelled
acceptance,

> ' Jesus saith to him
> Go thy way
> Thy son liveth.'

The man heard and obeyed. He had come with the
hope of bringing Jesus back to Capharnaum ; by his
authority he had thought to be able to induce Him ; he
now turned away with that hope gone, but there was
another in his heart. Men looked on and wondered. This
was a disappointing end ; the ruler would surely be annoyed,
chagrined, perhaps even insulted that so little notice had
been taken of his request. And yet it was not so. On the
contrary he seemed contented ; the parting glance he cast
upon the Nazarene might have suggested that these two
had met before. There was nothing more to say ; there
was nothing to keep him in Cana ; the ruler with a bow
took his leave, joined his bodyguard outside and leapt into
the saddle. There was a clank and jingle in the street and
they rode away, while Jesus was left once more among the
common folk of Cana.

They did not return to Capharnaum that night. Their
horses were tired, the darkness had set in, travelling by
night in Galilee was not easy ; on a plain outside Cana they
encamped. Next morning they were up betimes and took
the road again. As they came nearer to Capharnaum, up
the valley they saw messengers hurrying towards them,
evidently excited, evidently bringing good news. They
rode on, waiting what would be ; in his heart the ruler
knew what it was: When at length they met he halted.
The horses were reined up, the chief messenger approached
the ruler's saddle ; he made his salaam of reverence, and
then, almost breathless, for he had hurried and he was
excited, he gave the ruler the good tidings that his son was
alive and well.

The ruler was moved ; but by this time, more than his
dying son, another had begun to occupy his thoughts. Do
what he might, on the journey down the figure of Jesus of
Nazareth had refused to be banished from his mind ; that
transparent face, those compelling eyes, the mouth which
tightened with affection, the solemn brow with truth written

right across it, the flush on that cheek which spoke of love and knowledge and understanding, as if they had been intimates all their lives. In the cottage at Cana the vision had conquered him, and still it held him in thrall; when the news was given to him he could only recall what the Man from Nazareth had said. One further test, and the proof for him would be conclusive.

> ' He asked therefore of them
> The hour wherein he grew better.'

That was easily answered. It had been last evening, at the hour when commonly fevers are at their height. So suddenly had the change come that it had impressed itself on everyone. They had been standing round the bed, the women prepared to begin their wailing, the men silent and uneasy, when in a moment the sick boy had opened his eyes, and had spoken sensibly, and they knew that he was saved.

> ' And they said to him
> Yesterday at the seventh hour
> The fever left him.'

The ruler sat silent; what he was thinking was for himself alone; these men would never have understood. At that same hour he had met Jesus of Nazareth; at that same hour he had been dismissed with the assurance that his son was safe; at that same hour something had come over him, convincing him that what he heard was true. From that hour he had been another man, and in spite of his trouble had come along his journey light-hearted; so light-hearted, that he had not cared to press home to see the end.

The cavalcade started once more and soon dropped over the hill into Capharnaum. Already the news had spread through the little town, and the people were out on the highway, waiting to welcome and congratulate their sympathetic ruler. He received their tokens of joy, but he answered little. Instead he hurried to his house; that all understood; it was natural that a father should hurry to a son come back to life. When he arrived, then he spoke. He gathered his household together; he told them what had befallen him at Cana; he explained to them his previous studies and reflexions which had induced him to make this journey. He dwelt on the beliefs of these Jews,

the Messias that they looked for, the proof that this gave
that this was He. He told them how this Messias was, in
the mind of thoughtful men, not for the Jews only but for
Gentiles also ; he drew his conclusion, with an earnestness
and an authority that impelled them to do the same. To
what it would lead he did not know, but he would be true
to the light that had been given him ; Gentile though he
was,

'Himself believed
and his whole house.'

15. The Beggar at the Probatic Pool

At this point the harmonist of the Gospels is brought up
against an event which it is most difficult to locate. Everything seems to indicate that it should be placed later in the
narrative ; the fact that the Galilæan ministry had now
begun in earnest, the introductory words

'After these things',

which in S. John usually imply an interval of time, the
difficulty of fixing the festival day of which the Evangelist
speaks, the depth of the discussion with which the scene
concludes, implying, it would seem, many other preceding
visits to Jerusalem. Still, for the purpose of this study, it
need not trouble us ; the event stands apart, and as such
it may be treated. It is a link in the chain of visits to the
Holy City, and in that sense it certainly is in its right
place ; as for the Galilæan development, it is enough for
us to know that some time during the early part of that
ministry Jesus interrupted His labours and went up again
to Jerusalem.

'After these things
Was a festival day of the Jews
And Jesus went up to Jerusalem.'

In the north-east of the city, close behind the prætorium
and the house of Pilate, is a deep, broad well cut into the
solid rock. It is reached by many steps ; there are dry
tanks which show that once upon a time the well supplied
different pools with water. At the bottom of the steps at
this day water is in abundance ; could the surrounding
debris be removed and the place explored, there can be
no doubt that this lowest tank would be found to be very

large. This would seem beyond question to be the pool of which S. John speaks :

> ' Now there is at Jerusalem a pool
> Called Probatica
> Which in Hebrew is named Bethsaida
> Having four porches.'

This pool, with its porches and its colonnades, was a sacred spot among the Jews. In those days it would have been outside the northern city wall ; a place where many would congregate, seeking water both for themselves and for their beasts ; probably, too, to sit together under the porches and discuss the events of the day. Moreover, the water had healing properties, and that it would seem in a miraculous way. From time to time it was noticed that its surface, usually still and quiet, was by some strange power disturbed ; when this happened, then it was commonly believed that the first sick man, of whatever disease, who bathed in the water was cured.

For these two reasons the pool was a resort of many more than just drawers of water and gossips ; it was the gathering-place for all the wretched cases of the city. There they staked out their claims, men of all sorts and conditions of disease, blind men, lame men, men with withered limbs and running sores ; the East to-day has them in abundance, in those days they must have been many more. At every entrance they occupied the sides of the steps ; under the porches their mats were stretched out, one beside another. There was the continuous cry, the monotonous appeal, here and there the jingle of little castanets which is the blind man's privilege. All day long they lay or sat in rows, begging of the passers-by, receiving enough to make it worth their while to stay ; waiting for the moving of the waters, in the hope that when they were moved some kindly hand might help them down and they might be healed. It was a gruesome company ; and the diseases to be seen there, to one who understood, told often a gruesome tale.

It was in the spring, when the rains had practically ceased, and the country was green, and the Feast of Purim, Esther's feast, was being celebrated. To this feast, it would seem certain, Jesus had come up alone, which argues that it was still very early in the Galilæan period, and that it was not the Pasch. After the festival celebration—it was

the Sabbath Day—He strolled alone and unknown to the
pool at the north-east corner of the city. He could still
move unnoticed along the narrow streets, could still be
jostled by the crowd with impunity. He had been away
from the city long enough for the scene in the Temple to
be forgotten, even by those who witnessed it, and there
were many to whom it had been a tale and no more.

Among the groups which came about the place Jesus
passed on alone. He noticed the pitiable sights around
Him ; to some He may have given an alms ; but not yet
did He show that power which soon elsewhere was to be
so lavish. Presently He stood still before a case that might
well have been described as the most wretched of all that
wretched crew. On a mat behind a pillar, alone and
derelict, as if even in that grim assembly he were an outcast,
lay a man, filthy and deformed, with a disease upon him
that was only too well understood. He had been there
a very long time, so long that there was not a visitor to the
pool but knew him ; for thirty-eight years he had hobbled
to his corner every morning, and had begged his alms
every day, and at evening had hobbled back again to his
lonely hovel in the city. It had been a dreary existence,
a dull, grey thing without heart or interest or care, that
could scarcely be called living ; the one hope that had
kept him alive had been that one day he might take his turn
at the water and be cured.

But even that hope had of late begun to wane ; or rather
it had become so fixed, so stereotyped and monotonous,
that it was now a dead thing, petrified by time, a form of
words and nothing more. The man had grown old in his
corner ; he had seen his fellow-sufferers pass away, a few
to the pool for a cure, many more to death. He had come
to look on life with a fatalistic eye, a doom with another
to follow it. He would lie where he was till the end, whatever the end was to be ; he was nothing to anybody,
nobody cared, why he went on living he did not know.

So with dull vision he had come to look upon the world
around him, or on such of the world as passed beneath the
porch where he lay. It took little notice of him, and of it
he took little notice ; even those who dropped an alms into
his pot as they passed by were thanked with little more than
a stare. Before this man Jesus stood. He took in all the
loathsome condition of that body ; He saw the withered

soul within, scarcely any longer human ; He read the tale
of the long years of waiting, stretching far beyond the years
of His own life ; and He was pitiful.   When He was born
in Bethlehem this man had already become a fixture on the
spot.   When as a boy He had first come to the Temple
close by, this poor creature had completed twenty years.
During the long period of waiting and labour in Nazareth,
he, too, had waited here, aimlessly, hopelessly, with no end
in sight.   Truly it was a case for His compassion ; He
would make it much more.

At first the man took no notice of Him ; he was used
to looks of pity from strangers, especially those who beheld
him for the first time.   But this stranger did not seem
inclined to pass on like the rest ; He stood and looked and
looked ; He seemed to read him through and to know
him ; His eyes seemed to recognize a friend.   The poor
sufferer raised his head and looked back in return ; he
knew at once that this Man was, or meant to be, more than
a passing stranger.   For a moment there was silence between
them ; presently, when they had so far read each other,

> ' Jesus saith to him
> Wilt thou be made whole ? '

Such a question at once fanned to flame the dying embers
of hope in the poor cripple's soul.   Was his opportunity
about to come at last ?   Had at last a man appeared who
would be compassionate enough, when the water was next
stirred, to carry him down and to see that he was put in
first ?   It was too good to be true.   But perhaps the man
himself, being a stranger,—he had not seen him there
before—did not fully understand the meaning of his own
words ; perhaps he meant something wholly different.
Yet no, he was clearly in earnest, evidently he had compassion and would help if he could ; he would hint to him
what that help implied.   He would not ask for it, he would
state the simple fact, and see what would be the effect.

> ' The infirm man answered
> Sir
> I have no man
> When the water is troubled
> To put me into the pond
> For whilst I am coming
> Another cometh down before me.'

Patiently, if it can any longer be called patience, the man told his tale of thirty-eight years of endurance ; the moving of the waters, the news of it flying up the steps, the noise and confusion among the crippled and diseased beneath the porches, the immediate struggle among them, the fighting and jostling to be first, the rush to the stone stairway, the tumbling rather than walking down the steps, the rolling into the water, the healing of one, the failure of many, the jubilation, the sullen return of the rest to their lairs. How often he had seen it ! How often he had taken part in it ! And always with the same result ; always he had come back again, more bruised than before, to his lonely mat behind the pillar.

The stranger listened and took in the whole scene. He did not seem to change ; or if there was a change, it was from compassion to encouragement, from sorrow to hope, from sadness to a light as of joy behind a cloud, a something which made the cripple know that somehow, somewhere all was and would be well. There was a long pause. Not a soul was within hearing ; the rustle of their feet could be heard along the stone pavement beyond. Here and there other cripples rolled on their mats and talked in low tones to one another ; what this stranger said could easily reach the diseased man's ears, but his only. Quietly, slowly, so clearly that the words could not be mistaken, so emphatically that they compelled obedience,

> ' Jesus saith to him
> Arise
> Take up thy bed
> And walk.'

At once a strange thing happened. As he lay on his carpet the man felt his crippled limbs stretch themselves and tingle. He rolled over on his side ; the motion cost no effort, it was no longer painful. His mind adverted to his stiffened legs ; they at once responded. He looked down at them ; they were no longer bent, they had a human shape. He put down his arms, he helped himself to sit up, he moved his body forward, he rose to his knees, he stood up, first lifting one leg then the other. It was all impossibly easy, he might never have gone through these eight-and-thirty years. Dazed, preoccupied, mechanically as in a dream, he stepped to the corner of his mat, to do as he had been bidden. He bent down and his body yielded ; he rolled the mat up from one end to the other ; he tucked the roll under his arm and prepared to go. As he turned he seemed to awaken. He came to himself ; he was cured, he was whole and well, and that at the word of a Stranger. He must show the Stranger some gratitude ; he looked for Him, but He was gone.

He could not stay to search further. Overcome with gladness at his fortune, mystified by the way it had happened, the old man, a cripple no longer, hurried down the steps into the street. But here he had a check. He hastened along, rejoicing in his strength, looking neither to left nor to right, caring nothing for all about him, ignoring every-thing in his fulness of joy, with his bundle under his arm, taking no heed of the crowd of passers-by, who stepped away from him as he came along, and drew their robes about them when he neared, and looked back on him in amazement. It was the Sabbath day, the day on which no man might work, not even carry a bundle, much less such a bundle as a rolled-up mat. It was the Sabbath day and yet this was being done before their very eyes ! At last some man, some indignant champion of the Law, stood boldly in his path and stopped him. They looked at each other, the one angry and threatening, the other wondering and anxious. What did this mean ? Were his fellow-men in arms against him ? Were they, perhaps, jealous of him because of his exceeding gladness ? Would they rob him thus early of the freedom he had gained ? Or was it all a dream, and was this the shock of the awaken-ing ? The poor man looked up, deprecating, pleading, while the crowd gathered round in now no longer silent condemnation.

At last the accusation came. It came from many mouths :

'It is the sabbath
It is not lawful
For thee to take up thy bed.'

The Sabbath ? Why, of course it was. In his excitement he had forgotten it. Not that the Sabbath had meant much to him, but at least he had been compelled to keep the Law. And yet what could he do ? No doubt these men around him, some of whom must have known him as the long-time beggar at the pool, supposed that at last he had been cured as others had been cured before him, that at last he had found his way to the water's edge in time. If that were the cause of the commotion he would enlighten them ; in any case he had his defence and he would use it. His courage returned ; he had enough on his side to justify himself. Sabbath day or no Sabbath day, he had been given a command by one who had a right to command him and he would obey ; whether these men were to be his friends or not, he had been an outcast long enough not to mind. There was a note of triumph, almost of defiance in his words as boldly

'He answered them
He that made me whole
He said to me
Take up thy bed and walk.'

He that made him whole ? What did the worthless creature mean ? Was he mad, and had he only exchanged one malady for a worse ? Had the cure turned his head ? When he had come out of the water, had the heat of the midday sun affected him ? Or was this not one of the ordinary cases at the pool, and had he been cured in some other way ? Had someone, as he said, really healed him ? In that case, for a double reason, it would be well to discover who he was ; first because he did such things, and therefore could be no common man, secondly because he did them on the Sabbath, and therefore must be held in suspicion. Whoever he was, he could be no good influence ; however good the work he did, a truly good man would not break the Sabbath. Half-incredulous, for the man before them might be raving, half-suspicious, for he might be speaking only truth, they cross-examined him.

'They asked him therefore
Who is that man who said to thee
Take up thy bed and walk ? '

The beggar stood silent. At once his conscience struck him. Who was the man who had healed him ? He did not know ; he had taken little trouble to know. In the excitement of the moment of his cure he had scarcely noticed that his Benefactor had slipped away and had not been seen again. Since then he had not given Him another thought. He could scarcely even recall His appearance. He had seemed like any other man ; all he could remember were those eyes which had looked him through and through and had given him hope. But to tell them only that was useless ; they would never understand. He could only cast down his eyes, and shake his head, and slink away, muttering to himself that he did not know, he had not had time to notice, blaming himself for his own discourtesy. He had said all he was able ; he pushed past them all and went on, and they scornfully made room for him. His mat was still under his arm ; let them say what they had a mind to say, Sabbath day or not, he would still obey the Man who had healed him ; if he did not who could say but the hand that had restored him might strike him again ?

Meanwhile Jesus had gone on His own way. He passed through the crowd that was gathered about the pool, one among them all, in nothing remarkable, not yet known enough in Jerusalem to be pointed out. He turned to the right down the road that ran outside the northern wall, then again sharply to the right at the corner of the city. A few minutes more and He was at the Golden Gate of the Temple ; He passed in, and again was lost among the hustling crowd, gathered in the outer court to celebrate the festival. He was alone ; yet no, He was not alone, for His Father was with Him. Here in His Father's house, built though it was by Herod, desecrated though it was by traffickers and dealers, with priests and Levites farming it worse than did the sons of Eli, still could He stand before the Holy of Holies and commune with His Father, in this as in all things else a faithful observer of the Law.

While Jesus thus prayed and waited, the man He had healed went to his home. There he laid aside his bundle, and at once made his way to the Temple. There were many things to take him there, the simple attraction of the Jew, the fact that he had been so long absent, the desire of thanksgiving, the festival which drew everyone that day. He entered by the Golden Gate, and made across the court towards the steps that led up to the sanctuary ; as he went he came face to face with Jesus, who had turned to leave. Their eyes met ; they recognized each other. The adventure of the morning made the beggar keen to observe ; what was more, his Healer seemed willing, nay anxious, that He should be recognized. The poor beggar-man was grateful. He would have expressed his gratitude, but he knew not what to say or do ; he stood there mute and confused, but none the less glad and grateful. Jesus understood; He took that silent thanks; then in that same voice which the man had heard before, the same assurance and emphasis, the same kindness and deep sympathy, yet also the same authority which compelled respect,

> ' Jesus saith to him
> Behold thou art made whole
> Sin no more
> Lest some worse thing happen to thee ' ;

and again He passed on and was lost in the crowd.

Do the words give us a clue as to the nature of the man's disease? And is the suspicion confirmed by the way the Evangelist has concealed it? If so, then all the more must we marvel at the infinite condescension of our Lord Jesus Christ.

He had gone again, but the man had learned all he needed; he could now defend himself and prove his case. He hurried from the Temple; he sought out those in the street to the north not far away, who had objected to his doings that morning. In his confused but convincing way he told them how at last he could point out his Benefactor; he had met Him but now in the Temple court. He described Him, His features, His stature, His Galilæan dress; whether he was able to give the name or not, Jesus of Nazareth was soon identified.

So around the name of Jesus the talk began to revive. It soon reached the ears of the Pharisees and doctors, and at once they were on the alert. Was He then back among them in Judæa? Since He had left the Jordan they had given Him little thought. In Galilee He was of no concern; there it was to be hoped that He would follow the example of His predecessor John the Baptist, commit Himself by some imprudent interference, and fall in time into the clutches of Herod. But now this maker of mischief was back once more among them, and they must look to it. This time they must not be so passive as they had been before.

And they did look to it, for fortunately He had given them their opportunity. He had done a miracle, that could hardly be denied; but He had overlooked the fact that He had done it on the Sabbath day. The miracle might awe the people, but the breach of the Sabbath would certainly shock them, had already shocked them, and on that they must take their stand. They made their preparations ; they waited cautiously, apparently unconcerned, till He came again to the Temple ; when He came He was easily identified. It was indeed He ; the Man who, at the last paschal season, had caused the disturbance in the courts, the Man who later by the Jordan ford had given so much cause for anxiety. In those days it had been difficult to frame any clear charge against Him ; in sheer despair some had urged that for the sake of the public peace, cause or no cause He must be got out of the way. Now He had played into their hands ; He had broken the Sabbath ; with a clear conscience they could proceed against Him.

> ' Therefore did the Jews persecute Jesus
> Because He did these things on the Sabbath.'

It is not difficult to picture the interview, the first of many, repeated again and again in Jerusalem, but never to the same degree elsewhere. On the one hand were the Scribes and Pharisees, the lawyers and doctors, the priests and Levites, the masters in Israel, not all but by far the majority, who in their hearts were by no means so secure as outwardly they affected. Already thirty years before they had betrayed their suspicions by interpreting the prophecies for Herod, that the Messias was due, that He would be born in Bethlehem, yet even then had shown no eagerness to welcome Him. On the other hand was this single Man, alone and unaided, with no prejudice to warp Him, no interest to defend, nothing within to conceal or crush down, under whose unassuming Galilæan mien John had discerned the Word of God, the Life, the Light, come at last and waiting to be owned. On the one hand was an over-eager group of men, whose decision was already taken before the evidence was adduced, united to support one another lest any one might fail ; by their aggressive vehemence betraying their unwillingness to listen to the truth ; clinging to a clause, a detail, any seeming flaw, that thereby they might wreck the whole. On the other the white Light shone that never once flickered, shining through the darkness true and steady, always consistently the same, refusing to be broken into prismatic colours lest the truth of the whole might be lost. On the one side was hostility and self-seeking, on the other proffered friendship and surrender ; on the one side hatred and confusion, and justice knowingly perverted though its semblance was always preserved ; on the other peace and quiet, and disconcerting affection, which only made hatred more intense till nothing but blood would content it.

Such a scene we now have for the first time. It explains why Jesus seldom came into Jerusalem till the end, and why when He came He did not stay long. Elsewhere opposition was of a different kind. In one place, as in Samaria, it might come from sheer ignorance, in another, as in Nazareth, from over-familiarity and contempt. At one time, as at Capharnaum, it might arise from childish vanity which resents instruction, or will not acknowledge a greater than itself ; at another, as at Magdala, from a proneness to take scandal, seeing in Jesus no more than it saw in itself. When deeper causes were its source, at least it expressed itself in the shape of questions, of carping criticisms, of complaints. But in Jerusalem, from beginning to end, it was different. Here there was always determined opposition, merciless persecution, the hatred of an enemy that knew. There was no enquiry that the truth might appear, no letting things take their course as being no concern of theirs. From the beginning they were hot on the scent, they hunted Him down without mercy ; they knew whom they pursued, or if they did not know it was because they would not, positively they refused to learn.

This may to some extent explain why the Evangelists Matthew, Mark, and Luke, till they come to Palm Sunday, say practically nothing of the work of Jesus in Jerusalem. To them it was a thankless and a fruitless task ; there were other things to tell of elsewhere which would better illustrate the coming of the King and the founding of the Kingdom ; when they had to give the story of His death, then they could come to the Holy City. On the other hand it may suggest why S. John gives it so much attention. After all, however much He might show Himself in Galilee, it was in Judæa, in Jerusalem, in the Temple that prophecy placed Him ; and unless He had declared Himself there, then in a vital matter the Scriptures would not have been fulfilled. Indeed in the Church's early days this was a charge brought by the unbelieving Jews ; and according to one scholar, whose judgement has profoundly influenced more, it was mainly to refute this obstinate charge that the Gospel of S. John was written.

But apart from this possibly primary motive, there is that other which has been already mentioned, and which lies behind everything that S. John has written. To 'the disciple whom Jesus loved' the rejection of Jesus is an ever-abiding agony.

> ' He was in the world
> And the world was made by him
> And the world knew him not
> He came unto his own
> And his own received him not,'

is a cry that constantly recurs. The astounding truth of the rejection he can never set aside ; and he writes with the hope that the portrayal of Him who was rejected, and the manner of it, will compel men at length to accept the one gift of God.

> ' These are written
> That you may believe
> That Jesus is the Christ
> The Son of God
> And that believing
> You may have life in his name.'
>
> John xx, 31.

S. John saw what others could not or would not see ; beneath the human shell the Word of God, beneath the language of Jesus the inner truth which it conveyed. As the years had gone on, and he had meditated more and more, on the one hand proofs failed him and he could only assert that what he said was true, but with an emphasis stronger than all argument ; on the other hand, with the same simplicity, with the same emphatic despair of making human words express spiritual things, he read boldly through them and into them the truth he had seen, even though as a result he leaves us sometimes more mystified than before.

> ' That which was from the beginning
> Which we have heard
> Which we have seen with our eyes
> Which we have looked upon
> And our hands have handled
> Of the word of life
> For the life was manifested

And we have seen
And do bear witness
And declare unto you
The life eternal
Which was with the Father
And hath appeared to us
That which we have seen
And have heard
We declare unto you
That you also may have fellowship with us
And our fellowship may be with the Father
And with his Son Jesus Christ.'

1 John i, 1–3.

The same half-despairing earnestness of these words is to be read in the efforts made by the Evangelist to describe the mind of Jesus when face to face with men. We have seen it in the conversation with Nicodemus ; we have seen it in the account of the meeting at Jacob's well ; even more we see it in the present scene. S. John knows what in their hearts these Pharisees know, however cleverly they may hide it. He looks through this and other interviews, before or after, which he has not chosen to describe. What he has seen with the eyes of the soul, what he has heard with the ears of spiritual understanding, that he now sets down with that emphasis and reiteration which is so peculiarly his own.

When we have said this we have said enough ; further explanation would demand a treatise of theology. S. John has told the story of the cripple's healing ; he makes use of it to state the forces at work in the city, the two chief causes of rancour and resentment on the part of the enemy, the sublime, unflinching attitude of Jesus. So quickly does he move, that he allows no time or opportunity to watch the development ; let it suffice, he seems to say, that on one side was the constant accusation that Jesus broke the Sabbath and therefore contemned the Law, that He made Himself one with God and therefore blasphemed ; on the other side was the constant affirmation of Jesus, that He came from the Father and was one with Him, that He alone could manifest the Father, that to know Him, and the Father through Him, was a new thing, even Eternal Life.

' Therefore did the Jews persecute Jesus
Because he did these things on the Sabbath.'

'These things', not 'this thing' ; the words tell their own tale. They refer to a period, a series of occasions, not to a single event.

> 'But Jesus answered them
> My Father worketh until now
> And I work
> Hereupon therefore
> The Jews sought the more to kill him
> Because he did not only break the Sabbath
> But also said God was his Father
> Making himself equal to God.'

Again as it were the laying down of a thesis. In reality the charge contains very much more than is contained in the words of Jesus just quoted ; but S. John is anxious to push forward, he gives the beginning and the end of the process, the intervening steps are a detail. What he has said is enough to introduce the attitude of Jesus, and that is all he requires.

'Then Jesus answered and said to them : Amen, amen, I say unto you, the Son cannot do anything of himself, but what he seeth the Father doing. For what things soever he doth, these the Son doth in like manner. For the Father loveth the Son, and sheweth him all things which himself doth. And greater works than these will he shew him, that you may wonder, for as the Father raiseth up the dead and giveth life, so the Son also giveth life to whom he will. For neither doth the Father judge any man, but hath given all judgement to the Son ; that all men may honour the Son as they honour the Father. He who honoureth not the Son honoureth not the Father who sent him.

'Amen, amen, I say unto you, that he who heareth my word and believeth him who sent me hath everlasting life ; and cometh not into judgement, but is passed from death to life. Amen, amen, I say unto you, that the hour cometh and now is, when the dead shall hear the voice of the Son of God ; and they that hear shall live. For as the Father hath life in himself, so he hath given to the Son to have life in himself. And he hath given him power to do judgement, because he is the Son of Man.

'Wonder not at this ; for the hour cometh wherein all that are in the graves shall hear the voice of the Son of God ; and they that have done good things shall come forth unto the resurrection of life ; but they that have done evil unto the resurrection of judgement.

'I cannot of myself do anything ; as I hear, so I judge ; and my judgement is just ; because I seek not my own will, but the will of him that sent me. If I bear witness of myself, my witness is not true ; there is another that beareth witness of me ; and I know that the witness which he witnesseth of me is true. You sent to John, and he gave testimony to the truth ; but I receive not testimony from men. But I say these things that you may be saved.

'He was a burning and a shining light, and you were willing for a time to rejoice in his light ; but I have greater testimony than that of John. For the works which the Father hath given me to perfect, the works themselves which I do, give testimony of me that the Father hath sent me. And the Father himself who hath sent me hath given testimony of me. Neither have you heard his voice at any time, nor seen his shape ; and you have not his word abiding in you. For whom he hath sent, him you believe not.

'Search the scriptures ; for you think in them to have life everlasting, and the same are they that give testimony of me. And you will not come to me that you may have life.

'I receive not glory from men ; but I know you, that you have not the love of God in you. I am come in the name of my Father, and you receive me not ; if another shall come in his own name, him you will receive. How can you believe, who receive glory one from another, and the glory which is from God alone you do not seek ?

'Think not that I will accuse you to the Father ; there is one that accuseth you, Moses, in whom you trust ; for if you did believe Moses, you would perhaps believe me also : for he wrote of me. But if you do not believe his writings, how will you believe my words ? '

When we come to analyse this address we find it marvellously well ordered. Jesus has been charged with ' making Himself equal to God ' ; S. John replies by defining, in the words of Jesus, wherein precisely that equality lies, and where there is inequality. Then he appeals to the people themselves, showing them the blessing that comes to all who will acknowledge the Son of God made Man. Next, given the claim and its consequent blessing, he traces the evidence on which they rest. Last of all, he concludes with the reasons why those evidences have not been received.

First, then, concerning the relation between Jesus and the Father. Being the Son, He derives all from the Father :

> ' The Son cannot do anything
> Of himself ' ;

But being the Son He has all the Father's love, and with that love has everything ; all the vision of the Father :

> ' For the Father loveth the Son
> And sheweth him all things
> Which himself doth ' ;

all His power :

> ' For as the Father raiseth up the dead
> And giveth life
> So the Son also giveth life
> To whom he will ' ;

all His care of men :

> ' For neither doth the Father judge any man
> But hath given all judgement to the Son ' ;

an equal share in His honour :

> ' That all men may honour the Son
> As they honour the Father
> He who honoureth not the Son
> Honoureth not the Father
> Who sent him.'

Next with regard to men themselves. He has come that they may ' have life ', that they may be ' born again ', that from being mere creatures they may become ' sons of God ', that they may be lifted from the earthly ' valley of this death ' to a new state which death can never touch :

> ' Amen, amen, I say to you
> That he who heareth my word
> And believeth him that sent me
> Hath life everlasting
> And cometh not into judgement
> But is passed from death to life.'

This life is to be not only for the just, but even for those who are dead, who by their own hand have spiritually killed themselves :

> ' Amen, amen, I say unto you
> That the hour cometh
> And now is
> When the dead shall hear the voice of the Son of God
> And they that hear shall live.'

This is a truth that he must emphasize, and in three ways he repeats it ; first by again telling of the power of the Son :

> ' For as the Father hath life in himself
> So he hath given to the Son
> To have life in himself.'

then by proclaiming Him judge of all mankind :

> ' And he hath given him power to do judgement
> Because he is the Son of Man ' ;

lastly by again declaring that His appeal is for all alike, good and bad, saints and sinners, living and dead.

> ' Wonder not at this
> For the hour cometh
> Wherein all that are in the graves
> Shall hear the voice of the Son of God
> And they that have done good things
> Shall come forth unto the resurrection of life
> And they that have done evil
> Unto the resurrection of the judgement.'

But on what evidence does all this rest ? For those who see, His own evidence would be enough ; but since those of Jerusalem will not see, for the time being He sets it aside.

> ' If I (alone) bear witness of myself
> (To you) my witness is not true.'

Therefore He will bring other evidence which even they will acknowledge, indeed which already they have acknowledged. First, there is that of John the Baptist :

> ' You sent to John
> And he gave testimony to the truth
> He was a burning and a shining light
> And you were willing for a time
> To rejoice in his light.'

Still even John was but a human witness :

> ' But I receive not testimony from men ' ;

there is a stronger evidence than that of John in the life of Jesus Himself, who came ' not to destroy but to perfect ', whose every word and deed rang true, who later could demand :

> ' Which of you shall convince me of sin ? ' ;

that evidence which gave certainty to every man of goodwill, every right-minded Jew, as it had done to Nathanael and Nicodemus.

> ' But I have a greater testimony
> Than that of John
> For the works
> Which the Father hath given me to perfect
> The works themselves which I do
> Give testimony of me
> That the Father hath sent me.'

Nay more, the Father Himself has spoken in His favour ; He has proclaimed Him to be ' His beloved Son ' :

> ' And the Father himself who hath sent me
> Hath given testimony of me.'

Last, since above all things else they take their stand upon the Scriptures, to these He will appeal ; they too, for one who will but read them aright, give ample witness of Him.

> ' Search the Scriptures
> For you think in them to have life everlasting
> And the same are they
> That give testimony of me.'

John the Baptist, the life of Jesus, God the Father, the Scriptures,—to a believing and truth-seeking Jew the argument is overwhelming and conclusive. It has accepted his premises and no more, the rest has followed. It will be noticed that miracles, in the strict sense, do not enter in apart ; if they are considered at all, they are included under the more general heading, ' works '.

How then comes it that they have failed to recognize Him ? With this, given in the manner of a warning, He concludes.

First he reminds them that with all their show of religious observance they have not God within their hearts.

> ' But I know you
> That you have not the love of God in you.'

This is the first and deepest cause of their blindness ; in their observance of the Law, the first commandment of the Law has been ignored. But the second cause is like to the first ; their putting men in the place of God, making men their judges, receiving from them their reward, measuring all things by their standards.

> ' I am come in the name of my Father
> And you receive me not
> If another shall come in his own name
> Him you will receive
> How can you believe
> Who receive glory from one another
> And the glory which is from God alone
> You do not seek ? '

Hence has followed their third source of blindness, their false interpretation of the Law. They have read it with human eyes alone, made of it a religion for man alone to see. The sense they have misunderstood ; in the end they have disbelieved, misconstrued, the author. Let then the author be their judge ; He will not judge them.

> ' Think not that I will accuse you to the Father
> There is one that accuseth you
> Moses
> In whom you trust
> For if you did believe Moses
> You would perhaps believe me also
> For of me he wrote
> But if you do not believe his writings
> How will you believe my words ? '

As usual with S. John, the scene ends as abruptly as it began. In other words, what he has given us is not so much a scene as an episode. He has caught hold of a single event that by its means he may depict the minds of men and of Jesus alike, as they developed in the turmoil of Jerusalem. He would almost seem to be telling us in this story why it was that for the immediate future Jesus gave Himself to Galilee rather than to Judæa. Judæa had the knowledge but made no use of it ; it had the first grace but rejected it ; if it had been given more, if it had received the evidence of miracles, it would easily have perverted their significance, as indeed it did.

6

16. The First Rejection at Nazareth

WE left Jesus in Galilee at Cana. The ruler from Capharnaum had gone; the men of Cana knew nothing of the favour that had been granted to him. We next hear of Him back at Nazareth. Nevertheless, in the meeting with His fellow-townsmen there described, there is a statement which proves that He had been for some time at Capharnaum, and there had begun His working of miracles.

> ' As great things as we have heard done
>   In Capharnaum
>   Do also here
> In thy own country.'

Since this could be said, and since the time of miracles has still to be deferred for some weeks, it seems clear that the first visit to Nazareth must also be deferred, perhaps to the time of His first missionary tour through Galilee. Still, as has just been done with the visit to Jerusalem, the visit to Nazareth may well be placed here. It stands apart as an event by itself; if the former explains why He left Jerusalem alone, this explains why He left Nazareth, which may account for its place in the Gospel narrative.

On one day, then, early in His ministry in Galilee Jesus made His way back to Nazareth, by a winding and undulating road which at the end rises over a ridge and drops into a large amphitheatre, round the sides of which the town of Nazareth clings. Beyond it to the south the hills slope again gently upward; beyond these is a drop, almost precipitous, into the beautiful valley of Esdraelon. In truth Nazareth is a backwater, is nowhere; an ideal spot for a hermitage, but wholly off the beaten track of life, where no man would live who loved the ways of men, or whose ambitions rose beyond those of the tillers of the soil. Such is Nazareth even at this day, when it lives in great part on the tourists and pilgrims who visit it ; in the days of Jesus it must have been the same, left far to the west by the road from Judæa into Galilee, far to the south by the caravan route from the sea coast to Damascus, pitched up among the hills out of sight, and wellnigh out of mind, ignored even by the people of Galilee.

And yet was it Jesus' own city. There He had been brought up, there for close on thirty years He had had a happy home. The hills about were entwined in all the memories of His boyhood, the life of the town was His own. With His natural tendency to love those with whom He had lived, with that fidelity in love which never failed anyone, it was inevitable that much of His heart should still linger in the little town that clung on that hill-side. To it He would return, in it He would make His first declaration ; after Jerusalem, He would give it the first opportunity. Though He knew it would fail Him yet would He not fail it ; He would take up His life in Galilee where He had laid it down.

He waited till the Sabbath. On the Sabbath day, as had always been His custom, He made His way across the village to the synagogue. His reputation had gone before Him. The talk concerning Him and His assumption of authority had long since come into Nazareth ; how He had done a wonder at Cana; how, before the Pasch, He had taken up His abode at Capharnaum ; how He had gathered certain followers about Him and had trained them to preach and baptize by the Jordan in Judæa. Wiseacres in the village had put their heads together ; they had compared these present rumours with the record of His past, and knowingly had shaken their heads. When at last He had returned, quiet, unassuming, silent, apart, a mixture of lowliness and yet peaceful assurance about Him, they had eyed Him with suspicion, the first inclination to respect crushed beneath what they thought to be the evidence of facts. They had waited for Him to come out and speak, but so far He had said nothing. He had retired to His Mother's house, He seemed just to have come home to rest, and to take up the old, unobtrusive habits which had marked His days of old.

But on the Sabbath morning He was to be seen making His way through the narrow streets to the synagogue. There in the old days He had taken His turn in reading

and expounding the Scriptures, and it had to be confessed
that there was always something that held them in His
exposition. They would ask Him to take His turn again ;
if He would, He might have something to say about Himself.
The report spread through the bazaar and soon the little
synagogue was full. But not full of friends ; there were
watchful, critical eyes turned upon Him, blinked with a
Nazarene outlook, of men who knew their own minds, that
they did, and would brook no nonsense, that they would
not, above all, would not brook airs or assumptions in one
who after all was no more than one of themselves, a villager
of Nazareth, and a young, untaught, inexperienced one at
that.

But they would wait and see. They would give this
youth a hearing ; in case He had any claim to make, He
should have an opportunity of proving it. When they had
assembled, in greater numbers than usual, He was invited
to the pulpit to read. He accepted, without any demonstration ; as if this were but one more ordinary occasion, Jesus
rose from His seat against the wall and came forward. It
chanced that that day the book to be read was that of the
prophet Isaias. The attendant offered it to Him ; He
unrolled the scroll, and read where it opened ; it was the
beginning of the sixty-first chapter.

> ' The spirit of the Lord is upon me
> Because the Lord hath anointed me
> He hath sent me to preach to the meek
> To heal the contrite of heart
> And to preach a release to the captives
> And deliverance to them that are shut up
> To proclaim the acceptable year of the Lord
> And the day of vengeance of our God
> To comfort all that mourn
> To appoint to the mourners of Sion
> And to give them a crown for ashes
> The oil of joy for mourning
> A garment of praise for the spirit of grief
> And they shall be called in it the mighty ones of justice
> The planting of the Lord to glorify him.'
>
> Isaias lxi, 1–3.

He stopped reading and rolled up the book ; He restored
it to the attendant and sat down. He was strangely quiet,

and calm, and self-possessed ; His manner held them all,
every eye was fixed upon Him.   Then firmly, as would
speak a master in Israel who knew, winningly, as from one
who would be a benefactor, the words rang through the
silence of the synogague :

'This day
Is fulfilled this scripture in your ears.'

What followed this introduction who shall attempt to
substitute ?   He had chosen for His text one of the tenderest,
one of the most hopeful of the prophecies of the Messias.
Elaborating it He spoke to them of meekness, of a contrite
heart, of captives, and of them that were in bondage ; as
He spoke they knew that they themselves were included by
Him in these categories.   He spoke as one who Himself
was meek, who Himself could fathom the depths of contrition,
who had lived with them in bondage and knew the weight
of chains ; as one who had been released, and had come to
share His lot with others.   Gently He spoke to them, as one
who understood ; sympathetically, as one who knew how
hard it would be for them to bend ; encouragingly, as to
those who had already yielded to despair and were content
to remain prone upon the ground in their prison cell ;
hopefully, as one who pointed to a new horizon, and strength
restored, and a future of bright things.   Gracefully He
drew them on, unconsciously they followed ; under the
spell of His attraction they were dumb ; as they listened to
His invitation, telling them that He was there to lead them,
to teach them, to heal them, to set them free, to give them
all their heart's desire if they would but take it, they did
not know that even as He spoke He had begun to cast His
spell about them, and that they had but to yield to be
entirely won.   The eloquence of Jesus !   Founded on
crystal sincerity, and unspeakable truth, and a sympathy
that included every human heart, and a companionship
that endured with them all ; and behind it an authority
which carried beyond argument, and compelled men to say
that never did man speak as He spoke! It was not eloquence,
it was much more ; it was utter truth uttering itself, convincing by its own transparency, blinding and subduing by
the brightness of its light, conquering beyond possibility of
doubt every man of goodwill who heard it.

The address was ended, and Jesus sat back, as it were to

rest. For a moment there was silence, the silence of the
Eastern sky before the dawn. At length a head moved and
the spell was broken. The men looked round ; they cast
enthusiastic glances at each other ; there was admiration,
and joy, and satisfaction unto tears in their eyes and hearts
as they woke from their trance and began to speak.

> ' And all gave testimony to him
> And they wondered at the words of grace
> That proceeded from his mouth.'

Would that they could have remained as this, with the
freshness of the morning dew upon them ! But it was not
to be. Like Simon, and Nathanael, and Nicodemus, and
others in the days gone by, they had come to judge of this
new preacher for themselves ; but unlike them, they had
come with narrow, carping minds, prejudiced by previous
disparaging experience. Their first impulse, almost irresistible, had been one of admiration and surrender ; now, as
they looked at one another, the old tone revived, and they
affected to be doubtful. They owned to the beauty of all
that He had said ; but memory was slippery, and criticism
was sharp, and very soon they were able to forget it. Instead
they remembered the carpenter Joseph, plying his trade in
his dark little workshop at the northern corner of the
village ; they remembered Jesus, boy, youth, and man,
just a follower of His father's trade and no more. They
knew exactly the school at which He had studied, and
precisely how much learning it was possible for Him to
acquire ; it was no more than their own, indeed it was less,
for they had the added learning of age and experience.
For the village to submit to such a man, for the elders to be
taught by a carpenter, was not to be endured ; let Him say
what He liked, it was not to be endured. The force of the
reaction was strong ; it soon found expression ; the remark
passed from mouth to mouth ;

> ' And they said
> Is not this the son of Joseph ? '

The corner once turned, other things quickly followed.
There was a grudge they had against Him. If He was in
truth what He now claimed to be, how was it that He had
deserted Nazareth ? He had made Himself notorious
elsewhere, in Cana, in Capharnaum, in Judæa, in places
where He was not known ; if He were true, ought He not

to have begun at Nazareth, where He was known, and men
might the better have judged ?   It was being said that He
had healed the sick elsewhere, were there not sick enough
in Nazareth, that He must needs go to others ?   They put
it all together, His previous history which was nothing, His
present methods which were at least evasive ;   they would
be prudent and reserve their judgement, they would see
what else He might say or do, they would say not a
word.

Jesus read their thoughts.   ' He knew what was in man ' ;
by long, enduring, wearisome experience of them, He
knew what was in these men of Nazareth.   They would
not speak ;   then He would express their thoughts for
them.

> ' And He said to them
> Doubtless you will say to me this similitude
> Physician, heal thyself
> As great things as we have heard done in Capharnaum
> Do also here
> In thy own country.'

Yes, He had read their thoughts, and by their looks and
nods they acknowledged it.   What answer would He give ?
Had they but been willing to take it, even as He spoke He
was giving them their answer ;   but their eyes were blinded
and they saw only that which they had decided that they
would see—the carpenter of Nazareth and no more.   So is
it with all who seek Him ;   let them fix the limits of their
knowledge, and they will see no further ;   let them be men
of goodwill, ' true Israelites in whom there is no guile ', and
they will see ' the Son of God, the King of Israel '.

Sadly therefore Jesus answered the question which He
Himself had put.   He answered it by a series of warnings,
and they but too quickly understood them.   He had quoted
one proverb, He would answer with another.   They were
self-confident ;   as in Judæa so here they relied on their
election as his fellow-Nazarenes.   He would remind them
of times in the past when their forefathers had been passed
over, and the favours of God had instead been granted to
outcast but faithful Gentiles.   Let them not rely too much
on their own judgement ;   if they would hear Him, all that
He had promised would come to them—if only they would
hear Him.

' And he said
Amen, I say to you
That no prophet is accepted in his own country
In truth I say to you
In the days of Elias
There were many widows in Israel
When heaven was shut up
Three years and six months
When there was a great famine throughout all the earth
But to none of them was Elias sent
But to Sarepta of Sidor
To a widow woman
And there were many lepers in Israel
In the time of Eliseus the prophet
And none of them was cleansed
But Naaman the Syrian.'

The insinuation was quickly understood. True, it was only a warning, but it was taken as a charge. This Man, one from among themselves, before they had allowed it to Him, had taken on Himself the rôle of a prophet; should they think to refuse Him, their decision was already rejected. He had ended by suggesting that not only Capharnaites but Gentiles, men of Syria and women of Sarepta, might yet be more favoured by God than they. The insult was clear; it was manifest to all; there was not one dissentient voice; do we need other proof that in all the preceding thirty years in nothing had Jesus differed from the plainest among them?

So these men took His words, and acted accordingly. A cry of execration rose up and filled that little synagogue; if Jesus had not spoken blasphemy, at least He had insulted His fellow-Nazarenes beyond any hope of forgiveness. In their excitement they rushed to Him; they forced Him from His seat; they hustled Him and thrust Him forth, into the street of the bazaar outside. Acting together, as is the way with a mob, their fury gathered strength; forgetting themselves in the tumult they grew reckless. Down through the village they hurried Him along, past the very door of the little house in which, thirty years before, His Mother had received the visit of an angel; round the curve of the valley below the town, and up the gentle slope which ends suddenly and drops abruptly over the Vale of

Esdraelon. It was a noisy throng that pushed Him, forgetful of the Sabbath, its decorum and its laws ; passion had been roused and was master. As they went along they fixed His doom ; not only should He be driven from the village, He should be thrown over the precipice beyond, and meet the death that He deserved. Women at their cottage doors looked on dismayed, their children clinging about them ; old men on the house-tops raised their eyes from their scrolls and shook their heads. It was long since such a rabble had disturbed the streets of Nazareth, never before upon a Sabbath day.

And to a point Jesus permitted it. If they wished they could drive Him from the synagogue, they could hound Him through their streets, they could push Him to and fro, they could hurry Him along, they could pull Him back, they could strike Him, they could befoul Him with the mire of the road, they could jeer at Him and make mockery of what He had said, they could shriek their cat-calls in His ears, they could acclaim His death as a thing to be desired ; Jesus in that crowd, in His own village, knew that He had not a friend that would defend Him, in spite of all those preceding thirty years. It was a strange requital ; it tells a strange tale.

Yet for all that would He not abandon them ; they should not reap the bitter fruits of their own mad folly. He might have let them throw Him over that mountain-side, and angels might have held Him up, lest perchance He strike His foot against a stone ; now indeed the offer of Satan might have been in place. He might have turned on them, as later upon a like occasion He turned upon another crowd, and they would have fallen one and all to the ground. But He did neither. However uncouth, however barbarous, they were after all His fellow-citizens ; by merely living with Him all these years they had won a special place in His heart. He would spare them the last remorse ; they should not be guilty of His death. Some day, perhaps, they would awaken to what they had already done, and they would be sorry, and He would forgive them.

They had neared the summit of the hill ; as they reached it, their very fear of what they were about to do made them the more uproarious. They called to one another, encouraged one another in their deed of evil ; they were occupied more with themselves, and the great show they were making, than with Him. Suddenly they became aware that something had gone wrong. Their cries of bravado sounded hollow ; some of their company had ceased to shout at all. They looked at one another, enquiring ; they looked for their Victim in their midst ; He was no longer there. Instantly they were sobered ; that He could have escaped by an ordinary ruse was not possible. Like drunken men awakened they were smitten with shame ; they turned about, they slunk back to the town, muttering to themselves as they went, by foolish words of self-defence sulkily silencing their consciences. Arrived at the village they slipped away into their cottages, and there the Sabbath pall covered them ; when again they met in the streets, that evening or the next morning, the folly of that day was a forbidden topic.

But there was one in Nazareth that day on whom tradition has affectionately meditated. In the midst of all the turmoil where was His Mother ? She could not but have known what was going forward ; the confusion in the little town, disturbing the silence of the Sabbath, could not have failed to reach her ears, as it reached the ears of everyone. Some neighbour who had seen would have thought of her ; out of common pity she would have run to her door, and broken to her the news of this new plight of her Son. And Mary would have heard, and would have risen to follow, and none would have been able to prevent her ; she who was one day to stand by her Son, watching Him while He bled to death, now when she heard of this first danger could never have left Him to die alone ? Was this, then, the fulfilment of prophecy ? Had the doom she had foreknown come so soon ? She hastened from her cottage, she followed along the track of that shouting mob ; if her Son were to die, how could she do other than die with Him ?

And yet what is this ? Up there on the hill, before the fatal edge is reached, there is confusion. Soon the shouting dies down, soon all is quiet, soon the mob comes slinking past her where she stands unnoticed, in the shadow of a cottage by the roadside. He is not with them, and she understands. In some way they have been thwarted, somehow her Son has escaped them, somewhere He is safe, and her Mother's anxious heart is relieved.

So tradition has pondered on the Mother ; and to commemorate this first deep shadow of what in no long time was to befall her in real earnest, a chapel in her honour stands in its little garden, crowning the hill where her Son would not yet allow His own to drive Him to death. It is called the Chapel of Mary Weeping.

17. Settlement at Capharnaum

Jesus escaped from His would-be destroyers, and made His way once more down the valleys to Capharnaum. Definitely now His own people of Nazareth had rejected Him ; they had been wise in their own conceit, and had accepted the result. He passed from their midst, as He would again, when He chose, pass from the midst of others ; 'their hour' was not yet come, and therefore not yet might they kill Him. In Nazareth especially He would not die. With all their sinfulness these people were His own ; He loved them still with a special love, and He would not allow them to be guilty of so terrible a crime. He would leave them for a time ; later, when perhaps they would be more pacified, He would come back and try again.

In the meantime at Capharnaum, by the Sea of Galilee, there was a better centre from which He could set out. There already He had been well received ; the King's officer lived there whose son He had cured, as well as the relatives of Simon ; close by, at Bethsaida, hardly separated from Capharnaum, dwelt most of those who had already in some way owned Him for what He was. The country, too, was according to His heart. There was the peaceful lake in front, shut in by the mountains beyond, making the spot look like a hiding-place from all the unnecessary world. There were the sloping hills behind, to which when He was so minded He could fly and pray as much as He had done on the hills round Nazareth. Moreover, Capharnaum itself was central. All Galilee lay to the west ; to the east was the lake with its easy means of passage ; beyond were Trachonitis, and Ituræa, and Decapolis with its many towns, and Perœa over the Jordan. Capharnaum itself was a busy little market centre to which many roads, overland and across the lake, converged.

Besides there was a prophecy to be fulfilled. It had been foretold that He should be born in Bethlehem, and so it had been done ; that like His people He should come up out of Egypt, and it had come about ; that He should live so long in Nazareth as to be called a Nazarene, and by close on thirty years' sojourn there He had earned that name. It was also said that over the way of the sea beyond the Jordan, over the land of Zabulon, and Nephthali, over Galilee of the Gentiles, the great light should appear.

'At the first time
The land of Zabulon
And the land of Nephthali
Was lightly touched[1]
And at the last
The way of the sea beyond the Jordan
Of the Galilee of the Gentiles
Was heavily loaded[2]
The people that walked in darkness
Have seen a great light
To them that dwelt in the region of the shadow of death
Light is risen.'

Isaias ix, 1, 2.

This prophecy, too, He must fulfil. Round about that lake He must preach His chief sermons ; along its shore He must pour out His miracles. In the neighbourhood would come the occasion to lay the foundation of His Church ; on its hill-side He would give His last commission. In Capharnaum, then, He would take up His abode, so far as He would have any fixed abode at all. He went down the valleys from Nazareth, a full day's journey on foot ; at Capharnaum they received Him, for they were friends already, and gladly took Him to their own. In recompense for the trial of the day before it was some consolation ; if consolation there could be that could heal the wound, caused by the collapse of such a friendship, by the snapping of so strong a bond of love.

Jesus settled at Capharnaum, to begin His work in real earnest. And yet even here, after all this lapse of time, He was in no hurry. During the week, while the hills and valleys were teeming rich after the rains, men were busy in the fields or on the lake and He would not interrupt their labours. Instead He spent His days in quiet ; that was ever His inclination ; there were always the crannies in the rocks in which He could hide, and there was always His

---

[1] Was brought into contempt (R.V.)
[2] He hath made it glorious (R.V.)

Father with whom He could converse. Only on the Sabbath days, at first, did He let Himself be heard.

> ' And there He taught them
> On the Sabbath days.'

Then He would go with them to their synagogue ; there He would speak to them, leading them on, giving them little that was new, starting from the teaching of John which they had already learnt, still preparing them, still waiting, repeating again and again the same doctrine :

> ' Do penance
> For the kingdom of heaven is at hand.'

It was familiar teaching ; and yet about it, as it came from Him, there was something very different from anything they had heard before. The truth He taught was the same, but it was more real ; it went more home ; men left Him with not only a conviction that penance must be done, but with a desire to do it. The ' kingdom ', too, became more and more full of meaning. It was in the air ; it was part of their atmosphere ; what in the end it was to mean they could not know, but somehow along the shores of that lake among themselves it was finding its foundations. All this and more, as they listened to Him on succeeding Sabbath days, began to sink unconsciously into their minds. He did not argue with them, He did not prove, scarcely did He appeal, He stated and little more ; but it was with a power, an authority, a quiet contentment that was sure of itself, which told them without need of argument that He was right.

18. The Call of the Four

Thus had Jesus settled at Capharnaum. In this quiet, patient way He had begun to teach, but so far we do not hear that He worked any miracles. He still waited on ; there was still work of preparation to be done by prayer, and He was never loth to give Himself to prayer. It was still possible for Him to go about alone without creating disturbance. As He went down the street, or out on the lanes beyond, men would let Him pass them by with little more than a look, and perhaps a remark among themselves ; the time was not yet when the crowds would throng about Him wherever He appeared.

Hence very early one morning we find Him wandering

alone by the lake-side from Capharnaum towards Bethsaida, even as a year ago we saw Him wandering alone along the banks of the Jordan. Then the Baptist had declared Him, and two men had followed in His track; Andrew and John, men from the Lake of Galilee. The memory of that day had never been forgotten, either by them or by their brothers, Simon and James. Then He had said : ' Come and see ' ; and they had gone, and

> ' Saw where he abode
> And stayed with him all that day.'

And though of late He had passed away from them, preferring to be alone while they returned to their fishing, still the esteem, and reverence, and love remained in their hearts, and, when they spoke among themselves, His name was often on their lips. Often, when the night's work was done, and they had drawn their boats high up on the shore in the morning, they would sit together on the stones, slipping their nets through their fingers, mending a broken string here, there disentangling a piece of wood or weed, making all clean and ready for the next expedition ; and as they sat and worked they would talk together, in their rambling, disconnected way, not looking up, one interrupting another, one supplementing another, sometimes all together, sometimes a single voice apparently speaking to itself ; and the subject would regularly be the wonderful adventure by the Jordan, and the utter truth of the Man they had met there, and all that had followed after, in Cana, and Jerusalem, and Judæa, and Samaria, and what must yet be destined to come.

Now during these last weeks He had again appeared in their neighbourhood. They had heard of His coming once more to Capharnaum, and they had noticed how His Sabbath-day discourses were impressing and winning the people of the place. What He said was nothing very new ; they had heard it before in Judæa ; but it was the Man behind the words that was growing upon them, even as at the first He had grown upon themselves. They discussed these things together ; they began to draw conclusions ; soon, they were sure, something momentous would happen. He would make Himself a leader and men would follow, and when He did they would not be slow to join the movement.

So pondering, but keeping their secret to themselves, these brothers had returned to their fishing and resumed their routine life; when on this particular morning, before most people were astir, they saw Him walking towards them along the water's edge. Andrew and his brother Simon were still in their boat off the shore; perhaps a sign that the sun had not yet risen over the hills in the distance. They saw Him coming and were glad; why they could hardly say. Still they could make no claim upon Him; there was no reason to interrupt their task; they would give Him a sign of recognition and greeting, a nod of the head and a morning salaam, for their hands were occupied, and then go on with their labour.

But not so Jesus. At last, at long last, the hour had struck, and He must begin to gather men about Him for His work. These had been His first companions. First of all men they had corresponded with the light given to them by John; they had stood with Him in His first days of waiting, baptizing at the Jordan ford. They had followed Him into Galilee; at Cana He had parted with them but had not forgotten; He never forgot. Hitherto they had been faithful; that fidelity He must reward in the way He always did. He must give them a further call, to things yet higher and more intimate.

He walked down the side of the lake till He reached the spot nearest to where the little boat lay upon the waters. The ripple of the waves lapped against the vessel; as the net was slowly drawn in, silver beads ran along the strings. The men pursued their task in silence; the peace upon the lake at that hour held them beneath its spell. He came, and stood there, and watched them, as might a man from up-country, to whom the fisherman's trade is new. When at last the net had been hauled in, they looked up at Him. He too was gazing at them; He had been waiting for that look; He raised His hand, beckoned to them:

'Come!'

He called across the water, and they seemed to hear the echo of that other 'Come!' which had won them in Judæa:

'Come after me
And I will make you to become fishers of men.'

There was something almost playful in the tone of His speech, playfulness in the form of the words. Yet beneath

it all there was earnestness, telling them that this was no
mere jest about their trade, no mere pretty compliment ;
but that the words came from One who gave a real call and
meant it.

Such confidence, linked with such assurance, who could
resist ? Certainly not such men as Andrew and Simon.
All these last months, how they had longed for something
of the kind ! They made no delay ; down into the boat
went all their fishing-tackle ; they rubbed their hard hands
together to clean them, and along their clothes to make
them dry. More by look and action than by word they
entrusted their vessel and its contents to their fellow-
fishermen. They were soon in the water, soon they were
on the shore, soon by the side of this Man who again by a
word had captured them, recklessly glorying in the wild
choice they were making.

The three for a moment stood together on the beach.
Not much was said ; there was not much that could be
said ; for the hearts of all three were very full. On one
side was unutterable love for these two men who had
blindly left their all for Him ; on the other was that which
had destroyed all power of speech within them, they could
now only be and follow. Jesus turned to move forward.
A little further on was the stake of the elderly fisherman
Zebedee. He was a prosperous tradesman ; his name was
esteemed in Bethsaida. His boat was lying on its side inshore,
for the fishing of the morning was done. Zebedee was
seated in it, with his sons, James and John, and the men of
his crew about him ; the black nets lay across their knees
while they searched with their fingers for the broken strings
and joined them together. Again it was a silent group ;
they had done a hard night's work ; this was the end of
their morning's task, and soon they would be off to their
cottages to rest.

With Andrew and Simon beside Him, Jesus came near
the ship, and stood as if to watch the fishermen at their
work. At first they did not notice Him, they were too
preoccupied ; soon they looked up, and first John, then
James, knew who was standing before them. Holding his
hand still, with silent reverence John gazed ; already that
deep affection had begun to work in him which tied his
tongue, but on which he was to feed all his life. In return
he was greeted with a look of recognition, and welcome,

and it seemed of invitation ; the Master had come for something. James sat beside him silent ; he, too, it was clear, was included in the call. Jesus raised His hand and beckoned to them both. The look in His face, of friendship, of desire, of encouragement, was not to be mistaken, to one who cared it was irresistible.

> ' Come,' again He said
> ' And I will make you fishers of men.'

At that instant James and John were won. They did not stop to think ; no other words were wanted. They laid down their nets and their needles, stepped out of the boat, and soon were at the side of Andrew, and Simon, and Jesus ; John, the young man of keen ambitions, to whom the great little world of Bethsaida was just then opening with all its prospects ; John, the son of the elder, Zebedee, who might some day come to be the master fisherman of all the lake ; James his brother, who had little ambition for himself alone, but for John, and in company with John, had great dreams ; they set it all aside and they followed, into the great unknown.

And poor Zebedee, they left him too. During these last weeks the old man had heard much of his sons' adventures in Judæa. He had noticed how deeply they had been affected by the Stranger from Nazareth ; how their native enthusiasm had taken a new turn, how John in particular had been moved, partly by a personal devotion to the Man,—he was inclined to extremes,—partly by new notions about a coming kingdom, and he had already begun to be anxious for the future. He had brought them up well ; he had spared himself in nothing ; he had built up for them a thriving business. And they had responded ; the sons of Zebedee had promised fair to carry on a good tradition ; if he had won an honourable place on the lakeside, they might be expected to make it more honoured. Yet now it had all come to this ! A strange Man from Nazareth—from Nazareth of all places !—had passed them by and apparently had turned their heads. He had beckoned to them and they had obeyed, He had called to them and they had followed, forgetting all else, forgetting even him, their self-sacrificing father. As he watched them pass out of sight, with never a glance behind them, the old man's eyes filled with tears, his old head shook anxiously, his hands set down the net they had been mending and rested idly on his knees. He did not call them back ; he made no remonstrance ; he knew his sons too well to doubt their choice ; but his head hung low, and his long beard drooped upon his chest, and his arms grew listless, and the heart of Zebedee was very lonely, as he watched his two boys pass away to be made into fishers of men.

19. The Demoniac in the Temple

The five returned together to Capharnaum. They had friends and relations there, and it was easy to find a home. Again Jesus sat through the days and waited for the Sabbath ; but now a new thing had come into His life. He had chosen four men ; with these four men He would shake the foundations of the world and upon the ruins would rebuild it.

The Sabbath day came round and as usual He made His way to the synagogue. Capharnaum boasted quite a good synagogue. It had been fortunate in winning the favour of a Roman official ; and he, because he liked the Jews, and sympathized with their deep religious spirit, and knew how much religion meant for their development, had built them a synagogue, in the centre of the town, alongside of the forum, with the sea in front and the hill sloping up behind, lifting it up on noble steps and decorating it with ornamental work far superior to any other synagogue in that neighbourhood. The people of Capharnaum were proud of their possession ; its steps, with the square outside, were their common meeting-place. There, too, in consequence of this, gathered the poor of the town.

The hour of prayer was over, and the congregation was making its way home. Jesus again had taught ; He had spoken once more of the Kingdom, and of the need of penance in preparation for it ; this time the four had stood about Him, and had been given their first object-lesson in their training. Then He too made to go ; as He came near the door a strange thing occurred. There within the porch lay a particularly loathsome beggar, whose sole excuse for his condition was that he was a lunatic ; a crouching, forbidding creature, seemingly more animal than man, to which even a kind heart had to make an effort to be kind. Jesus came near ; the groups about the door and upon the steps outside were making room for Him to pass. Suddenly, without any provocation, the poor thing in the corner behind them grew restless. It shrank against the wall ; it hissed an angry defiance ; hatred was written on its features, in its livid eyes, on the clenched teeth between the parted lips ; like a rat in presence of a snake it shook with fear, like a rat at bay it poised itself to spring and fight. In alarm the people stood aside, and Jesus was before it ; then, with a loud shriek that rang through the synagogue, a shriek unearthly, discordant, as if the very mouth of hell were speaking, it cried out :

> ' Let us alone
> What have we to do with thee
> Jesus of Nazareth
> Art thou come to destroy us
> I know thee who thou art
> The holy one of God.'

The shriek was followed with dead silence ; it was a cry to strike fear into anyone that heard it. Then there was a rush to the spot ; men behind strained their necks to see, those in front pressed the further back, in terror of the thing that now looked no longer human. From it they turned to Him at whom the horrid creature glared, and of whom it had said so strange a thing. It had recognized Him ; it had said that it knew Him ; it had called Him ' Jesus of Nazareth ', yet had it also declared Him ' the Holy One of God '. It had addressed Him as an enemy, with whom it was at war, whom it feared even unto death. What was it ? Who was He ? It was a mystery of awe and fear. Jesus stood before the creature motionless. The time had come at last ; this was the hour for which He had so long waited. More than a year ago He had crossed swords with Satan, and had ended by merely dismissing him ; now Satan was again before Him, this time in more subtle garb. Then he had said : ' If thou be the Son of God ', and had waited to see the effect ; now he called Him ' the holy one of God ', a yet more convincing flattery. Then he had met Him in the privacy of the desert ; now it was in the open synagogue, for all the world to hear. Before he had spoken as a master, now he cried out like any cringing slave. Surely all this would satisfy the pride of the Man from Nazareth.

Still Jesus stood and looked at the poor wretch cowering before Him. His glance went through its eyes ; behind those eyes He saw others, of another creature living within ; through those eyes He looked into another world. Then He spoke ; His words were the fewest possible, His tone was one of withering contempt ; a new thing to those who thought they had known Him well, and who had deemed that contempt in Him was not possible.

> ' And Jesus threatened
> And rebuked him saying
> Hold thy peace
> Speak no more
> And go out of the man.'

Immediately there followed a new phenomenon. The creature ceased to stare ; it turned and writhed, and twisted ; it strained and tore at itself, as if it would let loose some power, some fire that raged within its body. There was another hideous yell that rang round the building ; a leap forward, into the midst of the terrified people gathered about ; and the creature lay among them, panting, unconscious. At length it opened its eyes ; frightened it looked about it, from one side to the other ; at once men saw another expression in its face. It was no longer fiendish, it was human ; no longer one of hatred, and passion, and violence, but of fear, and helplessness, and appeal for pity. The onlookers drew nearer ; they lifted the poor victim up ; they looked for the wounds which they had seen him inflict upon himself ; there were none at all.

> ' And when the unclean spirit tearing him
> Had thrown him into the midst
> Crying with a loud voice he went out of him
> And hurt him not at all.'

There were serious faces in the synagogue that Sabbath day. A portent such as this was a new thing. It was more than an ordinary miracle, it implied a power over the other world ; and the very nearness of it made them fear the more. They looked at the delivered man, pondering ; they looked at one another and their eyes were eloquent ; they began to talk among themselves, and always their conversation ended in questions. A Man had done this thing before their eyes ; who then could He be ? Of late He had held them by the beauty of His teaching ; had this deed been done to confirm what He had taught ? For weeks He had been living in their midst, come down from Nazareth, and had scarcely been observed ; yet all the time, almost unconsciously, Capharnaum had been yielding more and more every day to His attraction. What did it mean ? He had spoken much of a Kingdom, and to-day He had acted like a King ; but it had been in a Kingdom that was beyond this world. Their thoughts went round and round, but always came back to the same enquiry. This Man among them, this Jesus of Nazareth, who was He ? They must study Him, they must learn Him better ; they must know Him. The work had now begun in real earnest.

> ' And they were all amazed
> And there came fear upon them all
> Insomuch that they talked
> And questioned among themselves saying
> What thing is this
> What is this new doctrine
> What word is this
> For with authority and power
> He commandeth even the unclean spirits
> And they obey him
> And go out ? '

If this was not the first public miracle of Jesus in Capharnaum, at least it was the first of which we have any record, and as being the first the Evangelists treat it. They tell us of the sensation it created, not only in Capharnaum but throughout all Galilee ; it was the beginning of the fame of Jesus as a worker of wonders.

> ' And the fame of him was spread
> And published forthwith
> Into every place of the country of Galilee.'

20. Simon's mother-in-law

While in the synagogue the witnesses of this scene were recovering from their wonder, Jesus had passed out and gone. Such, we shall see, was His usual custom. He worked His miracles and passed on, as if they were ordinary things ; only when He had some particular occasion did He draw attention to them. He left the synagogue that Sabbath day, turned to the left across the street in the direction of the lake, and with Andrew and Simon, James and John, came to the house called Simon's, but probably the home of Simon's relatives. Tradition places it nearer to the sea, but a few minutes' walk from the synagogue. The ruins of Capharnaum would indicate that it was a town of about a mile long, stretched along the shore. The rising ground behind gave little encouragement for other arrangements ; at its greatest depth it could not have been more than a quarter of a mile.

As they came on their way these four turned over among themselves the wonderful scene they had witnessed. They were not of Capharnaum, and therefore were able more easily to escape from the throng ; they had not yet become identified with Him as His companions, and therefore were not liable to be cross-examined. No less than the others they had been impressed by what had taken place before their eyes ; they, too, no less than the rest, asked themselves what it might mean. But better than the others they were able to answer their own question. There was their untrammelled goodwill to help them, as it had already helped them before, their inclination to believe, their trust in Him now long assured, the beginning of that devotedness to Him which, though they scarcely knew it, in reality was love ; all this enabled them to see far more than others saw, and to reach conclusions that reached far beyond.

In addition there was their past experience. They had heard their former revered master, John, declare Him to be the Lamb of God, saying he had discovered Him by the witness of the Dove. They themselves, won by no miracle, but because He had shown them that He could read their hearts and yet would give them His friendship, because of His look, of His words, of His personal attraction that could not be resisted, of His strength and yet of His lowliness, had hailed Him as the Messias, the Son of God, the King of Israel. Before their eyes at Cana, just that men might be made more humanly contented, He had converted water into wine. In the very Temple court, because, as He had said, His Father's house had been desecrated, He had brought to His feet both Pharisees and people. By the Jordan they had sat with Him, and He had taught them, and all they had seen and learnt had been stamped indelibly upon them. They had seen Him hold out His hand even to heretic Samaritans, and in two days had won them. From Cana, as they now knew, He had healed at Capharnaum the son of the ruler who had appealed to Him. He had again come to them in their homes, He had again

called them after Him, and even at this moment their
hearts were warm and joyful under the glow of their glad
adventure. Who was He ? Who was He not ? And what
might not be expected of Him ?   No ; it was not strange
that devils feared and obeyed Him ; it was not strange that
they called Him ' the holy one of God '.

All this and more poured through their minds as they
walked close behind Him down the narrow street.   They
reached the house where they had to stay, and where their
morning meal awaited them, a little two-roomed cottage
close upon the shore belonging to Simon's relatives.   But
here was something to distract them.   Jesus entered, and
took His place apart, waiting for the meal to be served ;
when the others followed it was whispered to them that
there was trouble in the place.   The mistress of the house,
the old mother-in-law of Simon, was seriously ill ; she was
lying in the inner room, shivering with fever.   She was
unable to receive them ; she could not serve them ; what
was to be done ?

But they did not hesitate.   The enthusiasm roused by the
scene of that morning was still hot within them ;   the
thoughts that had since been running through their minds
had left their mark.   He who at His mother's hint, to
relieve a household trouble, had changed water into wine,
what would He not do in a much more serious household
trouble of their own ?   They came to Him where He had
sat down ; they told Him of the sick woman in the inner
chamber ; what He would do they did not know, but they
were very confident.

> ' And forthwith they tell him of her
> And besought him for her.'

And the heart of Jesus was glad.   It was glad because at
last, nay, so soon, they had shown this confidence in Him.
They had responded so quickly to the evidence before
them, and thus far at least had believed.   It was a good
beginning ; it should be encouraged ; even while they
spoke He rose from His seat, obeying them ' as he that
serveth '.   They led Him through the door that opened
into the sick woman's room.   There on a low bed against
the wall the sufferer lay, shivering all over with fever, her
face an unnatural red as with great heat, yet the body bent
and heavily covered, as if it were cold ; her eyes vague and

glassy, seeming scarcely to see what was going on around her.

Jesus went across to her and took her hot hand into His own. He said nothing ; He looked into her eyes, and they grew fixed and steady. He drew her arm upwards towards Him and the whole body followed and sat up. While He did this He spoke ; He commanded the fever, as if it were some living thing ; He bade it go out of the woman. And immediately she knew that she was well. The throbbing in the brain was at an end ; the beat of the pulse was normal ; the intolerable heat was gone, her limbs were supple with their natural warmth ; she no longer wished to lie down. Not a word was spoken ; the poor woman could say nothing, too overcome with the relief that had been given to her ; the four that stood around were equally dumb, with awe, with gratitude, with bursting devotion. It was an eloquent silence which Jesus of all men on earth always understood.

The five moved back to the outer room. On a low table in the middle a simple meal had been prepared ; they reclined around it, leaning on their cushions, waiting for the hot food to be brought in. Suddenly, to the surprise of the four, to the increased gratitude of Jesus, she who had been healed came through the doorway, herself bringing in the food to be eaten. She had no words to utter, but she could act ; then this should be her way of showing gratitude. In one house at least in Capharnaum, no matter what might happen, Jesus would be always welcome ; that house alone in the town is commemorated to this day.

CHAPTER

7

21. A First Evening of Miracles

ALREADY this had been an eventful day, but it had not yet by any means ended. Since the hour when Jesus had left the synagogue that morning, the news of what He had done had spread like fire around the neighbourhood. During the few preceding weeks He had been preparing this poor people. Sabbath after Sabbath He had spoken to them, words which had completely, however unconsciously, won their hearts ; when at last He had cast out a devil before their very eyes, it is true at first they were astonished, and yet on reflexion they were not. As the day wore on, and as they recovered from their wonder, they found themselves seeing in this but a fitting expression of the Man as already they knew Him. Yes ; He was ' the holy one of God ' ; and it was no more than becoming that He should have power to do such things. Now it was recollected that a few weeks before the healing of a local magnate's son had been attributed to Him ; to-day He had followed this up by another spontaneous act of mercy ; soon the news sped down the street of what He had done in the house where He was resting. There was only one conclusion, at least for those who had any belief in Him whatever ; He had only to be shown a sufferer, He had only to be asked, and who could say what He might not be willing to do ?

Hence the afternoon became a busy one in all that quarter of Capharnaum. It was the Sabbath day ; while the sun was up it was not permitted to do much ; but no sooner had the sun gone down, and the Sabbath was at an end, than every street and by-lane was astir. Jesus was still hidden in the house, but He would come to them if they asked Him. Just because His attention had been called to her, with a touch of His hand He had cured an old woman of fever ; what He had so easily done for one He could do for more. They would try Him ; they would

show Him their sick and would appeal to Him; already
the confidence that comes to simple faith had awakened.
They wheeled or carried out their sick and diseased, and
placed them in rows down the street; the memory of the
morning encouraged them to go further; they gathered
together their lunatics as well as their possessed. By sunset
a weary assembly was ranged in an avenue from the cottage
door; around it the whole neighbourhood had gathered,
men and women chattering, some making much demonstration, others pompously maintaining order as they marched
to and fro.

> ' And when it was evening
> After sunset
> They brought to Him all that were sick with divers diseases
> And many that were possessed with devils
> And all the city was gathered at the door.'

Jesus came into the street; as He stood before them a
great silence fell upon them all, broken only by the shuffling
of feet, the whispering of final directions, the hurrying of
a few to find a place in the line. He looked down the
narrow lane, and again for the third time that day His
heart was glad; this was indeed the beginning of the
Kingdom. He stepped across the threshold; on His right,
at His feet, lay a sick sufferer. He looked at him, He loved
him, He made the patient know that He was loved, that
individually he was cared for and not as merely one of a
company. He stooped down to him; He laid His hand
upon his weary head; He whispered a word into his ear;
He blessed him; He passed on. But even as He passed
the man knew he was cured; in every inch of his body he
knew it. Jesus had scarcely moved to the next bedside
when he was sitting up, anxious to stand upon his feet, to
walk, to jump into the air for very joy.

Jesus passed down the line, and in each case it was the
same; the same individual care, and interest, and affection,
the same individual touch of the hand; the Evangelist
calls attention to the fact that He laid His hand on every
one.

> ' But he laying his hands on every one of them
> Healed them.'

He was more to them than their physician; He was their

intimate, He was their friend, and He longed that they should be the same to Him. The eyes which looked down into theirs were the same as those which by the Jordan had conquered Andrew, and Simon, and Nathanael, the same understanding yet never patronizing eyes as those which had won the woman by the well of Jacob. He moved on, He touched them every one, and every one rose up cured. But as He took His time with each some of the bearers became anxious. He cured all He touched, but would He be able to attend to their case? It was growing dark ; soon He would have to stop ; we can see them coming to Him, crowding in about Him, offering to lead Him, telling Him all together of the special need of their particular friend, forgetting Him in their eagerness for their own gain, taking the very miracles as ordinary things. The shadow of that which later He would blame so bitterly was already falling upon them.

Among the sufferers were some of those weird cases, the possessed. Of these a few had been dragged there in chains, and were held like wild beasts before Him ; others skulked in His presence as if they feared His punishment ; one and all sought to escape Him, and only force could keep them on the spot. As He came down the line towards them, their unrest could scarcely be held down ; they writhed, they bit, they screamed, they howled, they laughed in scorn ; hatred and fear, conviction and yet contempt, mingled in the sound of their voices as they shrieked :

'Thou art the Son of God.'

That morning in the synagogue for the first time Satan had found his Master. He was now satisfied that indeed this was the Christ, and he would howl out his claim in derision. The evidence of a witness such as himself would never count for much, by those who were ill-disposed might even be brought as evidence against Him.

Jesus knew this. From such a quarter He would not accept any confession of Himself. For that, if there were need, He could ask His Father and angels would be sent to confess Him ; devils He would not have. Besides it was man who was on his trial, and He would wait till man of his own accord discovered Him. He turned on the howling spirits ; He rebuked them and brought them to silence. For a moment He wore that look which made men tremble

before Him ; then He passed on, and where He had passed
there was peace.

> ' And devils went out of many
> With his word
> Crying out and saying
> Thou art the Son of God
> And he rebuking them suffered them not to speak
> For they knew that he was the Christ.'

S. Matthew closes the account of this scene by again
reverting to prophecy. He says :

> ' That it might be fulfilled
> Which was spoken by the prophet Isaias saying
> He took our infirmities
> And bore our diseases.'

It is a strange application of a passage that was well known.
We know it to have been said of the suffering Messias :

> ' Surely he hath borne our iniquities
> And carried our sorrows
> And we have thought him as it were a leper
> And as one struck by God and afflicted.'

Nevertheless this further application was according to the
Jewish mind. Prophecy was the very food of the Jewish
soul ; he turned it over and over ; he would look for
applications of its phrases, as the student to-day might
apply the phrases of an ancient classic ; if there was no
more than a parallel meaning it was enough.

There is, however, a further question. Even more
literally, in the case of miracles, may not the prophecy be
true ? Is it not possible that with every miracle Jesus
wrought something was, as it were, laid upon Him, and
something taken from Him ? Elsewhere we find Him
unable to work miracles because of the people's unbelief ;
in another place He says that ' virtue went out of Him '.
Again a certain miracle could not be worked except through
prayer and fasting ; once or twice the effecting of a cure
costs Him groans and labour. If this were so, if the working
of miracles entailed that in some real way

> ' He took our infirmities
> And bore our diseases ' ;

then all the more may we realize and marvel at His infinite
condescension.

22. The Beginning of His Tours

Darkness at length put an end to the excitement and rejoicing. Jesus and the four entered again into the little cottage, and the crowd could not but let them go ; it was the close of a wonderful day, the first formal opening of the Kingdom. Down the little side streets the people slipped away to their homes, talking without ceasing as they went, talking without ceasing far into the night, whether together round a flickering lamp, or stretched out on their mats to sleep. In their cottages or under sheds, or out in the open road, it mattered very little at this time of the year where they took their rest ; wherever it was convenient they would make their bed, roll themselves in a blanket, and then, till sleep overcame them, would talk unendingly of the wonderful things they had seen that day, of the wonderful things they had heard, of the wonderful Man who had spoken and done those things, and who had so won their hearts.

In the cottage lay Jesus, stretched out alongside of His four. It had been a strenuous day, for all that it had been the Sabbath, and both He and they were tired ; silence had come with the darkness, the deadly still silence of the East, and they were soon asleep. Next morning as soon as the dawn had made the sky grey, and it was possible to see, He was awake and up betimes. Capharnaum still slumbered ; His own lay beside Him ; He rose gently from among them, stepped to the door, opened it and passed out, through the street made straight for the long hill that rises behind the town, as He went stepping over prostrate forms of men sleeping in the open. Here and there a pariah dog opened an eye and looked at Him, but it was too weary to bark ; so long as He left it alone at this hour He might pass unheeded.

He was soon out of the town. Once on the hill it was easy to find a lonely spot. There were slight ravines made by water-courses ; here and there the surface of the hill curved outward and afforded convenient hiding-places. In one of these recesses Jesus stopped. He stood still ; He looked up to heaven ; He raised His hands, as does a priest at the altar ; He was soon lost to earth in the presence of His Father ; Jesus of Nazareth prayed, like any mortal man He prayed. And we know why on this particular morning out of many the Evangelist draws attention to it ; this morning marked the beginning of a new phase in the campaign.

We must leave Him there in prayer, while the sun comes over the hills across the lake, flashes across the water, awakens Capharnaum and Bethsaida, and at length shortens the shadow on the hill, prying into nooks and crannies till it finds Him. It marked the hour for rising ; in the East so many sleep in the open air that as soon as the sun is up all the town seems to rise together. Their first thought was the memory of all they had witnessed the day before. They sat together, performing their morning ablutions, nibbling at a morning meal, but always the same conversation continued. As soon as they bethought them to move, those who were free, and they were many, found themselves drawn again to the door of the cottage where they knew He had made His lodging.

But inside the house was disturbance. Simon and the others had awakened, and had found He was not among them. They had looked at one another, then at the place where they knew He had lain down. They asked each other questions ; they looked again, as if by repeatedly looking they might find Him there at last. Simon would endure it no longer ; if He was lost He must be found, for He could not be far away ; perhaps already he had learnt his Master's fondness for lonely prayers on the hills. To the hills at all events he led the way, and the others followed ; with eyes searching everywhere it was not long before His standing figure was spied against the grey background.

> ' And when it was day
> Rising very early in the morning
> Going out he went into a desert place
> And there he prayed
> And the multitudes sought him
> And Simon and those who were with him followed after him.'

They hurried towards Him ; though He was absorbed in prayer He must be interrupted. Surely He could not know what an opportunity He was missing. Why, if He chose, He had all Capharnaum in His hands. He could not know that the excitement of the day before had continued till the morning ; that already at this early hour crowds had come to the house to look for Him. He must not let them go ;

prayer was very well, but now He must be among them ; such a favourable moment for the founding of the Kingdom might never come again.

> ' And when they had found him
> They said to him
> All men seek for thee.'

Jesus came to them out of His prayer. They wanted Him and He would give Himself to them, the while He pitied the petty ambition that to the end was never far away from the minds of His poor followers. At the same time, even to please them, He must not confine Himself ; though Capharnaum was to be His centre, He must not shut Himself off from the wider field, which the Father had given Him to traverse. There is true friendship in His answer ; it is almost apologetic ; He is compelled to refuse, but to lighten the refusal He invites them to come with Him.

> ' And he said to them
> Let us go
> Into the neighbouring towns and cities
> That I may preach there also
> For to this purpose am I come.'

They came down the hill together, making for the road which passed up through Capharnaum, and led to Corozain and the hills. As they came down they were sighted by the crowd that had followed in search of Him. They hurried to meet Him ; they surrounded Him talking all together ; they would know where He had hidden away, they would have Him back in Capharnaum ; there was much there that He might yet do, there were many sick yet to be cured. He answered little, but the important four were not slow to speak. They whispered to one and another that He was not to stay in Capharnaum ; that even at that moment He was on His way to other places. The people listened in dismay, they protested noisily, they would keep Him by force if they dared ; they begged of Him to make His home in Capharnaum, and not to go elsewhere.

> ' And the multitudes came to him
> And they detained him
> That he should not depart from them.'

A different treatment this from that which He had received—or was soon to receive—from His fellow-citizens of Nazareth. Shallow enough as later this devotedness proved to be, for the moment He felt it. Nevertheless, for the present, He could not stay. He must move ; the time was short, and the will of the Father must be done. They walked down the hill ; Capharnaum lay on the right below them ; infinite in compassion, with gratitude expressed in look and voice for this show of appreciation,

> ' He said to them
> I must preach the kingdom of God
> To other cities also
> For therefore am I sent.'

With this farewell He parted from them. True, it was to be only for a few days or weeks at most. He would return soon ; Capharnaum would henceforth be His base ; still its people now knew that for the future He was not to be wholly their own.

The time that follows is summed up by the Evangelists in a comprehensive sentence, pregnant with meaning.

> ' And Jesus went about all Galilee
> Teaching in their synagogues
> And preaching the gospel of the kingdom
> And healing every manner of sickness
> And every infirmity among the people
> And casting out devils.'

In other words, at last the work had begun in real earnest. We can see Him making His progress through the country. The report of what was done on that memorable Sabbath day has already gone before Him ; men throng to see Him, if only because of all that was being said. During the midday hours He moves from one town to another ; in the afternoon and evening, when men are more at leisure, He comes into a synagogue and they gather round Him. There is no longer need to confine Himself, as He did at first, to the Sabbath day, though it appears that in this first tour He teaches only in the synagogues. He sits among them and discourses, and it is always the same subject ; the Kingdom has come, and its blessings have come with it. There follows the daily procession of healing ; in every town the scene of Capharnaum is repeated. The sick are brought out that He may touch them ; cripples hobble up asking for more than alms ; possessed creatures are set in His path, and go away released from their bondage. The enthusiasm of Capharnaum spreads and grows ; once the floodgates have been opened the torrent sweeps over all Galilee.

23. The Miracle in Simon's Boat

During this time, though Simon and Andrew, James and John, had definitely cast in their lot with Jesus, and were ready to answer whenever He should call, still it was not yet clear that all else had to be surrendered. There was their livelihood to be earned ; there were family ties to be respected ; so far as they were able they must still from time to time return to Bethsaida, and there help in carrying on their trade.

Meanwhile, when Jesus had ended His tour, and had come back to Capharnaum, a new state of things had obviously arisen. It was no longer for Him as it had been in the early days, when He could walk alone down the side of the lake in quiet meditation ; now, whenever He appeared, crowds would gather round Him and would refuse to leave Him alone. He belonged to them, they claimed Him ; He spoke to them things that went deep into their souls, and they were ever eager to listen, no longer only in the synagogue, no longer only on the Sabbath, but every day, on the open road, in the market-place, by the border of the lake, anywhere at any time, this restless, generous, fickle, and thoughtless people would gather about Him, would press familiarly upon Him, so that at times He would need to be defended. So much like one of themselves, in spite of His wonderful words and deeds, did He still remain among them.

It was on one such occasion, in the early morning, that He found Himself on the lake-side at Bethsaida, at the very spot where, a few weeks before, He had shown such friendship to Andrew and Simon, James and John. He had appeared in the street and the people had thronged about Him, not this time for miracles, but that they might induce Him to speak. He had come to the edge of the lake and they had followed Him. Those in front loudly endeavoured to hold the others back, loudly protesting that He should be given space in which to move ; those behind pressed on, shouting and protesting no less, so that there was danger that some might be pushed into the water. They were a chattering, elbowing crowd ; their very enthusiasm was demonstrative, annoying ; they had little thought for the convenience of Him whom they pursued with their attentions ; in their familiarity they almost forgot Him.   Yet for the present they were men of goodwill ; therefore He would bear with them, let them be as offensive as they might ; always to the end He would have compassion on them.

They had pressed Him down to the shore ; it was impossible to go further.   And yet where He stood, with men crowded close around Him, and others on the rising ground above, He could not speak to them as He would.   In the little bay in front of them, riding on the water, moored to stakes, were two fishing-boats, both quite empty, though evidently both had been but recently hauled in.   On the stony beach hard by were seated their crews, cleaning their nets after the night's labour, though there were no fish in their baskets.   Jesus turned His eyes from the crowd, and looked at the boats and the fishermen.   One of the boats He recognized as Simon's ; Simon himself He saw at work among the little group.   He climbed into the boat ; standing in the stern, He beckoned to Simon to join Him ; in a moment Simon laid down his net and was on board beside Him, filled with satisfaction at the honour that was done to him.   Jesus bade him put out a little from the shore, then swing round the boat so that He could face the people ; thus from Simon's boat, as from the pulpit of the world, Jesus

> ' Sitting
> Taught the multitudes
> Out of the ship.'

This is the first and one of the few occasions when we find Jesus making a formal discourse to the people in the open air.   Hitherto, as has been pointed out, He has spoken to them only in the synagogues, and that at first only on the Sabbath day.   Now both time and place are disregarded ; they long to hear Him whenever and wherever He will speak, and He responds to their longing.   He spoke not as the Scribes, discussing, arguing, sifting, suggesting conclusions with a query ; He imposed no external rite or law ; He spoke with authority, as one not groping, who knew beforehand what He had to say, and that what He had to say was true.   He spoke of His Father and theirs, of His Kingdom and theirs, of the way into that Kingdom,

which was through their own hearts and His ; when later
S. Matthew gives us the Sermon on the Mount, it is evident
that these things were already familiar to them.   And for
His manner, He spoke as one of themselves.   He used their
ideas, their thoughts, their experiences, so intimately, so
clearly, so accommodated to their own understanding, that
anyone among them might suppose it was himself who
spoke, and wonder why he could not say the same.   And to
it all they listened in glad silence.   As the sermon advanced
the silence grew more and more intense.   The voice rose
from that little boat and ranged up that hill-side reaching
every ear.   All eyes were upon Him, all hearts were lost to
Him, in the stillness they forgot that they belonged to this
world.

He ceased, and yet they were silent.   He moved from
His place in the little ship, and slowly the spell was broken.
He left them on the shore to come to themselves ; meanwhile He motioned to Simon, and bade him put out to
deep water.

' Launch into the deep,' He said,
' And let down your nets for a draught.'

It was a sudden and strange ending to His discourse ;
moreover it contained a strange order.   The Man from
Nazareth could not know much of fishing ;   He could not
know that this hour of the morning, with the sunlight
dancing on the water, was not a favourable moment ;   at
this time of the year in particular it was always better to
fish by night.   That very night they had been out, but with
no success ;   much less were they likely to make any catch
in the morning.

Still, an order from Him was an order to be obeyed ;   to
this degree of love at least Simon had already arrived.
He would humour the Master, He would do His bidding ;
still there was his own reputation to consider.   He must
defend himself from seeming foolish ;   he must encourage
his fellow-fishermen to follow his example.

' And Simon answering said to him
Master
We have laboured all the night
And have taken nothing
But at thy word
I will let down the net.'

They swung the vessel round and rowed into deep water. The crowd on shore saw them moving outward, and dispersed once more over Bethsaida and Capharnaum. The boatmen reached a likely spot ; they let the nets down, they rowed on dragging the nets after them. Suddenly the boat stood still ; they could move no further ; the nets were so loaded as to stop them. They pulled them in ; they were full of fish ; hand over hand they hauled and the silver streaks fell wriggling in hundreds into the hold. In the process a net broke, but so great a catch was not to be lost. They shouted to the shore ; there were James and John, the sons of Zebedee, who worked with Andrew and Simon as partners. Their boat was soon manned and beside them ; they too let down their nets ; in an incredibly short time both vessels were so full that they seemed in danger of sinking.

It was indeed an exciting adventure. The crews shouted to each other, they congratulated one another, they calculated the value of their capture ; in all their experience such a haul had never been made before. In the excitement of the moment they never thought of Him, their Benefactor, who sat back in the stern looking at them, loving them, glad that they were glad, suffering Himself to be ignored ; —in moments of excitement and prosperity Jesus of Nazareth is easily ignored. He sat back and looked at them ; He would let them have their pleasure to the full ; the day would come when they would better understand the significance of what had just happened ; Jesus preaching from the bark of Peter, Jesus present in the boat while the crew of Peter laboured, Jesus giving orders and Peter blindly obeying, Jesus in a moment rewarding the fruitless toil of a weary, dark night. It was the first of those prophetic miracles performed for the training of His own.

But soon, while the noise and rejoicing continued, on one man in the ship the truth began to dawn. Simon all the time had been at the helm, in the stern behind the Master. He had steered the ship from the shore ; he had directed the casting of the nets ; as fold after fold was gathered in, and the fish came leaping in a ceaseless stream into the vessel, it grew upon him that this was no mere fortunate coincidence. He knew every inch of that water ; he knew besides that at this time of the day the fish were usually shy ; in any case never had so great a shoal been found so near the shore. It was the Master who had done this thing, the Master seated there below him; silently, spontaneously, unobtrusively, generously He had done it. It was possible that the men to whom this draught of fish had been given might never recognize the hand from which it came, might never think of thanking Him, and yet He would not mind. It might be the same as it had been at the marriage feast at Cana, as it had been with the cripple at Jerusalem; He might just be content to do good, and slip away, and be ignored.

This was not to be endured. Jesus must be thanked; and the responsibility for that, Simon quickly saw, rested with himself. It was his ship that Jesus had chosen; to him He had given the order, under his direction the men had worked; this was but a further proof of His special favour, after the calling of a few weeks before. Simon looked back and saw what was happening. He recalled the first meeting by the Jordan in Judæa, when Jesus had greeted him and said that one day he would be called the Rock; he remembered the favour that had been done in the house of his relatives at Capharnaum; he put it all together, from the first day to this, and saw beyond a doubt that it portended something momentous in the future.

But how could he dare to face it? Think who this Jesus was, and who was he himself. The more he had seen of Him, the more he had been filled with awe and reverence. He had watched Him from the first, keenly he had studied His every gesture; long since he had discovered, what others had not discovered, the deep beyond deep of trans-parent truth, and understanding, and insight, and love of men, and love of God, and at the same time the strength, the independence, the utter selflessness, the single-minded motive, that lay hidden beneath the rough, outward garb of this Man from Nazareth. He had listened to His words, and none more than he had discerned their plain sincerity and self-confident conviction, their authority and force, the vision they raised of ideals never before imagined, the yearning they instilled to high aspirations and endeavour; to listen to this Man was light and life, and longing desire, and joy in the glory of sacrifice. He had watched all this, he had listened to it all, he had drunk it all in; he had seen it all confirmed by deeds beyond explanation. He who could turn one thing into another, He who could make devils shriek in fear as He passed them by, He who with the simple touch of His hand could cure every manner of disease, what was there He would not do ? What was there He might not be ? What might not be contained beneath that word of John the Baptist :

'Behold the Lamb of God ' ?

And on the other side was himself. Simon knew himself, only too well ; spontaneous, generous, eager, devoted, with a strong man's power to admire and love, and a strong man's power to command and win allegiance ; indeed, he knew this well enough. But there were the other things ; his impetuosity and lack of thought, his foolish extravagance in word and deed, making him say that which a moment's reflexion would never have permitted, making him do things of which he was everlastingly ashamed, always sanguine, always making others sanguine, but always failing everybody, always in the end disappointing everybody, and himself most of all. He could be so brave, yet at unexpected moments what a coward he could be ! How could he ever trust himself? How could he allow anyone else to trust him ? Above all this splendid, glorious, confiding, loving and lovable Jesus of Nazareth !

No, it was not to be permitted. Simon's great heart was full to bursting and he must speak. The nets had at last been drawn in, the two little boats would hold no more ; the fishermen were standing over their haul, their noisy congratulation turning to astonished silence ; on them too the truth was beginning to dawn. Suddenly, with his usual spontaneity, Simon rose from his place beside the helm. Jesus was close by ; Simon turned to Him. His eyes glistened bright, he wanted to be grateful, he longed to make Him some return, but he was afraid. All this was in his voice, and his words and his actions, as he fell down before the feet of Jesus, and placed his joined hands upon His knees, and looked up like a child into His face, and cried with a child's cry of mingled joy and sorrow, great hope and shivering fear :

'Depart from me
For I am a sinful man
O Lord.'

The scene drew the eyes of all upon the two. Simon's words brought home to them what had been done ; at last they realized the miracle, and the honour bestowed on Simon first of all, and on themselves as his fellow-labourers. James and John, standing in the other ship alongside, understood more than the rest. Their thoughts, too, went back down the line of events to the first meeting by the Jordan, and in this preference of Simon they saw the beginning of fulfilment of that first prophecy of Jesus. They looked at Simon kneeling at His feet, oblivious to all else, expressing in his eyes his utter soul ; when the months passed on, and Simon became Peter, when the years followed, and Peter still was at the helm, they never forgot that first attitude of homage and humility.

Neither did Jesus forget it. He looked down on Simon and was satisfied. As with a certain Maid at Nazareth, great things had been done to him, and it had only made him realize the more his own unfitness. He had discovered himself and owned it ; the rest was assured. True, he would yet make blunders, he would have many falls ; with all his generosity, and desire to do great things, Simon would still be Simon. But Jesus would endure all that ; He would wait for him in patience till he learnt ; patient waiting was a marked feature in Him ; He knew that in the end Simon would not fail Him. He looked gently on Simon ; He put His hands on the hands clinging to His knees ; the words came sweet as honey from His mouth :

'Fear not
From henceforth thou shalt catch men ',

and the courage that passed into Simon with the words made him long to follow to the end of the world.

All the men on board heard the words. They heard them and they were glad. For with all his faults his comrades loved Simon, and thought great things of him, and were proud in their hearts that one of themselves should be given such a greeting. Yet was there no demonstration ; it was a moment of too much awe for that ; now that they understood they felt the event too full of future things. They took again to their oars ; they rowed the boats to shore, laden with their prize ; Jesus alighted and they followed. The morning they spent in assorting their fish, but from that moment there was no longer doubt about the entire service of the four ; the call of a few weeks ago had now been signed and sealed for ever.

24. The Leper

Again, when His time of rest was over, Jesus left Capharnaum and Bethsaida, and went abroad through Galilee. On this second tour it would seem the four were with Him, taking their first lesson in the apostolate. Though all Galilee was now alive to His name, still down in the deep valleys were tiny hamlets where He was less known, or less considered,—the inhabitants would think themselves too insignificant for His notice.

In hamlets such as these, just a row of huts alongside of the road, too small to have any municipal governance of their own, the laws of hygiene, of cleanliness, were less exactingly observed. Whereas in larger towns, for example, lepers were kept at a distance and on no account might come into the main streets, in these hamlets people were more negligent, and more tolerant, and a leper might keep his hut in their midst unmolested.

Jesus had come to one of these hamlets. As He passed down the lane a leper spied Him from the hut in which he passed his weary days. He had heard of Jesus, as by this time all Galilee had heard of Him. From a distance he saw Him ; inevitably he asked himself whether his own day of release would ever come, as apparently it had come to so many. The wondering led to hope, the hope to courage ; the opportunity was before him and he resolved to try. As Jesus came near he limped from his place of hiding ; in the middle of the road he fell down, first upon his knees, then upon his face ; prostrate he showed the Stranger how deeply already he believed. Then he spoke ; but it was not by way of petition. He did not ask to be cured ; his faith went deeper down than that ; years of endurance, besides, had given him that quiet patience which is prepared for any doom. He did not ask ; he but said what he believed, and waited.

'Lord,' he said,
'If thou wilt
Thou canst make me clean.'

The response was immediate. Jesus understood ; He always understood ; the secret of this silent power over men was this all-understanding, which centred on the individual man before Him, as if for Him at that moment

there were no other interest in all the world. He looked
down on the poor creature stretched out on the ground at
His feet, who would not so much as raise his head ; clearly
he was something more than the ordinary victim who
clamoured about Him to be cured. He knew the sufferer's
longing, yet also recognized his beautiful restraint. Here
was one who had learnt the one lesson of life, and was willing
to abide by it, acceptance of the will of God ; and He was
touched to the heart because of him. He bent down to him
where he lay ; His hands reached out and touched him, a
quite gratuitous condescension, and therefore all the more
significantly mentioned by each of the three Evangelists
who tell the story ; for who without need would put his
hands upon a leper ? Then the words were promptly
uttered, as if the Speaker were no longer able to keep them
back.

> ' And Jesus having compassion on him
> Stretched forth his hand
> And touching him saith to him
> I will
> Be thou made clean.'

> ' If thou wilt
> Thou canst make me clean.'
> ' I will
> Be thou made clean.'

Was ever so much contained in so few words ? A perfect
prayer, perfect because of its utter simplicity, and therefore
receiving a perfect answer. A perfect petition, though the
leper asked for nothing ; he knew that Jesus knew, and was
content to leave it there ; such bribery Jesus could not
resist. At once the change. Scarcely had the words been
uttered than the leper felt his healing. The dead extremities
took life, the muscles of his body softened down, supple
once more, to their proper place and function ; the joints
responded to the brain, no longer stiff and hampered ; the
fresh blood rushed through the veins, tingling with the glow
of health. And Jesus stood over him, smiling with interested
eyes, glad for the healed man's gladness, made a yet more
assured friend because of the upturned face, flushed with
unutterable gratitude and love.

But the meeting could not last long. It is not the way
with Jesus to linger among those on whom He confers His

choicest benefits. He read all the man wished to say ; in
return He bade him say nothing, not even to others. It is
the first of such injunctions, which afterwards were common ;
already it was becoming manifest how the repute for working
miracles was being perverted, made a hindrance instead of
a help to recognizing Him for what He was.

> ' And he strictly charged him
> And forthwith sent him away
> And Jesus saith to him
> See thou tell no man
> But go shew thyself to the priest
> And offer for thy cleansing
> The things which Moses commanded
> For a testimony unto them.'

Did Jesus, on these occasions, mean strictly what He said ?
Were His words not rather a protest against the growing
tendency to magnify His miracles at the expense of Himself ;
to make too much of the material deed, and forget the spirit
which inspired it ? For in matter of fact, how could the
man obey the order ? He had been a leper, and all the
village knew it ; Jesus had Himself commanded that he
should go to the priest, and receive the official declaration
of his cure, and how could this be secured without mentioning Him who had healed him ? Even if he said no more
than that, in the gossiping East the story must soon spread
all over that country-side.

No ; the poor man had been given a hopeless task. Do
what he might, when Jesus had passed out of sight, he could
not refuse to answer the enquiries that were made from
every quarter ; much less could he restrain the exuberant
joy within himself which clamoured for expression. He
went his way ; ' went out ', says one Evangelist, as if the
scene had taken place inside some building ; and forthwith
began to spread abroad the news of the blessing that had
befallen him. He did not wait for enquirers ; he himself
became the herald, not so much of what had been done,
but of the glory of Him who had done it. Thus in spirit,
at least, was he obedient.

> ' But he being gone out
> Began to publish and to blaze abroad
> The word.'

In this way did the story spread. Much concerning Him was known along the country-side already ; but now here was one, more insistent than the rest, whose case was unique, whose enthusiasm was catching, who would not let the fame of his Benefactor sleep. In greater crowds, therefore, than ever did they gather in the towns and hamlets about Him. They thronged in to see Him ; they sat to hear Him speak ; wherever there were sick they were brought out, for they knew very well by this time that when He passed by they would be healed. In their eagerness, in their devotedness, they took little notice of the weary strain they put upon Jesus Himself.

> ' And the fame of him went abroad the more
> And great multitudes came together to hear
> And to be healed by him of their infirmities
> So that he could not go openly into the city
> But was without in desert places
> And they flocked to him from all sides
> And he retired into the desert
> And prayed.'

Thus we are shown, beyond any doubt, that this winning of the multitude was not one of the main ambitions of Jesus. On the contrary, the more the following grew, the more He seemed anxious to avoid it. He permitted it and no more ; when at last it was at its highest tide He openly rebuked it. Not on this did He count for the foundation of His Kingdom. ' He knew what was in man ', in Galilee as well as in Judæa ; this enthusiastic devotion, with all its genuine ring, once it was thwarted would die as quickly as it had grown. For the present He would let them have their satisfaction. He would yield to them ; He would humour them ; He would draw them by means which their material minds would understand. He would let them throng about Him and molest Him in their rough, uncouth, careless way, whenever He appeared in the streets, till they became a burthen to Him ; nevertheless His chief aim lay deeper down than that.

That was gained in solitude more than in public display ; by the winning of a few, however small the number, who were in real earnest, and would follow Him into the wilderness, rather than by this noisy army, however for the moment devoted. Already it was showing its own misguidance. When He came near a larger town the noise and confusion were becoming uncontrolled. He had perforce to avoid them ; soon, till the excitement settled down, He had to avoid them altogether. First He went to places where the people were fewer ; when they followed Him there, He disappeared altogether, up on the lonely hills where no man lived. It is to be remembered that in the midst of His most crowded preaching days this was the way He spent much of His time ; from the beginning to the end of His life His attraction for the desert places, and for the loneliness of the mountain-side, is too plain to be doubted. There He stayed, and while men talked loudly in the streets, and looked out for Him where He might appear, He spent hours and days apart from them in prayer ; so the Evangelists explicitly tell us. And yet this was He who had just said :

> ' Let us go into other towns and villages
> For to these also am I sent ' ;

and who in other places complained of the fewness of the labourers in the vineyard.

8

25. The First Forgiving of Sins

THUS did the days pass as He went about on this second tour through the towns and villages of Galilee. There was great success of a kind, but not of the kind He most looked for ; men who were won by miracles only would fail Him in the day of trial. What He sought was faith, however faltering ; faith in Himself for what He was, a humble and contrite heart that would inevitably follow it, trust and love, towards Himself and towards the Father. He sought for men like Simon and John ; and these were few indeed. He found His way back to Capharnaum ; it was the end of another campaign ; though He needed rest, He knew that there would be little for Him. A new phase in His career was about to begin, and with it a new plan of battle.

It was not to be expected that a movement such as this could pass over a whole province without disturbing those who were in authority. Already we have seen, in Jerusalem and Judæa, the anxiety that was roused by the appearance and preaching of John the Baptist. When John had yielded to Jesus his place at the Jordan crossing, the suspicion had been transferred to Him ; the affair in the Temple had angered them, the crowds that went to His baptism had annoyed them, their animosity had so far shown itself that Jesus had found it prudent to transfer His labour from Judæa into Galilee. Since then had occurred the visit to the feast at Jerusalem, when at the Pool, on the Sabbath day, Jesus had healed the cripple, and had scandalized the leaders of the Jews by His claim. The upshot of that visit S. John summed up in the words :

‘ Hereupon therefore
The Jews sought the more to kill him
Because he did not only break the Sabbath
But also said God was his Father
Making himself equal to God.’

Undoubtedly, therefore, down in Judæa, and particularly in Jerusalem, among the chief men of the Jews, the tide of feeling had run steadily against Him. The fact that in no point could they prove Him in error was nothing in His favour. They were determined to be right ; He was against them and therefore was wrong ; all that had to be acknowledged concerning Him only made them hate Him the more. When then He transferred Himself to Galilee, glad and relieved as they were to be rid of Him, it was not to be supposed that they would allow Him to drop out of sight.

In Galilee itself they could easily find allies. In the various little towns of the province, hanging about the synagogues, lived comfortable priests and doctors of the Law, secure little kings of Israel in their petty surroundings. The people of the towns partly revered them, partly feared them ; it was hard to say which was the more prevalent, reverence or fear. They listened to their interpretation of the Law, they accepted their impositions without venturing a word of complaint, they fed them, as they passed down the streets they honoured them. Altogether they were little gods, these Pharisees and Scribes, these priests and doctors of the Law, quite content with the yoke of the Old Dispensation, and not very anxious for a Messias who would be likely to disturb the existing condition of affairs.

When, then, Jesus did appear, and began to move from town to town up and down Galilee, fearlessly preaching a new order of things, asking no leave from anyone, filling the synagogues whenever He appeared, still worse, teaching in the open air, speaking in a manner that compelled the people to contrast it with their own, and always to their disadvantage, it was inevitable that they should take it ill, and should become uneasy for themselves and their own authority. They would watch Him when He came and went ; they would treat Him with a cold independence, at the same time ever on the alert to detect any flaw in His speech or His behaviour. They would communicate with Jerusalem, and Jerusalem would gladly respond ; the brains and skill and experience of the metropolis would be put at the service of the less sophisticated brethren in Galilee. Miracles would count for nothing ; by those who do not wish to believe miracles are easily ignored. As the influence of Jesus grew greater, the bitterness and fear in these men would become more aggressive. They would confer with one another ; where argument and proof were wanting they would support themselves by numbers. They would close up their ranks, they would follow Him more nearly and study Him ; though the cleverness of their criticism would be less brilliant than that of their friends in Jerusalem, still not less manifest would be their decided opposition.

Such in matter of fact we find to have been the case. Hitherto, during all the time in Galilee, not a word has been said of Scribes and Pharisees, doctors or priests ; of them we have only heard in Jerusalem and by the Jordan. Now on a sudden, when Jesus returns to Capharnaum after His second Galilæan tour, He finds Himself confronted with a determined little army, gathered there from every quarter, drawn up for battle against Him ; evidently it had been assembled there in His absence, as if to occupy His own chosen citadel. They had come to the place and made their enquiries ; they had been surprised and alarmed at the esteem He had secured among the people. The evidence of the reports they received told only in His favour. If they wished to regain the ground He had captured from them they would need to go with caution ; step by step they would have to follow Him and watch Him until their opportunity came.

Thus we find them, for the first time, in the first scene after the return of Jesus to Capharnaum :

'And again after some days
He came and entered into his own city Capharnaum
And it came to pass on a certain day
As He sat teaching
That there were also Pharisees and doctors of the law
Sitting by
That were come out of every town of Galilee
And Judæa and Jerusalem.'

The meeting was being held in a house in the town ; one of those familiar gatherings in which Jesus specially delighted, and to which, it would seem, these Pharisees and doctors of the Law had secured admission.

At first all went quietly enough. Jesus had come back to Capharnaum unexpectedly, and had slipped into the house without being much molested. But He could not be hidden long. As usual the news of His arrival spread quickly through the town, and many were anxious to greet Him. The door of the house was open, and He was easily discovered. As is common in the East, men entered the house unannounced, sat down or stood about Him till the place was full ; then the crowd stretched far beyond, down the little street outside.

> ' And it was heard that he was in the house
> And many came together
> So that there was no room
> No not even at the door
> And he spoke to them the word.'

It was again the old story. He had returned to Capharnaum to rest, and from the moment of His coming rest was denied Him. He had begun to speak to a few, and the few had grown to a multitude. But this time there was a difference, and His sensitive heart at once knew it ; there were enemies in the camp.

Meanwhile in the town there were others who were busy about other things. Jesus had healed their sick before ; if He were asked He would heal more. While He was in the town they must seize their opportunity ; since He had begun to go about so much one never knew how long He would stay among them. Now there was one case, particularly painful, in a house not very far away from the place where He was staying. A poor man with palsy, trembling all day from head to foot, unable to do for himself anything at all, lay there from morning to night, from day to day, upon his mat, a pitiful wreck, and indeed very much compassionated by his neighbours. When Jesus was before in Capharnaum, and had let loose His torrent of mercy, and with a touch of His hand had healed every sick person that was laid before Him, this poor sufferer had been forgotten ; in the excitement he had been left behind. But this must not happen a second time ; when next Jesus came into the town means must be found to bring the man to Him.

Now their opportunity had come. That evening Jesus was among them ; whether He would be there next day they did not know. They must take the sufferer at once to make sure ; formalities were quite unnecessary, they would take him, mat and all, just as he lay. Four of them were told off, each took up a corner of the mat ; in this way, surrounded by other determined friends, they proceeded down the street to the house where Jesus was engaged. But here there was likely to be trouble. The crowd was thick about the house ; all heads were turned towards the door, all ears strained to catch whatever was being said. Of those behind no one took any notice ; they were packed close to one another, peering between each other's necks, a thick wall of humanity that it would be quite impossible to pierce.

But the bearers of the burthen were not to be so easily defeated ; they had made up their minds and somehow they would gain their end. The house was one of the usual sort ; a single-storeyed building with a stone staircase outside, leading up to the flat roof above, on which in hot weather men could sleep comfortably at night. A stone balustrade ran all round ; there was a slight slope upwards to the centre, to take off the rain in the wet season ; in the centre itself a square patch was covered with loose tiles, resting on thin poles, which in the very hot season could be removed, and so give air and coolness to the room below. To remove these tiles, therefore, was no difficulty.

The men who bore their burthen soon took in the situation and were quick to make their plans. The crowd filled up the street and blocked the doors ; by that way there was no access. But the sides of the house were free. By another route they slipped round to the narrow passage where the stone staircase was built, and there, unobserved by any of the throng below, hauled up their burthen on to the roof. They laid the shaking man beside the parapet, then turned to the tiles. Though it was not yet the season for removing them, still it was drawing near. In any case those in the crowded room below need not have been much surprised by any commotion overhead ; they might well have supposed that the master of the house was taking means to provide more air and light.

So the removing of the tiles went on without causing any disturbance. But what followed was more unexpected. Scarcely had the opening been cleared, and the welcome light and air begun to pour in, than a black mass appeared above them. It looked like a long piece of sackcloth ; it contained something alive, for it was trembling from head to foot ; it was hanging by ropes from the four corners ;

men were seen above handling the ropes, and preparing to let the weird thing down. Those standing in the middle of the room stepped back, pressing hard on those behind ; almost at once the space they left vacant was filled by the prostrate, shaking body of the palsied man. The carriers had calculated aright ; the bed had been so let down that their burthen had come to earth at the very feet of Jesus where He sat.

While it was descending Jesus stopped His discourse. His eyes looked up, and followed the apparition with the rest. In a minute the man lay quivering before Him, and at once His face was lit with a new light ; new at least to those who knew Him less, but to Simon and Andrew, James and John, it was already becoming familiar. There was pity in it, and individual sympathy ; there was simple affection and love ; there was encouragement which said that all would yet be well ; there was behind all an un-accountable something which instilled peace and resigna-tion ; even if he were not cured, so the patient began to feel, after this it would not matter very much.

So Jesus looked on the sufferer, and then again He turned His eyes upwards. Over the ledge above Him He saw peering faces ; eager, zealous, appreciative faces, though of plain, rough working men ; faces that told Him how proud they were of their performance, how proud they were of Him. There was no sign of apology for this untoward interruption, there was no utterance of words, there was no request ; there was only a silent appeal that did not fear to look back into His eyes, and a hope that was already certain.

Jesus saw all this and, as always, their faith, even such faith, must be rewarded. But to-day that alone should not be all. It was now the time for yet another manifestation of Himself, and the opportunity was before Him. In Jerusalem, in presence of the Pharisees, He had already spoken with terrifying clearness of Himself and His claim, of His Father and His own Sonship ; so clearly that they had wished to kill Him for it. At Nazareth His claim had been less ; there, to the less instructed, He had been content to announce Himself as the Messias ; yet there too His life had been in danger. Now for the first time in Capharnaum the Pharisees and doctors were about Him, men from Judæa, men from all over Galilee ; such a

combination had not faced Him before. Miracles of
themselves had made and would make on them little
impression ; miracles could always be explained. They
were capable of more ; from their training and status and
knowledge of the Law they understood more. What He
had already revealed of Himself they had rejected but had
not refuted ; they looked for yet a further sign, and He
would give it to them.

The silence in the room was tense. The common folk
knew what would come ; still a fresh miracle was always
a fresh excitement. The doctors of the Law sat still, expecting nothing, prepared for anything, determined whatever
came to be unmoved, whatever was done ready to criticize.
Jesus ignored them ; in the midst of the silence He spoke ;
gently, as always with a sufferer, but this time it seemed
with even greater tenderness.

> ‘ And when Jesus had seen their faith
> He saith to the man sick of the palsy
> Man, Son
> Be of good heart.’

He paused ; the crowd waited for the word to be uttered
that would heal, but it did not come. Instead, what was
their astonishment when there went clearly round the
room :

> ‘ Man, Son
> Be of good heart
> Thy sins are forgiven thee.’

‘ Thy sins are forgiven thee ! ’ This was indeed something
new. The palsied man still lay there, uncured ; the people
listened, and did not understand. The Pharisees and
Scribes understood, and looked up at Him, astonished
beyond words at such audacity, indignant, insulted that
this should be said in their presence. They dared not speak ;
they dared scarcely glance at one another ; they could only
turn over and over in their minds the paralysing words, and
draw the unavoidable conclusion. The Man who would
say this on His own authority, who could claim such
power as by right,—who could He be ? They had come
to judge this so-called worker of miracles ; they were
confronted with One who claimed to be much more. How
was this to be endured ?

> ' And thinking in their hearts
> They said within themselves
> Why doth this man speak thus ?
> He blasphemeth
> Who is this that speaketh blasphemies ?
> Who can forgive sins
> But God alone ? '

He read their hearts ; in their hard, indignant, unforgiv-
ing faces He read them. From His own face in part the
gentleness faded, and it grew harder. Yet not wholly hard ;
it was the first time He had met these men here in open
conflict, and He knew that the words He had spoken were
a challenge. Though others might not see what they
implied, these had done so ; they had interpreted them
aright, they had concluded they were blasphemy, and how
could it be proved that in fact sin had been forgiven ? He
would bear with them ; the time for threatening and
defiance was not yet. He would appeal to their reason ;
He would ask them to lay aside their prejudice and judge
impartially. He would for once go against His usual
custom ; He would work a miracle in their presence, not
this time in confirmation of faith already confessed, but to
encourage it in those who would not believe. He would
stoop to these men as He would stoop many a time again,
though not in quite the same way ; when the end came it
should never be said that He had not given them every
opportunity. And

> ' Jesus presently
> Knowing in his spirit
> That they so thought within themselves
> He said to them
> What is it you think ?
> Why do you think evil ?
> Why think you these things in your hearts ?
> Which is easier
> To say to the sick of the palsy
> Thy sins are forgiven thee
> Or to say
> Arise, take up thy bed and walk ?
> But that you may know
> That the Son of Man hath power on earth
> To forgive sins

> Then said he to the man sick of the palsy
> Arise
> Take up thy bed
> And go into thy house.'

As He spoke, there was a dignity in His words which could not be mistaken. Now for the first time we hear Him assume a title which was later to become His usual description of Himself; a title, humble in sound and meaning, but here at once endowed with high authority; the ' Son of Man ' indeed, but with ' power on earth to forgive sins '. It was the old lesson again enforced; Jesus is at once the lowest and the highest; as at the Jordan, when He had lowered Himself to the meanest sinner, then He had first been called ' the Son of God ', so now, when for the first time He called Himself ' the Son of Man ', He exerted that right of infinite mercy which belonged to God alone.

The effect of the words was instantaneous. The shaking of the body that lay on the mat before them ceased; the man grew still, then sat up; rising to his feet, regardless of all around him, mechanically he proceeded to carry out the order given to him. He loosed the mat from the ropes; he rolled it up into a bundle; in his eagerness, in his excitement, he had no words for Him who had healed him. He made for the door, and a passage through the crowd was opened for him. The people stared in astonishment, they asked each other what had happened, they pursued him with questions which he could not and made no attempt to answer. Only, as he came to himself, and as he walked on steady feet, and realized what had been done, he broke into cries of joy and thanksgiving and glory to God who had bestowed this favour upon him.

> ' And immediately rising up before them
> He took up the bed on which he lay
> And went his way in the sight of all
> Glorifying God.'

The crowd too was moved more than usual. Jesus had healed others before, sometimes in great numbers; so easily had this been done that it had almost ceased to make any further impression. But this was a special case; it was akin to the healing of the man possessed that famous Sabbath morning in the synagogue. Besides He had said such things, such mysterious things, about the forgiveness of sin, and that in presence of the Scribes and doctors. Before these learned teachers of the Law He had set aside the Law itself, and by this miracle He had proved that He had the right and the power to do it. They were more than astonished ; they wondered what it signified ; a kind of fear came over them, but it was a happy fear, a fear that inspired confidence and thanksgiving. The multitude scattered, but many that day knew that God was among them.

> ' But all the multitudes seeing it were astonished
> And were filled with fear
> And wondered
> And glorified God that gave such power to men
> Saying, We have seen wonderful things to-day
> We never saw the like.'

Obvious words, very platitudes ; yet were they a proof that these men had been impressed as they had never been before. Would that they had followed the light further !

26. The Call of Levi

After this event Jesus stayed some little time in Capharnaum. Perhaps the gathering of the Scribes and doctors kept Him there ; He would not leave His own to the mercy of ravening wolves. It is true that we notice from this moment a steady waning of the spirit of the people ; though they follow Him and proclaim Him, the angle begins to change. Nevertheless, not till they desert Him will He desert them, and it was not yet time for Him to fly before His persecuting enemies.

It would seem from various indications that Jesus often began His day by a walk along the shore of the lake. When He had first come to Capharnaum He had been able to wander alone ; now that had become quite impossible. As soon as He appeared in the morning groups would begin to gather round Him ; to many in the town labour was seldom very pressing, beneath the beating sun leisure was easily accepted as an essential of life. And at this time He still had their hearts. They loved Him in their way ; they esteemed Him for what He was, they were grateful for what He did among them, they relished what He said to them and always sought for more. Whatever was to happen to them later, now at least they were devoted to Him.

And Jesus responded. Two things we notice in our Lord's dealings with men ; on the one hand He forced Himself on no one, on the other He gave Himself to any who would have Him, whether in themselves they deserved it or not. He never passed anyone over ; He gave His hand to each and all, no matter who they might be. If they declined it, He would not compel ; if they took it, though He might foresee that in the end they would fail Him, and that all His labour would be wasted, yet He never said or hinted that it was not worth while. This is no generalization ; proofs and examples appear at most unexpected places, from Nathanael, and Nicodemus, and the Woman of Samaria, and the men of Sichar, all of whom must have seemed doubtful cases, and most of little use for the main end in view, to the little children, and the Rich Young Man, and the publican Zachæus, and Judas, and the Penitent Thief, and Thomas. In His heart there was room for them all ; with individual souls, no matter who they were, His patience was never exhausted. This, and all that lies behind it, is at the root of every understanding of the character of Jesus ; in this all-comprehending harmony with every man He meets He is essentially the perfect Man.

An example of this we have now to record. On one of these mornings while He was in Capharnaum He had gone as usual to the shore, and the people had gone after Him. There, seated on a weather-smoothed boulder, with the water lapping at His feet, and the sun rising over the hills across the sea behind Him, with great quiet in the air, and the green on the land above turning into fruitful gold, He had been among them and taught them. Now His word was ended for that day and He dismissed them to their work. When they were gone, with the four who were now always with Him, He returned to the town. He passed down a main street, running parallel with the shore ; on one side the water with boats of many kinds lying at anchor, on the other side a row of tiny shops, with fruit and vegetables, grain and nuts, meat and game, earthenware pots, cheap articles of clothing, trinkets and jewellery in locked cases, sweets and delicacies over which flies swarmed in thousands ; here a carpenter's workshop, there a store of barrels where a man might stand and drink, again a cook-house where he might buy hot food for a meal. At a corner, where another street crossed leading up to the heart of the town, was a man in his little shop who seemed to attract His attention. He was seated on a mattress, his legs doubled under him ; he leaned on a rounded bolster at his side ; mattress and bolster suggested that he spent his nights there as well as his days. In front of him was a low table ; on it were rolls of parchment, books of record, ledgers and account books ; by his side a carefully locked box containing coins of many nations. This shop was the custom-house, and the man was the collector of customs.

His name was Levi Bar-Alpheus. He was a good man enough and had many friends, for all that he was a customs officer ; and though these friends, taken all together, were a very mixed crew, still, for a tax-collector, Levi had no bad name. Moreover, as later years were to show, he was a faithful Jew, who loved his people and studied his Scripture ; in spite of his profession, though he himself scarcely knew it, he had a soul and an eye for better things. But he submitted to his destiny ; it was his lot to be a tax-collector, and there at his desk he must remain, even while underneath there beat a heart that could be generous and true.

As Jesus came up the street from the lake Levi watched Him, and a longing came into his soul. He had heard of the doings up there in the town behind ; he had heard something of the teaching of Jesus. The men who were with Him, Andrew and Simon, James and John, were not unknown to him ; they had often had to deal with him concerning customs and taxes and exchange. As they came up the street in the company of Jesus, Levi recognized them, and just for a moment wished that he could be where they were. But he quickly put the wish aside ; such a lot was not for such as he. He was just a tax-collector and no more, and tax-collectors never changed their spots ; they were fishermen, a respectable trade, and might with reason hope to be more highly favoured.

With thoughts like these running through his brain, as the group came nearer Levi turned down his eyes and occupied himself once more with his accounts. Yet what was this ? Jesus and the four came along. He stood at Levi's counter ; He looked down attentively at Levi ; Levi was quite aware of it, but did not dare to look up. Jesus stood and waited, a touch of gentle humour lighting up His face. Levi at last could endure it no longer ; he raised his eyes from his book and turned them up to those which were looking down upon him. Jesus caught those eyes; once more at a glance these two knew that they knew each other. He smiled encouragement and friendship; He raised His hand and beckoned:

'Follow me,' He said,

and Levi, the customs officer, became in an instant Matthew the disciple.

27. The Banquet at Levi's House

Levi went home that day a happy but mystified man. He could scarcely believe the favour that had befallen him; it was greater than any miracle. That Andrew and John should have been chosen he could easily understand, but for himself!—It was too good to be true. He must celebrate the event; in the only way he knew he must celebrate it. All the world must be told what had happened; he must give a dinner in his new Master's honour.

Hence the next thing we hear of Jesus is something we would never have expected. He who loved to be alone, who sought by choice the hill-sides and the water's edge and the desert places, who on the other hand when duty called must be up and about His Father's business, wandering over Galilee from town to town, preaching repentance and the Kingdom, He who had won all Capharnaum to respect Him, and the Pharisees and scribes to fear and hate Him, is found here in an open place, where everyone can watch Him as he passes by, seated at table, the chief guest of the publican, Levi, with whom no man who cared for his own good name would be associated, much less would sit down to dine. And in His company what a crew! The roisterers of Capharnaum were there; the men of Levi's profession, all the tax-collectors of the place, who lived to themselves because no one else would have them, and made their money and spent it as they would, finding in a life of indulgence compensation for their social ostracism. With them were their hangers-on; men of easy manners and loose morals who are always to be found where money is abundant, to whom vice was a vulgar boast, whose language and behaviour, when the wine began to flow, was enough to sicken any honest man. There were others, too; men of all sorts and conditions, to whom a banquet

was an irresistible attraction, and who in one way or another
had secured an invitation from Levi.   For Levi was a free
soul, and this time above all he was prepared to be lavish.
He had invited so many that all Capharnaum and Bethsaida
might know how highly he valued the honour that had been
done to him.

In the midst of all these Jesus reclined and ate, and in
imitation of Him His disciples reclined and ate with Him.
Of themselves they would never have dared, but since He
did it they might venture, too.   He reclined in their midst ;
He let them treat Him as they would.   They might forget
He was among them, in their merriment they might forget
themselves, in action and speech their coarseness might
offend Him, and He would say nothing.   He who had stood
to be baptized with sinners at the Jordan, who had shocked
the disciples by holding converse with the sinful Woman
in Samaria, who had befriended the poor sinner in Jerusalem, here in Capharnaum, ' His own city ', would not
be ashamed of sinful men, would not pass them by ; if they
wished it they should have Him as much as anyone else,
cost what it might to Himself.

But there were others who judged Him differently.   The
Scribes and Pharisees who had watched Him since the day
when He had healed the palsied man before their eyes, and
had claimed for Himself the power of forgiving sins, were
not likely to leave such a scene as this alone.   The news of
the banquet soon reached their ears, and they were determined to see for themselves.   With affected carelessness, as
if on some other business, they strolled down the street
where the house of Levi stood.   What Levi and his companions did was no concern of theirs ; his profession made
him an outcast, and his manner of living, with all its noisy
demonstration, was a curse to be endured and ignored.
They walked down the street ; as they neared the house
they crossed to the other side and thence cast a contemptuous
glance at the party.   They knew who was there, but they
affected not to know it ; when, as if by chance, they caught
sight of Jesus, and disciples of His in that gathering, they
stood still and stared.   They could not believe their eyes ;
here at last, they said to one another, with shock and scandal
written on their faces, here at last this Man had given
Himself away.   Was He after all no more than a wine-
bibber ?   With all His grand preaching, had He succumbed

to the temptation of a dinner? He had taught penance, and was this the example that He set of it? A Kingdom, and were these His army? In spite of all His reputed power over devils was the companionship of wealth too much for Him? He who claimed the right to forgive sins, could He so publicly, so flagrantly, violate every law of common decency?

They were indeed shocked, and this time, as it seemed to them, with the best of reasons, with full justification. Still they would not complain to Him; something warned them that might not be safe. It would be wiser to speak to some of His admirers, by insinuations whispered to them they might make a beginning of defection from Him. They crossed the street again; they came nearer and stood by some of the disciples; half indignant, half complaining, they questioned them:

> ' Why doth your Master
> Why do you
> Eat and drink with publicans and sinners?'

It was certainly a question that might well give trouble to their unsophisticated minds. Truth to tell, it had not occurred to them. He had come, and they had followed Him, that had been enough; why He had come they could not say. They were uneasy; they could answer nothing. But the Master came to their relief; it is the first of many such occasions; here as always He would never allow His own to be put in the wrong. The Pharisees and Scribes were yet to learn by experience that it was always more prudent to attack Him than them. When they complained of Him they were answered as they deserved; when they complained of them they received short shrift. So was it here. He turned to the questioners; the old look of command came over Him; He answered their complaint in the manner that was henceforth to be common when He spoke to men like these. He answered in a parable, which had a double application; it was an answer to their question, but more than that, if they had goodwill it was a grace offered to themselves.

> ' And Jesus hearing this
> Answering saith to them
> They that are in health have no need of a physician
> But they that are sick.'

But neither would He stop there. These men were
Pharisees, learned in the Law and the prophets ; yet was
it their besetting sin that they closed their eyes to many
prophecies which did not suit their purpose. He would
remind them of one ; one that marked the fatal cleavage
between Him and themselves. His voice grew a little
harder, his tone a little more indignant ; He seemed to
throw His protecting shadow over the sorry assembly
around Him as He added :

'Go then
And learn what this meaneth
I will have mercy
And not sacrifice.'

Had they chosen, these men might have recalled one of
those many denunciations of the prophets of old, warning
their people of this very danger.

'What shall I do to thee, O Ephraim?
What shall I do to thee, O Juda?
Your mercy is as a morning cloud
And as the dew that goeth away in the morning
For this reason
Have I hewed them by the prophets
I have slain them by the words of my mouth
And thy judgements shall go forth as the light
For I desired mercy
And not sacrifice
And the knowledge of God
More than holocausts
And they like Adam have transgressed the covenant
There have they dealt treacherously against me.'
Osee vi, 4–7.

Thus on their own ground did He meet them. He
proved to them that He was a better observer of the Law
than they. Then again He altered His tone ; His anger
was again turned to peace. He looked round that banquet-
table and claimed its rude assembly for His own. His
mission was not for those who thought themselves good
enough without Him. From the beginning He had identified Himself with sinners, with those who knew their need
and looked to Him for their satisfaction. He had begun
His preaching on the note of penance ; among sinners,
those who knew and acknowledged their poverty before the

Lord, He was most at home. This the men about Him felt as He spoke, and they loved Him for it.

> ' I am come,' He said,
> ' Not to call the just
> But sinners
> To repentance.'

28. The Disciples of John the Baptist

During these last months there had been in the neighbourhood another group of men of whom hitherto we have heard little. The disciples of John the Baptist, deprived all this time of their master, had continued his work by the Jordan and elsewhere. John, as we have already seen, had encouraged his followers to leave him for the still greater One in Judæa, but, like Jesus, he had used force with none. He had been patient with them ; as long as they had preferred to remain with him, till the light to see and the grace to act had been given to them from above, he had continued to instruct and train them. In time, as the truth dawned upon them, they would listen to the truth and all would be well.

At this point a further insight is gained into the method of John with his disciples. We have already heard how he gathered about him a special group of men and gave them a special training so that, if need be, when his own end came, they might continue the work of preparation. Now we learn more. From his childhood John had grown up in the school of prayer and fasting, and from experience had discovered how much is learnt in that school. This same he had taught to them ; if they would learn aright they, too, must gain the light to see by means of fasting and prayer.

Nor was this any strange thing. To them, from all they saw around them, prayer and fasting were but accompaniments of a higher life. The pagan priests beyond their borders practised it, the Law inculcated it. Sackcloth and ashes, as a means of appeal to God, was an ordinary term ; the Pharisees with their disciples made of it a kind of display. And yet, now that John was taken from them, when they came about Jesus who was said by some to be their master's successor, and looked for the signs which should distinguish Him as such, this sign at least was wanting. Jesus Himself did not seem to fast; on the contrary He dined with such men as Levi in the light of day; if He prayed, it was chiefly in secret, and apart from the haunts of men. As for His disciples, even those who had once been with John, it would seem that they ate and drank, and otherwise behaved, very much as did other men. Surely there was something wrong in this. His miracles could not well be denied; His preaching coincided with the preaching of their leader; but how could He be a worthy successor of John, if He made so little of a matter so essential?

Before they would go any further they must find a solution to their problem. The affair at the house of Levi had been no little scandal to them as well as to the Pharisees, and they wished to understand. Moreover, what Jesus had then done had demeaned them also in the eyes of their rivals; the disciples of the Pharisees rated them about this Jesus and His ways. Therefore, on a day soon after this event, they came to Jesus and asked Him. It was in no carping mood; it was simply in mystification that they put their question.

> ' Then came the disciples of John
> Now the disciples of John and the Pharisees used to fast
> And they say to him
> Why do the disciples of John fast often
> And make prayers
> And the disciples of the Pharisees in like manner
> But thy disciples do not fast
> But eat and drink ? '

It was a sincere difficulty, and Jesus understood and bore with them. That they should criticize His method He did not mind; He welcomed enquiry, He was there to lead and not to drive, to serve and not to command. As was always His way with enquirers, He would take them on their own ground; thinking their thoughts with them, beginning with that which they already knew. Months before, when by the Jordan these same men had taken alarm because He had seemed to be superseding John, and had come to their master to warn him, John had answered them by a beautiful comparison. If to the Jews he had spoken of himself as the voice crying in the wilderness going before the Lord, to them he was the bridegroom's friend going before the bridegroom.

' You yourselves do bear me witness
That I said that I am not the Christ
But that I am sent before him
He that hath the bride is the bridegroom
But the friend of the bridegroom
Who standeth and heareth him
Rejoiceth with joy
Because of the bridegroom's voice
This my joy therefore is fulfilled.'

Jesus reminded them of this. He was the bridegroom ;
the presence of the bridegroom is pure joy ; whether it be
shown in eating and drinking, or in that greater joy of soul
which only He can give. Tolerantly He looked at them ;
poor men, they were inevitably tinged with the spirit of
their surroundings, and outward show was to them a great
matter. There was truth in their criticism, but it was
unbalanced. For their own sakes pain, unhappiness,
mortification were nothing to be desired ; even in this
world man was not made to be unhappy. But the secret
of true happiness was known to very few. He had come

' That you may have life
And may have it more abundantly ' ;
He had come
' That my joy may be in you
And your joy may be filled ' ;
that their ' sorrow might be turned into joy ', which ' no
man should take from them '. When He had given them
this, when they had discovered the secret, then fasting and
the driest prayer, yes, even suffering, and persecution, and
death, would become a joy. Then they would
' Go out rejoicing
That they were accounted worthy
To suffer something for the name of Jesus.'
' And Jesus saith to them
Can you make the children of the bridegroom
Fast and mourn
As long as the bridegroom is with them ?
As long as they have the bridegroom with them
They cannot fast
But the days will come
When the bridegroom shall be taken from them
And then they shall fast
In those days.'

Here we have a first, far-off echo of that which later was to become more clear, until it ended, first in grim reality, and then in that awakening which could find no better description than the metaphor of the bridegroom and the bride. By the majority of men Jesus is not known at all; He is observed, He is watched, He is dissected, He is discussed, He is summed up, sentence is passed upon Him, and He is voted to be after all little more than others. The secret of Himself, the Light, the Life, the Way, the Truth, the Love, the All-in-all, is absolutely missed; only a few, who have looked with self-forgetting eyes, and have caught the vision, and in turn have themselves been captured, awake to a new understanding, and are lost in an all-consuming love to which all other love is as nothing, and live to a new life from which all other life drops away. They cannot speak of it to others, even to themselves it cannot be expressed; if they attempt it their words seem almost a mockery, a description of a shadow and no more. Nevertheless they know it to be true, even as a man knows he is alive and can say no more about it; they know it to be true, and can only say so. Others may listen, and may smile at their folly, and may call them 'drunk with new wine', and so may pass them by as out of hinge with the world of men about them, but they cannot change. They know what they have seen and they know it to be true, and they can do no more than reassert it, in the hope that at least some few, nay, let it be only one, may listen, and catch a glimmering of the light, and fall in love with it, and then go forth as they go forth, crying to all the world:

'Jesus Christ
Yesterday, to-day and the same for ever.'
'I am sure
That neither death nor life
Nor angels nor principalities nor powers
Nor things present nor things to come
Nor might nor height nor depth
Nor any other creature
Shall be able to separate us
From the love of God
Which is in Christ Jesus our Lord.'
Romans viii, 38, 39.

This, to the children of the Bridegroom, is the Bridegroom

Himself ; and since He is this how can they mourn ? And yet the day would come when mourn they would ; when the Light would grow dim, and the Master would pass away from them, and His sun would be eclipsed, and before their very eyes He would die ; when they would be left wanderers in ' the valley of this death ', and there would be nothing but darkness about them ; when they would begin to wonder, and to question, and to doubt, and to look backward, saying to themselves : ' We once thought, we once hoped '. Then they would mourn, and their mourning would be greater than any other in all the world, and life itself would seem no longer to have a meaning. The Bridegroom would be taken away, and they would look where they had laid Him, and after that His very corpse would vanish.

But the trial would not end there.

> ' A little while
> And now you shall not see me
> And again a little while
> And you shall see me.'
> ' Amen, amen, I say to you
> That you shall lament and weep
> But the world shall rejoice
> And you shall be made sorrowful
> But your sorrow shall be turned into joy.'
> ' You now indeed have sorrow
> But I will see you again
> And your heart shall rejoice
> And your joy no man shall take from you.'

Love left rejoicing in the possession of its beloved does not know its own joy ; only when it has been separated from that which it loves does it awaken to all that its own life means. Then it learns how the life of another has become its own life, the light from another its only guiding star. The agony of separation, still worse of utter loss, is death, except that true love can never die. But when it has gone through the throes of death, when it has been buried and trampled down, then in the tomb it awakens to the truth that it has been laid alongside of its beloved, and that in his death, and its own, it lives again. It lives again and its beloved lives, and life is love, and love is life ; and nothing but the cross, and death, and separation, and the blackness approaching to despair, could ever have shown in all its glory this overwhelming light, to which the light seen and basked in before was but a shadow. Then it is not content to go forth sounding the name,

'Jesus Christ
Yesterday, to-day and the same for ever ' ;

it must add to its song another stanza, and there is further triumph in the cry :

' I know not anything
But Jesus Christ
And him crucified.'
' For me to live is Christ
And to die is gain.'

' To suffer or to die '.—' Not to die but to suffer '.—The cry has rung down the centuries, caught up from one and passed on to another among those who have seen and understood the meaning of this coming of the Bridegroom into the world, His living and His dying, and His rising again,

' With us all days
Even to the consummation of the world.'
' Therefore
If you be risen with Christ
Seek the things that are above
Where Christ is sitting at the right hand of God
Mind the things that are above
Not the things that are upon the earth
For you are dead
And your life is hid with Christ
In God.'
Colossians iii, 1-3.

' You are a chosen generation
A kingly priesthood
A holy nation
A purchased people
That you may declare his virtues
Who hath called you out of darkness
Into his marvellous light.'
1 Peter ii, 9.

'Blessed be the God
And Father of our Lord Jesus Christ
Who according to his great mercy
Hath regenerated us unto a lively hope
By the resurrection of Jesus Christ from the dead

.   .   .   .   .   .

Whom having not seen you love
In whom also now you believe
Though you see him not
And believing shall rejoice
With joy unspeakable and glorified.'

1 Peter i, 3–8.

The world looks on and can make nothing of all this. But those who have seen know ; and those who know have no words that can contain it ; it is a truth which can only be lived, and so alone realized, even unto life eternal.

Thus under the similitude of the Bridegroom, again following the lead of John the Baptist, did Jesus begin that further course of teaching which was to conclude at the Last Supper, and was to receive its fulfilment in the Resurrection and after. The shadow of it was already there, the development would follow, consistently and faithfully, according as the minds of these simple people opened to receive it ; not until all was over would the full meaning of the words appear. Meanwhile He must still bear with them ; to lift them up He must descend yet lower to their level ; if they could understand only language of a certain sort, that language He must talk with them.

In all the Scripture there is perhaps no passage whicl more illustrates the depths of the condescension of Jesus than that which follows. He is talking to poor men of a poor country town, to whom new clothing was a very rare possession ; men accustomed to tatters and patches, and those patches told their own tale ; old clothes cut up to mend those which still seemed wearable, with a motley effect that could not but catch a stranger's eye. He is talking to men to whom an empty wine-skin is a matter of both wealth and significance. Old skins are stored up in their huts, not to be lightly thrown away ; of all their treasures a skin of old wine is one of their chief possessions. He is speaking to hard-working sons of the soil, who, of an evening, when the day's work is done, and the sun has gone down beyond the Galilæan hills, would gather round the wine-shop at the corner of the street, and sit upon the stone benches fixed into the wall, and discuss the doings of the day, and would end with many a merry joke on their favourite topic, the relative value of the wine they drank.

Even down to such things does Jesus condescend. He has listened to their gossip ; in the old days in Nazareth He had ample opportunity for this. He has measured their limited ideas, their narrow horizon. He has taken hold of them ; even by means such as these He has lifted the minds of these men to higher things ; their patches, their wine-skins and their wine are all made to serve His purpose. And yet without the loss of a single spark of dignity ; though His language is homely none the less is it sublime ; while He speaks to these men as one of themselves, they cannot lose sight of the Master among them.

> ' And he spoke also a similitude to them
> That no man seweth a piece of raw cloth
> Or a piece from a new garment
> To an old garment
> Otherwise the new piecing
> Taketh away from the old
> And the piece taken away from the new
> Agreeth not with the old
> And there is made a greater rent
> And no man putteth new wine into old bottles
> Otherwise the new wine will burst the bottles
> And both the wine will be spilled
> And the bottles will be lost
> But new wine must be put into new bottles
> And both are preserved
> And no man drinking old wine
> Hath presently a mind for new
> For he saith, The old is better.'

In seeking to be understood of men, could the Word of God descend lower ?

CHAPTER
9

29. The Disciples and the Ears of Corn

TO any observer it was now fairly evident that the manner of Jesus had adopted a definite policy. His miracles as facts could not be denied ; the most that could be done with them was to question their significance. His teaching to the people could not be gainsaid ; He preached to them respect for authority, He lifted them up to higher things, criticism He answered by appeal to Scripture in ways that defied counter-argument. In Himself He stood before them utterly without blame, and this was the most disconcerting fact of all ; simple, humble, submissive, unambitious, sinless, selfless, preferring prayer and hiddenness to publicity, calling Himself no more than the Son of Man, whatever others might say of Him. It was true He showed a certain independence, both of the Pharisees and of the people ; but the more they put it to the test the more did it appear that it was the independence of One who knew that He was right, and needed not to depend on anyone.

On one point only did He seem somewhat careless, at times even contemptuous ; He made light of the restrictions of the Law. This had been particularly marked in His attitude towards the Sabbath day. On a Sabbath day, in Capharnaum, at the door of the synagogue itself, He had first cast a devil out of a man possessed. That same day He had healed an old woman in a fisherman's cottage near the lake. In the evening of that day, though after sunset, He had cured a whole streetful of sick people, preparations for which had disturbed the Sabbath silence in the whole town. He had been up to Jerusalem for the feast of Purim, and there, on a Sabbath day, not only had He healed a beggar, but He had encouraged him, too, to break the Sabbath. There more than here He had shocked the people ; and when He had been challenged for what He had done He had merely evaded the charge. It was evident that here His enemies might have their opportunity; if He showed such continuous contempt for the Sabbath regulations, some day they might catch Him tripping. They must concentrate on this; on the Sabbath days, as far as possible, they must never let Him out of their sight. By accumulating evidence like this against Him, in time they would be able to convince the people that He could be no faithful Jew.

This will explain the next situation in which Jesus is found. The matter seems at first so paltry that one wonders how the Evangelists could have found it worthy of mention. The answer would seem to lie in the evidence it gives of the close watch that was already being kept upon Him. It is another Sabbath day; the meeting in the synagogue is over, and the work of the morning is done. For once, being the Sabbath, the people have left Him alone, and have scattered to their homes to spend the remainder of the day in pious idleness. Jesus has been left with the little group of men whom He has now drawn closely around Him; as a friend among friends He has gone out with them into the cornfields beyond the little town. The spring-time is past, the sun is high overhead, the stalks in the fields along the hill-side are tall, the ears of corn are hardening for the harvest.

They have come out together to be alone, and to enjoy each other's company, but they have been followed. The Pharisees have not so easily permitted Him to escape them; at the risk of breaking the Law themselves they must keep Him in sight. Perhaps He will violate the Sabbath regulations by walking further than the doctors allow; since He has worked no miracle this morning in the town, perhaps He will so favour some leper or other outcast in the lane beyond; or perhaps He will have something to say to His disciples apart, which it will be well for them to hear. At all events they must follow Him; they must keep at a prudent distance, but not beyond sight or hearing; if He oversteps the lawful Sabbath limit there they can stop, but to have discovered that would be something definitely gained.

As Jesus and His companions walk along they have not much to say to one another. They are happy in each other's company and it is enough; He in theirs, because they have come to Him of their own accord, because they have accepted His friendship, because He loves them with an everlasting love, a love which no man shall take from Him ; they in His, they cannot say why, perhaps because at such times as this He is always most Himself, most like them, and no more. On occasions such as this there is little restraint ; among themselves they can talk as it pleases them, almost forgetting His presence. Only from time to time, when they discuss a topic of which they know little, for instance the Kingdom and all that it will mean, then they will talk foolishly, and suddenly remember He is there, and will look round a little guiltily, and hope He has not overheard.

In this happy, careless way on that quiet Sabbath morning the group had become a little scattered. The cornfields, with the stalks almost a man's height and the pathways winding through them, were a delight to every sense ; soon they became a temptation. In the East there are few hedges ; pathways are made across a field as they are needed, and whatever grows over them, corn, or rice, or grapes, or other fruit, is considered a common right of any passer-by. Hence this morning the ripening corn beside them, in the condition when it is sweetest, was an easy attraction ; it was still some time before the late morning meal and they were hungry. Thoughtlessly, with a kind of merry eagerness natural in these grown-up children, they went on ahead and began to pluck the ears, to rub them in their hands till the husks fell away, and to put the white grain into their mouths.

This was indeed an opportunity which the worthy Pharisees had least anticipated. Plucking corn on the Sabbath ? And Jesus seeing it and making no objection ? But perhaps He did not notice ; perhaps He was distracted. He was the last in the company, left behind by most who had gone forward ; the Pharisees further in the rear were able to come up and speak to Him. They pushed along the path through the corn ; they drew close beside Him ; then the first in the row pointed to the scene going on before them.

'And it came to pass again
On the second first Sabbath
As the Lord walked through the cornfields
That His disciples being hungry began to go forward
And to pluck the ears of corn
And did eat

Rubbing them in their hands
And the Pharisees seeing them said to him
Thy disciples do that which is not lawful to do
On the Sabbath days
Why do they ? '

Jesus turned round and looked at them. For a third time the actions of His own were being called in question ; as we have already seen, such accusations had short shrift. These men still preserved that attitude of enquiry which they had affected before the house of Levi ; they still found it prudent to conceal their sense of criticism and enmity. He would take them again on their own ground ; as He had always done before, He would answer these men from the Scriptures in which they placed their all. There was no anger but there was withering irony in His tone as He answered them :

' Have you not read so much as this
What David did when he had need
And was hungry himself
And they that were with him
How he entered into the house of God
Under Abiathar the priest
And took and ate the loaves of proposition
And gave to them that were with him
Which it was not lawful for him to eat
Nor for them that were with him
But for the priests only.'

' And David came to Nobe to Achimelech the priest, and Achimelech was astonished at David's coming. And he said to him : Why art thou alone, and no man with thee ? And David said to Achimelech the priest : The king hath commanded me a business and said : Let no man know the thing for which thou art sent by me, and what manner of commands I have given thee. And I have appointed my servants to such and such a place. Now therefore if thou have anything at hand, though it were but five loaves, give me, or whatever thou canst find. And the priest answered David, saying : I have no common bread at hand but only holy bread, if the young men be clean, especially from women. And David answered the priest, and said to him : Truly, as to what concerneth women, we have refrained ourselves from yesterday and the day before, when we came out, and the vessels of the young men were holy. Now this way is defiled ; but it shall also be sanctified this day in the vessels. The priest therefore gave him hallowed bread ; for there was no bread there, but only the loaves of proposition, which had been taken away from before the face of the Lord, that hot loaves might be set there.'

1 Kings xxi, 1–6.

The allusion was manifest and the Pharisees could not escape it. However rigid might be the law of eating, there were circumstances under which it might be broken ; and if for his followers David would break it, so would He. Much more could He break that which had been bound about the Law by human hands, artificial, rigid, utterly intolerable.

But that was not all He would say. As the men stood before Him silenced, He clenched one argument with another :

> ' Or have you not read in the law
> That on the Sabbath days
> The priests in the Temple break the Sabbath
> And are without blame ? '

' And on the Sabbath day you shall offer two lambs a year old without blemish : and two-tenths of flour tempered with oil in sacrifice : and the libations, which regularly are poured out every Sabbath for the perpetual holocaust.'

Numbers xxviii, 9, 10.

It was true. No matter how strict the Law it admitted of exceptions ; even the Law itself made them, and that for priests, and that too in the very service of the Temple.

Jesus again had answered them, as on all former occasions, not by confining Himself to the petty affair against which they carped, but by raising a greater question which would bring them back, if they chose, to a study of Himself. Once more, while with the poor and ignorant He was patient, waiting for them to be drawn, with Pharisees He was emphatic, for they had the means to find Him if they would. For the inference was obvious. If David might break the Law, and Jesus also, then He claimed to be at least as great as David. If the Temple service could allow an exception for priests, and He had the same authority, then who did He claim to be ?

Thus they could not but argue in their minds, and Jesus accepted their conclusion. Before they had time to assert it or reject it, and add to it their now common corollary

that He blasphemed, He took the words out of their mouths.
In no hesitating terms He told them :

> ' But I tell you
> That there is here a greater than the Temple.'

This was more explicit than anything He had hitherto
said in Galilee ; perhaps it is on that account that the event
has been thought worthy of record. Then He turned on
His critics. The prophecy He quotes He has already
quoted elsewhere ; He will use it again. For it contained
the root of the whole matter. Long ago the prophet had
foreseen the danger that awaited his people. They were
by nature hard ; hard hearts would make them merciless
and rigid ; mercilessness would petrify the interpretation of
the Law till it would yield to nothing ; such interpretation
would frustrate the purpose of the Law itself, since it would
rule out Him whom the Law was destined to foreshadow.
It would put the letter before the spirit ; the very Sabbath
itself would come to supersede the observance of the Law
of God. Of all this He now reminded them.

> ' And if you knew what this meaneth
> I will have mercy and not sacrifice
> You would never have condemned the innocent
> And he said to them
> The Sabbath was made for man
> And not man for the Sabbath
> Therefore the Son of Man is Lord
> Even of the Sabbath.'

30. The Man with the Withered Hand

The Sabbath passed away and the week that followed.
The enemy had again been silenced, but that was all.
What He had done, and had approved in others, was stored
up as evidence against Him ; what He had said convinced
none of them, it only rankled in their minds. They would
bide their time ; the proofs were accumulating, of a kind
at least to suit their purpose when the day came to use it.

Another Sabbath day came round, and as usual at the
hour of prayer Jesus went to the synagogue. It was again
the same experience ; He had the ear of all. When the
Pharisees spoke, their own disciples listened and no more ;
when He appeared, the whole town flocked to hear Him.
And yet He did not seem to wish it. He passed it by as if

it were of no concern ; only when He sat down to speak, and His eyes were afire, and He leaned forward in His earnestness, and appealing arms were stretched out as if they would draw all that motley audience to His heart, and the words came pouring forth, hot and true and overwhelming like a torrent that could not be stemmed, yet, no less, words such as every man who heard them could understand and speak, only then was it manifest, to anyone who had eyes to see and ears to hear, that indeed this was more than man, wherever that conclusion might lead.

But His enemies had not eyes to see, and had not ears to hear. To them this transformation was a pose. This Man, who manifested power more than theirs, and because He had power more than theirs, must be suppressed ; it was a duty of their state to suppress Him. In the assembly that day there stood a man who, as soon as they beheld him, seemed suited to their purpose. He had a withered right arm ; it clung stiff and white to his side and refused to move ; the rest of his body showed signs of a stroke which had left this permanent disablement behind. Even while Jesus was yet speaking, His enemies thought out their plan. They would push this man forward in front of them ; they would tempt Jesus to heal him. If He refused, as it was the Sabbath day, and moreover He did not always give men like them His attention, the people looking on might be disappointed, might be drawn to believe in Him a little less ; if He consented and worked the miracle, why this could be adduced as another instance of His disregard of the Sabbath.

The address was over and the men in the synagogue had recovered from the sweet fascination of His word. Jesus was silent ; He again slipped back and was one among them all ; imprisoned in the body of that flesh the Son of God was Jesus of Capharnaum, and to most of them nothing more. As He sat down to rest, for a moment lost to everything, the Pharisees brought up the crippled man and set him close beside Him. Then they themselves came near ; they assumed their usual independent air ; He and His views were of no concern to them, but they did not mind showing Him some consideration. They would ask His opinion on a certain abstract, and chiefly theoretical question. Suppose, they said, that a man had the power to work miracles ; would he be justified in using it at any time ? For instance, on the Sabbath day ; would he be justified in using it then ?

> ' And the Scribes and Pharisees watched him
> Whether he would heal on the Sabbath days
> And they asked him saying
> Is it lawful
> To heal on the Sabbath days ?
> That they might find an accusation against him.'

It is not hard to imagine the malice that lay behind this question. As the weeks advance, and the evidence impelling to belief in Jesus is made manifest, more and more hardens the determination of these men not to believe. ' Thou wouldst not ', said Jesus later ; they would not from the beginning. When the Child was born in Bethlehem they would not ; then it might have compromised them with the mighty man of blood, Herod. When He stood by the Jordan and called to them they would not ; then to yield would have touched their personal prestige. When He came to them in the Temple at Jerusalem they would not ; by that time malice had set in, and they were able to resist even supernatural evidence. When they came to Him here in Galilee, though they had followed Him so far, yet they would not ; the witness of miracles had come to mean nothing. They were a trick, they were magic, they were just the use of a power as yet unknown to others, they were diabolic, they were ordinary phenomena highly developed by an overwrought imagination, they were merely mysterious puzzles meaning nothing ; at the last, when no other explanation would avail, they were performances which no self-respecting, thinking, educated man could for a moment take seriously, much less accept as evidence of the supernatural. Whatever may have happened in the good old days of Elias and his pupil Eliseus, miracles like prophets had long since ceased. Hence, let Jesus do what He liked, and that right before their eyes, miracle or no miracle it would matter nothing to them ; if on the other hand He healed this man on the Sabbath, that would matter much.

If it is easy to realize the hardening heart of these men, it is difficult to fathom the condescension of Jesus in submitting to deal with them as on a footing of equality. That He should condescend to Andrew and Simon was something ; when He stooped to Nicodemus it was more ; still more when He taught the poor woman of Samaria ; when last of all He had sat out that banquet with the publicans and sinners at the house of Levi in Capharnaum, one might have thought that He could not go much lower. Yet here, and many times afterwards, we find Him treating these hypocrites, these His determined enemies, as honest men ; answering their questions by words out of their own mouths, defending Himself against their arguments as if their objections were sincere, appealing to the best that was in them, or to that which ought to have been there and was not, teaching them in particular what they would understand, but what to others, even His own, must have been as yet wholly unintelligible, never compelling, never using force, never threatening till the end began to draw near ; gentle with them, patient with them, except when wrath and indignation were the only kind of mercy ; and yet never once flinching, never yielding, making more clear to them than to any others both the bold extent of His claim and the breadth of His forgiveness.

Thus again, and more pointedly than ever before, were these two camps opposed to one another in the synagogue that Sabbath morning. Jesus, seated after His discourse, looked up at these men as they stood before Him and asked Him their soft question. He looked up at them ; He pitied them ; those who saw the pity in His eyes might well have wondered whether it were the pity of contempt. He looked at them ; then slowly He turned His glance upon the man with the crippled arm seated close beside Him. He knew how he came to be there ; He knew very well why these miserable men had asked their seemingly innocent question. He was aware of the trap they fancied they had laid for Him. But that should not alter His manner ; the time for that would come all too soon. They should still be treated in the old way ; they should still have mercy ; the man before Him should be healed, none the less should all be sent away without a doubt who was the Master.

In the scene that followed there was something dramatic, as if Jesus would do what He did upon a stage for all the world to see. In front of Him a space had been cleared ; in a circle all round spectators stood, eager to watch this contest between the Pharisees and Jesus. With the ease of a wrestler who knows beforehand which way the fight will end, He turned again to the cripple. He said, as a Master who commands :

> ' Arise
> And stand forth in the midst.'

The man obeyed. Then, before He acted, He turned once more to the Pharisees. Those in the circle around were poor country people ; few among them all but had their sick at home, or until His coming had had them ; few but possessed their sheep on the hill, some a little flock, for others a single one was a precious treasure. The Pharisees had come to injure Him in their eyes ; before those same poor people He would humble them, and so would teach them their lesson.

Yet would He deal with them gently. He would appeal to their candour, to their own first principles of right and wrong, below which even they could not go. Simple truth appealed to simple truth as He said :

> ' I ask you
> If it be lawful on the sabbath days
> To do good or to do evil
> To save a life or destroy ? '

It was a simple question, and the answer seemed obvious. But to what might it lead ? To say that it was not lawful to do good on the Sabbath must make those observers of the Law appear very foolish, and to save life was to do good ; on the other hand to say that it was lawful was to sweep away all they hoped to gain by this experiment. It was wiser to say nothing ; silence would be non-committal ; silence is the commonest, the easiest, the cheapest, the most contemptible subterfuge of the deceiver. So, grimly, with faces that refused to reveal anything one way or the other,

> ' They held their peace.'

But if they would not speak He would. In the language of their daily lives, and of the lives of those standing round Him, He would convict them.

> ' But he said to them
> What man shall there be among you
> That hath one sheep
> And if the same fall into a pit
> On the sabbath day

> Will he not take hold on it and lift it up
> Much better is a man than a sheep
> Therefore it is lawful
> To do a good deed on the sabbath days.'

It was a simple illustration, such as might have happened that very morning, and none would have found fault. It was also wonderful arguing, from the single detail which no one could deny, to the general principle at which they pretended to demur, and again from the general principle to the particular case before them. It was rhetoric of the most perfect kind, in fewest words, adapted in every phrase to the minds and lives of those who listened to Him ; it was the language of the perfect Man.

What follows is something entirely new in the character of Jesus as it has so far revealed itself. We are told that He

> ' Looked round about on them all with anger ',

and that He was

> ' Grieved for the hardness of their hearts.'

We have read no such word of Him before. When Nathanael said of Him, in undisguised contempt :

> ' Can any good come out of Nazareth ? '

we do not hear that Jesus ' looked on him with anger '. When Nicodemus questioned Him and argued with Him, and tended even to ridicule in his query :

> ' How can a man be born again ? '

Jesus was firm even to hardness, but He was not angry. When the miserable woman of Samaria affected to make light of Him, He was in no way angry. There was a show of indignation in His face and manner when, on the paschal visit, He drove the traffickers from the Temple ; but the Evangelist finds it more true to describe His demeanour by the phrase :

> ' The zeal of thy house hath eaten me up.'

Even at Nazareth when, if He had allowed them, His own fellow-townsmen would have done Him to death, we are only told that He ' passed from their midst ', and not a word is said of His anger, or any sense of wrong. Here at Capharnaum, and elsewhere in Galilee, He has been dogged, and criticized, and accused, and thwarted, and contradicted, and denied, but so far we have only been given the impression that though He felt it keenly yet He met it all with patient meekness.

Now on a sudden this new thing appears ; the meek Christ is roused to anger. And the reason is given to us. These men were blind, blind of their own accord, blind because they wished to be. That they were His enemies was only secondary. Men might be His enemies and He would not of necessity on that account be angry with them ; in another place He expressly says so. But they were blinded in their hearts ; not only would they not see Him whom they had before them, they had steeled themselves against every feeling of affection in regard to Him. They would not believe, they would not love, therefore they could only disbelieve and hate ; Jesus Christ knew that these men from their hearts detested Him. They were blind, they were blind in their hearts, He knew it and the knowledge grieved Him. They might deceive others, under that cloak they might deceive themselves, but Him they could not deceive. His heart was sensitive to the quick, alive to every shadow that passed over the hearts of others ; it was made to love and to be loved as was that of the tenderest human being, keen to give, keen to receive, keen to make return of gratitude. To know that it was disliked, even by one, however without cause or blame, was an unending agony ; how much more when He knew that He was not disliked only but detested, not by one only but by a whole company, not without cause but with evidence accumulating against Him ! They hated Him bitterly and it hurt Him ; more than that, it grieved Him ; already His Passion had begun, here in Capharnaum, here in the midst of His seeming triumph. They were deliberately blind, they were blind in their hearts, and it grieved Him ; and the grief now at length roused His anger.

Jesus looked at these hard men who had so hoped to make of His very generosity evidence against Him. Then He turned from them to the silent figure in the midst. He gave a word of command ; He spoke as one having authority, not a word too much, not a word too little.

‘ Stretch forth thy hand ’,

He said, and automatically the man obeyed. He stretched it forth, he held it out, he drew it in again. When he had recovered from his astonishment, he raised it to his eyes and looked at it. With his other hand he felt and pressed

it, and the hand that had been dead returned the pressure.
It reached out to other things, and the sense of touch was
in all the fingers.

> ' It was restored to health to him
> Even as the other.'

Jesus left the scene and went His way. His anger had
not checked His generosity; His enemies had not made
Him pause; let them make of His deeds what they would
He would still be the Lord of mercy. As soon as He had
gone the crowd pressed in on the man who had been
healed. They spoke to him, they questioned him, they
congratulated him; they talked among themselves, they
drew their limited but honest conclusions. As for the
Pharisees, they were forgotten in the hubbub; they and
their Sabbath-day strictures were utterly ignored.

To these last it was evident that the synagogue, their
own citadel, was no place for them any more that day.
The healed man was of no interest; miracle or no miracle,
he was outside their horizon. The people, too, for the
moment were beyond their control; while they were in
this state of mind it would be useless to speak to them, it
might even be dangerous. Though they held their heads
high, though they assumed their air of independence, and
contempt, and self-righteousness, they knew that they had
been beaten; they could only retire. As quickly as their
dignity permitted they withdrew, mad with rage within
and scarcely able to restrain it. In one of their own houses
they came together again; behind closed doors they
discussed the situation. It seemed evident, now, that they
would never be able by ordinary devices to catch this
Jesus of Nazareth. In spite of His contemptible low breed-
ing, in spite of His lack of education, clearly He was too
much for them. They must have recourse to some other
strategy, somehow He must be destroyed.

And here they bethought them of allies. Before this
Jesus came about, a man called John the Baptist had
threatened to give no less trouble. But he had been success-
fully silenced, and had been removed, by the simple device
of bringing him across the path of the tetrarch, Herod.
Could not the same be tried with this Man? Herod was
detested, that was true; but even Herod was preferable
to Jesus. He was a brute, he was a man of whims and

fancies, but he left them alone ; on one point only was he suspicious, and that was his power. To keep this secure he had his party in the land to stand by him, and to see that others did the same. They even took his name ; they called themselves Herodians ; under that shield they could ignore the detestation they shared with their overlord. If only these men could be induced to think ill of Jesus, what might not follow ?

Thus, before the day was ended, the Pharisees and the Herodians became friends in a common cause, however much before they might have been ' at enmity, one with another '.

31. Retirement from Capharnaum

Jesus had been driven from Judæa ; He had found it impossible to live in Nazareth ; now at length here in Capharnaum it was becoming dangerous for Him to stay. This last scene in the synagogue had shown that the hostility was bitter ; on that very account He had taken up this new attitude and had acted with a kind of defiance. But their hour was not yet come ; besides it was not to be that He should die in Galilee. He must use human prudence and avoid a crisis, at least until His work was done.

Therefore again He left Capharnaum for a time, though He still lingered by the lake. It would seem that He went north of the town. There the inhabited places were fewer ; had He gone south He would have come to the plain of Genesareth, and Magdala, and Tiberias, and other centres where His enemies might trouble Him. But here, outside the city, He had some consolation. If His enemies were bitter, they were still comparatively few in number ; even to the last day of His life they were always in fear of the multitude. Now, as He walked with His own along the shore, He was secure against them. For the crowds still thronged after Him, and stayed with Him wherever He stayed, and were a bodyguard which as yet no enemy would venture to defy.

They were indeed a strange gathering. As has been already seen, the report of His miracles and His teaching had spread far on every country-side. From all Galilee they came in ; that was to be expected. They came up from Judæa and Jerusalem ; the tide set in motion by the Baptist had not yet ceased to flow, and the reports that had been brought from the lake-side had strengthened it. They came from beyond the Jordan ; from Perœa and Idumæa ; all along the river as it meandered to the Dead Sea, the talk in the villages had been of these two men who had so disturbed the spiritual atmosphere. Even from far-away Tyre and Sidon, in Syria by the sea, where the shipping and trading and pagan wealth found employment for many a Jewish labourer, they came in numbers, ' a great multitude ', to see the Man who did the things of which they had heard, and to hear from Him the tidings of the Kingdom.

To anyone accustomed to the religious manifestations of the East, gatherings such as this are no strange thing. Pilgrimages to some hallowed shrine, still more at times to some sacred person, are an everyday experience ; at fixed seasons men, women, and children will flock in their hundreds to the spot, tramping for days and even weeks across the country, enduring every hardship on the way, striking the stranger when they pass with the willing sacrifice which is written on their faces. Time and distance are of no account ; food they will get as they move on, should their own little supply run out. They will rest anywhere, night or day, as it may be found convenient ; if they have to suffer on the route, it is the will of the god and they are satisfied. When they reach their goal it is a mixture of prayer and festival. Poor people all of them, they have still a few coins saved for this event, and these they will spend partly at the sweet stalls set up for their pleasure, partly at the shrine where their devotions are performed. All day long these devotions are going on, and day after day, till the festival is over, and the signal is given for the long tramp home to begin.

Thus we can easily picture the groups that gathered along the lake-side beyond Capharnaum. They consisted of the poorest of the poor. They were illiterate ; for the most part they were country people. Those from the towns were the commonest of labourers ; of the upper classes, or the wealthier castes, there is no sign of a single representative. Not that these had been left wholly untouched. Here and there grace had reached a few ; for one at least a remarkable miracle had been worked. But by far the greater number had hitherto passed the movement by. It was no concern of theirs, there was no money in it, one way or the other ; it was only another of the popular excitements with which the lower castes were amused. With such beginnings was Jesus Christ content.

We see Him, then, doing the will of His Father in surroundings such as these. In that motley crowd there are many with ailments of one kind or another ; indeed there are few who are not in some way diseased. This is no exaggeration ; poverty in the East is stricken with diseases, and contortions, and debilities of every kind. Of medical aid there is little, and was less in those days ; what there is might, as often as not, be more dangerous than the disease ; hospitals and nurses, as we understand them, are none. Cripples crawl about till they develop ways of moving entirely uncanny ; fever lies on the roadside, waiting for the open air to cure it ; smallpox leaves its mark on thousands. Hence when these men come to Jesus, their one ambition is to get near Him, so that by so little as touching Him they may possibly find relief. They jostle one another ; there is ceaseless noise about Him ; He is pressed upon by those that are nearest, between these, hands are pushed that they may touch or pull at His clothing ; lunatics lie down at His approach, blocking the way, foaming at the mouth, adding to the hubbub by their cries. It becomes unbearable ; to protect Himself He must get aloof. He sends down His fishermen disciples to Bethsaida ; He bids them bring round a boat to this part of the shore. In the boat He is able to escape for a time from the throng, and either rest or speak to them as they sit down on the shore.

> ' And he spoke to his disciples
> That a small ship should wait on him
> Because of the multitude
> Lest they should throng him
> For he healed many
> He healed them all
> So that they pressed upon him
> For to touch him
> As many as had evils
> And the unclean spirits when they saw him
> Fell down before him
> And they cried saying
> Thou art the Son of God
> And he strictly charged them
> That they should not make him known.'

Such a scene as this S. Matthew chooses to remind his

readers of another prophecy. It is not the miracles which strike him ; they are not so much as mentioned. It is not the crowds over whom Jesus has cast such a spell ; they are but the objects of His bounty. Rather he looks back from this assembly to the day on which he himself was first called, and finds in the prophet Isaias the words that sum up this impression. He has seen Jesus criticized, and Jesus has not quarrelled ; he has seen Him insulted, and He has not cried out in protest ; he has seen Him molested by friends and enemies in the streets, and He has passed it by as meaning nothing. Broken souls like his own He has not disregarded as worthless ; wistful souls like that of Simon He has fanned into flame. Again and again He has been put upon His trial ; every time He has made Himself the judge of His judges, and has come from the ordeal victorious. He has broken down the man-made barriers of the Law, He has opened out a wider hope to everyone, He has made life another thing to many a man who had begun to despair, even to such as himself, the publican, yes, even to the Gentile world. Matthew looks back on all this ; to him this picture is a stronger argument than anything Jesus says or does.

'That it might be fulfilled
Which was spoken by the prophet Isaias saying
Behold my servant whom I have chosen
My beloved
In whom I am well pleased
I will put my spirit upon him
And he shall shew judgement to the Gentiles
He shall not contend nor cry out
Neither shall any man hear his voice in the streets
The bruised reed he shall not break
And smoking flax he shall not extinguish
Till he send forth judgement unto victory
And in his name
The Gentiles shall hope.'

10

32. The Choice of the Twelve

THE time had now come for something yet more definite to be done. In these last days His enemies had gone so far as to plot together for His death; the shadow of the end was already appearing. In His turn, then, it was fitting that He should gather His forces, that He should choose the leaders who were to succeed Him, and give them their powers and authority. True, He did not strictly need them; if He so chose, He could conquer the world without them; He had but to ask His Father, and He would give Him legions of angels to do His bidding. But from all eternity it had been otherwise decreed. Though to conquer the world as the Son of God would have been easier than easy, He had chosen to conquer it as the Son of Man; though angels might well have made up His armies, He preferred them to be made of mortal men. This was to be the great triumph; as for ever the song was to be sung of man redeemed by Man, and for this He had become incarnate, so should eternity ring with the pæan of the world won back by human weapons.

Still was it a momentous hour, the hour when He would choose these men, and in the way of men He must prepare for it. One evening as the sun went down He slipped away. He went high up the mountain that rose straight from the lake at this point. There, alone, He stood to pray; that was nothing new or strange. All the night He stayed there;

'He passed the whole night in the prayer of God';

perhaps that, too, was not a thing unknown. He buried Himself in the blackness of the night, lifted His thoughts from the weary earth about Him, sank His own mind and will in the will and mind of His Father, and through that mind looked once again upon the men from whom He would choose. In that light what the light of this world had to show went for very little; He looked only for the life, or for the germ of life, which could be made to live for Him alone, for Him and for the Kingdom. He looked for the soul that would dare to set aside its own existence, and to put on Him, and to lose itself in Him, even as He was lost in the Father ; simply, singly, unreservedly would reckon this world and all that was in it as nothing, in the glorious folly that would come from the realization and love of Him. According to this gauge He chose, the rest mattered little ; He chose 'whom He would Himself', and none should interfere ; let them but be true to their calling, He would give them whatever else they needed.

Day dawned, and He began to descend the mountain-side. As usual on such occasions, the crowd had begun to ascend the hill to meet Him. They drew near and He stood still ; He held out His hand and bade them come no further. Then with authority, beckoning in turn to one and to another, He called to Him twelve from the gathering before Him. Each one, as he was called, came forward ; He took them apart, the rest He bade await His return. Then He told these twelve what it was that He had done. He had chosen them apart from the rest to be to Him a special company ; in a very special sense they were to be all His own. Henceforth they should be always with Him ; henceforth He would concentrate all His energies on them. For them and for their training He would continue to preach, and teach, and deal with the people. He would call them His apostles, His messengers ; very soon He would send them out to preach in His stead.

But He would not stop there. He had chosen them, He loved them, they were now His very own ; therefore wonderfully would He trust them. Not only would He commit to them the preaching of His word, He would give them His own powers ; and what He gave them now would be as nothing in comparison with what He would give them later. They wondered at the miracles He wrought, at the sick He healed ; when they were sent to preach in His name the same power should be theirs. Nay, greater things than He did they should do, even so that those who did not understand would wish to revere them as divine. He cast out devils ; they too should cast out devils ; yea, the time would come when in His name they would cleanse the very souls of men. Oh ! Indeed He did love them ! Indeed He would do so much for them ! We can

hear the quiver in His voice as for the first time He spoke
to His Twelve on that momentous morning, on that
mountain-side ; the quiver is preserved in the words of
S. Mark :

> ' And going up into a mountain
> He called unto him
> Whom he would himself
> And they came to him
> And he made that twelve should be with him
> And that he might send them to preach
> And he gave them power
> To heal sicknesses
> And to cast out devils.'

For what He did and gave on that morning was but the
beginning ; it did but foreshadow that outpouring of His
Sacred Heart at the Supper-room later on, and in the many
proofs of tenderness He gave them in the too short days
after He was risen from the dead. Always He was the same
Jesus ; but never more manifestly than from this day
whenever He was apart with His own. Always He was
their Master, yet had He been their mother He could not
have shown greater tenderness and sympathy :

> ' My little children ! '

When we look at the group of men to whom this outpouring was addressed, still more when we consider the crude
condition of their training, we may well pause and marvel
at what we can only call the divine courage of their Lord.
A man who knows his powers, or who has a work to do and
must needs face it whatever be his capacity, needs courage
in proportion to carry his work through ; but to entrust
a work to others whom he knows to be unfit, who are wanting
even in essentials, who from the nature of things must often
fail, to trust such men and to give them powers which almost
inevitably they will abuse, this requires courage of another
kind, one which can rise only from combined magnanimity
and trust and love. Jesus Christ asked for faith in Himself ;
yet did He first show how much faith He put in worthless
men. He asked for love ; but not before He had first
loved men with a superhuman love. He asked for trust ;
but was it more than the trust He Himself placed in instruments so frail and fickle ?

For who were these men? Simon and Andrew, James

and John, we have already long known. When by the lake-side they were called to follow Him, we saw what manner of men they were ; only of the latter two we now learn another trait, when in gentle humour Jesus calls them, no longer sons of Zebedee, but Sons of Thunder. There was Philip, accommodating, gentle Philip, enthusiastic, admiring Philip, whose admiration made him see so quickly, whom all men loved and trusted, yet somehow would never have selected for a post so momentous. There was Philip's strong friend, Nathanael of Cana, now called Bartholomew, who knew Nazareth better than the men from Bethsaida knew it, and had begun with a prejudice against anything that came from it. There was Levi, the publican, now Matthew ; his election might well have seemed to many a defiant challenge to all the world. There was Thomas, hard-headed, stubborn Thomas, who even in his moments of devotedness might have made one question whether his devotedness were not only another form of obstinacy. There were James Bar-Alphæus and his brother Jude, known also as Thaddeus, and Simon, called the Cananæan and sometimes the Zealot, all three kinsmen of the Lord, the least educated of the group, the most inclined to act without reason. Lastly there was Judas, the man from Carioth, the one man among them all who seemed most fitted for his post, prudent, experienced, man of affairs, who always had reason on his side, always acted with forethought, with whom when he spoke all instinctively agreed, so full was he of practical sense, so wise. Had the Twelve been bidden to elect their own leader, they might well have chosen Judas ; to the end they looked on him as one to be trusted, one whom it was safe to follow. And yet at the end that happened which compelled them always to put his name last upon the list :

'Judas Iscariot
Who also betrayed him.'

Jesus knew what would be, yet did He make this choice. He chose Judas, and lived with him, and instructed him as the rest, and gave him the power to work miracles, and trusted him with His all. The nature of that trust brought them often intimately together ; there was therefore the daily agony of meeting one who, He knew, would in the end turn traitor to Him. Yet said He not a word ; on the contrary, if we may judge from many evidences, from the sense of security of Judas, from the tender words of Jesus at the end, from the abiding esteem of the others, resting, no doubt, on the example of the Master, then was Judas treated all the time with a regard and a consideration perhaps even greater than any of the rest.

33. The Sermon on the Mount

We have now come to an event which has caused no small discussion among students of the life of Jesus. It is the time and place of the Sermon on the Mount. In the Gospel of S. Luke which, to this point at least, strives to preserve the actual order of events, the choice of the Twelve is immediately followed by a sermon. This sermon, when compared with S. Matthew's Sermon on the Mount, has resemblances so striking that many commentators, probably most, are convinced that the one is no more than a synopsis of the other. Intrinsically there is little to contradict this conclusion ; the only real source of controversy lies in the fact that S. Matthew says the sermon was delivered on a mountain, while S. Luke brings Jesus down into a plain. From this apparently deliberate difference some conclude that the sermon was delivered twice, in two different places ; for that Jesus often repeated what He said, as He often repeated His miracles, is both natural to suppose and at times evident enough.

Nevertheless, in this particular instance, to one who has studied the traditional spot, the difficulty may be less than at first sight appears. Sloping up behind Capharnaum and the shore of the lake along which it lies there steadily ascends a rolling mountain, running very high, but with many curves, and many more or less even places. At one point in particular, about half-way up the hill, an hour's climb or less from the town, the mountain-side bends into a large amphitheatre which, in comparison with all that surrounds it, may well be called ' a plain place ' (Luke vi, 17). Above this again tradition marks the spot where the Twelve were said to have been chosen. If this tradition is correct, indeed, whether it is correct or not, the site fulfils both the statements of the Evangelists ; with S. Matthew the sermon was delivered on the mountain, with S. Luke Jesus came lower down from the place where He had chosen the Twelve, and

' Stood in a plain place,'

But whether this be correct or not, the more one considers the point the less material does it seem to be for our purpose. That the Sermon on the Mount actually was delivered, that it was looked upon by the Twelve as a distinct stage in their career, a definite statement by Jesus of His teaching such as He had never made before, laying down in what He differed from the common teaching of men, in what His New Law differed from the Old, what were His ideals and what the means by which they were to be attained, it would seem impossible to doubt. Definitely on a particular day Jesus enlarged His scope. No longer was it merely

> ' The Kingdom of Heaven is at hand
> Do penance
> And believe the Gospel ',

but from that moment it began to be a positive, built-up thing, active in its sphere, and even aggressive, a clear challenge with no alternatives, a ' magna charta ' on which future teachers and followers might rely.

This much, it would seem, must certainly be allowed. On the other hand it may be asked, and students generally question it, whether the Sermon as S. Matthew gives it is precisely that which Jesus spoke on that occasion. We know the method of S. Matthew. He writes, not so much in order of time, but rather in compartments. He groups together his events, prophecies, miracles, parables, and so forth. It would not, therefore, be unnatural to suppose that in the Sermon on the Mount he has given not only what was spoken on that occasion, but much more of the positive teaching given by our Lord elsewhere ; even as at the end, in another long sermon on Mount Olivet, he would seem to have grouped together many of the warnings of the later days.

If this be so, and the evidence is strong, then the chief matter of importance for us is to know that either on the very day on which He chose the Twelve, and this seems the more probable, or else on a day immediately following, Jesus, in presence of a large gathering of people, gave to the disciples a clear message, showing the principles of life which He Himself taught, and which, when their turn came, they must go forth and teach. To describe this gathering S. Luke makes use of almost the very words used by S. Mark, when, as we have seen, he described the crowds that followed Jesus from Capharnaum along the northern shore of the lake. The mountain rises straight from that lake-side ; the interval of time was at most a matter of only a few days ; therefore it would seem that S. Luke means to tell us that the crowd gathered round Him on the shore was practically the same as that which went up to Him on the mountain.

Hence, immediately following the account of the choosing of the Twelve, he goes on :

'And coming down with them
He stood in a plain place
And the company of his disciples
And a very great multitude of people
From all Judæa and Jerusalem
And the sea coasts both of Tyre and Sidon
Who were come to hear him
And to be healed of their diseases
And they that were troubled with unclean spirits
Were cured
And all the multitudes sought to touch him
For virtue went out from him
And healed all
And he
Lifting up his eyes on his disciples
Said ' :

and there follows immediately what is known as the Sermon on the Plain.

The introduction of S. Matthew is no less significant and formal. Though on various other occasions he spends more time than either S. Mark or S. Luke in giving the words of Jesus, yet nowhere else does he speak with such solemn dignity as here. With him the Sermon on the Mount is opened and closed by words which seem to say that it is a thing apart ; here we have the teaching of Jesus applied to human life at its best. He has omitted mention of the night spent in prayer, and of the choosing of the Twelve which has followed ; he is intent only on the words that were spoken. Therefore he begins :

'And seeing the multitude
He went up into a mountain
And when he was sat down
His disciples came to him
And opening his mouth
He taught them saying ' :

and immediately there follow the Eight Beatitudes, introducing the Sermon on the Mount.

To attempt to draw out in detail the personality and character of Jesus as it is shown in the actual teaching of the Sermon on the Mount would occupy many volumes. We must be content with a summary. But first let Him speak for Himself, without interruption on our part; the impression at the end, however unspoken, cannot fail to be like that of which S. Matthew speaks:

> ' And it came to pass
> When Jesus had fully ended these words
> The people were in admiration
> At his doctrine
> For he was teaching them as one having power
> And not as the Scribes
> And Pharisees.'

We would suggest only one thing. Here and there in the Sermon passages occur which have their parallels in the New Testament; often allusion is made to, and passages are quoted from, the Old. By blending these parallels and allusions we form a kind of commentary on the teaching of Jesus made by Jesus Himself; and since we have supposed the mind of S. Matthew to have been to give us a general conspectus of His doctrine, an amplification such as this may not be out of place.

See Jesus then, seated on that mountain-side, with His chosen Twelve standing close around Him, now for the first time set apart, for the first time placed above the rest, receiving their first official lesson in what they were to say, and how they were to say it. See before Him this gathered multitude, Galilæans and Judæans, men from Tyre and Sidon in the east, and from Perœa in the west; such an assembly as but recently had come together about Him; poor men, on whom life pressed heavily, simple men, drawn there by their readiness to believe, hungering men, to whom religion and the hope it held out meant very much indeed, and in whom it created a great craving. The enemy was not there; the morning was early, the hill was high, the place was away from the city; they had remained below content to be masters in Capharnaum. For this occasion, perhaps the last in His life, He need not consider them at all. The rich and agnostic were not there; or if they were, these were men of goodwill, and were prepared to submit to His warnings. He could speak freely from His soul ; He could let it show itself without reserve ; no one there would misinterpret Him, or would put false meanings to His words. Moreover, what He was about to say was to be the model on which His own were to frame their future discourses ; then at all costs must He speak with abounding generosity.

'And opening his mouth, he taught them, saying : Blessed are the poor in spirit, for theirs is the kingdom of heaven. Blessed are ye poor, for yours is the kingdom of heaven. Blessed are the meek, for they shall possess the land.

'The meek shall inherit the land, and shall delight in abundance of peace (Psalm xxxvi, 11).

'Blessed are they that mourn, for they shall be comforted. Blessed are ye that weep now, for you shall laugh. Blessed are they that hunger and thirst after justice, for they shall have their fill. Blessed are ye that hunger now, for you shall be filled. Blessed are the merciful, for they shall obtain mercy. Blessed are the clean of heart, for they shall see God.

'Who shall ascend into the mountain of the Lord, or who shall stand in his holy place ? The innocent in hands and clean of heart (Psalm xxiii, 3, 4).

'Blessed are the peacemakers, for they shall be called the children of God. Blessed are they that suffer persecution for justice' sake, for theirs is the kingdom of heaven. Blessed are ye when men shall hate you and revile you and persecute you, and shall separate you, and shall reproach you and cast out your name as evil, and speak all that is evil against you untruly, for my sake : for the Son of Man's sake. Be glad in that day, and rejoice : for behold your reward is very great in heaven ; for according to these things did their fathers persecute the prophets that were before you.

'But woe to you that are rich, for you have your consolation. Woe to you that are filled, for you shall hunger. Woe to you that now laugh, for you shall mourn and weep. Woe to you when men shall bless you ; for according to these things did their fathers to the false prophets.

'You are the salt of the earth. Salt is good ; but if the salt shall lose its savour, wherewith shall it be seasoned ? It is good for nothing any more : it is profitable neither for the land nor for the dung-hill ; but shall be cast out to be trodden on by men. He that hath ears to hear, let him hear. Have salt in you, and have peace among you.

'You are the light of the world. A city seated on a mountain cannot be hid ; neither do men light a candle and put it under a bushel, but upon a candlestick, that it may shine to all that are in the house. So let your light shine before men that they may see your good works, and glorify your Father who is in heaven.

'Do not think that I am come to destroy the law or the prophets ; I am not come to destroy, but to fulfil. For amen, amen I say unto you, till heaven and earth pass, one jot or one tittle of the law shall not pass till all be fulfilled. He therefore that shall break one of these least commandments, and shall so teach men, shall be called the least in the kingdom of heaven ; but he that shall do and teach, he shall be great in the kingdom of heaven. For I tell you that unless your justice abound more than that of the scribes and Pharisees, you shall not enter into the kingdom of heaven.

'You have heard that it was said to them of old ; thou shalt not kill ; and whosoever shall kill shall be in danger of the judgement ; but I say to you that whosoever is angry with his brother shall be in danger of the judgement ; and whosoever shall say to his brother : Raca, shall be in danger of the council ; and whosoever shall say : Thou fool, shall be in danger of hell fire. If therefore thou offer thy gift at the altar, and there thou remember that thy brother hath anything against thee, leave there thy offering before the altar, and then coming thou shalt offer thy gift. And when thou goest with thy adversary to the prince, whilst thou art in the way with him, endeavour to be delivered from him ; be at agreement with him, lest perhaps the adversary deliver thee to the judge, and the judge deliver thee to the exacter, and the exacter cast thee into prison. Amen I say to thee, thou shalt not go from thence until thou pay the very last mite.

'You have heard that it was said to them of old : Thou shalt not commit adultery ; but I say to you that whosoever shall look on a woman to lust after her hath already committed adultery with her in his heart. And if thy right eye scandalize thee, pluck it out and cast it from thee ; for it is expedient for thee that one of thy members should perish, rather than that thy whole body be cast into hell ; it is better for thee to enter into life maimed, than having two hands to go into hell, into unquenchable fire, where their worm dieth not, and the fire is not extinguished. And if thy foot scandalize thee, cut it off; for it is better for thee to enter lame into life everlasting, than having two feet to be cast into the hell of unquenchable fire, where their worm dieth not and the fire is not extinguished. And if thy eye scandalize thee, pluck it out; it is better for thee with one eye to enter into the kingdom of God, than having two eyes to be cast into the hell of fire, where their worm dieth not, and the fire is not extinguished.

'Their worm shall not die and their fire shall not be quenched; and they shall be a loathsome sight to all flesh (Isaias lxvi, 24).

'And it hath been said: Whosoever shall put away his wife, let him give her a bill of divorce; if a man take a wife and have her, and she find not favour in his eyes for some uncleanness, he shall write a bill of divorce, and shall give it in her hand; and send her out of his house. But I say to you, that whosoever shall put away his wife, excepting for the cause of fornication, maketh her to commit adultery; and he that shall marry her that is put away committeth adultery. And whosoever shall put away his wife and marry another committeth adultery against her. And if the wife shall put away her husband and be married to another, she committeth adultery.

'Again you have heard that it was said to them of old: thou shalt not forswear thyself, but thou shalt perform thy oaths to the Lord; thou shalt not take the name of the Lord thy God in vain; for the Lord will not hold him guiltless that shall take the name of the Lord his God in vain (Exodus xx, 7). Thou shalt not swear falsely by my name, nor profane the name of thy God: I am the Lord (Leviticus xix, 12). For he shall not be unpunished that taketh his name upon a vain thing (Deuteronomy v, 11).

'But I say to you not to swear at all; neither by heaven, for it is the throne of God; nor by the earth, for it is his footstool; nor by Jerusalem, for it is the city of the great king; neither shalt thou swear by thy head, because thou canst not make one hair white or black. But let your speech be Yea, yea: No, no: and that which is over and above these is of evil.

'You have heard that it hath been said, An eye for an eye and a tooth for a tooth.

'Eye for eye, tooth for tooth, hand for hand, foot for foot, burning for burning, wound for wound, stripe for stripe (Exodus xxi, 24, 25).

'He that giveth a blemish to any of his neighbours, as he hath done, so shall it be done to him : breach for breach, eye for eye, tooth for tooth shall he restore ; what blemish he gave, the like shall he be compelled to suffer (Leviticus xxiv, 19, 20).

'Thou shalt not pity him, but shalt require life for life, eye for eye, tooth for tooth, hand for hand, foot for foot (Deuteronomy xix, 21).

'But I say to you not to resist evil ; but if one strike thee on thy right cheek, turn to him also the other ; and if a man will contend with thee in judgement and take away thy coat, forbid not to take thy cloak also. And whosoever will force thee one mile, go with him other two. Give to everyone that asketh of thee, and from him that would borrow of thee turn not away ; and of him that taketh away thy goods ask them not again. And as you would that men should do to you, do also to them in like manner.

'You have heard that it hath been said, Thou shalt love thy neighbour and hate thy enemy : but I say to you that hear : love your enemies, do good to them that hate you, bless them that curse you, and pray for them that persecute and calumniate you, that you may be the children of your Father who is in heaven, who maketh his sun to rise upon the good and bad, and raineth upon the just and the unjust. For if you love them that love you, what thanks are to you ? what reward shall you have ? Do not even the publicans this ? For sinners also love them that love them. And if you salute your brethren only, what do you more ? Do not also the heathens this ? And if you do good to them who do good to you, what thanks are to you ? For sinners also lend to sinners for to receive as much. But love ye your enemies ; do good and lend, hoping for nothing thereby ; and your reward shall be great and you shall be the sons of the Highest ; for he is kind to the unthankful and to the evil. Be ye therefore merciful as your Father also is merciful ; be you perfect as also your heavenly Father is perfect.

'Take heed that you do not your justice before men, to be seen by them ; otherwise you shall not have reward of your Father who is in heaven. Therefore when thou dost an alms-deed, sound not a trumpet before thee, as the hypocrites do in the synagogues and in the streets, that they may be honoured by men. Amen I say to you, they have received their reward. And when thou dost alms, let not thy left hand know what thy right hand doth, that thy alms may be in secret ; and thy Father who seeth in secret will repay thee. And when ye pray, ye shall not be as the hypocrites, that love to stand and pray in the synagogues and corners of the streets, that they may be seen by men. Amen I say to you, they have received their reward. But thou when thou shalt pray, enter into thy chamber ; and having shut the door, pray to thy Father in secret ; and thy Father who seeth in secret will repay thee. And when you are praying, speak not much, as the heathens ; for they think that in their much speaking they may be heard. Be not therefore you like to them ; for your Father knoweth what is needful for you before you ask him.

'Thus therefore shall you pray : Our Father, who art in heaven, hallowed be thy name ; Thy kingdom come ; Thy will be done on earth, as it is in heaven. Give us this day our daily, our supersubstantial bread ; and forgive us our sins, our debts, as we also forgive everyone that is indebted to us ; and lead us not into temptation but deliver us from evil, Amen. For if you will forgive men their offences, your heavenly Father will forgive you also your offences. But if you will not forgive men, neither will your Father forgive you your offences. So shall my heavenly Father do to you if you forgive not everyone his brother from your hearts. So when you shall stand to pray, forgive, if you have aught against any man ; that your Father also who is in heaven may forgive you your sins.

'He that seeketh to revenge himself shall find vengeance from the Lord ; and he will surely keep his sins in remembrance. Forgive thy neighbour if he hath hurt thee, and then shall thy sins be forgiven to thee when thou prayest. Man to man reserveth anger, and doth he seek remedy of God ? He hath no mercy on a man like himself, and doth he entreat for his own sins ? He that is but flesh nourisheth anger, and doth he ask forgiveness of God ? Remember thy last things, and let enmity cease ; for corruption and death hang over in his commandments. Remember the fear of God and be not angry with thy neighbour ; remember the covenant of the Most High, and overlook the ignorance of thy neighbour. Refrain from strife, and thou shalt diminish thy sins (Ecclesiasticus xxviii, 1–10).

'And when you fast, be not as the hypocrites, sad ; for they disfigure their faces, that they may appear unto men to fast. Amen I say to you, they have received their reward. But thou, when thou fastest, anoint thy head and wash thy face ; that thou appear not to men to fast, but to thy Father who is in secret ; and thy Father who seeth in secret will repay thee.

'Lay not up to yourselves treasures on earth, where the rust and moth consume, and where thieves break through and steal ; but lay up to yourselves treasures in heaven. Sell what you possess and give alms ; make to yourselves bags which grow not old, a treasure in heaven which faileth not ; where neither the rust nor moth doth consume and where thieves do not break through nor steal, where no thief approacheth ; for where your treasure is, there will your heart be also.

'The light of thy body is thy eye : if thy eye be single, thy whole body will be lightsome ; but if thy eye be evil, thy whole body will be darksome. If then the light that is in thee be darkness, the darkness itself, how great shall it be ! Take heed therefore that the light which is in thee be not darkness. If thy whole body be lightsome, having no part of darkness, the whole shall be lightsome, and as a bright lamp shall enlighten thee. No man can serve two masters ; for either he will hate the one and love the other, or he will sustain the one and despise the other. You cannot serve God and mammon. Therefore I say to you : Be not solicitous for your life, what you shall eat, nor for your body, what you shall put on ; is not the life more than the meat, and the body more than the raiment ? Behold the birds of the air ; consider the ravens for they neither sow nor do they reap ; neither have they storehouse nor barn ; and your heavenly Father feedeth them ; are not you of much more value than they ? how much are you more valuable than they ! And which of you by taking thought can add to his stature one cubit ? If then ye be not able to do so much as the least thing, why are you solicitous for the rest ? And for raiment why are you solicitous ? Consider the lilies of the field how they grow ; they labour not, neither do they spin ; but I say to you that not even Solomon in all his glory was arrayed as one of these. And if the grass of the field, which is to-day, and to-morrow is cast into the oven, God doth so clothe, how much more you, O ye of little faith? Be not solicitous therefore, saying : What shall we eat or what shall we drink or wherewith shall we be clothed? And be not lifted up on high ; for after all these things do the heathens seek. For your Father knoweth that you have need of all these things. But seek ye first the kingdom of God and his justice ; and all these things shall be added unto you.

'Fear not, little flock : for it hath pleased your Father to give you a kingdom. Be not therefore solicitous for to-morrow, for the morrow will be solicitous for itself. Sufficient for the day is the evil thereof.

'Judge not, that you may not be judged ; condemn not, and you shall not be condemned. Forgive, and you shall be forgiven. Give, and it shall be given to you ; good measure, and pressed down, and shaken together, and running over, shall they give into your bosom. For with what judgement you judge, you shall be judged ; for with the same measure that you shall mete withal it shall be measured to you again.

'And he spoke also to them a similitude : Can the blind lead the blind? Do they not both fall into the ditch? The disciple is not above his master, but every one shall be perfect if he be as his master. And why seest thou the mote that is in thy brother's eye, and the beam that is in thy own eye thou considerest not? Or how canst thou say to thy brother : Brother, let me pull the mote out of thy eye, when thou thyself seest not the beam in thy own eye? Thou hypocrite, cast out first the beam out of thy own eye, and then shalt thou see clearly to take out the mote from thy brother's eye. Give not that which is holy to dogs, neither cast ye your pearls before swine, lest perhaps they trample them under their feet, and turning upon you they tear you.

'But I say to you : Ask, and it shall be given you ; seek, and you shall find ; knock, and it shall be opened to you : for every one that asketh, receiveth ; and he that seeketh, findeth ; and to him that knocketh it shall be opened. And he said to them : Which of you shall have a friend, and shall go to him at midnight and shall say to him : Friend, lend me three loaves ; because a friend of mine is come off his journey to me, and I have not what to set before him. And he from within should answer and say : Trouble me not ; the door is now shut and my children are with me in bed ; I cannot rise and give thee. Yet if he shall continue knocking, I say to you, although he will not rise and give him because he is his friend, yet because of his importunity he will rise and give him as many as he needeth. Or what man is there among you of whom, if his son shall ask bread, will he reach him a stone ? or if he shall ask him a fish, will he give him a serpent ? or if he shall ask an egg, will he reach him a scorpion ? If you then, being evil, know how to give good gifts to your children, how much more will your Father who is in heaven give good things to them that ask him ? All things therefore whatsoever you would that men should do to you, do you also to them ; for this is the law and the prophets.

'Enter ye in at the narrow gate ; for wide is the gate and broad is the way that leadeth to destruction, and many there are who go in thereat. How narrow is the gate and strait is the way that leadeth to life ; and few there are that find it. Beware of false prophets, who come to you in the clothing of sheep, but inwardly they are ravening wolves. By their fruits you shall know them. Do men gather grapes of thorns, or figs of thistles ? Even so every good tree bringeth forth good fruit, and the evil tree bringeth forth evil fruit. A good tree cannot bring forth evil fruit, neither can an evil tree bring forth good fruit. Every tree that bringeth not forth good fruit shall be cut down and shall be cast into the fire. A good man, out of the good treasure of his heart, bringeth forth that which is good ; and an evil man out of the evil treasure bringeth forth that which is bad. For out of the abundance of the heart the mouth speaketh. Wherefore by their fruits you shall know them.

'And why call you me, Lord, Lord, and do not the things which I say ? Not every one that saith to me : Lord, Lord, shall enter into the kingdom of heaven ; but he that doth the will of my Father who is in heaven, he shall enter into the kingdom of heaven. Many will say to me in that day : Lord, Lord, have we not prophesied in thy name, and done many miracles in thy name ? And then will I profess unto them : I never knew you ; depart from me, you that work iniquity. Strive to enter in by the narrow gate ; for many, I say to you, shall seek to enter, and shall not be able. But when the master of the house shall be gone in, and shall shut the door, you shall begin to stand without and knock at the door, saying : Lord, open to us ! And he answering shall say to you : I know not whence you are. Then you shall begin to say : We have eaten and drunk in thy presence, and thou hast taught in our streets. And he shall say to you : I know you not whence you are ; depart from me, all ye workers of iniquity. There shall be weeping and gnashing of teeth, when you shall see Abraham and Isaac and Jacob and all the prophets in the kingdom of God, and you yourselves thrust out. And there shall come from the east and from the west and the north and the south, and shall sit down in the kingdom of God ; and behold they are last that shall be first, and they are first that shall be last.

'Every one therefore that cometh to me and heareth these my words and doth them, I will shew you to whom he is like ; he is like to a wise man that built a house, who digged deep, and laid the foundation upon a rock. And the rain fell, and the floods came, and the winds blew, and they and the stream beat vehemently upon that house, and could not shake it ; and it fell not, for it was founded on a rock. And every one that heareth these my words and doth them not, shall be like a foolish man that built his house upon the sand, without a foundation ; and the rain fell, and the floods came, and the winds blew, and the stream beat vehemently, and immediately it fell. And great was the ruin thereof. And it came to pass, when Jesus had fully ended these words, the people were in admiration at his doctrine ; for he was teaching them as one having power, and not as the scribes and Pharisees.'

As one attempts to write the story of Jesus Christ, one's eyes are inevitably riveted to the central figure. But there are times when one's vision expands, when the figure in the centre seems to rise out of its surroundings, and occupy at once, first the whole of that period of years during which it has lived, then the whole of this world's history :

Jesus Christ
Yesterday, to-day and the same for ever.

Such a moment is that which S. Matthew here mentions. It is comparatively early in His public life. Hitherto He has confined Himself, for the most part, in and about Capharnaum. By overflowing generosity He has won the hearts of the people ; by personal contact He has stirred the enthusiasm of His disciples ; now the moment has come for the more formal opening of the Kingdom. For an hour or more that morning, on the mountain-side that runs up behind the little town, Jesus has been speaking and the people have listened ; they have listened in silence, and the fascination of His words has carried them out of themselves. For an hour or more that single voice has been pouring itself out, and has lifted them above their sordid surroundings, into a world where sorrow has been turned into blessedness ; has given them new joy and courage in the good tidings that after all they are of some account in the eyes of their Father ; has freed them from the bondage of the Law, making it a glory to brave things yet harder than the Law had ever enjoined ; has given them a new understanding of sin, till innocence, and truth, and simplicity, and forgiveness, and loving-kindness, and charity have shone out as the real honour of mankind ; has given the noblest possible ideal for life and character, even the ideal of the Father God Himself : ' Be you therefore perfect, as your heavenly Father is perfect ' ; has taught them to pray, to speak to that Father, in terms that can never be forgotten ; has cut through all hypocrisy and brought to perfect light the genuine truth of the soul ; has shown them where absolute confidence can reach, higher than the flight of the birds of the air, lower than the grass beneath their feet ; has defined and vindicated true justice, which is also mercy, and equality, and meekness ; and though what has been said has ended on a note of warning, still has it been with joy, and hope, and love unutterable in the air.

He has said all this, and He has said it in their own language. Never once has He needed to go beyond their own vocabulary, the vocabulary of that Galilæan countryside, their own ideas, their own surroundings, to teach and to illustrate His teaching ; they have caught and understood every word. As on a former occasion, speaking to poor working men at their street corner, He had made use of their patched clothing, their bottles, and their wine, to bring home to them the truth of the Kingdom, so now He has caught hold of the things about Him and them by which to teach them the word. He speaks of their everyday joys and sorrows, the salt of their everyday meal ; the village perched up there on the hill above them ; the candlestick in the window-sill ; their daily conversation with its oaths and loose language ; their daily bickerings before the local judge ; their household quarrels ; the local thief ; the local borrower of money ; the sun now beating down upon them ; the rain which had but recently ceased for the season ; the pompous display of religion in the streets ; their daily toil and their daily wages, carefully stored and hidden away in their money-bags at home, the rust and the moth which were a constant trouble ; the raven at that moment hovering above them ; the flowers flourishing abundantly around them ; the green grass on the plain with all its rich promise ; their food, their drink, their clothing, their need of daily sustenance ; the ditch over there between the fields ; their dogs ; their swine ; their fish and their eggs ; the stones on the hill-side with the danger of snakes and scorpions beneath them ; the gate in the wall hard by ; their sheep and the wolves they knew only too well ; their vines and their fig-trees ; their thorns and thistles ; their fruit trees good and bad ; their house of detention ; last, down there below on the lake-side, a cottage that has fallen to ruins in a storm, and another that stands secure.

He has spoken to them in their own language. He has said what He has said in the language of their lives. He has seen them in their poverty. He has seen them broken and weighed down by cruelty and injustice and misunderstanding, and has blessed them for it all ; He has blessed them for it and has poured oil into their wounds ; He has listened to them in their heated quarrels, a brother against a brother, and has given them the means of reconciliation ; He has noticed their proneness to coarse vices and has forewarned them ; He has heard their loose talk, their ribald oaths, their cursing that has led to other abuses, their rising hatred one of another with revenge to follow as an imagined duty, and has pulled them up with a word that has swept all rancour aside. He has watched them at their prayer, in their almsgiving, during the fasting season, and has warned them against mere outward show. He has compassionated with them in their daily cares, their anxiety for their daily bread and their daily clothing, their eagerness to hoard their daily earnings, their eyes keenly watching the tradesman's scales in the bazaar, and has boldly and assuringly lifted them above it all. He has weighed the love of father and son, of friend and neighbour, and has accurately gauged how far they can be tried. He has gazed on the good workman and the negligent, and has judged the value of their work. He has lived their lives, He is one of themselves, He knows them through and through, their good points and their bad points, and He loves them ; in spite of all, He loves them and gives them all this.

And yet on the other side, while He remains but one among them, how much above not only them but all others does He claim to be ! With an assurance such as no man, no, not even any prophet before Him had ever ventured to assume, He pronounces blessing upon them ; with the might of a monarch He pronounces woe on others. He speaks as of His own authority : ' I am come to fulfil ' ; ' I say to you ' ; ' I tell you '. Who is this who so speaks of Himself ? He quotes Moses and the prophets, and sets up Himself and His new doctrine as something that shall transcend them all. He gives them commands beyond those of the Law, boldly contradicting those of Scribes and Pharisees, yet promises rewards of which neither Law nor Pharisees have ever dreamt : ' Your reward shall be great ' ; ' You shall be the children of the Father ' ; ' Your heavenly Father shall repay you '. He takes it upon Himself to teach all men how to pray, how to commune with Almighty God, and God He boldly calls His own Father and theirs. He speaks of this Father as of one with whom He is personally familiar, tells them of His providence and care for them as something with which He is intimate, of His mercy as of a characteristic trait, of His perfection as an ideal towards which they themselves, as being sons, might hope to aspire. He speaks of the Kingdom of Heaven as if it were His own, promises it to whom He will, strange things indeed He adds about the value of His word and the keeping of it, as if the very being of men and of the world depended on it.

Still with it all there has been no arrogance, no sense of false assumption, not a single word that has not rung true ; assurance, yes, and certainty, and dignity, and grandeur of ideal, but no arrogance. Truth has sounded in every word He has said, human truth, the truth that lies at the root of all that is best in man, to which the heart of man instantly responds ; bravery in face of trial, moral courage to its last extreme, which has sent a thrill of honour and glory tingling through the veins of all who have heard Him ;

at the same time a lowliness, a submissiveness, a contentment, a joy in whatever might befall, which has made the
most crushed life noble. And with it has gone a gentleness
of touch upon the most sensitive of suffering, a compassion
that has entered into, and condoned, and lifted up, and
made bright again the most downcast and the most sinful ;
an understanding of the love of friend and enemy, and the
extremes to which it would venture ; a love of the Father,
an unquestioning surrender to the Father, a familiar dealing
with the Father, as became a well-loved son, a simple
reliance on the Father, tender and human as that of any
child, even while He sat there Master of them all, as strong
as adamant.

Thus inevitably from the words He said did these people
come to gaze at and think upon the Man who said them.
All gazed at Him ; all alike were drawn to Him ; none of
any kind were omitted. The little children gazed open-
mouthed, and under the spell forgot their mothers whose
arms were around them ; the mothers gazed and for the
time forgot their children. Old age bent double leaning
on its stick looked up at Him where He sat upon His stone
and was stirred to new life ; youth with its dreams looked,
and was fascinated, and longed to do great things. Ignorance, stupidity listened and rejoiced that it heard what it
could understand ; learning, cleverness listened, and was
weighed down with the burthen of thought that it bore
away. Men in high station came, with intent to test Him,
and stood before Him paralysed, feeling the force of His
every word ; crawling men of low degree and stricken
down sat on the edge of the crowd, and knew no less that
the message was for them. Innocent, true souls were
there, and came away rejoicing, spurred to yet more truth
of life and sacrifice ; guilty souls, shameless hearts felt
their guilt the more, yet through it all were able to brush
away the tears of despair, and look up with hope such
as they had never known before, and love revived within
them, the love that came out from and went back to that
Man.

Who was He ? What was He ? What should they think
of Him ? How should they describe Him to themselves ?
What portrait of Him should they bear away, stamped upon
their hearts ? They gazed and gazed, speechless and
entranced, longing to enter into His soul. They saw the

fire of zeal flashing from His eyes, flying from His words like sparks from iron, yet never a shadow fell upon the patience, the patience without limit, revealed in His face. They bowed before the grandeur, the nobility, the fervour for the truth, and for all that was best in men, yet did they recognize the lenient condoning, the gentle indulgence and compassion where they failed. They felt the holiness, the earnestness, the seriousness of purpose that compelled to silence, yet with it all was there a brightness, a gaiety of heart, a cheerful vision, a pouring out of blessing and reward that made all life a sheer joy. They were awed by His extolling of prayer, and of self-surrender, as if nothing else were of moment, yet alongside was a knowledge of the active things of life which only experience could have taught. They were lifted up by the sight of a greatness of soul, and of outlook, and of ideal, and of endeavour that might have paralysed them, were it not for the deep lowliness and union with them every one, that made them feel He was their servant even while He was their Master ; and along with Him all things were possible, they could do all things in Him that strengthened them.

They looked at Him and they saw much that lay beneath. There was determination that never looked aside, that never for a moment flinched or hesitated, never bent or swerved, pressing on to a goal straight before it ; yet was it ever gentle, ever considerate, ever forbearing, taking poor weakness by the hand, lifting up the fallen, carrying the cripple on its shoulder. There was energy, action, a daring to rush forward that carried all before it, yet none the less never losing self-control, always composed, always at peace within itself, a sense of quiet reigning all around it. There was hatred of everything evil, indignation, wrath, condemnation, fire and death, death undying, meted out in fierce anger against it ; yet never did a sinner feel himself condemned or his hope extinguished, but only knew that forgiveness, and love, and warm pressure to a warm heart awaited him if he would have it. There was a keen sense of justice, justice idealized, justice defended, strict justice without favour, yet was the hand that dealt it out soft and tender and soothing. There was passionate love of truth, truth that feared nothing, truth open and outspoken, to saint and sinner, to selfish rich and to sensitive poor, to men in high places and to those downtrodden ; yet for them all an attraction none of them could resist, a sincerity that forestalled opposition or resentment. He was tolerant and He was stern ; He bent to the weakest, yet He stood up like a tower ; He yielded, yet He held His own ; He was a mountain of strength, yet a mother could not be more gentle ; He was lost like a child in the arms of His Father, yet was He ever fully conscious and master of Himself. All this was uttered in every word He spoke, was expressed in every look and gesture. Who was this Man ? What was He ? They longed to know Him more, and they did not know that the longing within them was the first-fruit of love.

For indeed throughout His address love, and love only, had spoken all the time. Nothing else could have given such insight into the souls of other men ; nothing else could have fostered so great a craving to bless, and to give, and to receive back, and to make secure. There was love for the poor, for the meek and lowly, for the sorrowful ; love for the hungry of heart, for the merciful of heart, for the clean of heart ; love for the makers of peace, and for those who failed to make peace and therefore endured persecution ; love on the other side for the rich, and the happy, and the contented, warning them against false security ; love for them all, both the motley crowd before Him, and the chosen Twelve who stood around the throne where He sat. Indeed, for these last He had special affection ; they were His own, the salt of the earth, the light of the world, the apostles that were to be. For them in particular He had come ; He had chosen them, He was living for them, soon He would die for them, and for them would rise again from the dead. With them He would always abide, with them and with all who would have Him, the Lover of each, longing for each, speaking to each the same winning words He had just spoken on that mountain-side, the bosom friend of every hungry soul and its complete satisfaction, if only it would come up the hill and look for Him, and find Him, and listen to Him, and lose its heart to Him, as He had already lost His own to it. In the light of all that came after, it is not too much to say that this was the Jesus Christ men saw as He spoke to them on the mountain-side.

'We have found the Messias.'
'We have found him
Of whom Moses in the law

And the prophets did write
Jesus
The Son of Joseph
Of Nazareth.'
' Rabbi
Thou art the Son of God
Thou art the King of Israel.'

Since that time they had followed Him and watched Him.
They had seen Him change water into wine, and had

' Believed in him ' ;

though what exactly they had believed it would have been
hard for them to define. ' They believed in him ' ; they
knew He was true, they knew He was mighty, they knew
He was already Master of their hearts, and that for the
moment was enough.

Then they had seen Him in the Temple, in indignation
cleansing His Father's house,—He had actually called God
His Father !—and they had stored up what He had said
on that occasion for their future meditation.

' When therefore he was risen from the dead
The apostles remembered
That he had said this
And they believed the Scripture
And the word that Jesus had said.'

Later they had stood by Him and had baptized under
His direction at the Jordan, the first to obey their former
leader, and to transfer their allegiance from John to Him ;
and in those months of quiet labour, the time of their
novitiate, they had learnt the peace which He gave, and the
familiar ease and equality of His ways, the patient hope,
the confident waiting, the eyes ever lifted up above the mountains, which had made their faith a yet more living thing.
They had parted with Him for a time at Cana, but again
at Bethsaida by the lake He had come back to them, and
again had called them to Him, and they had been astonished
that one such as He should pay so much heed to men like
them ; and faith and love had been deepened into glad
surrender to this Man because of the joy and glory of His
love for them.

And now had come this last event of all. Another time
He had chosen them ; that morning, before all the world,
He had picked them out : He had set them by His side

while He showed them what was the message they were to take to men, and how they were to take it.

When that address was over there fell a deep silence on them all. On other occasions we find the crowds about Him boisterous, expressing their approval in rough ways; not often after He has spoken to them, on this day not at all. He passed down the hill; as He went through their midst they made room for Him; when at last His back was seen, then they began to talk among themselves. What authority He had shown! Not a doubt or a question anywhere; nowhere so much as a conjecture. How unlike was this to that which they had usually heard in their synagogues! There men spoke to them in riddles, and left the riddles unanswered; their Pharisees made so much of the interpretation of the Law that it was assumed to be beyond men like them. But with this Man all was different. His word all could understand, it was definite and sure; yet was it not less sublime, or indeed less visibly the word of God.

They talked among themselves, at first in awed whispers, gathering courage as they followed Him down the hill. Capharnaum lay white below them, stretched along the water's edge, reaching on to Bethsaida where the rows of square cottages yielded to the green plain of Genesareth. Out from Capharnaum as they approached it other crowds were coming. Their Master had been away from them long enough; Pharisees or no Pharisees, enemy or no enemy, they would have Him back. In this mind they met Him, and surrounded Him, and took Him along with them into the town, the people from Capharnaum His vanguard, the crowd from the mountain bringing up the rear; while at the gate the Pharisees stood by and hated, and pondered all the more how and when their own day would come.

11

34. The Centurion's Servant

I T would seem to have been on this same day that the next event occurred of which we have record. Away down in the town, in the direction of Bethsaida, stood the Roman barracks. It was not a large one, for a company of men would have sufficed to keep Capharnaum in order should trouble ever occur; if more were ever needed, there was Magdala not far away, and Tiberias, the centre of Roman rule, a few miles along the shore. It was well for Capharnaum that the officer in charge of this station was a human soul. He knew the people about him; Roman though he was he could sympathize with their national ideals. He helped them when he could; even their new synagogue, with its characteristic mixture of Jewish and Western decoration, they owed in great measure to him, and the grants from the public treasury which he had been able to procure.

In another way also he showed his humanity, not too common a thing in Roman officials of his standing; he had interest in and affection for his servants. One of these at this very moment was lying ill in the servants' quarters behind the Centurion's house; probably his 'boy', as in the East the body-servant is called, almost certainly a Jew from the neighbourhood. Between the master and the servant, as is not uncommon in such cases, a special tie had arisen, amounting almost to friendship. The officer now was anxious for his servant; with the fever that was on him, signs of palsy had come; the trembling caused by the fever had increased, and now the youth was permanently shaking from head to foot. The Centurion was loth to lose so faithful a servant; besides the man was suffering, and it hurt the master to see it. But the doctors could do nothing, and gave no hope of recovery.

What was he to do? While he pondered, suddenly the news came to him that Jesus was again in Capharnaum.

Such news reached him quickly, for he was responsible for good order in the town ; and of late, when Jesus had appeared in the streets, there had been a tendency for crowds to gather and there were signs of trouble brewing. But this time a new thought occurred to him. That Jesus healed the sick there was no doubt. Though he was himself a Roman, still his servant was a Jew ; perhaps on that account Jesus might be induced to extend His favour to the sufferer.

At once he acted. Close to where he lived, in the respectable quarter of the town, were the houses of the little aristocracy of Capharnaum, the ancients of the people, the Pharisees, the owners of the fields on the hills. He called some of the elders to him ; he showed them the boy and explained to them his desire. He was himself only a Roman, and moreover a soldier, so he could not expect to be heard ; perhaps they would go in his stead, would speak to Jesus on his behalf, and see whether He would condescend to come. But they need not urge their petition ; if they but stated his case it would be enough. Should the Prophet be disposed to come, that would suffice to bring Him ; if He would not, He would be saved the trouble of refusing. Let them be content with the simple message :

'Lord
My servant is lying at home
Sick of the palsy
And is grievously tormented.'

The ancients understood. Though they had little love for the dominating Romans as a race, who held them in firm bondage, yet this man was an exception ; and, as often happens, because he was an exception they loved him all the more. Certainly they would carry the message ; and though their Roman friend had framed it very modestly, there was no reason why they should not strengthen it with arguments of their own. Though he was a Roman, and Romans had their own peculiar standards, still even judged by Jewish standards this Centurion was a good man. Though he was a Roman, yet he had respect and even showed affection for the Jews ; that would have influence on Him who said He had been sent to the lost sheep of the house of Israel. Though he was a Roman, and therefore by birth and profession an idolator, still in his heart it was evident that he revered the one true God; he had shown this in a practical way by helping them to build their synagogue.

They made their bow to the Centurion, gathered their robes about them, and hurried through the narrow streets. No time was to be lost; Jesus had been at work all the morning up the hill, therefore, if they did not reach Him soon, He would go down to Simon's house to rest. They came to the edge of the crowd; an opening to Jesus was easily made for them; when the ancients needed Him, whether for good or for evil, a way to Him was always found. They stood in His presence almost breathless, less with the hurrying than because of the message they brought. For it was to be remembered that they were doing an unusual thing. They were acting for a Roman officer, a man whom they were anxious to oblige, and they were by no means sure how their request would be received. They salaamed to Jesus; one of them delivered the message; then first one and then another put in further arguments. The man was a good man; he deserved to be favoured; he was a friend of the Jews; why, he had built, or had helped to build, the very synagogue in which Jesus Himself had taught and prayed.

> ' And when they came to Jesus
> They besought him earnestly saying
> He is worthy that thou shouldst do this for him
> For he loveth our nation
> And hath built us a synagogue.'

What singular arguments were these to use with Jesus Christ! How little did they understand! And because they did not understand, the very arguments they used were a shadow of the great misunderstanding that was one day to come. 'He loveth our nation!' Soon they would round on Him, urging against Him that He loved it not. 'He hath built us a synagogue!' Soon it would be cried against Him that He was a destroyer of the Temple of God.

But Jesus, it would seem, was not so hard to move as they expected. He stood there quietly and heard them; the effect of that morning's discourse was still upon Him. He did not need to be persuaded; it was enough to be told that

His help was needed, and that someone had asked Him for
it. They talked themselves to silence ; without more ado
He said to them :

> ' I will come
> And heal him.'

Immediately the procession began through the streets
towards the Centurion's dwelling. The nodding, chattering,
approving, self-congratulating ancients led the way, and
Jesus went with them ; Jesus the Master, while they hung
obsequiously around Him, Jesus peaceful without, while
within He knew, only too well, the depth and value of all
this pomp and ceremony. He would endure this show a
little longer ; perhaps with time, and further evidence such
as this, it would deepen into something more real. Soon
He would have to try them, in the very synagogue of which
they had just boasted, to see how far their faith would go ;
but for the present He would give them every opportunity
of knowing Him a little more. Around Him the crowd
pressed in, the same that had been with Him by the lake,
the same that had listened to Him on the mountain. There
was excitement, and talk, and enthusiasm, but for the
moment more suppressed than usual ; all that had happened
that morning had sobered them a little, and besides they
were waiting for what was about to be done.

Naturally the news that He was actually on the way
quickly went ahead before Him. The Roman was told
that He was coming ; immediately there was bustle in the
house, for due preparations must be made. After all,
though he was well-to-do, and his house was better furnished
than most, and more refined as became the home of a
ruling Roman, yet was it a pagan house, and here and there
might be found in it that which would ill suit the eyes of
one like Jesus. He must not be offended or angered ; if
He were, He might refuse to act ; in any case instinct told
them that things which were familiar and of no account
to them might well be offensive to Him.

But while the servants were so occupied, the thoughts of
the soldier went further. In other instances we have
already seen how one good act has led to another ; especially
we have seen how a simple act of faith or trust has been
rewarded by a deeper faith and trust, and has been made
to see more and ever more. The

' Master, where dwellest thou ? '

with its answer,

' They came and they saw ',

and its reward,

' We have found the Messias ',

is repeated many a time in the life of Jesus, and since.

It was so in this case. The Roman had begun with the dream that perhaps this strange Man might be induced to come and heal his servant. Now to his surprise he heard that He was actually coming ; what was more He had said that He would heal the boy where he lay. He was confused ; now that it had happened, as is often the experience, he was as if taken by surprise. It was too much. After all he was only a Roman soldier, and this Man Jesus was the grand ideal of the Jews, whatever that might mean. Was it essential that He should be compelled to step across the threshold of a pagan ? There occurred to him the story he had been told of the civil commissioner and his son. It had occurred only a month or two ago ; the commissioner had himself gone to Cana, and had invited Jesus down to Capharnaum. Jesus had not come ; from Cana He had healed the child without needing to make the journey. Might He not do the same now ? Certainly if He would He could ; then why should He not ?

Thus beautifully did the heart of that Roman soldier grow, and quickly, even as did later the heart of the criminal on the Cross. It had begun with a little faith in this Wonder-worker ; it had gone on to an act of hope, expressed in his appeal ; reverence and self-humiliation had followed ; and now there was greater faith, and greater hope, and mingled with them not a little love, warming the whole into something glorious, into something which to this day we can have set before us for our model. When we repeat our : ' Lord, I am not worthy ', and that at the moment of our greatest proof of faith, it is well to bear in mind that the prayer was first uttered, not by a Jew, not by a follower of Jesus, but by a poor pagan Roman.

As he had done before, so now he was quick to decide. This soldier was a man of action ; he was accustomed to command and to be obeyed. Friends were in the house with him ; from one like him they were seldom absent. He called them to him ; he asked them to do for him an

errand like the one he had asked before. He gave them a
message and bade them deliver it to Jesus, even while He
was yet on the road.

'Lord ', was his message,
'Trouble not thyself
For I am not worthy
That thou shouldst enter under my roof
For which cause
Neither did I think myself worthy
To come to thee
But only say the word
And my servant shall be healed
For I also am a man subject to authority
Having under me soldiers
And I say to this Go
And he goeth
And to another Come
And he cometh
And to my servant Do this
And he doeth it.'

It was a singular message ; but coming from a Roman
officer, and to a subject Jew, it was more singular still.
That one in his position should speak of his house as unfit
for Jesus to enter, that was indeed strange hearing for those
Jewish ancients. Why, Jesus was a Nazarene, Jesus was a
carpenter, Jesus put up in Simon's cottage by the lake ; at
most, with all His miracles, and teaching, and army of
followers, Jesus was no more than one of themselves. That
this Roman should think himself unworthy to meet Jesus
was surely an extravagance ; it could be due only to the
fact that he had never yet met Him. With them the trouble
was the opposite ; He was too easily accessible, to anyone and
everyone, countrymen of Galilee and aristocrats of Judæa,
educated Scribes and unlettered fishermen ; even men like
Levi and his sort could win Him to sit with them at table.

Then there was the curious argument he had bade them
use. These Romans, with all their greatness, were certainly
a strange people. Because he was a Roman officer, representing the almighty arm of Rome, therefore he was not
worthy to meet Jesus ! Because he commanded Roman
soldiers and, alone in that city, could make them come and
go at will, therefore he was not fit that Jesus should come

under his roof ! Curious reasons. But they did not see what Jesus saw, and what the Roman soldier dimly saw. The man had argued rightly. If he could command men to do his bidding, no less could Jesus, if He chose, command powers that were not of man. If he could bid men come and go and act as he appointed, then could Jesus bid His angels act for Him. And on the other hand, officer as he was, representing the Roman Emperor, yet should the great Tiberius ever come to Capharnaum he would hesitate to take him to his house ; how could he then not hesitate to receive this Jesus, who for all His rough garments, and His lowly way of living, was evidently more than Tiberius ?

So had that Roman soldier revealed the steps of his growth in faith. Quickly and surely, grace following grace, it had leaped beyond the limits that others yet had reached ; even Simon and John, with all their devotion, had not yet gone so far. For with them still, and for long after, nay, to the very end, the idea of the Kingdom to come held them confined. Not till He was dead, and risen again, and gone from this world, and they were left to carry the word to Gentiles and kings far away, were they able to break through the barrier which held their Jesus and His Kingdom within the kingdom of Israel. But this man, by a single bound, had transcended not Israel alone but even Rome itself and its Empire. Jesus, he confessed, if He was any-thing, was greater than David, greater than Cæsar, greater than the world with all its kings.

The two Evangelists who relate this narrative tell us that

' Jesus hearing this marvelled ',

and the word has given rise to much discussion. But for us the simple statement is sufficient. The heart of Jesus went out to that man, even as later it was to go out yet more fully to Simon. For throughout His life the one desire of Jesus was that He should be discovered ; that He should be discovered, and recognized, and owned. For every step made in that discovery He was grateful ; no man made it but met with reward overflowing. The one thread of interest running through the whole drama of His life is the growth of this discovery. And on this occasion it was as on others ; as at the beginning by the Jordan, as later in the lane leading up to Cæsarea Philippi, so here, when Jesus heard the message brought to Him, His human heart beat quicker, and His eyes flashed brighter, and a greater keenness spread across His face, and the joy on His brow might well be taken for surprise, at the thought that he who made this confession was no Jew, but a Roman and a pagan.

'And Jesus hearing this marvelled.'

Indeed it was a great moment, a reward for the work of that day ; though, as usual with the rewards of God, it had come from an unexpected quarter. The confession, from such a man, opened out the vision which, sooner or later, He would have to make known to His Jewish country-men. One day He would have to show them that His Kingdom was not for them alone but for all men ; indeed that in the end the stranger, untrammelled by prejudice and tradition, might prove to be the true heir. Here and now He would give them a glimmering of the truth, and yet as He spoke He knew that in His words must be contained another shadow of the coming doom. It was a strange appendix to the great address of that very morning ; yet by it the Great Charter of Judaism became the Great Charter of all mankind.

'And Jesus hearing this marvelled
And turning about to the multitude that followed him
He said : Amen I say to you
I have not found so great faith
Not even in Israel
And I say to you
That many shall come from the east and the west
And shall sit down in the kingdom of heaven
With Abraham and Isaac and Jacob
But the children of the kingdom
Shall be cast out into the exterior darkness
There shall be weeping and gnashing of teeth.'

As He spoke He looked out over the crowd about Him. The message of warning was for them indeed ; it was the first of many. Then He turned again to the bringers of the message. Men strained to catch His words, for they knew that they would be momentous. He had regained His composure, He spoke with that solemn ease which, on like occasions, we have already seen. As if it were an everyday matter for this Monarch, and Judge, and Recompenser of men, He bade them take back His answer :

' Go
And as thou hast believed
So be it done to thee.'

The messengers took a hurried leave, and many from the crowd went with them. They had not far to go ; but long before they reached the Roman's house they knew. There was confusion about it and excited rejoicing ; men were busily comparing notes with one another, men were heaping on the Centurion their congratulations, and were making their way into the servants' quarters to see the youth where he sat, sound and whole, upon his mattress. They put it all together. So many minutes ago Jesus had spoken the word ; so many minutes ago the youth had sat up, well. There was no doubt ; the Roman's prayer had been heard ; yet none but he dreamt to what extent this was true.

35. The Widow's Son

From a word of S. Luke, who characteristically records the next event, it would seem that on the following day Jesus left Capharnaum and made His way to Naim. It was a journey of about a day on foot. The road led over or around the hills which skirt the western side of the Lake of Galilee ; then, going almost due south, by midday travellers would reach the foot of Thabor. Rounding Thabor they would come out upon the upper end of the Valley of Esdraelon, stretching thence to their right due west till below the Carmel range it reached the sea. North of the valley they would leave behind them the range of hills among which Nazareth lay hidden ; opposite them to the south, dividing the valley from Samaria, was the range of Little Hermon. At the eastern end of this, a little above the level of the valley, stood a white village with a wall about it. It was Naim. There they intended to stay for the night ; on foot from Thabor they would reach it in at most three hours.

The company that went with Jesus that day from Capharnaum was a large one. There were the disciples, henceforth His inseparable companions. There were also many of those who have already been twice described, who had come up from other places, Judæa and Peræa, Tyre and Sidon, and who had been with Him during all these last days. For them Capharnaum had no other attraction but Himself; they had come to be with Him, therefore wherever He went they would follow. They had come over the hills in the morning; at midday, at the foot of Thabor, they rested; in the afternoon across the valley which just now, in the spring-time, was looking its best; towards evening, as the sun was stooping on their right over Carmel, the noisy company came to the little arched gateway that led into Naim.

But here they were brought to silence. As they reached the city gate sounds of wailing and mournful singing were heard coming down the street within. Soon a procession emerged; men leading the way; behind them four others carrying a corpse upon a light bier of two poles and a piece of matting; the body wrapped in white, a face-cloth covering the face, the mouth, chin, and neck visible. Behind it walked an elderly woman, or so she seemed, robed in black, leaning on the arms of two others; behind her again a group of other women, some friends, others trained in the art of weird wailing. Beyond and around them followed the crowd, drawn there some from curiosity, others out of pity; it was evident that this funeral was one of special interest in the little town. As it left the city gate the mourners turned to the right, making for the caves in the mountain-side which was the place of burial.

The procession told its own tale. It was composed of such men and women as showed that the mourning family was of some consideration in the place. The corpse on the bier was that of a young man, little more than a boy; that a promising young life should have been so cut off was one of the themes of the mourners in the rear. But the chief object of sympathy was the figure that moved behind the corpse. She was alone in her sorrow, no immediate relatives were mourning with her, no husband, no other children; those supporting her were only kindly neighbours. It was clear at a glance that she was the mother, and that this was her only son. She was, moreover, draped in a widow's garb; she was a very lonely woman.

> ' And when he came nigh to the city
> Behold a dead man was carried out
> The only son of his mother
> And she was a widow
> And a great multitude of the city was with her.'

Jesus walked in front of the enthusiastic crowd that had come with Him across the valley ; closest around Him walked the Twelve. At a meeting of the roads outside the city gate the two processions met. With one glance He took in the scene, the evidently sympathetic mourners, the dead boy, above all the poor woman staggering behind the corpse. At once His human heart went out to her ; because she was suffering He also suffered ; does not this tell us something of the wound within which constant separation from His own Mother gave Him ? He had left her at twelve years of age, and because He had caused her sorrow, He, too, had felt it deeply. He had left her at Nazareth, after thirty years of companionship, and down in Judæa His heart had often flown back to her. He had her with Him in Capharnaum, but because of His Father's business, more than ever before, He had been compelled to leave her aside. He was human, as we know, very human ; He had felt the separation every time ; but His agony had been doubled by the thought that He had made her suffer too. If He ' knew what was in man ', He knew no less what was in woman ; above all that particular agony of hers when she craves for support and cannot find it, or still worse when, having found it, it is suddenly taken away.

Jesus knew all this ; therefore He understood the woman's broken heart before Him. The power to suffer when others suffer is the richest gift of man, and in this special gift Jesus was not wanting.

> ' He hath truly borne our sorrows
> And he hath carried our griefs.'

He looked at her, He understood what this separation meant to her, He was sorry for her, He suffered with her, He would help her in what way He could ; it was just that and nothing more. No one asked Him ; no one pleaded for her, as the day before the ancients had done for the Centurion in Capharnaum ; what He did was a spontaneous act of human generosity. And what an act it was !

> ' Whom when the Lord had seen
> Being moved with mercy towards her
> He said to her, Weep not.'

Jesus spoke to the widow ; gently He asked her not to cry. He stepped a little backward, and put His hand upon the pole that was resting on the two men's shoulders.

Instinctively they stood still and the whole procession stopped. The widow's tears ceased, checked by this sudden distraction; her eyes looked up and followed Him, for the rest she stood there, an effigy of anxious suspense. Behind her the wailing also ceased; the women wondered what was the reason of the halt, and stared at the Man who had caused it. All about the crowd was silent. To interrupt a funeral procession was a thing most unbecoming, almost a scandal; but then it was Jesus who had done it, and when the Carpenter of Nazareth commanded it had by now become accepted to obey.

Thus for the moment dead silence reigned over the multitude in that country lane. In the midst of it all Jesus stood, His hand still resting on the pole. All eyes were fixed on Him; there was not one that did not strain his neck to see what He would do. Then clearly, looking at the corpse before Him, with a voice that everyone could hear, with eyes that seemed to penetrate beyond that corpse into another world, He said:

'Young man
I say to thee
Arise.'

No, He did not quite say that. He called him, not 'Young man', but 'Little boy'. He spoke as the mother would have spoken; for the moment He was one with her.

Immediately there was a disturbance. A tremor ran along the death-clothes; the corpse on the bier began to move. It raised itself and sat up; the arms that had lain by its side, stiffened in death, were full of life; they went to the face and lifted up the face-cloth. The eyes opened, they looked straight in front of them, straight into the mother's eyes who was standing paralysed at the feet. Then at once the risen boy began to speak. 'Mother!—Where am I?—What is the meaning of all this?—What has happened?—Where have I been?—What is this crowd?—What this strange gathering in this strange public place?'—and the boy looked from her all around him, and began to talk, to anyone and to everyone in the old familiar way. He was indeed alive, alive and the same. The men who carried him nervously lifted the poles from off their shoulders and placed their burthen on the ground. The boy rose to his feet; he stood up in their midst sound and well.

Then followed a pretty little ceremony. Jesus came nearer to the boy ; He took the boy by the hand ; a step or two and they were by the mother's side. He placed the boy's now warm hand in the hands of the mother that were cold. Formally He gave him to her and her to him ; and His own heart showed that He was happy in their joy.

'And he gave him to his mother.'

Meanwhile all around them silence had prevailed, silence nurtured by fear. Gradually the truth dawned upon them. First the carriers, then all the rest, saw before their eyes what could not be mistaken ; the boy that was dead was now alive. They saw son and mother locked in each other's arms and marvelled ; they looked at the Man who had done this thing, who had commanded death itself, and they were afraid. But soon they recovered ; there was too much peace reigning for fear to last long. Jesus had done His work ; with His Twelve He passed on, through the gateway into the town. The crowd pressed in upon the boy ; it remembered all that had of late been done ; those from Capharnaum related the sermon and the miracle of the day before. Then He had spoken 'as one having authority', as one who was a messenger from God ; to-day He had indeed proved it, more completely than ever before. As Jesus passed out of sight He heard the crowd crying behind Him :

'A great prophet is risen up among us
And God hath visited his people.'

He passed on His way from Naim, but what had been done that day could not remain unnoticed. Other miracles He had wrought, now in such abundance that men were ceasing to marvel. But this was different, it was unique, it revealed a power not hitherto suspected. The news of it spread far and wide ; it went over the hill to Samaria, and into Judæa beyond, and there in particular, by friend and enemy, it was much discussed. And friends were confirmed in their friendship, and enemies were confirmed in their hate.

36. The Embassy from John the Baptist

Meanwhile, down in Peræa, on the lonely mountain-side that overlooked the eastern shore of the Dead Sea, in the lonely palace perched high aloft, where Herod and his court held their revels, during all these months John the Baptist had been lingering in prison. Young man as he was, barely thirty-two, his life's work had been done. He could now look back upon it all. Patiently he had lived through his long thirty years of lonely preparation ; when the time came he had gone forth, a solitary voice crying in the wilderness. At the Baptism of Jesus he had had his first reward, being given to know the Messias without a doubt. He had pointed Him out to others as the Lamb of God ; he had yielded place to Him at the Jordan ; he had seen Him increase while he himself decreased ; he had rejoiced as the friend of the bridegroom in the bridegroom's triumph. Since he had been held in prison his disciples had still clung to him, and from time to time he had contrived to bring them under the Master's influence ; in this at least there was still work to do.

Nevertheless these disciples continued to hesitate. They brought him news of the wonders being done in Galilee, but they could not so easily set aside their devotion and reverence for John. John had taught them, John had trained them, the vision of God which they had learnt, the newness of life which had come to them, were all due to John. What then was he to do ? As plainly as he could he had told them the truth ; to do more, to dismiss them abruptly, might end in injury. He could only encourage them again and again to learn of Jesus first-hand that in the end they might be convinced. His own end, he knew, could not be far off ; before that end came it was essential that their future should be secured. He would send them on a formal embassy ; he would allow the Master Himself to speak, and so use His personal influence upon them. That they respected Him they knew ; their doubt was whether Jesus was in fact ' He that was to come ', or whether He was only a successor of John, further carrying on the work of preparation. For to say truth there was so much against Him. He was from Nazareth ; He was so much like other men ; in austerity, in outspokenness, in life of prayer, even John seemed to excel Him.

With this in mind John selected two of those who were still devoted to him. He would say no more himself ; he would bid them carry to Jesus a message in the form of a question. In answering that question Jesus would have His opportunity ; even if His answer were cryptic, as it so

often was when men doubted, it would give him something
which he could unravel to these men, and so convince them.

' Now when John had heard in prison the works of Christ
    He called to him two of his disciples
    And sent them to Jesus saying
    Art thou he that art to come
    Or look we for another ? '

The messenger-disciples took their leave of their master,
wondering in their hearts what would be the answer to this
question. For it was indeed the one vital question. If
Jesus was truly the Messias whom John had foretold, then
must they, as others had already done, surrender the latter
for Him. But this, as has been said, they were loth to do.
John they knew, John they had learnt to love with their
whole hearts ; they would gladly follow him and preach
his doctrine to the uttermost parts of the earth, they would
be his companions in prison. In him they believed, and
they knew they could trust his utter truthfulness ; how
could they desert him in this his hour of need ?

But this Jesus, after all, who was He ? Were they yet
sure of Him ? Could they rely upon Him ? They had
heard much concerning Him, and it could not be denied
that all He said, and all He did, were evidence in His
favour. On the other hand there were doubtful signs.
For instance John, by his very appearance, his life in the
desert, his clothing of camel's hair, had from the beginning
been marked out from other men. This Jesus, on the other
hand, had had no such preparation or training. He had
no distinguishing attire, He had been a village carpenter
and nothing else ; even now, in outward appearance at
least, He made no pretence at being anything more. John,
again, had lived his life as he had begun it. He had been
severely austere ; he had practised penance openly, setting
an example of the penance that he preached ; he had
taught and insisted on the same with those who would
attach themselves to him as his disciples. This Jesus had
apparently done nothing of all this ; though He said : ' Do
penance ! ' yet He took life as He found it, ate and drank
with other men, even at times with well-known reprobates ;
so far as could be seen no kind of penance was performed
by those whom He had taken for disciples. Moreover,
John made much of prayer. He prayed in the sight of men

for an example ; to his disciples he gave special instructions on the way to commune with God ; there were some who gave themselves, under his guidance, entirely to the life of prayer. Jesus, it seemed, did nothing of the kind. True, it was said that He was wont to slip away from men, and that He had been found alone on the hill-sides lost in prayer ; but His disciples, what did they do ? They had learnt from Him a simple form of prayer, but He had taught them little more.

Altogether, then, the evidences, as they saw them, were by no means clear. So at least concluded these men as they came down the mountain from Machærus, and went together up the coast of the Dead Sea, and took the road by Jordan through Peræa, passing the spots where, in the old, happy, enthusiastic days John had baptized, and they with him, and they had won so many to conversion from their evil ways, and hope had risen like the sun over the eastern hills, and it had been good to be alive. As they went along memories such as these only served to deepen their prejudice. They believed in John, they wished only to believe in John ; whatever their suspicions of Jesus and His claim, they could only look upon Him as in some sense an intruder. At all costs they must uphold the good name of John, to whom they owed everything they valued. So it came about that their very truthfulness and loyalty tended only to make them the less inclined to accept the very Truth ; and so it has been with many since.

At the southern end of the lake they crossed the Jordan into Galilee. Jesus had been last heard of at Naim, at no great distance up the valley ; from there it was easy to trace Him. In another place, not in Capharnaum, they came up with Him on His tour ; from some indications one suspects it was in Corozain, up on the hill to the north-west of Capharnaum. They arrived at one of those striking moments when by lavish, almost extravagant outpouring of generosity Jesus was appealing to the hearts of the people. It was evening. Jesus had come into the city after another day of labour. As soon as He had come the sick, and the diseased, and the maimed, and the possessed had been ranged in rows along the street ; at that very moment He was passing down among them, and was laying a gentle hand on every one in turn, and each, as soon as he was touched, was healed. And the whole city was gathered about, seeing, believing in this Worker of wonders, enthusiastic, hustling to and fro, delighted with its good fortune, but alas ! and He knew it, still far from drawing the obvious conclusion.

Into this excited crowd the disciples of John came, and witnessed all that went forward. Certainly it was striking ; their master, John, had never done anything of the kind. If miracles alone were a convincing proof, then they must accept this new Leader. Still there were the other things to be considered. He was working wonders, that could not be denied, but who could tell by what power He worked them ? Thus would prejudice, even a noble prejudice, hold them back from accepting the evidence patent to their eyes.

While the ceremony proceeded the two men looked on in silence. They were reverent, they were thoughtful ; they stood in marked contrast with the noisy crowd about them. Their very unbelief added to their attitude of respectability ; almost they might have been mistaken for Pharisees. They would see the ceremony through ; they would suspend their judgement ; when they had received an answer to their message, then, perhaps, there would be more light.

At length came their opportunity. The end of the row of sufferers had been reached, the sick had been touched and healed, the disciples had done their work of keeping order, and they might now take their rest. As they turned to go to their khan, the two men from John came before them. Could they be allowed to speak to Jesus ? They had a message from their master, the Baptist, who had sent them with it from his prison. Of course, to the disciples, such a petition must be granted. These were old friends ; Andrew and Simon knew them, and James and John, and Bartholomew and Philip ; and Philip was always accessible to anyone who would come to Jesus. Jesus Himself was told. There was a message from the Baptist ; a message from one in prison could never be refused, least of all from one for whom His heart was ever bleeding.

Thus at the corner of the street they met. There was something formal about the meeting ; it was an embassy from one monarch to another. The men stood before Him, conscious that much depended on the answer to their question. Jesus received them, patient, encouraging, the Master sure of His right, and in His strength able to yield, and sympathize, and help, and give. It was a short message, only an enquiry ; the disciples standing round, when they heard it, wondered what it might signify.

> ' And when the men were come unto him they said
> John the Baptist hath sent us to thee saying
> Art thou he that art to come
> Or look we for another ? '

Jesus looked on these men and loved them ; and in the light of love He understood. He knew their hearts, their doubts and their hesitations, their true devotedness to His beloved John, which nevertheless kept them from Himself. He would not condemn their incredulity ; but neither, as always, would He compel their faith. He would give them new light according to their understanding, which, if they chose, they could follow. These men were steeped in the prophets ; under John in particular they had studied the signs ; the words of the prophets ran through their minds, and their prayer was their interpretation. Jesus would then speak to them in this their own language ; as He had spoken to the Woman at the Well through the medium of water, as to the poor of Capharnaum by means of their patched clothes, as to the men on the hill-side in terms of the sun, and the birds, and the lilies, so with these men He would speak in the language of the prophets. He would take one of these prophets ; He would gather up his hints, given in various places ; all this He would focus on Himself and on the scene before them, and that should be His sufficing answer.

Isaias was their favourite prophet ; he more than any other had foretold the coming of their master, John. One phrase of that prophet had been :

> ' The dead men shall live
> My slain shall rise again
> Awake and give praise
> Ye that dwell in the dust.'
>
> Isaias xxvi, 19.

Again, in another place it was written :

> ' And in that day
> The deaf shall hear the words of the book
> And out of darkness and obscurity
> The eyes of the blind shall see

And the meek shall increase their joy in the Lord
And the poor man shall rejoice in the Holy One of Israel.'
Isaias xxix, 18, 19.

And yet again :
' They shall see the glory of the Lord
And the beauty of our God
Strengthen ye the feeble hands
And confirm the weak knees
Say to the faint-hearted
Take courage and fear not
Behold your God will bring the reward of recompense
God himself will come
And will save you
Then shall the eyes of the blind be opened
And the ears of the deaf shall be unstopped
Then shall the lame man leap as a hart
And the tongue of the dumb shall be free
For waters are broken out in the desert
And streams in the wilderness.'
Isaias xxxv, 2–6.

Phrases such as these were familiar to these men ; out of them there had grown an idea of the signs that were to be, though how they would finally be fulfilled they did not know. Jesus took that idea ; He made it concrete and real ; far more vividly and really than they had ever dreamt, the prophecy was being fulfilled before their eyes. He stood before them ; He would treat them as they were, ambassadors from John. They had asked their question, not in the carping spirit of the Pharisees ; then they should have their sufficient answer. Yet should it be an answer that would not compel ; even after it was given they should be free to come to Him by choice or not at all.

He looked round on the crowd gathered in the street, preoccupied now with their own affairs ; who they were, what they had been, what had been done to them, these two men had witnessed for themselves. Then, with the firmness of truth, He said :

' Go
And relate to John what you have heard
And seen
The blind see
The lame walk

The lepers are made clean
The deaf hear
The dead rise again
The poor have the gospel preached to them.'

This, for them, was His sufficient answer ; the rest they would be able to add or deduce for themselves. Still would He not leave them without a word of guidance. However prejudiced, these were good men ; there were others prejudiced because they were not good. Then they should be differently treated. Evil-minded men He would whip with threats and warnings ; these He would lead kindly by the hand. They had suspected Him ; they had been shocked by His behaviour ; in their zeal for the truth they had suspected Him as untrue. Let that be ; He would not crush the bruised reed ; in spite of their suspicion He would show them that He understood, and cared, and forgave, and would gladly take them to His own if they would come. After He had drawn the picture for them He looked on them compassionately and added :

' And blessed is he
That shall not be scandalized in me.'

The two disciples of John went their way. They had received their answer ; they had both heard and seen ; before they drew their own conclusions they must hear what their master in his prison had to say. During the three days of their pilgrimage back to Machærus they could not but turn the matter over between themselves. They knew it was a crisis in their lives. They had come that way strengthening each other in their prejudices ; now they went back, struggling still in their hearts for John, but softened, less able to condemn the other, won, or at least given pause, by the gentle words with which they had been dismissed :

' Blessed is he
That shall not be scandalized in me.'

They were gone, but their visit had not been without its effect in other ways. In spite of his imprisonment, the name of John was still a power in the land ; to many besides his immediate disciples he was still a distinct rival to Jesus. He had come of a priestly family ; the circumstances of his birth were well known. His sincerity had been proved by the life he had lived ; his fearless doctrine had conquered many hearts. By his baptism sinners had been utterly transformed ; what all men, what Judæa and Galilee in particular owed to him could not be measured ; withal he had won the love of many. Now at this moment he was lying in prison, unable to do good any more, awaiting his doom ; truly their prophet, their guide, their hero, their martyr. All this was established and certain ; Jesus on the other hand was still on His trial. He was only from Nazareth ; His family was of no religious significance ; His birth was unknown ; He had lived a life in no way different from that of anyone among them ; the effect of His teaching was still to be seen.

Jesus knew all this. It was a conflict of conclusions that must needs be faced, and here was an opportunity to face it. And He did so. That He was greater than John they must be plainly shown ; yet in the showing not one tittle must be taken from the honour due to John. Indeed it should be magnified ; He would prove to this people that if they esteemed John, He esteemed him more. Nowhere does the human nobility of Jesus more appear than in the magnificent way He speaks of John, at the very moment when on John's account His own reputation was in danger. It is still the language of the men whom He addresses, still their own ideas that He uses, their own memory and experience ; and yet all is raised to a noble oratory which only a magnanimous nature could have uttered.

> ' When the messengers of John were departed
> And went their way
> Jesus began to speak to the multitudes
> Concerning John
> What went you out into the desert to see ?
> A reed shaken with the wind ?
> But what went you out to see ?
> A man clothed in soft garments ?
> Behold they that are clothed in costly apparel
> And live delicately
> Are in the houses of kings
> But what went you out to see ?
> A prophet ?
> Yea I tell you
> And more than a prophet
> For this is he of whom it is written

> Behold I send my angel before thy face
> For Amen I say to you
> Among those that are born of women
> There hath not risen a greater prophet
> A greater man
> Than John the Baptist.'

Would it be possible to say more than this of any man ? Certainly Jesus had given John his due, full measure and flowing over. Still He would not stop there. Let Him leave it there and He would have gained nothing. This people was a material people ; it judged by material standards ; let Him leave what He had said unqualified, and many would take it as proof of His capitulation to John. Great then as John had been declared to be in himself, that greatness was as nothing when compared with his greatness as a member of the Kingdom of God. Nay, not only John, but every faithful member of that Kingdom was greater. Indeed since the days of John himself, when the Kingdom had begun to be announced, it had been the failure to grasp the meaning of that Kingdom that had caused endless trouble and persecution. On this account the enemies of John had rejected him ; on this account his friends had tended to make too much of him ; both alike had failed to recognize his proper rôle, as the end of the line of prophets, as a prophet of a greater One to come, as the new Elias. His tone changed a little ; the warning note, not untinged with sadness, appears now in His words : henceforth it is destined to grow. In this strain He added to what He had already said :

> ' Yet he that is lesser in the kingdom of heaven
> Is greater than he
> And from the days of John the Baptist until now
> The kingdom of heaven suffereth violence
> And the violent bear it away
> For all the prophets and the law prophesied
> Until John
> And if you will receive it
> He is Elias that is to come
> He that hath ears to hear
> Let him hear.'

In these last words we have the first clear sign that already two camps were forming among His hearers in regard to Jesus. For a long time, even as we have seen from the beginning, the Pharisees and Scribes had been at their work. They had begun with contempt at the movement, initiated by John, continued by Jesus. At the signs of revival they had become suspicious ; later they had left John to do as he thought fit, and he had ended as Herod's victim in prison. Instead they had seen that not John but Jesus was the real enemy. In consequence they had so worked against Him in Judæa that He had transferred Himself to Galilee. Here they had had Him carefully dogged and watched ; they had pursued Him with carping questions and complaints, and every time they had received an answer, sometimes defiant, sometimes appealing, but always such as put them in the wrong. The experience had in no wise converted them, it had only galled them, till they had determined on other means by which to undermine Him. They had whispered behind His back against Him ; they had allied themselves with those who, on grounds of their own, were not likely to be His friends ; they had assumed a yet stronger attitude of contempt for one who was an outsider, for one who broke the Law, for one who mixed with low people, for one whose own manner of life was so far below their own, for one who, with all His wonder-working and His preaching, laid claim to that which no man of reason could allow. On these grounds they secured themselves in their opposition ; with arguments such as these, specious, convincing to many poor folk who knew no better, they drew around themselves not a few both high and low.

On the other side were, for the most part, the common people. More and more was it becoming apparent that

'The poor have the gospel preached to them.'

These from the first had come to Him down in Judæa. They had followed John's guidance and come to Him, more simply, more unconventionally, less critically, than had John's own more enlightened disciples. Up in Jerusalem, the only two great events of which we have record had won them to Him, the Cleansing of the Temple at the Pasch, and, on the occasion of another feast, the Healing of the Beggar at the Probatic Pool. After this last there had followed a controversy, lost on the leaders, but not forgotten by the crowd. In Capharnaum He had carried them away.

He had given them His all, He had spared Himself in nothing. He had stood aloof from the authorities, ecclesiastical, civil, and military ; He had shown Himself the Master of each and had brought them one by one to His feet. Yet with all that, instead of rising as one might have expected Him to rise, higher and higher in esteem as a leader in Israel, He had gone down lower and lower. He had made Himself the friend of publicans not Pharisees, of sinners not Scribes, of poor women not hard Sadducees, even of pagan soldiers and strangers from Tyre. Simply at first they had gone to John and all this had followed ; they had a Friend and they were satisfied.

The sharp division between these two camps S. Luke has in mind when suddenly at this point he pauses in his narrative to write the following significant sentence :

> ' And all the people hearing and the publicans
> Justified God
> Being baptized with John's baptism
> But the Pharisees and the lawyers
> Despised the counsel of God against themselves
> Being not baptized by him.'

He writes it here because it is now that Jesus gives His first warning of the dividing camps. In His own beautiful way does He show it. He has just done John the fullest honour ; while doing so He has also justified Himself, as well as the poor and the sinners who stood by Him, and who might have been shaken in their confidence by the coming of John's disciples. By it too, He has put in a class apart those superior persons who stood upon the edge of the crowd, and shrank from the contaminating touch of these vulgar people, and curled the lip in affected pity for this deluded and deluding Man who so played upon the ignorance of the mob. At the end of the street the market square opened out before them. There, a short time ago the sick had been ranged in rows, waiting for His saving blessing ; now, at a distant corner, children were playing a game that He knew. They sat in two parties, one over against the other. One side played imaginary instruments, nursery tunes which only children know, and hand on to one another through the ages ; the other side responded, in its own way, now picking up the rhythm and dancing to it, now catching a mournful wail and breaking into tears, now missing both and failing, till they grew tired and the game was at an end.

Jesus watched these children at their play. With His accustomed readiness He took for His illustration what lay before Him. The men who would not have Him, who held themselves too wise and grand for Him, what were they but mere children, sulking apart and saying that they would not play ? They would not play with John, they would not play with Him ; they thought themselves wise, but little children playing and happy in their games were wiser than they.

> ' And the Lord said
> Whereunto shall I liken
> The men of this generation ?
> And to what are they like ?
> They are like to children sitting in the market-place
> And crying to their companions one to another
> And saying
> We have piped to you
> And you have not danced
> We have lamented
> And you have not wept
> For John the Baptist came
> Neither eating bread nor drinking wine
> And you say he hath a devil
> The Son of Man is come
> Eating and drinking
> And you say Behold a man
> That is a glutton and a wine-drinker
> A friend of publicans and sinners
> And wisdom is justified by all her children
> And by her works.'

12

37. The Woman who was a Sinner

AT the southern end of the beautiful little plain of Genesareth, corresponding exactly to Bethsaida on the north, was the small but fashionable town of Magdala. Between Capharnaum to the north and Tiberias to the south it was conveniently half-way. Hence from Capharnaum and its poor labouring population it could obtain all it needed, both of provisions and of service ; from Tiberias could come the leisured classes, Romans and Jews alike, who fancied a villa by the sea. It was a gay town ; its industries were chiefly those which pandered to the rich and luxurious ; among the ordinary people of the country round about Magdala had no good name.

Anyone coming up on foot from Tiberias or the south to Capharnaum had inevitably to pass through Magdala. For between the two towns the only road clings to the side of the lake, on the other side the mountain rises almost abruptly. It is only after Magdala is reached that the route can bend inward and branch in other directions. It would therefore have often been the lot of Jesus, on His tours, to pass through this contaminated town ; indeed, being the friend of sinners, it is likely enough that He often stopped there, and was heard by not a few.

Magdala was nothing if not fashionable, and one affectation of the fashion of the day was a pretended religious broad-mindedness. However crude and primitive the fanaticism of Capharnaum and Galilee in general, however intolerant the harshness of Jerusalem, however indifferent to everything religious romanized Tiberias might be, luxurious, self-satisfied, comfortable, conscienceless Magdala possessed what is called an open mind. It was not irreligious, for that in such a city was bad form ; it was not fanatically tied to any sect, for that belonged to boorish Galilæans ; it was not exclusive, for that was narrow-minded. Though, of course, Judaism was ' the thing ', still even the Roman gods must have something in them, seeing the fine stuff their worship produced ; yes, even the Carpenter from Nazareth, about whom such an indecent stir was being made, might at least be interesting, might afford some little religious excitement. In any case, to make some show of notice of Him when He passed that way could do no harm ; it would be consistent with their tenets, it would show they were not afraid of Him, it would probably keep Him in His place, a little notice from the élite of the land might reveal His weak point. Such revivalists are usually best tested by a little notice.

Accordingly, on one occasion about this time, when it was heard that He was in the town, an invitation was sent to Him, asking Him to dine with a certain leading magnate of the place, whose name was Simon. He was a Pharisee, but, of course, had broader views than his friends in Judæa. He had heard that the countrymen up the road held Jesus for a prophet ; indeed the other day, at Naim across the valley, they had openly proclaimed Him to be one. On the other hand He was unlike other prophets ; particularly was He unlike the Baptist, who had been such an interesting figure the year before. For whereas the Baptist lived the life of a fanatic, eating nothing but the produce of the desert, this Man was known to be quite amenable to a good dinner, and did not seem to mind the kind of company He met at table. Altogether, said Simon to himself, the Man was worth meeting ; to have Him to dinner would be an interesting experience.

But, of course, it would not do to let Him give Himself airs. Though He might dine, by special invitation, with the aristocracy of Magdala, it must not be forgotten, it would be unfair on the Man to forget, that after all He was only a carpenter and, of all places, from Nazareth. He had had no education, He had lived only with country people, He was bound to be a little rough. No doubt His manners would be uncouth, that would be only what one should expect ; perhaps, suddenly finding Himself among so many of His betters, He might be a little shy, or again a little extravagant. Simon would make it as easy for Him as he could, for Simon was above all things a gentleman. He would dispense with the usual ceremonies performed in receiving guests. He would pass over the washing of the feet at the door, the formal embrace inside ; Jesus, in His degree of life, would be unaccustomed to these things and might find them awkward. Besides, there were the other guests to be considered. After all they were Simon's friends, and Jesus was no one in particular ; they were the real guests, Jesus was only a stranger. They would need to be treated with respect, to give Jesus the same attention would seem a little too extravagant.

The invitation was accepted. Jesus went to Simon's house, and was received by the host, with politeness indeed but with little ceremony. From the beginning, by Simon and the other guests, Jesus was put in His place ; by that delicate touch which only the trained worldling can cover with the suavest of manners, Jesus was made to feel the honour that was being done to Him. He came and accepted it all ; He said nothing, He seemed not to notice the condescension ; with the rest He reclined in the place allotted to Him. The meal began, conversation was made ; Jesus was spoken to and He responded, He was asked questions and He answered them. Rather ordinary, rather disappointing, rather commonplace, thought these gentry to themselves ; rather difficult to see what there was in Him that had so caught the fancy of the crowd. Simon began to be uneasy. He had hoped to give his friends an interesting evening, and the dinner was falling flat. He might have known better ; had he been wise in inviting this countryman to dine in a company where He would be so much out of His element ?

On a sudden a strange thing occurred. The dining-hall was open to the world at large ; it was not difficult for anyone who chose to gain access. Suddenly on the verandah separating the room from the street stood a woman. Her dress was brilliant, of striking colours, prominent were yellow, and red, and black ; a skirt of many folds hung about her. There were flashing rings on her fingers, golden bracelets on her bare arms, rings of silver round her ankles, about her neck a necklace of gold coins. Her hair was long, and black, and flowing ; if it had been caught up, the ribbon had fallen away. Her face was strong and commanding, firm set, powerful, handsome rather than beautiful ; it was the face of a woman born to rule, born to be great, in either good or evil. There was no smile upon the square mouth ; the steady eyes flashed, almost dangerously, as if they dared anyone to thwart her. In her hand she carried a little alabaster box, the well-known box of precious ointment. She stood in the doorway, a queen, caring nothing, it would seem, either for the distinguished guests that reclined before her, or for the servants who gathered near, but did not dare to touch her.

For a moment she stood, and searched the faces of the men at table. Simon the host? No, it was not he she wanted. She tried another and another; it was none of these. At length her eyes met those of Jesus. He did not move; alone in that room He was very quiet; but His glance was responsive, and spoke to her of one who understood. Instantly she rushed across the room. Before a hand could be raised to hinder her, while all were still struck dumb by this appalling apparition, the woman was standing at the feet of Jesus, stretched out upon the couch. Then she flung herself upon her knees; in a torrent the tears began to flow; they fell on those feet, her eager hands seized them; she spread the water of the tears over them, washing away the dust that was there. As she stooped, her mass of hair fell forward. She wrapped them in it, she wiped them with it, she pushed the hair away and kissed them. Then she seized her alabaster box, her precious alabaster box of ointment. Between her finger and thumb she crushed it; instantly the room was filled with the richest odour. She poured the ointment out, every little drop of it, upon those precious feet; again with caressing hands she spread it over them; again she kissed them; again they were lost beneath the face that lay upon them, and the hair that covered them like a veil.

All the time He reclined there and allowed it. He moved not a muscle; He let her have her way to the uttermost. Quietly He leaned against His cushion; only the face was turned towards her, and the eyes looked down upon her, and in them was a strange light. There was evident approval of all that was being done; there was gratitude; there was joy; there was pity; there was sympathy; there was friendship; there was love; yes, there was love, even for this strange woman.

For who she was could not be mistaken. She was known in Magdala; even in wicked Magdala she was notorious; had she not been known, her very dress would have proclaimed what manner of creature she was. Such a woman, so the Law declared, must not so much as be passed by in the street. Should one see her coming, then must an honest and self-respecting man step to the other side, lest he be contaminated by her mere shadow. That such a creature should intrude into such a place as this was audacity incredible ; that she should touch any man unsolicited was a crime unforgivable ; that she should single out one Man for her attentions, that she should handle Him, and play with Him, and show in His company unmixed delight, and that He should show no resentment, should permit it all, should seemingly approve it, nay, should let it appear that they knew one another, understood one another, even that there was love between them,—what a paralysing, damning discovery ! Surely the impostor had at last been unmasked ! Surely there was now no need of further evidence ! That He was known to be the friend of publicans and sinners was bad enough ; to be this creature's friend was to be beyond all hope of justification.

In this wise, when they had recovered from their first astonishment, the guests at that table argued with them-selves. They had ample time for thought ; the scene before them was protracted ; Jesus seemed to show no sign of wishing it to end. Gradually they looked at one another. They dared not utter words, but their eyes told clearly their thoughts. Horror was changing into triumph, fear into malicious joy. They had caught Him out at last ; their own contamination, in that this woman was in the room with them, was forgotten in the glory of the discovery of His greater degradation.

But there was one among them who was more thoughtful. Simon, the host, watched the scene and was frankly puzzled. That this woman's demonstrative affection betrayed any hidden secret in the life of Jesus he could not believe ; the Man and all His ways were too well known for that. But might it not betray His limitations ? Could it be that He did not know the kind of creature that was touching Him, or the consequences of this approval of her behaviour ? If that were the case, then He could not be the wonderful prophet of whom he had heard so much ; with all His reputation, one who could make so fatal a mistake could only be something very common. He did not wish to judge rashly ; he wanted to be fair ; but this was an offence against all rules and conventions, both of society and of the Law, and he knew not what to think.

> ' And the Pharisee who had invited him
> Seeing it
> Spoke within himself saying
> This man
> If he were a prophet
> Would know surely
> Who and what manner of woman this is
> That toucheth him
> That she is a sinner.'

Jesus knew what was passing through the Pharisee's mind ; had He known it no otherwise He might have read it in the look of perplexity, not unmixed with scandal, on his face. He would not leave him so. With all his treatment of Him, Simon was well-intentioned, well-disposed ; he should have the reward of that. With all his external affectation and submission to convention, in his heart he felt deeper, and pondered with less obstinate prejudice than the others ; for that he should be given further light. The woman had finished the anointing ; she could do no more. Over the feet she lay prone, blissfully content to remain there, oblivious of all else. She had not been repulsed, she knew she was welcome, this for her was enough. And Jesus all the time had kept His eyes upon her ; He too had been content.

But now the next step must be taken. He had won the sinful woman ; through the sinful woman He might win the self-righteous host. He turned His head towards him ; the authority that His companions well knew came into His eyes. He held the mastery, He spoke as a master and there was no choice but to answer ; nevertheless as He spoke were His words gentle and winning.

> ' And Jesus answering said
> Simon
> I have something to say to thee.'

The rest of the company had been ignored ; the grace was given to one, and it was accepted ; in the address there was true friendliness expressed, and Simon responded. Somehow, he told himself, there was some explanation of this mystery. He looked back at Jesus ; he welcomed the sign and replied :

' Master
Say it.'

Immediately silence reigned again throughout the room.
He was about to offer His defence for this unwarrantable
conduct, and enemies and friends leaned forward that they
might catch every word. But it was to Simon alone that
Jesus spoke. The rest might hear if they wished ; He did
not fear them ; but neither did He forget that their hearts
were stony ground. Simon was a magnate in the town ;
he dealt in money and finance ; he was a man of means as
this banquet showed, and indeed was intended to show.
He had his creditors and debtors ; some of these last, at
times, he had forgiven out of pity. Jesus knew all this ;
and here, as elsewhere, He would speak to this man in
language of his own. There was something almost disconcerting in the way He turned the subject as He began :

' A certain man had two debtors
The one owed five hundred pence
The other fifty
And whereas they had not wherewith to pay
He forgave them both
Which therefore of the two loveth him most ? '

Truly a curious question. Love introduced into a mere
business transaction ? Love between creditor and debtor ?
Love and business did not go together. Besides, what had
this to do with the matter before them ? Could it be that
Jesus was trying to turn their minds away ? Was He
shirking His difficulty ? Was He hoping to win back what
He had certainly lost in these few minutes, by a display of
His wonderful powers of persuasion ? Simon must be
cautious. He must not be led off the track. He would
answer, but there was almost resentment in his words as he
replied :

' I suppose
That he to whom he forgave most.'

Jesus took him up at once.

' Thou hast answered rightly ',

He said ; and straightway His manner altered. He had
three things to do. He must show Simon that He had been
hurt, yet must He do it with kindness. He must reinstate
the sinner before Him, yet must He allow all the painful

truth in her regard. He must defend Himself, His own sinless honour must be untarnished ; on that point there must never be the least misunderstanding. How beautifully He did all three ! His eyes turned again to the woman where she lay, with her face and hands still covering His feet. He pointed down to her ; He invited the Pharisee to look upon her. He would shirk nothing ; His tone grew more vigorous as He looked up again and said :

> ' Dost thou see this woman ?
> I entered into thy house
> Thou gavest me no water for my feet
> But she with tears
> Hath washed my feet
> And with her hairs hath wiped them
> Thou gavest me no kiss
> But she since she came in
> Hath not ceased to kiss my feet
> My head with oil thou didst not anoint
> But she with ointment
> Hath anointed my feet.'

For a moment He paused. He let His words sink in. There was no gainsaying what He had said ; in one respect at least, whatever men had against her, the poor, sinful, contemned woman at His feet had shown herself superior to His host ; before all present Simon was rebuked. And yet it was not with contempt. Jesus had been hurt, but He was not angry ; He had only told the simple truth in a simple way. Simon knew it ; he took it well ; he hung his head a little in acknowledgement. Then, seizing the moment of his sorrow, Jesus lifted him to a higher plane. The woman had surpassed him in her demonstration, yet was that as nothing in comparison with that which the demonstration implied. She had done all this because she loved Him ; sinner as she was she loved Him, more than Simon, much more than anyone there present, however righteous he might be. And because she loved more she should be more rewarded ; she should receive the true reward of love ; she should be forgiven all, she should be reinstated, she should be given love for love.

Thus for the first time at that Pharisee's table did Jesus propound His central doctrine ; the one great truth that lies at the root of all Christian ideal. Without it Christianity is dead ; with it she stands alone, and unique, and sublime in all the world ; the doctrine of the personal love of Himself, and of the restoration of all things and of all men through that love.

He paused but for a moment.   Then, a little more loudly, so that every man, friend or enemy, in that room might distinctly hear, He continued :

> ' Wherefore I say to thee
> Her many sins are forgiven her
> Because she hath loved much
> But to whom less is forgiven
> He loveth less.'

That for the moment was enough.   He had taught His lesson ; independently of miracles He had taught it, for these men were not amenable to miracles.   He had now only to act on what He had said.   He leaned forward to the woman lying at His feet.   Hitherto not a word had passed between them ; what she had done had been expression enough for her, for love finds its expression more in deeds than in words.   It was now His turn.   For Him the place and the people about Him became as nothing, He gave Himself entirely to her.   He expressed for her the fulness of her heart, which could not express itself.   He bore her sorrow, He carried her grief, with a little word He lifted from her the whole of her weary burthen.   He spoke to her gently, almost in a whisper, in a quiet, soothing whisper, yet such as in the tense silence could be distinctly heard by all :

> ' Thy sins are forgiven thee.'

They were momentous words ; no sooner were they uttered than it was as if a spell had been removed from that company.   The poor woman heard Him ; He was speaking to her.   She had not looked for this ; she did not know what she had looked for ; she only knew that somehow this Man had won her love, and winning it had taught her what love was.   She had learnt what love was, and had shown it ; nothing had been able to prevent her.   She had shown it, and He had allowed her, and she had been satisfied. She was content now to go away, back into the darkness, and to take her burthen with her ; in the memory of that ecstatic moment she would be able to carry it.   Let men say what they would, let them do what they pleased, let them treat her as an outcast as she deserved, she could now endure it.   He had let her come to His feet ; He had accepted the offer of her love ; she wanted no more, she could look for nothing in return.

But what was this ?

'Thy sins are forgiven thee ' ?

Slowly the woman raised her head.   The hands still clung about His feet ; the body still lay prone beyond them. She looked up, she shook the hanging hair from her eyes. She looked up to Him and His eyes were upon her, loving eyes, all-understanding eyes, all-powerful, all-assuring, eyes whose assurance, and strength, and forgiveness, and forgetfulness, and encouragement, and friendship, and equality, and fulness of affection could not be doubted.   She saw it all there written ; she saw more.   This Man she had loved ; now she saw that He was more than Man.   Whatever He was He was more than mere man ; she saw it, she knew it to be true, and her love leaped up to this higher level and grew the greater.   He had forgiven her her sins. He could do it.   The burthen was gone, she was another creature.   Henceforth she belonged to Him ; henceforth her one delight would be to repeat this utter joy, to fling herself at His feet.

He gave her this ecstasy.   Then with another word He recalled her back to life.   The work of that hour was done, and they must separate.   She had come in a sinner ; as the Master, the Judge, He had treated her ; now He spoke with the intimacy of friendship, and with an assurance that it would abide :

'Thy faith hath made thee safe
Go in peace.'

Instantly she rose from the ground.   It was easy now to go ; as she walked her feet scarcely seemed to touch the ground.   She saw none of those around her.   Let them shrink from her, stare in indignation at her, draw aside their robes from her as she passed ; poor things, they were only human beings and this kind of dealing was but human. While they contemned her, she could only pity them the more.   Let them have their way ; her heart was beyond it all, it had fled away to Him, and He had not treated her like that. He had taken her, He had restored her, He had made her His friend ; the rest mattered nothing at all. The woman in the city, a sinner, was the happiest woman in the world.

Meanwhile, from the rest of the company in that banquet-chamber the spell had also been lifted. They had sat there all the time in silence ; they had taken in the scene in its every detail. They had begun with horror and indignation, they had gone on to a suppressed glee at the discomfiture of this so-called prophet ; when He had spoken their satisfaction had received a check. What He had said, though it had been addressed alone to Simon, had sobered them. He had spoken of love, and even their callous hearts had been affected. He had spoken of forgiveness as the fruit of love, and that, too, coming from Him they had understood. Hardened as they were, and contemptuous, still they were not there to catch Him. Unlike the Pharisees at Capharnaum, that day when He was first heard to forgive a sinner his sins, they had not come with the set purpose to disbelieve. He had done what He had done in their presence, openly, spontaneously, not as a challenge, not in defiance. When the banquet was over and He had gone, they had much to discuss among themselves as they asked one another :

' Who is this
That forgiveth sins also ? '

It would seem, then, that sinful Magdala had received these good tidings better than the more highly favoured Capharnaum.

38. A Tour of Galilee

Jesus left Magdala and again set out on His tour. By this time the country-side had been thoroughly aroused. The reports of the miracles had gone abroad and done their work ; the words He had spoken, so unlike those to which they had been accustomed, had been passed on from mouth to mouth, and had been again and again turned over by the village sages, as they sat at evening after the day's work was done at their cottage doors. His defiance of the Pharisees and Scribes had been noticed, even while He paid them the recognition that was their due. Many remained loyal to the latter, partly from respect, partly from fear, partly from a sense, not divorced from prejudice, of loyalty to the Law, partly from the human tendency to be well with the powers that be, telling themselves that in the end they must triumph. Still there were many who were won to this new Prophet, so sincere was He, so strong and safe, so human, so eager to do good ; whose every word corresponded with His life, whose deeds were those of more than Man. They discussed Him, they looked for Him ; whenever He appeared along their country lanes they went out to meet Him. Outside of Nazareth it had already been forgotten that He was only a Nazarene ; that at least He had lived down ; instead He was welcomed as ' a prophet '.

Hence at this time His tours through the towns and villages of Galilee were very different from what they had been at the beginning. Then He had gone about more or less alone ; then He had been able, when He so chose, to slip away up the mountains or into hidden places to commune with His Father in prayer. Now He was beset on all sides ; night and day He was in the midst of people ; an inconsiderate, unthinking, boorish, self-centred, loud-mouthed people, who had not the mind to realize the utter weariness which their unceasing, importunate, noisy attentions caused. Jesus bore it all. That it was a keen trial to Him we have already had reason to see ; it was all the more keen because He knew how shallow in matter of fact it was, how soon, when the day of testing came, it would take scandal, and be disillusioned, and turn away, and walk with Him no more.

But thus the work had to be done, and thus unflinchingly He would do it. After all, though He preached to them, and gave to them all He had to give, it was not in this over-excited people that He trusted. Definitely now He had chosen another line ; He trusted in the training of the Twelve. A few days before He had set them apart from all the rest ; He had given them a model lesson in the art and subject-matter of their teaching ; He had shown them the breadth of His embrace in His award to the Roman soldier, and the value He set upon faith. At Naim He had proved to them His power over death, at Magdala His power over sin ; had there still remained a doubt in their minds as to His relations with their former master, John the Baptist, He had made that clear, too. All this He had done within the last few days, keeping them always by His side. Henceforth He would have them always with Him, He would take them along with Him from town to town, He would teach them by example how they were themselves to act, how to preach, how to handle men, how themselves to abide through it all meek and humble of heart. This in a true sense would seem to have been His chief aim in this second period of tours. The next time He would step aside, and would send these men in His name, to put into practice the lessons they had learnt.

Meanwhile, as they went on their way, He humoured them. These men, with all their limitations, were from the first devoted ; they longed to do something for Him ; and as members of a household He gave each his work to do. They had with them a little money to meet their needs should payment be ever required ; one was appointed to keep the common purse, to supply what was needed, to distribute the rest among the poor. When at evening they came to a town, a place of rest had to be found ; two or three would be chosen and sent forward, to see whether the khan was available, or whether friends were able and willing to receive them. On the road food might be needed ; it would almost seem that this was Philip's special charge. When the crowds gathered round Him, and there was danger of disorder, then all the Twelve would be at work, preserving peace and quiet, and roughly enough at times they seemed to go about it. Thus in many ways He made use of them ; thus He kept them humbly serving ; thus He trained them in obedience, even while He prepared them to become masters in Israel.

But these were not all His regular attendants ; besides the men there was a group of women. Though it may be noticed that up to this point only one miracle on a woman has been recorded, the healing of Simon's mother-in-law, still we have had beautiful proofs of the regard Jesus had for women. The miracle at Cana on a hint from His Mother, the astonishing condescension shown to the poor woman of Samaria, the miracle in Simon's house which has just been mentioned, the sympathy for the widow at Naim and the pure joy He found in comforting her, last of all, the defence He made for the sinful woman at Magdala, all these, spontaneous and sincere, proved the heart that was in Him. Now we are told that there were many more

of the kind ; many women He had healed of sicknesses,
many possessed or obsessed He had delivered ; and of
these, as was not to be wondered at, many now clung to
Him, many followed Him and served Him, looking for
opportunities to make Him some return.

Among these the first to be mentioned is

> ' Mary
> Who is called Magdalen
> Out of whom seven devils were gone forth.'

Who was Mary Magdalen ? This is no place for controversy ; we are painting a picture and no more. We will only
say here that we are unconvinced by all the arguments which
seek to destroy the popular tradition of the Church. Their
strength lies in ignoring the singular consistency of character
and action, the singular sameness of devotion and demonstration and almost reckless love which marks one woman from
the day we meet her at the feet of Jesus in Magdala to the day
we leave her at the same feet after the Resurrection. The
letter may be turned against her, the spirit of the Gospel
story seems to read entirely in her favour ; and S. Luke
who characteristically in the scene of her humiliation
declines to give her name, calls her only ' a woman in the
city, a sinner ', now immediately after, when she is installed
as the leader of the penitent women who followed Jesus and
served Him, delights to give her her full title, Mary Magdalen. We shall meet her again, and often ; perhaps when
we have met her more often we shall know her better.

Along with Mary Magdalen, two other women are here
given special mention. One is

> ' Joanna
> The wife of Chusa
> Herod's steward ' ;

the other is just

> ' Susanna ',

and of her we are told no more. Of Joanna we hear again
after the Resurrection ; she was one of the group of women
to whom Jesus first appeared, and who first announced to
the frightened disciples the fact of the empty tomb. But
these two facts alone tell us something. Joanna, Susanna,
and others were women of means and position. In one way
or another all had felt their indebtedness to Jesus ; some
had been cured of bodily infirmities, others had been

relieved of intolerable slaveries of the soul. Their upbringing had undermined their moral character ; their circumstances, particularly in and about the court of Herod, had depraved them ; their lives had been such as to kill all hope of peace within them ; and somewhere He had passed by, and had looked upon them, and had invited them, and they had believed in Him, and loved Him, and hope had revived, and delivery had come, and courage, and the joy and peace and devotedness which only He could give. No wonder they had now gone after Him, craving to put at His service themselves and all they possessed ; no wonder when they came together they formed themselves into a community

> ' Who ministered unto him
>   Of their substance.'

The spirit which drew them together for His service was the same as that which has drawn women together in millions through the ages ; in them, accepting their service along those Galilæan lanes, Jesus accepted and approved the women religious of the world.

39. The Charge of Beelzebub

To one who would discover the character of Jesus Christ as it revealed itself on earth nothing is more disconcerting than the matter-of-fact way the Evangelists handle the most solemn events ; and all the more since it is clear that by so doing they are only being true to their subject, giving a true picture of the matter-of-fact way Jesus was handled by the people about Him. With all His greatness and proof of power He remained always one of them ; however moved they were by Him, they could never for long treat Him as one apart. Though from the very beginning He never concealed His claim to be the Messias, and first insinuated, then urged, and finally convinced those who saw the truth that He was much more, still did He abide among them as the Man from Nazareth, their equal ; and they accepted Him as such. His miracles did not seem to give Him special distinction ; His teaching, the most sublime that had ever issued from the mouth of man, did not set Him on a pedestal. His life and the manner of it, with its prayer, its independence, its absolute perfection in every single detail, only seemed to make Him all the more familiar to them all.

Not only is this disconcerting ; it baffles every attempt

to circumscribe Him. We try to draw Him apart, we study Him alone, we catch at certain traits which we discover in Him, we look again that we may mark the lines more deeply, and behold when we look we find He has slipped away and is lost in the crowd. We search for Him there ; we try to distinguish Him from others ; and while again we note distinguishing features, we find His chief distinction lies in His likeness to all about Him. He is a kindred soul, not only to this one or to that, as is the case with every other human being, the necessary consequence of our limited nature, but with each and every man or woman that comes near Him. Among all those motley gatherings in Galilee there was not a person of goodwill but felt, as soon as he came in contact with Him, that here was a man like himself ; here was one who thought like him, who saw things as he saw them, who had like ambitions, like sufferings, like consolations. Here was one who was an equal in His heart, whatever the mob might make of Him. It was easier with such a one to be familiar than to do Him honour, to talk with Him than to praise Him, to be so contented in His company that one almost forgot He was there than to concentrate all one's thoughts upon Him.

And yet precisely this, however impossible to describe, or rather because impossible to describe, is the one distinguishing feature in the character of Jesus. It was His universality ; the understanding, the sympathy, the strength, which made Him able to enter the soul and heart of everyone who came near Him, and which made every soul know, if it chose to-know, that here was one on whom it could utterly rely, who would not misjudge, would not be prejudiced, would not be weary of listening, would not grow impatient with those who tried and failed, would not show sham sympathy, would not fail in trouble, would not take advantage either of His own power or of the poor soul's weakness, would not promise what He could not do. Here was one who rang true from top to bottom, who made every possible allowance for shortcomings, who saw all sides and gave them all full credit, who listened because He was interested, with His heart as well as with His ear, whose patience was infinite because it was sincere and selfless, whose sympathy was spontaneous and genuine, whose support was strong and reliable, whose word was safe.

All this each man discovered for himself, as soon as he

came within His atmosphere. Each man knew it, every man knew it, there was a personal contact with each and all. Crowds as such meant nothing to Jesus ; He took men one by one, individually He built them up, in mutual understanding, mutual confidence, mutual friendship, mutual love, mutual support, mutual giving to each other, sharing with each other all that they possessed, lifting up each other to the full height of their desires, mutual perfection in their union. However great the distance between Him and every other man, there was always with each one that came to Him this feeling as of equality which enabled one and all to leap the chasm.

This is no fanciful or exaggerated picture ; it is no *a priori* judgement that so it must have been. When we watch Him with individuals, or rather when we watch individuals with Him, the almost appalling truth is forced upon us. When we stand outside a crowd, in whose midst He is overwhelmed, and see for ourselves how He is treated, how every man speaks to Him as if He were His own special intimate, how familiarity leads almost to neglect, how He is pushed to and fro as any other, how His solemn greatness, His wonder-working, His power over devils, His command of death itself, His forgiving of sins, His claim of equality with God, are almost forgotten, are ignored, though not denied, in the happy, easy equality that exists between them and the Man from Nazareth ; when we find this illustrated at all times, under all conditions, with every class of people, from the beginning to the end ; in spite of ourselves we are compelled to acknowledge it, the veriest unbeliever must acknowledge it. In an effort to define Him we are driven to declare Him undefinable. And He is undefinable because He is so much like everybody else, every man, each man, all men, including you and me. Because His heart is so akin to every other, is so all-inclusive, is so easily understood by each and all, therefore we know Him, and yet therefore we cannot describe Him. Jesus Christ ! We know what we mean when we use the name, and look up at Him, and love Him, and long for we know not what ; but to say what we mean by the name is beyond the speech of man.

Baffling reflexions such as these crowd upon us when we come to scenes like that now before us. From the whole story it would seem that Jesus had come again into

Capharnaum.   His tour was over and He was returning
home.   Thereupon we are told :

> ' And they came to a house
> And the multitude cometh together again
> So that they could not so much as eat bread
> And when his friends had heard of it
> They went out to lay hold on him
> For they said
> He is become mad.'

What a sudden anti-climax !   In the last few days He
had filled them with admiration by the Sermon on the
Mount, with wonder by healing the servant at a distance,
with fear by commanding death, with awe by forgiving
sins ;   yet when He returned again into Capharnaum here
they were, pressing on Him more than ever, treating Him
with scant respect.   He might have been no more than
some winner in a contest of whom they were proud as
coming from themselves ;   in their boisterous applause
forgetting that even He needed at times to eat and drink.
And on the other side those who knew Him better, who now
were always with Him, ' His friends ' as they are expressly
called, forget the wisest and deepest of preachers, forget the
worker of miracles, forget Him who saw beyond death,
forget the Forgiver of sins, see before them only a Man
at the mercy of the crowd, apparently unable to help
Himself among them, nay, so weak and foolish as to yield
to them, needing to be rescued, to be saved from His own
folly, to be supplied by them with common sense !

> ' And when his friends had heard of it
> They went out to lay hold on him
> For they said
> He is become mad.'

Verily an anti-climax such as no man could have invented·
And yet how bafflingly true to life, how consistent with
everything else we know of this universal Jesus Christ, at
once the highest and the lowest, the strongest and the
weakest, the greatest and the least, the Master and the
servant, the Ruler and the subject, the commanding Lord
and the utterly self-effacing Lover.

Immediately after this we are brought up against another
striking contrast.   Jesus was rescued by ' His friends ' from
the crowd.   He was brought into a house, some humble

cottage in the street open to all the passers-by ; there He was given food and drink. While He rested there some had remembered a sorry case among them, a man blind and dumb, who was also possessed. They hunted out this man ; they seized him and dragged him to the house where Jesus was at meat. The whole story is told by the Evangelist in a single sentence :

' Then was offered to him
One possessed with a devil
Blind and dumb
And he healed him
So that he spoke and saw.'

Though we have heard of other cures of the kind in general, given to us along with other summaries of miracles, still this is only the second described apart and in detail. But in the telling what a difference ! The first had been at the door of the synagogue, that Sabbath day when Jesus had formally begun His career of wonder-working. On that day

' They talked
And questioned among themselves
Saying : What thing is this ?
What is this new doctrine ?
What word is this ?
For with authority and power
He commandeth even the unclean spirits
And they obey him
And go out
And the fame of him was spread and published forthwith
Into every place of the country of Galilee.'

Here all is changed, almost to the very opposite. The people do not fear, they are not amazed ; what happens is only what they have expected. The healing is performed with no dramatic circumstances ; it is done as if it were an ordinary, an everyday affair. Truly there had come a marked change ; in their outward bearing at least the multitude had already travelled very far.

But not in their outward bearing only. The Evangelist, S. Matthew, has recorded this event, though so like many another, and in itself in no way remarkable, to show to us how in two different directions the thoughts of men had been growing. On the one hand were those who had been making steps towards His discovery ; on the other was the enemy, hardening itself the more to every appeal, and finding fresh arguments with which to reject every further and more compelling piece of evidence. The first miracle, at the door of the synagogue some months before, had drawn from the people the question

> ' What thing is this ?
> What is this new doctrine ?
> What word is this ? '

Now they looked yet further. They looked from the prophet to the king. They were hoping for the kingdom that was to restore all things to Israel ; the kingdom was to be restored by one who in some sense would be a Son of David. This Man was Master of men ; this Man spoke as one with authority of His own. He made His own law ; by His deeds He proved that He came from God ; He commanded sin, He commanded devils. Might He not then be the One chosen to lead them to command the world ?

> ' And all the multitudes were amazed
> And said
> Is not this the Son of David ? '

In this way they pushed a little further the question they had asked themselves before.

But while Jesus left them to question as they would, there was another group whom He would not leave alone. We have already seen the enmity of the Pharisees growing ; they were the accepted guides and leaders of the people, therefore for the people's sake their false arguments should be denounced. By the Jordan ford they had begun, first with their suspicions, then with their condescending patronage of John the Baptist ; at the notorious scene in the Temple they had their first ground of attack by demanding the authority of Jesus and its proofs. By their wiles and schemes they had driven Him out of Judæa ; when He had returned, and had cured a well-known beggar in their very streets, they had begun the counter-attack against the obvious argument of His miracles. To keep an eye upon Him they had thence pursued Him into Galilee. They had denounced Him for breaking the Sabbath ; they had whispered against Him as a blasphemer in that He claimed to forgive sins ; they had affected righteous horror because He dined with publicans and sinners, and in addition had

declared Him a glutton and a drunkard. Sabbath after
Sabbath they had dogged His steps, and had lost no excuse
to prove Him a breaker of the Law. They had gone so far,
here in Galilee, as to plot to take His life, and for this had
demeaned themselves so as to ally themselves with men
whom they contemned. They had made even Capharnaum
no safe abode for Him, so that more and more He was
compelled to seek other resting places. Now they were
following Him more closely, watching Him, interpreting
His every word and deed according to their own desires,
by any argument that might serve their purpose counter-
acting His influence on the simple, ignorant, enthusiastic,
yet fickle and fearing multitude.

These men were here on this day. On the edge of the
crowd they stood about, some of them all the way from
Judæa, superior, contemptuous, not to be deceived, having
explanations always ready to explain this mountebank's
tricks. They saw the miracle that had just been performed
before their eyes. This time the Sabbath argument would
not serve. Besides, the miracle itself was more than an
ordinary case of healing ; supernatural in effect it must be
supernatural in its cause. But there were two supernatural
causes, the one good, the other evil. Now this Man, being
a trickster, could have no good cause behind Him. He was
a breaker of the Sabbath and could not be countenanced
by God. Above all He was their rival, and therefore at any
cost He must be crushed. The conclusion was obvious ;
He had no power from God, then He had it from the devil.
They turned away in dudgeon ; they discussed what they
had seen among themselves ; in low, inconsequent terms,
but carefully loud enough for the poor, credulous folk about
to hear, they murmured :

> ' This man hath Beelzebub
> And casteth out devils
> By the power of devils.'

It was not hard to let Jesus discover their murmurings ;
they intended that He should. In a mob such as was this
about the door there are never wanting those who would
appear more clever than the speaker, and who would show
their wit by posing a problem. This insinuation of the
Pharisees was too good to be lost ; it was not long before
it trickled through the crowd to His door. Then at once

the face of Jesus changed. Promptly He took action ; He would scotch such a serpent on its first appearance ; in this company at least the poison should have its antidote. He sent for the Pharisees to come to Him ; the call was of the nature of a challenge. Should they refuse, the refusal would convict them of fear, perhaps of deceit and insincerity ; they had no choice but to obey.

When they had come, then followed a solemn address, the most solemn that He had yet uttered, a new thing in His preaching. It was the first of those great and tremendous warnings which were henceforth to be common, and which would gather force and point as time went on. Let us take it without comment, watching the face, and hearing the beat of the heart of Jesus during this movement of high indignation. Somehow it is quite unlike anything we have seen or heard before, even in the moment of anger on that Sabbath day when He healed the man with the withered arm. For His face is not only aroused, it threatens. The warning is to a definite enemy that has determined never to be reconciled. To that enemy He lays down a line of demarcation, a step beyond which leaves no hope of recovery. He tells them, if they have ears to hear, that by the wicked charge they have made they have already put themselves beyond that line. Let them remain there and they are doomed.

'And Jesus, knowing their thoughts, after he had called them together, said to them in parables : How can Satan cast out Satan ? And if a kingdom be divided against itself, that kingdom cannot stand ; it shall be brought to desolation, and house upon house shall fall. And if a city or a house be divided against itself, it shall not stand ; and if Satan be risen up against himself and cast out Satan, he is divided against himself ; how then shall his kingdom stand ? It cannot stand, but hath an end. Because you say that through Beelzebub I cast out devils. Now if I cast out devils by Beelzebub, by whom do your children cast them out ? Therefore they shall be your judges. And if I by the spirit and finger of God cast out devils, doubtless the kingdom of God is come upon you.

' When a strong man armed keepeth his court, those things are in peace which he possesseth ; but if a stronger than he come upon him and overcome him, he will take away all his armour wherein he trusted, and will distribute his spoils. Or how can anyone enter into the house of a strong man and rifle his goods, unless he first bind the strong man? and then he will rifle his house. He that is not with me is against me ; and he that gathereth not with me scattereth.

'Therefore Amen I say to you, that all sins shall be forgiven unto the sons of men, and the blasphemies wherewith they shall blaspheme ; and whosoever shall speak a word against the Son of Man, it shall be forgiven him ; but he that shall blaspheme against the Holy Spirit, shall never have forgiveness, neither in this world nor in the world to come, but shall be guilty of an everlasting sin. (Because they said : He hath an unclean spirit.) O generation of vipers, how can you speak good things whereas you are evil ? for out of the abundance of the heart the mouth speaketh. A good man out of a good treasure bringeth forth good things ; and an evil man out of an evil treasure bringeth forth evil things. But I say unto you that every idle word that men shall speak, they shall render an account for it in the day of judgement ; for by thy words thou shalt be justified, and by thy words thou shalt be condemned.

'When the unclean spirit is gone out of a man, he walketh through dry places without water, seeking rest ; and findeth none ; then he saith : I will return into my house whence I came out ; and coming he findeth it empty, swept and garnished. Then he goeth and taketh with him seven other spirits more wicked than himself, and they enter in and dwell there ; and the last state of that man is made worse than the first. So shall it be with this wicked generation.'

We may leave to others more learned the exact significance of this denunciation. Let it be enough here to point out the signs it gives of the depth to which the heart of Jesus had been hurt. All this time He had been preaching and proving His Kingdom, by noble words and good deeds ; He was hurt to see it made one with the kingdom of Satan, His words ignored, His deeds distorted. He had shown this supreme act of power in the forgiving of sins, in the casting out of devils ; He was hurt to find Himself denounced, on this very account, as a blasphemer, and as being Himself possessed. He was hurt to have been rejected as the Son of Man ; but when the Spirit of God was despised He was indignant. The first He would endure, this last He would not ; in His defence of Himself He would still be content to continue to appeal, but for the last His wrath was eloquent to terror.

For the moment the Pharisees were silenced; their charge being so groundless, clearly when challenged they had no more to say. But on that very account were they only the more enraged against Him; evil, convicted of evil, is seldom reconciled. The people stood about, equally silenced, for never had the Master spoken with such vehemence. Many were there who feared for the consequences. It was the beginning of the parting of the ways, and they themselves must soon decide one way or the other.

But there were others in the crowd on whom thoughts such as these had little effect. These were the poor, the simple, the outcast, those for whom, as He had more than once plainly said, He had specially come; more spontaneous, less sophisticated, who were content with the truth as it came from Him, and did not look for subtle explanations. For such as these a single poor woman spoke; a brave witness in a trying hour. She stood there in the crowd, listening and looking. What He said she did not understand, nor had she any wish to do so; what she saw was enough. It was the Man Himself that held her; the certainty within Him, the authority without, the admirable bravery, the truth, the sincerity, the utter goodness; whatever He said, however much those learned men might be against Him, what a Son was this of whom any mother might be proud! Her mother's soul went dreaming backward to His childhood; from the childhood it wandered to the Mother. Such a Son, such a Mother, what a Mother she must have been! How many souls have reached the Mother in precisely the same way!

She could contain herself no longer. In the silence that followed the rebuke bestowed upon the Pharisees, scarcely reflecting upon what she said, regardless of all around her, as a woman will when deeply moved, she gave vent to her emotion and her heart:

> ' And it came to pass as he spoke these things
> A certain woman from the crowd
> Lifting up her voice said to him
> Blessed is the womb that bore thee
> And the breasts that gave thee suck.'

He heard her, everybody heard her; and a new vein of

thought was started in the minds of all, a vein which has never been exhausted.

> ' He hath regarded the lowliness
> Of his handmaid
> For behold from henceforth
> All generations shall call me blessed.'
> ' Hail full of grace
> The Lord is with thee
> Blessed art thou among women
> And blessed is the fruit of thy womb.'

That poor woman, in her simplicity, had discovered what the angel and Elizabeth had known and declared ; to discover that went far to the discovery of Himself, and that was eternal life. Still He would not acknowledge His gladness too much. His Mother's day would come ; for the present she too, like other men and women, was passing through her time of probation. Let her remain for the time in her humility, the handmaid of the Lord and no more, the little lowly woman whom people thought they knew. Let her continue saying :

> ' Be it done to me
> According to thy word.'

Meanwhile He would honour her in His own hidden way, which His hearers then would not recognize, but which we can recognize to-day. He would take that very offering of Mary and make it glorious.

> ' But he said
> Yea rather
> Blessed are they that hear the word of God
> And keep it.'

But this was only an interlude in the tragedy of that day. The Pharisees had been silenced in their insinuation ; with Asiatic subtlety they would change their front. Clearly the people for the moment were inclined towards Him ; they must keep them on their side. To abuse Jesus was useless ; it would not be useless to affect the manner of an enquirer. On another occasion, to the messengers from John, He had given miracles in proof that He was the Messias. But what were miracles to them ? To begin with were they genuine ? They had shown reason to suspect ; but even if they were, what did they prove ? Other men had worked miracles ;

this very day had Jesus appealed to the miracles worked
by their own fellow-men. That was a point to be secured ;
let them but undermine the faith that arose from the
miracles, and half the battle for the keeping of the people
would be won. Therefore they would ignore them ; they
would remind Him that, to educated men, miracles could
be no argument. They needed a deeper sign, more supernatural, more convincing ; He would not be able to deny
their demand, yet how would He be able to answer it ?

> ' Then some of the Scribes and Pharisees
> Answered him saying
> Master
> We would see a sign from heaven.'

Even as they drew themselves up for this challenge, the
people about them saw that something unusual was toward.
They gathered the closer together, curious ; such a dispute
was likely to be interesting ; so low for their sakes did Jesus
suffer Himself to be humbled. He let them come about
Him ; He gave them a full answer ; once more He gave
it in the language of those who asked Him, that of the Old
Testament. Nay He did more. They asked for a sign ;
He would give it to them, and that in a manner worthy of
Himself. They would not accept it ; neither now when
it was promised, nor later when it was fulfilled. Again in
their own language, in the language of the Scripture, He
would warn them of the doom that awaited them, of the
condemnation they would incur from the very pagans, who
in all their darkness had been more faithful than they to the
voice of God.

> ' And the multitudes running together
> He answering began to say
> This generation is a wicked generation
> An evil and adulterous generation
> Seeketh a sign
> And a sign shall not be given it
> But the sign of Jonas the prophet
> For as Jonas was a sign to the Ninivites
> So shall the Son of Man be
> To this generation
> As Jonas was in the whale's belly
> Three days and three nights
> So shall the Son of Man be

In the heart of the earth
Three days and three nights
The men of Ninive
Shall rise in judgement with this generation
And shall condemn it
Because they did penance
At the preaching of Jonas
And behold a greater than Jonas is here
The queen of the south
Shall rise in judgement
With the men of this generation
And shall condemn them
Because she came from the ends of the earth
To hear the wisdom of Solomon
And behold a greater than Solomon is here.'

40. The Coming of His Mother and Brethren

IT had been another heavy day, and it had thus far gone strangely. The dawn, when He came into the town, had been hopeful; with all their roughness towards Him the people had shown goodwill. The midday, too, had been bright; after His meal they had brought Him a miserable creature to be healed. But now, with this last interview the clouds had gathered; and a storm threatened as it had never threatened before. Never before had His enemies insulted Him so to His face as they had insulted Him to-day; never before had He answered them with such unflinching vehemence. He had said there was a sin which should never be forgiven; it was certain that on their side they would never forgive Him. The people looked at the rivals; there was war more emphatically declared than it had ever been declared before; no one who had a care for the human welfare of Jesus could fail to be anxious for Him.

We have seen how, late in the morning, His 'friends' had been compelled to rescue Him from the crowd, simply that He might be able to take His necessary food. Not far away were other friends, who were no less anxious than they; and among them one in particular. During all these months, since the day when Jesus first made His home in Capharnaum and took His Mother with Him, we have heard no word about her; now on a sudden we discover that she had been within hearing all the time. In Capharnaum it would seem that He had lived with Simon and the Twelve; but we now have evidence enough that she had been well cared for, nay more, that she had always been within reach. There were His relatives, especially the women. These same women we find later united with those others of whom mention has already been made, those who accompanied Him where He went and served Him. In the hands of these, when the final day of trial came, we find His Mother, and that in such a way as to imply that they had long been intimate. Then we may well understand with whom she dwelt in Capharnaum. No ; Mary had not been deserted. He had left her because He had to ' be about His Father's business ', but He had been very far from deserting her. And she understood, better than when He first seemed to leave her, even though still she ' kept all these things, pondering them in her heart '.

Now on a sudden, and for only a moment, she reappears on the scene. Can we guess its meaning and significance ? For weeks past the mere presence of Jesus in Capharnaum could not but have been to the Mother matter for constant anxiety. Let the evidence of fact guide us, and let our human sympathy have its way, and perhaps we may be able to read that Mother's heart. From the first she had known that her Son was born to trouble. She had not forgotten the sojourn in Egypt and the cause that had brought it about ; she could never forget that her Son's life had been saved only at the price of a deluge of infant blood. She had stored in her heart and had often pondered the words of the old man who had held her Child in the Temple :

' Behold this child is set
For the ruin and for the resurrection
Of many in Israel
And for a sign
That shall be contradicted
And thy own soul a sword shall pierce
That out of many hearts thoughts may be revealed.'

This had told her clearly, what the prophets, she knew, had long since foreshadowed, that her Son was indeed the Saviour, but that many would be His enemies ; nay, in the end would seem to conquer Him in their opposition.

So she had gone through the years, her Mother's heart never forgetting ; the shadow of the Cross, the background of doom, never wholly out of sight. The memory of this had added to her agony, that day when she had lost Him, at the age of twelve, in the Temple at the paschal season. When, at the age of thirty, He left her, and made His way alone to Judæa, she wondered whether then the dreaded day was at hand ; when He returned, and His own citizens of Nazareth rejected Him, and sought to take His life, we have seen how she was beside herself with fear. Since that time she had heard anxious stories ; above all the way He had been treated in Jerusalem whenever He had shown Himself there.

And now here in Capharnaum she had watched the tide ominously rising. True, on one side there was the enthusiasm of the people, but like Him she knew how little it was to be trusted. On the other hand was the growing opposition of the powerful Pharisees and Scribes, strengthening itself with recruits even from far-off Judæa, allying itself with the Herodians who, when it suited their purpose, like their master would stop at nothing. John the Baptist had fallen, and his doom was hanging now over his head ; she knew her Son had been already sentenced to follow when opportunity occurred. She had watched His hold upon the little town growing more precarious ; she had seen Him compelled to leave it for His own safety.

With all this in mind we are not surprised to find that when again He returned to the neighbourhood His Mother was soon within sight. She had come near with the rest ; in some cottage close by she had settled down and watched. Relatives and friends were with her, and as the day advanced they brought her the tidings. Jesus had come in the morning, and a multitude had come with Him ; others had joined these from round about, and in the crowds her Son had been almost overwhelmed. 'Friends' had rescued Him—this time He had not chosen to rescue Himself—had dragged Him into a house that He might rest, but here again He had been besieged. There He had healed a man possessed, but that had only led to further trouble. The enemy had begun to call Him evil names, attributed to Him all sorts of evil powers ; were whispering their wickedness among the fickle people. Who could tell where it might end ? The heart of the Mother trembled for her Boy, so worn He must be, so needing rest, so at the mercy of the mob which, as had happened at Nazareth, might at any moment turn on Him and rend Him, so utterly defenceless against the enemy, which had long since determined to have His life.

The Mother could endure the strain no longer. She must go and see for herself. She must see Him, and speak to Him, and give Him her Mother's love and sympathy. She must endeavour to persuade Him to rest awhile, to come away with her and be comforted. Once before He had listened to her, when she pleaded for a bride and bride-groom ; perhaps He would listen again to her now, when she pleaded for Himself.

The little party left the cottage and made for the spot where the crowd had gathered. But what were they to do then ? The throng was thick and closely packed ; around the doorway wherein Jesus sat the people had sat down likewise, as if they meant to stay. Beyond these again rows of standing men encircled Him like a wall.

'And as he was yet speaking to the multitudes
Behold his mother and his brethren came unto him
And they could not come at him for the crowd.'

Could not a message be sent through ? They must try. One of her companions drew the attention of a man in the crowd to the little trembling woman behind him. He told him who she was, told him what she wanted, asked him to have the word passed on. And the man did as he was asked. He looked at the simple widow. Perhaps he had been at Naim a few days before. On that day Jesus had restored a boy to life to comfort a lonely widow's heart ; surely He would restore Himself to her to comfort His lonely widow Mother. So the word went through the crowd ; it is a joy to know that so much sympathy Mary could command. The word went through and reached at last the men who were seated on the ground about the feet of Jesus. There was a pause in the discourse. The Pharisees who had come there to judgement had heard His rebuke and were not prepared to answer ; they had pleaded for further evidence, and in the spirit in which they asked for it it had been given them. The silence that followed was favourable ; one of those sitting there ventured to speak.

'Behold ', he said,
'Thy mother and thy brethren stand without
Seeking thee
Desiring to see thee.'

As soon as the words were uttered Jesus stood erect ; one might have supposed that He was about to make His way through the crowd and go to her. But not yet. Let us here notice another of the striking characteristics of Jesus, another of those baffling combinations of opposites of which we have already spoken. From this time it becomes more common, because the occasions become more frequent, until the climax is reached at the Last Supper and on Calvary. It is the close proximity of His anger and His love ; the way His wrath, when compelled to vent itself in threats, draws from Him yet more keen expressions of affection. When He is most indignant and hurt, then promptly after He is most loving ; when He has been driven to speak with greatest vehemence, then does He most easily react to the most childlike tenderness ; when He feels Himself most at bay, then is He most ready to smile on any who will stand by Him. From this time, when the opposition has definitely begun to take the field against Him, instances of this we shall find multiplied.

So it was on this occasion. Never before, in all their intercourse with Him, had the Twelve heard Jesus speak with such severity, such condemnation in His tone, as He had spoken to-day ; never before had He gone so far as to call His enemies to their faces :

' Ye generation of vipers.'

He had ended, moreover, on a harsh note, as though the very harmony of His life had been broken. The crowd around Him sat in awe ; the disciples by His side trembled at His vehemence. Could this portend that in time they too would be rejected ?

' Because they said
He hath an unclean spirit.'
' He that shall blaspheme against the Holy Spirit
Shall never have forgiveness
Neither in this world
Nor in the world to come
And shall be guilty of an everlasting sin.'

This was indeed new and terrible. Had His love been tried to the uttermost at last ?

Tried to the uttermost ? Jesus stood up among them. The message from His Mother was a joy ; on one heart at least in this world He could always safely rely. But there were others, too, in whom He trusted ; on them as well in time, after He had trained them, He would be able to depend. He loved them already ; He would love them more yet ; He would show them that He loved them. The Mother's word had won Him before, when His hour had not yet come ; so, now, the tone of wrath was softened to the opposite extreme at her message, as, standing there, He replied :

> ' Who is my mother ?
> And who are my brethren ? '

Then He looked around Him. The Pharisees and Scribes were dismissed from His mind ; for the present His business with them had been done with. Instead, the eyes were the same as those which had looked on the multitude on the mountain. The fire of wrath had gone out of them, the fire of compassion was restored ; it was the same Jesus once more. He looked round on them all ; those eyes rested last on the group of men close beside Him, His disciples, His own, His very own. His arm stretched out to them, as if it would draw them to Him ; it was a gesture that showed He claimed them. Then with a full voice, coming from a full heart, stirring emotion even to tears, He cried out :

> ' Behold my mother and my brethren
> For whosoever shall hear the word of God
> And do it
> Whosoever shall do the will of my Father
> Who is in heaven
> He is my brother
> And my sister
> And my mother.'

Here the Evangelists abruptly end their narrative. We long to know what happened next ; above all because there are those who would see in these last words some kind of slight of the Mother from the Son. The insinuation, be it noticed, does not injure her ; it injures Him. Effectually He has protected her. But ' are we without understanding ? ' Of one thing we are certain ; what for Himself He would not do, He did at the call of His Mother. The crowd which all that day had been thronging about Him, refusing to go away, now began to disperse ; in the evening of that same day we find it again, gathered in another place by the water's edge.

And this is only consistent with everything else we know. At the age of twelve He left her for a time ; when again they came together He merely said :

> ' Did you not know
> That I must be about my Father's business ? '

Yet He went down with her, and lived with her, and was subject to her, for eighteen long years after ; surely a sufficient interpretation of His words. At the marriage feast of Cana, when she spoke to Him, He said :

> ' Woman
> What is that to me and to thee ?
> My hour is not yet come.'

Had He stopped there we might have wondered. But He did not. At her request, and at her request only, He anticipated that hour, and there and then converted water into wine. When He started on His public career He left her, yet we are carefully and expressly told that He took her with Him to Capharnaum. And at the end of all, when He hung upon the Cross, and she again came

> ' Seeking him
> Desiring to see him ',

even with His last breath He was careful to provide her with a home and a friend ; the friend of His own bosom, one whom she could love as her own son, and who would love her in return as a Mother. If, then, on this occasion, Mary had presumed too much, if He had in any way wished to slight her, it would be strange indeed ; unlike Him, unlike everything else that we know of them.

Nor is that all ; the very strength of the words of Jesus is their defence. For in no way did they bring the Mother down, they only lifted the disciples up, as far as possible, to her level. ' I love you as I love my Mother ', is surely no disparagement to the Mother ; the Mother would have heard the words and, sure of His love, would have been glad to know that His love for her was set up as the standard of His love for others. Not only that ; He had given as the pledge of that love the way she herself had expressed it.

> ' Whosoever shall hear the word of God
> And keep it ' ;
> ' Behold the handmaid of the Lord
> Be it done to me according to thy word.'

The one is an echo and a confirmation of the other.

And on the other side the disciples were gladdened. They knew the love that existed between these two ; had it not been there, what could these words have meant ? Even had they not known it, this at least they knew ; their

Master could never have done to His Mother before all the world what it would have shamed any man who had any self-respect to do.

Jesus heard that Mother's appeal, as He had always heard her. He rose to go. He bade His disciples a temporary farewell, in words that came pouring from a heart that loved. He passed through the crowd ; His authority had again come upon Him and it had to yield. As He met the widow of Naim, so He met His Mother. He went down with her to her cottage, and there they were left alone ; when the evening came He sallied forth again to do His Father's work. Surely this is evidence enough of all she was to Him, and He to her.

41. The Beginning of Parables

It had been a heavy and a weary day, but it was by no means over. For a short time, it could not have been for long, He was permitted to stay with His Mother ; then, as it drew on to evening, He was out again to labour.

> ' The same day
> Jesus going out from the house
> Sat by the sea.'

For this was a momentous day, another of the landmarks on His route. It was the day on which the two camps had come to open battle, it should also be the day on which He would alter His whole method of campaign. Hitherto He had spoken plainly for everyone to hear ; henceforth He would speak more darkly ; clearly enough for those to understand who had goodwill and would hear, less clearly for those who would not. The camps were opposed ; in time the multitude would divide, to the one side or to the other. Let it be so ; He would compel none. Those who came to Him should come of their own free will ; for the rest, to teach them in such a way that they would not always understand was the greatest charity.

He left the cottage where His Mother stayed, and went down the narrow street to the water's edge ; one might have supposed that He was seeking a moment's quiet before sunset. But the people were on the watch. No sooner did He appear than they began again to gather round Him. During the day men had come in from other towns and villages, and the assembly was greater than it had been in the morning. By the side of the lake they pressed about Him, even more than they had done earlier in the day. Being near the water there was danger for many, owing to the noise, and jostling, and confusion ; under these conditions He could not speak. A boat was lying off the shore. Down in Bethsaida, some weeks before, on a similar occasion, He had made use of Simon's boat as a pulpit and the device had succeeded. He would do the same again. He had the boat brought round ; He stepped in ; and there, with a tiny strip of water between Him and the shore lapping the sides of the vessel, as the evening breeze began to freshen, He set about His new method of instruction. The multitude stood or sat upon the steeply sloping beach. Being apart in the boat He was visible to all ; it was easier now to order silence.

Jesus sat down in the boat and looked towards the land. The multitude was in the foreground before Him ; up the hill beyond, the crops were waving under the evening breeze, making the hill-side green and beautiful, with promise of a rich harvest soon to be ripe. But it was not all evenly green, as might have been a meadow on the plain. There were footpaths through the corn, leading from one village to another, broad enough even for donkeys and camels to march in single file ; footpaths not marked by any fixed boundary, but trampled into shape as occasion needed. Along these paths, even as they looked, men could be seen coming down the hill to the town, examining the crops as they came. Here and there among the fields, especially along the lower reaches, were crags and boulders, the bare rocky faces of the mountain-side, peering grey and white through the surrounding green ; in the crannies and narrow spaces between these, little yellow patches of corn, prematurely ripe. In the deeper hollows below, where the water trickled down among the rocks and made the ground sodden, there was growth of darker green, brambles and broad-leaved underwood appropriating all the soil.

As was usual with Him, Jesus took in the scene that rose up before Him, the people gathered on the shore, the hill with its richness and poverty rising up behind ; for His purposes it was enough. And now He would make use of it in a new way. Hitherto He had taken the sights and materials about Him to illustrate what He had to teach ;

now He would reverse the process. Henceforth men must discover for themselves the meaning of His words. It was indeed a complete transformation ; as they sat about, the disciples could not help observing it. Later they spoke of this day as one marking a distinct development ; only then did they realize all it signified. Hence the solemnity with which the Evangelists open their description :

' The same day Jesus, going out of the house, sat by the sea-side ; and great multitudes were gathered together and hastened out of the cities unto him, so that he went up into a boat and sat in the sea. And all the multitudes stood upon the land by the sea-side. And he taught them many things in parables, and said unto them in his own doctrine : Hear ye. Behold the sower went out to sow his seed ; and whilst he soweth some fell by the wayside, and it was trodden down and the birds of the air came and ate it up. And other some fell upon rocky ground, where it had not much earth ; and it shot up immediately, because it had no depth of earth. And when the sun was risen it was scorched, and because it had no root nor moisture it withered away. And some fell among thorns, and the thorns grew up and choked it ; and it yielded no fruit. And some fell upon good ground, and brought forth fruit that grew up and increased, and yielded some an hundredfold, some sixtyfold, and some thirtyfold.'

Certainly a beautiful and peaceful introduction ; an eclogue. There was a pause ; the people waited for the rest. But what is this ? There was a new expression on His face ; a shadow of the sadness He had shown, that morning when He had turned in anger on the Pharisees, seemed to pass over Him now. He seemed not happy, He seemed disappointed ; clearly the men in such numbers before Him, and the enthusiasm they professed, meant little to Him at this moment. Still they waited for what He next would say, for the doctrine He would draw from this story ; they were surprised, they wondered what He might mean, when, with an abrupt conclusion,

> ' He cried out
> He that hath ears to hear
> Let him hear.'

This is all that we are told ; the sermon ended there. To the astonishment of the gathered crowd He stepped out of the boat, and made as if He would go. The sun had now set behind the hill, and the shadows were gathering fast. It had been a long day; they let Him go. The crowd broke up and sought its rest; some in the town, most along the bank where the regular lapping of the waves invited all the world to silence.

To us after all these years, and after learning the interpretations given by the Master Himself, the meaning of the parables seems so clear as to be obvious. But if we take them apart, without any explanation whatsoever, it will easily be seen how mysterious, how like deep riddles, they must have appeared to those multitudes by the Lake of Galilee. Even to us there are parables still not finally interpreted; how much more must it have been to them! It was certainly a new beginning. Hitherto all that He had said had been plain and explicit, never more than in the culminating Sermon on the Mount. Now all was changed. He would have them discover for themselves; nay, He put before them doctrines which of themselves they would never interpret. For the key to His meaning they would need to apply to a definite teacher; the teaching by parables was the founding of the authority of the teaching Church.

It was more. The time was passing fast, and the end of all was already beginning to loom in sight. He had much yet to do and say; above all He had to tell men of things that were in themselves beyond the reach of human understanding. That they might be able to accept these things though they would not understand them; that their faith in Him as Man, which was all that at present He had won, might rise to faith in Him as truly Son of God; for this a new mind was needed. It was necessary now that they should be trained to accept truths and doctrines which at first they would not grasp, truths which they could take only on the authority of another. When they had become reconciled to this, then they would more easily receive the highest teaching of all that in no long time He would give them; teaching which, judged by their present human standard only, would be 'a hard saying', and wholly unacceptable. Thus step by step, without any harshness or compulsion, did Jesus lift up and train the minds of men to receive the full interpretation of Himself.

Some such realization as this came upon the Twelve

after they had listened to the sermon by the sea. Jesus did not waste His words ; He would not spend His time in just entertaining an interested audience. The picture He had drawn of the Sower and his Seed, though to many it seemed merely a picture, yet, because it came from Him, must have something deep beneath it. They discussed it with one another ; His last words,

> ' He that hath ears to hear
> Let him hear ',

had made them doubly serious ; yet could they not agree among themselves what exactly it might mean. Nevertheless they knew that it was vital that they should understand. They had been chosen ; He had expressly told them that soon He would send them out to teach others ; for their better training He was keeping them with Him wherever He went. They would go to Him ; they would confess their ignorance ; they would ask Him to give them light.

The evening had closed in and the Master had retired to His cottage to be alone. But the Twelve knew where to find Him ; they also knew that, come when they might, their coming would never be taken as an intrusion. He might at times escape from others ; there is never once a sign that He wished to escape from them, unless for their own sakes to keep them from sharing His danger. They could come to Him whenever they would ; His love of their company, at the end, grew to a great reliance ; to miss this trait, this ever-increasing love of, this trust in, this human dependence on the Twelve, binding them to Him by emptying Himself out before them till they knew He was in need of their support, their companionship, their affection, is to miss another of the characteristic features of Jesus, at once the strongest and the weakest of men.

Therefore without any fear these Twelve came to Him in the darkness of the night. They sat on the ground around Him. The oil-lamp lit up the little room. By it they saw His face. It had lost the pain they had noticed on it all the day ; He was glad they had come. They had come for a purpose ; they had something to ask Him. His manner encouraged them to speak.

Yes, indeed, they had two things to ask Him. That evening He had suddenly altered His manner of teaching :

why had He done it ? He had told the people a story :
what did it signify ?

> ' And when He was alone
> The twelve that were with him came to him
> And asked him what this parable might be
> And said to him
> Why speakest thou to them in parables ? '

Then at last, to His beloved Twelve, the heart of Jesus
was unburthened ; relieved itself of the load that had
weighed it down all the day. Had they been asked beforehand they would have said, in interpreting their own
anxiety, that it was the opposition and hatred of the Pharisees
that oppressed Him. Of late they had harassed Him more
than ever ; they had insulted Him that day beyond all
endurance. He had turned on them as He had never done
before ; for relief from the tension He had hidden Himself
away with His Mother. No wonder by evening He had
appeared depressed.

And yet He soon assured them that it was not that. The
opposition of the Pharisees hurt, but there was something
else which hurt Him more. It was not the Pharisees but the
people ; not the enemy but His avowed friends ; not those
who had said He had a devil, but those who had proclaimed
Him a prophet and had asked whether He were the Son
of David ; it was these who were making His very soul
bleed.

Yes, they were enthusiastic, but what did it all signify ?
They gathered from all sides about Him, but to what
purpose ? They spread abroad His fame as a worker of
miracles, but how few seemed to draw from them any
conclusion whatsoever ! They proclaimed Him by honoured
names, but that was because they would see in Him a leader,
the Man who would soon raise His standard and carry
them on to the prophesied victory. Beyond that how far
did they go ? Why, a Roman soldier, a common pagan
with none of their light or learning, had gone further than
any of these ; a poor, sinful woman, contemned by everyone,
had shown Him more of that which He longed for than all
of them together. From a handful of women, who had
thrown in their lot with Him and followed Him, He had
received more real faith and love than all this noise and
confusion represented. Could not the Twelve see where it

all tended? It was only human glory that they sought. They were proud of their fellow-Galilæan, they revelled in the miracles He wrought. On the other hand they were becoming used to Him; they evaded the lessons in His teaching; they turned them to their own purposes. In the end, and not long hence, they would fail Him because He would prove not to be that which they had fancied and ambitioned; that He was what He was they did not and would not see.

As Jesus prepared to speak, once more His thoughts went back to His favourite prophet, Isaias. He dwelt on that scene when the prophet had been chosen for his mission; when the angel had come, and with a burning coal taken from the altar had purified his lips; when by that purification the prophet had found the courage to offer himself for the service of the Lord, and had received his commission:

> ' And I heard the voice of the Lord saying
> Whom shall I send
> And who shall go for us?
> And I said
> Lo here am I
> Send me
> And he said Go
> And thou shalt say to this people
> Hearing hear and understand not
> And see the vision and know it not
> Blind the heart of this people
> And make their ears heavy
> And shut their eyes
> Lest they see with their eyes
> And hear with their ears
> And understand with their heart
> And be converted
> And live.'

Isaias vi, 8–10.

For indeed it was the same story; these people were worthy children of their fathers. They had eyes and would not see, ears and would not hear; therefore the time had come for Him to change His method. He had chosen His Twelve; soon He must make more active use of them; for the future they and their training should be His special aim, whatever might be done with the rest. He would open their eyes, He would fill their ears, He would give to them apart that which in their turn they would give to others ; from this moment, because of their special intimacy with Him, and their instruction at His hands, and commission from Him, they should become veritable masters in Israel.

This is the tremendous significance of the interpretation of the parables, dwelt upon at length by Matthew, Mark, and Luke. It is the last and crowning event of a tremendous day, marking another ending and beginning in the career of Jesus. Even at the time the Apostles recognized it ; long afterwards they realized all that it implied.

' And when he was alone, the twelve that were with him came to him and asked him what this parable might be, and said to him : Why speakest thou to them in parables ? Who answered and said to them : Because to you it is given to know the mysteries of the kingdom of heaven ; but to them that are without it is not given ; to them all things are done in parables. For he that hath, to him shall be be given, and he shall abound ; but he that hath not, from him shall be taken away that also which he hath. Therefore do I speak to them in parables, that seeing they may see, and not perceive ; and hearing they may hear, and not understand ; lest at any time they should be converted, and their sins should be forgiven. And the prophecy of Isaias is fulfilled in them, who saith : By hearing you shall hear and shall not understand, and seeing you shall see and shall not perceive. For the heart of this people is grown gross, and with their ears they have become dull of hearing, and their eyes they have shut, lest at any time they should see with their eyes and hear with their ears and understand with their hearts and be converted, and their sins should be forgiven them, and I should heal them. But blessed are your eyes, because they see ; and your ears, because they hear ; for amen I say to you, many prophets and just men have desired to see the things that you see, and have not seen them ; and to hear the things that you hear, and have not heard them.'

In this way He answered their first question. It was an answer full of disappointment, yet also of assured hope ; of sadness, yet none the less of deep affection ; throughout we have again the baffling contrast, ending on a note that is sublime. Then He turns to their second question. They shall have the parable explained to them, that afterwards they may have that which they may explain to others. Let Him again speak, uninterrupted ; what He says, above all His subtle sidelights and shadows, cannot be improved.

' And he saith to them : Are you ignorant of this parable ? And how shall you know all parables ? Hear ye therefore the parable of the sower. He that soweth soweth the word. The seed is the word of God ; and these are they by the wayside. When anyone heareth the word of the kingdom of God, and understandeth it not, and as soon as they have heard, immediately Satan cometh and catcheth away the word that was sown in their hearts ; lest believing they should be saved. And these likewise are they that are sown upon a rock upon stony ground ; who when they have heard the word, immediately receive it with joy ; yet have they not root in themselves, but they believe only for a time ; and then when tribulation and persecution ariseth because of the word, they are presently scandalized. And others there are who are sown among thorns ; these are they that hear the word and going their way, the cares of the world, and the deceitfulness of riches, and the lusts after other things, entering in choke the word, and it becometh fruitless. And these are they who are sown upon the good ground, who in a good and very good heart hear the word and understand it, and receive it, and keep it, and bring forth fruit in patience ; one thirtyfold, another sixty, and another a hundred.'

May it not be asked whether in so short a space the ways and characters of men have ever been so completely summed up ? A saint who knew men as few have known them divided them into three classes : those who see and do nothing, those who see and do their own will, those who see and surrender ; the division is not far removed from this. Jesus, as He had looked upon that crowd, with the green corn waving on the hill behind it, knew what was in man and what was in the corn ; the thoughtless who see, but pass on to something else, caught away by their immediate surroundings, too shallow to be of any worth, the despair of those who would draw them to great possibilities ; the more thoughtful but also the more self-willed ; who see, and appreciate, and rejoice in the better things, till trial comes, and difficulty arises, and perseverance is tested, and they yield to what seems to them to be inevitable, and come to nothing much ; again the more thoughtful and less frivolous, who nevertheless lose their way, and the fascination of trifles obscures the better things, and their resolves are drowned in the ocean of this world's preoccupations, and attractions, and aims, and accumulations, and ideals ; finally the true, who are devoted enough to take all consequences, who will give whatever the pursuit of greatness may cost, and who for that reason, and that only, ' with a good and very good heart ', provide rich ground for the sowing of the word. These may fail in part, they may not all produce full fruit, but they are faithful souls, and loved of God, and glorious.

It was indeed a wonderful first lesson for the Twelve in their study of human nature ; a wonderful opening of this new school. But before the scene ended He had a word to add for His pupils themselves. He had shown them men, and what in their ministry among them they were to expect ; He must also warn them of a corresponding danger. If men failed them, they were not to fail men ; they were to be the light, and must shine on men to guide them, whether men accepted the guidance or not. They were the interpreters of the truth, and must expound it, whether or not men chose to hear. They had received more than others, not for their own sakes, but that in their turn they might give the more ; in proportion as they gave, not as they received, should be their reward in this world and in the next. As He spoke He looked about the little hut in which they sat, lit up by the single light in their midst. In one corner stood the earthen pot containing the grain for their meal next morning, in another a mattress, in another scales for weighing what came in or went out. He took them in as He looked above the heads of those about Him and, as always elsewhere, they provided Him with His illustrations.

' And he said to them : Doth a candle come in to be put under a bushel, or under a bed, and not to be set on a candlestick, that they who come in may see the light ? For there is nothing hid which shall not be made manifest, neither was it made secret but that it may be known and come abroad. If any man have ears to hear, let him hear.

' And he said to them : Take heed therefore what you hear. In what measure you shall mete it shall be measured to you again ; and more shall be given to you. For he that hath, to him shall be given, and he shall abound ; and he that hath not, that also which he thinketh he hath shall be taken away from him.'

42. Further Parables

Not only does S. Matthew stop his narrative to collect together some of the parables of Jesus in one place. The other synoptists do likewise ; they are equally impressed by the sudden transformation in the method of His preaching ; in consequence there is confusion in the order of events. We may venture to make a few comments.

In the first place it would seem that we are dealing primarily with what happened on a single momentous day. It had begun with the thronging in the streets and the rescue of Jesus by His friends from the crowd ; there had followed the healing of the demoniac, the controversy with and the rebuke of the Pharisees, the call of His Mother and His response, the gathering by the lake and the opening of the teaching by parables, the assembling afterwards of the Twelve in private, and the expounding of the parable of the Sower. That same night, it would seem, they took ship and left the spot ; S. Mark explicitly tells us so :

> ' And he saith to them that day
> When evening was come
> Let us pass over to the other side.'

But secondly, if this background be correct, we have much that is difficult to insert into it. There are several parables, given to us one after another. Though at first some at least of these might seem to have been spoken to the Twelve in private, still there are hints that most, if not all, were publicly delivered ; for one of them, besides that of the Sower, the Twelve came and asked for and received an explanation. It seems obvious that these things could not have happened all in one day, much less in the day of which we are speaking.

It would appear, then, that Matthew, Mark, and Luke have alike been so impressed by the change that took place on this day, that they have thought it worth while to emphasize it by bringing together other and later illustrations to confirm what they say. It would seem that here, if anywhere, the theory of a previous collection of the teachings of Jesus may be applied. Of nothing would the first disciples have been more careful than these parables. They would have been at hand for anyone to use. When they were spoken they would have been in many cases entirely forgotten or ignored. The synoptists, wishing to make use of them, or some of them, would have been almost compelled to put them together in one place.

Thirdly it may be noticed that the parables here specially collected are all more or less connected with one another. Their subject is more or less common ; they deal with the farmer and his life, in the fields and at home. We are told of the sowing of seed and its results ; of the jealousy between two farmers and its consequences ; of the crops that grow while the farmer sleeps ; of the mustard seed growing to a tree in the plot of ground outside his door ; of the occasional find in the ground during the time of tilling, when the harvest is gathered in and the soil is being pre-pared for the coming rain. Then we are taken inside the house ; there are the candle, and the bin, and the bed, and the scales ; there is the housewife at her baking, whose rising bread can be made to serve the Master's purpose just as much as her husband's rising corn. There is the precious stone, the heirloom in the house, which travelling merchants have looked upon and desired to buy ; last of all, for these farmers in and about Capharnaum during a great part of the year were also fishermen, there is their fishing and the value of their take The combination of ideas is surely remarkable. Other parables we have else-where in abundance, but their subject for the most part is different, or else there has been evidence enough preserved to show when and where they were delivered. These of the farmer and his household form a group apart ; they have been given here together irrespective of their circumstances, and in spite of interrupting thereby the ordinary sequence of events.

It is therefore scarcely possible, in arranging a harmony at this point, to do otherwise than as the synoptists have chosen to arrange for us. Though we prefer to keep the background of the day, in a kind of parenthesis we add other parables, spoken and explained at other times, but quite impossible to locate. When this is said we have said enough. Of all parts of the Gospel none is more impossible to alter or develop than the parables. They are unique in the world ; simple, concise, absolutely to the point, vivid, familiar, living with the life of those to whom they are addressed, full of colour and reality, ringing true from the first word to the last, attractive, beautiful, complete, perfect. They are given in lavish abundance, pouring out from the mouth of Jesus as easily as water in a stream. Yet never before did any man utter anything so perfect ; never since, in spite of many efforts, has any man been able to imitate them. Let them then stand here alone, as they are given to us, in their sublime simplicity.

'Another parable he proposed to them, saying : The kingdom of heaven is likened to a man that soweth good seed in his field. But while men were asleep his enemy came and oversowed cockle among the wheat, and went his way. And when the blade was sprung up, and had brought forth fruit, then appeared also the cockle. And the servants of the good man of the house coming said to him : Sir, didst thou not sow good seed in thy field ? Whence then hath it cockle ? And he said to them : An enemy hath done this. And the servants said to him : Wilt thou that we go and gather it up ? And he said : No ; lest perhaps gathering up the cockle you root up the wheat also with it. Suffer both to grow until the harvest, and in the time of the harvest I will say to the reapers : Gather up first the cockle and bind it in bundles to burn, but the wheat gather ye into my barn.

'And he said : So is the kingdom of God as if a man should cast seed into the earth, and should sleep and rise night and day, and the seed should spring and grow up whilst he knoweth not. For the earth of itself bringeth forth fruit, first the blade, then the ear, afterwards the full corn in the ear. And when the fruit is brought forth, immediately he putteth in the sickle, because the harvest is come.

'Another parable he proposed to them, saying : To what shall we liken the kingdom of God, or to what parable shall we compare it ? It is like to a grain of mustard seed which a man took and sowed in his field, or cast into his garden ; which when it is sown in the earth is the least indeed of all seeds that are in the earth. And when it is sown it groweth up and becometh greater than all herbs, and shooteth out great branches, and becometh a tree, so that the birds of the air come and dwell under the shadow thereof.

'And again he said: Whereunto shall I esteem the king-dom of God to be like? It is like to leaven, which a woman took and hid in three measures of meal till the whole was leavened.

'All these things, with many such parables, Jesus spoke to the multitudes, according as they were able to hear the word. And without parables he did not speak to them; that it might be fulfilled which was spoken by the prophet, saying: I will open my mouth in parables, I will utter things hidden from the beginning of the world. But apart he explained all things to his disciples.

'Then having sent away the multitudes he came into the house. And his disciples came to him, saying: Expound to us the parable of the cockle of the field. Who made answer and said to them: He that soweth the good seed is the Son of Man; and the field is the world. And the good seed are the children of the kingdom; and the cockle are the children of the wicked one, and the enemy that sowed them is the devil. But the harvest is the end of the world, and the reapers are the angels. Even as cockle therefore is gathered up and burnt with fire, so shall it be at the end of the world. The Son of Man shall send his angels, and they shall gather out of his kingdom all scandals and them that work iniquity, and shall cast them into the furnace of fire. There shall be weeping and gnashing of teeth. Then shall the just shine as the sun in the kingdom of their Father. He that hath ears to hear, let him hear.

'The kingdom of heaven is like unto a treasure hidden in a field, which a man having found hid it, and for joy thereof goeth and selleth all that he hath and buyeth that field. Again, the kingdom of heaven is like to a merchant seeking good pearls; who when he had found one pearl of great price went his way and sold all that he had and bought it. Again, the kingdom of heaven is like to a net cast into the sea, and gathering together of all kinds of fishes; which when it was filled they drew out, and sitting by the shore they chose out the good into vessels, but the bad they cast forth. So shall it be at the end of the world. The angels shall go out and shall separate the wicked from among the just, and shall cast them into the furnace of fire. There shall be weeping and gnashing of teeth. Have ye under-stood all these things? They say to him, Yea. Therefore every scribe instructed in the kingdom of heaven is like to a man who is a householder, who bringeth forth out of his treasure new things and old. And it came to pass, when Jesus had finished these parables, he passed from thence.'

14

43. The Storm at Sea

IT had been a hard day, the last of a series of hard days. The weight of the burthen was pressing on Him heavily; the future was dark, and He knew it would be full of storm. It is easy, with all this, to understand the spirit which impelled His next movement. He was with His Twelve, in the cottage by the shore. In the streets outside, and along the water's edge, many of the people still hung about, squatting in their little groups and discussing far into the night the events of that day; others had settled down to rest here and there, wrapped from head to foot in their blankets. He must get away, if only for a night and a morning. The old desire to be alone at times was never long absent from Him; He must get away, and give Himself a few hours of peace. He turned to the fishermen; He looked towards the lake. The moon was up; there was a gentle ripple on the water.

> ' Let us go over the water ', He said,
> ' To the other side of the lake.'

It was a welcome order. These men had already learnt, and they were yet to learn more and more, what a different, what a wholly precious possession Jesus was when He was with them alone. In His company, when His heart would soften towards them, and He was with them as He was with no others, how different life became ! Then they felt they had power ; then they would do any deed, brave any danger, without so much as giving it a thought ; then they would ' do all things in him who strengthened them '. So it was on this occasion. Characteristically, with not a little noise and demonstration, they went out into the street ; pompously they bade the remnant of the people disperse. With their new-born authority they bustled about, and without more ado, without thought of further preparation, they escorted the Master to the shore.

'And sending away the multitude
They take him even as he was to the ship.'

There were several of their boats lying in. One was chosen for Him ; they scrambled in after Him and put out into the lake.

Let it be remembered that the Lake of Galilee is about fourteen miles long from north to south, and about six miles across at its broadest part, which is opposite Genesareth and Magdala. It lies more than seven hundred feet below the level of the Mediterranean, and is skirted on east and west by mountains, which shut it in as between two walls. On the north and south are open plains, though these too lie between mountain ridges. Through the plain on the north the Jordan flows into the lake, on the south it creeps out again, to make its way to the Dead Sea. From this it will be seen that a wind, especially a north wind, comes down upon the lake as through a tunnel, the mountains on either side confining it, the lower level of the lake's surface giving the wind greater force. Even a slight breeze, as may be seen almost any evening, will soon raise a ripple ; a gale, coming down this tunnel on a sudden, will stir a storm in a very short space of time.

The objective for the boatmen that night was Gerasa, a village, or rather valley, on the opposite shore. It lay somewhat south of Capharnaum, opposite Magdala, and therefore the trip would have been of about six miles, in a south-easterly direction, but much more east than south. A wind coming down the tunnel from the north would have caught the boat almost broadside ; hence, even without a storm, a sudden gust of wind might easily have brought danger with it. These fishermen were accustomed to be out in their boats at night, therefore the darkness in itself had no fears for them. Nevertheless we have many indications, some of which prevail to this day, that they did not care to cross the lake at night ; they feared the sudden winds that might catch them, especially in the springtide of the year. When the darkness came upon them they preferred to moor where they were and wait till morning.

It was evidently a quiet hour when the little boat put out. As it left the shore the lamp swung at the prow, its light reflected on the water. From behind them as they rowed a few lights glimmered, marking the long line of habitations

from Bethsaida to Capharnaum and beyond. Here and
there a pariah dog barked, one answering another. At a
distance, on the outskirts of the town, a band of foraging
jackals could be heard, with the laugh of a hyena added
to their shrill yelping. Once in a way a cock crew, and
another replied, a striking feature of an Eastern night. For
the rest all was silence, a silence only the more emphasized
by these cries. The boatmen submitted to the spell. They
went about their work saying nothing ; if they had to speak
they spoke in low whispers. As soon as they had got away
they put up their little sail, and nothing now was heard but
the swish of the water round the vessel, and the creak of a
mast.as the sail yielded to the wind or the guiding rope. In
the stern, on the boards between the sides of the ship, Jesus
lay down. A rough cushion had been found for His head,
and almost immediately He was fast asleep. This must
have been so, from the very nature of the voyage. Jesus,
the Son of God, was asleep, like any child, rocked in the
cradle of the bark of Simon.

For a time all went well, and the boatmen settled down
contented. The breeze from the north filled the sails, and
before daybreak they would be at Gerasa. They relieved
each other at the sheet and the rudder ; for the rest they,
too, settled themselves to sleep. But no sooner had they left
the shelter of the shore than trouble began to arise ; a mile
out, or a little more, and they caught the full force of the
wind coming down the upper valley. The wind grew
stronger, the cold air falling on the lake, following the heat
of the day, provoked it to a gale. Rapidly it increased, the
sail became difficult to control ; the route they were taking,
almost due east till they could come under the shelter of the
mountains opposite, exposed them to the full force of the
storm on their side ; they were in imminent danger of
capsizing. Presently the waters began to rise ; first an
ominous splash of spray flew across the deck, then a wave
curved over the edge and a stream of water ran down to the
stern. Wave followed wave and the ship began to fill.

Evidently there was serious danger, just the danger which
none of the fishermen living on those shores ever cared to
face. They had come on board without a thought ; the
excitement of the day had made them forget that at this
spring season the lake was particularly treacherous. Besides
He had asked them to take Him away by boat, and that had

driven every objection from their minds. But now they were anxious ; anxious for themselves, and anxious for Him. He was asleep and wholly in their keeping, so soundly asleep that neither the howling of the wind nor the splashing of the water nor the creaking of the vessel could awaken Him ; they had only one another to consult and were in a dilemma. To put back to Capharnaum was now impossible; they dared not attempt to turn the boat round. Their only hope was to run down the lake before the wind, or to keep on their course trusting that they might yet reach shelter ; in either case they knew their condition was perilous.

Still the storm increased. Soon the boat was utterly beyond control ; neither sail nor rudder could be governed. It was filling fast, a little more and it must go down, even if it did not capsize. The men began to lose courage ; presently they lost their nerve ; in a few minutes they were as helpless little children, seeking succour anywhere. And yet through it all He was lying there, fast asleep. As they clung to the sides and the thwarts they looked at Him where He lay. They loved Him, that none could deny ; still there began to creep over them the feeling that if He were awake, if He knew the trouble around them, all would cease. There came a little resentment ; while they were in such danger, while they were doing for Him all they could, and that at His own bidding, He was apparently indifferent, unconscious of it all. They could endure it no longer ; they were at the last extreme ; they dropped sheet and rudder, they let the vessel go where it would. In a panic they crept along the deck to where He lay, and began to cry in one voice :

'Master
Does it not concern thee
That we perish ?
Lord, save us
We perish.'

Instantly the sleeping Jesus opened His eyes. Through the noise of the storm which drowned every sound He nevertheless heard their appeal ; what the clamour of the elements had failed to do, their cry succeeded in doing, and He awoke. At once He took in the scene ; the howling wind above, the ship filling with water, the frightened men clinging to His feet. He made no delay ; He made no show ;

He acted as though it were an affair of every day. These were His Twelve, His own, and for them there must be no terms, or formalities, or conditions. He stood up where He was ; He stretched out His arm to the wind, looking at it, speaking to it, rebuking it, as if it were a thing of life. He turned to the water lashing round Him, as a master would turn to a barking hound.

'Peace
Be still,'

He said ; no more.

The obedience was instantaneous. The wind ceased ; there was a dead calm on the surface of the water. The battered sails hung listlessly about the masts ; the boat rocked gently up and down, to and fro and from side to side, staying where it was, as if it rested after a heavy struggle. The men crouched still beside Him ; for the moment they were paralysed. They had come to Him expecting succour. If only He were awake among them they had felt they would be safe, but they had never expected anything like this. They had feared the storm, but now fear of a new kind crept over them. They did not know what to say or think.

Meanwhile Jesus looked down upon them where He stood. They did not yet recognize what He had done. He had worked this wonder, not for the multitude, but for His own, His Twelve. He had worked it in their own vessel, where He was always with them. He had worked it under conditions which, by all the laws of nature, were hopeless. He had worked this wonder, and He had worked it for them ; why did they not see ? But the time would come when they would. If that day He had begun to speak to the people in parables, that night He had begun to act in parables to them. One day they would read its meaning and would know that so long as He was with them in the boat, not till the end of time would any storm, would the gates of hell itself, be able to prevail against them.

All this they would one day understand, but at present they were only little children. They had much yet to learn, and as little children He must continue to teach them, now drawing them gently on, now with seeming sternness urging them. He would seize this moment for the latter. True, they had been in trouble and had come to Him ; true, they had appealed to Him for help. All this shewed faith, and He loved them and in His heart thanked them for it. But He wanted more, He for ever wanted more, and not till He got that more could He be content. So He would rebuke them ; gently He would urge them ; He would stir them to things yet greater, to faith that would ride over every storm. He said :

'Why are ye fearful
O ye of little faith ?
Have you not faith in you yet ?
Where is your faith ? '

The men awoke from their paralysis. The boat was still, and if they would reach Gerasa by morning they must take to their oars. He seemed not to need them any more, He wished them to return to their labour. They stepped down the deck and settled to their tasks, each man in his place. But as the boat began again to move forward, as the late moon rose above the hills and streaked the waves with silver, they would whisper in awe to one another :

'What manner of man is this ?
Who is this, think you
That he commandeth both the winds and the sea
And they obey him ? '

It was indeed another discovery, a new revelation of this Man who had already won their hearts and their allegiance. It would not now be long before they would find for themselves a full answer to their question, even on the very spot where they were then sailing, and under not unlike conditions.

44. The Demoniac at Gerasa

In the morning the little boat came down the eastern coast and put in at Gerasa. It was a little hollow between the mountains, with a few tiny villages running up the hill-sides, at a distance from the shore. The mountains held it in a semi-circle ; at the northern end a spur ran right into the sea, ending in a steep crag. It was a somewhat isolated spot, with the lake in front, while beyond the hills was desert country. The little valley was rich and green ; the people, more or less cut off from their neighbours, had a character of their own. They were a mixed race, partly Jewish, but more aboriginal, content to remain as they were, desirous only to be left alone, tilling the soil, rearing their herds upon the upland plains.

In this hidden spot Jesus landed with His Twelve, to rest awhile from His labours. It was not the first time He had taken them apart, nor would it by any means be the last. But scarcely had they come ashore than an unpleasant incident occurred. The spot where they moored the boat was secluded ; the main town lay further inland, trailing up the hill-side ; between them and it, cut into the mountain, were holes and recesses, and here and there a monument, which showed that it was a place of burial. Alongside of these a rough path led up to the town but, except when a funeral procession came that way, it was mainly unfrequented. Along this path they were walking from the water's edge when suddenly, from one of the rock chambers in front of them, two horrible creatures rushed out ; unclean from head to foot, with hair dishevelled, nails that had grown into claws, bloodshot eyes, beards wild and shaggy, the remnants of broken shackles hanging from their wrists and ankles ; one of them was entirely naked. Like wild beasts they came, as it were, seeking whom they might devour ; being human, which evidently they were, they were therefore more terrible than wild beasts.

Later the Twelve came to know the story of these creatures, especially of one, the most frightful of the pair. He had been like this for years. For years a devil had possessed him. He had lived away from human habitation, had made himself a home in the tombs, had discarded every sign of humanity even to his clothing, had wandered thence on the mountain-side just a dangerous animal, a terror to all who came across him. Night and day he would lie in his lair and no man could find him ; then on a sudden he would break out, rushing anywhere, up the hill and into the desert, howling and shrieking, and threatening whomsoever he might meet. Or again he would remain in his own neighbourhood, as it were taking vengeance on himself ; with like shrieks and howls seizing the stones beside him, with them beating and tearing his body till it was a mass of hideous cuts and flowing blood. Often enough, when these paroxysms had seized him, he had been hunted down and put in irons. But it had been all in vain. He had snapped the chains like thread, fetters he had crushed to pieces, and men had ceased all attempts to tame him. He had been left to his fate ; he had been suffered to live among the tombs, since such had been his preference. If any wished to pass that way they went in groups and armed ; otherwise, so long as he molested no one, he was himself left unmolested.

Such was the poor creature that suddenly rose up with its companion before the eyes of the disciples when they rounded the corner of the hill. For a few moments it came on with a bound ; then, as suddenly as it had appeared, it stood still. Its attention had been caught by something strange ; it was fascinated, its neck strained forward, its bloodshot eyes opened wide and held fast. Next, as if it could not resist the attraction, it began to move slowly forward, its body bent, its arms seeming to grope as in the dark. When it grew nearer the pace became quicker ; nearer still, and it began to bound along, heeding nothing and no one. It made straight for Jesus where He stood, erect, silent, alone in the middle of the road ; instinctively the others had stepped back behind Him, in natural horror and fear. Arrived in front of Him, it fell down cringing at His feet, grovelling, struggling with itself, obviously owning that it had before it its Master.

For a few moments there reigned an awful silence. The creature lay beaten and subdued. Onlookers crept cautiously nearer ; Jesus stood still, looking down with pity on the sight before Him. Presently the crouching figure raised its head ; the arms followed, held up aloft as if to defend itself from some impending blow. Then, with a howl that none could think human, it cried :

> ' What have I to do with thee
> Jesus
> The Son of the Most High God ?
> Art thou come hither to torment us
> Before the time ?
> I adjure thee by God
> That thou torment me not.'

They were tremendous words, whatever they might signify. The Twelve heard them and wondered. Were they the answer to the question they had asked one another as they came that night across the lake :

> ' What manner of man is this ?
> Who is this, think you
> That he commandeth both the winds and the sea
> And they obey him ? '

They thought of that opening miracle in the synagogue at Capharnaum, when the man possessed had roused Him by crying :

> ' Let us alone
> What have we to do with thee
> Jesus of Nazareth ?
> Art thou come to destroy us ?
> I know thee who thou art
> The Holy one of God.'

They thought of the various occasions since then, when other devils had been ejected uttering the same despairing cry. They recalled the criticism of the Pharisees only the day before :

> ' This man hath Beelzebub
> And casteth out devils
> By the prince of devils ',

and His own indignant and scathing response. As He stood there, peaceful, assured Master of the creature at His feet, as the human animal looked up at Him, trembling in abject fear from head to foot, who that saw could doubt the reality of the battle between two powers, or who could doubt its issue ? If the day before the Pharisees had raised such a doubt in any mind, the scene before them was its sufficient answer. For His own at least Jesus would not leave the problem unsolved. The miracle to-day should surpass every other of its kind ; it should be one never to be forgotten.

Therefore before He dismissed the devil in the easy way He had done the like at other times, He would give them a lesson. The evil voice from within the man had called Him by His name, far more explicitly than it had ever done before. It was no longer

> ' Jesus of Nazareth ' ;

no longer only

> ' The Holy one of God ' ;

this time it was,

> ' Jesus
> The Son of the Most High God.'

It should also give its own name.

> ' What is thy name ? '

He asked, and again the answer was weird.

> ' Legion ', it said,
> ' For we are many.' .

Then He gave His command :
> ' Go out of the man
> Thou unclean spirit.'

Certainly this was not the language of one who cast out devils by the prince of devils.

And yet there was a pause. Not as on other occasions did the devil flee on the instant, tearing and tossing the poor human being as he went. Instead the man grovelled on the ground more than ever before. He writhed like a worm in agony ; he put on a look of piteous appeal, in all manner of ways he began to implore for mercy. He could not and would not ask for forgiveness, but at least he could hope for some respite. Let him not be sent back to the hell from which he had come ; let him not be hurled down for ever into the abyss ; not yet, not yet. Let him be allowed to remain above a little longer ; it did not matter where, it did not matter in what place. On the plateau above was a herd of swine ; filthy swine, which a Jew abominated, yet they would serve their purpose. If they could no longer dwell in men, let them at least be permitted to enter into the swine.

> ' And he besought him much
> That he would not drive him away
> Out of the country
> Nor command them to go into the abyss
> And there was there
> Not far from them near the mountain
> A great herd of swine feeding
> And the spirits besought him saying
> If thou cast us out hence
> Send us into the herd of swine
> That we may enter into them.'

It was a degrading appeal indeed. To a Jew the very sight of the swine grazing on the hill was as of a thing obscene ; a proof that they were in a land of unbelieving pagans. The Law forbade their use for food ; when the prophet had condemned a fallen people, the eating of the flesh of swine was given as a sign of their apostasy. The heathen knew of this abhorrence ; when he would most degrade a Jew he would stuff the flesh of swine into his mouth ; and in return a faithful Jew would die rather than obey. The very name of swine signified all uncleanness ;

the keepers of swine were men to be shunned. Even Jesus
Himself in His teaching had made use of the proverb :
> ' Cast not your pearls before swine
> Lest perhaps they trample them under their feet
> And turning upon you tear you.'

Thus did Jesus utilize the Jewish mind to emphasize the
abomination of Satan.   The prince of devils with his crew
would of their own accord choose to live in swine, and would
appeal to Jesus for the licence to do it.   Could degradation
in their eyes go lower ?
> ' And Jesus immediately suffered them
> And gave them leave
> And said to them
> Go.'

It was an echo of His former command :
> ' Begone, Satan.'

But the wonder did not end there.   Down at His feet the
poor creature suddenly lay quiet.   He seemed to grow
conscious of the shame of his condition ; he crept even
nearer, he drew over himself the mantle of Jesus, and hid
his nakedness beneath it.   Let us leave him there for the
moment.   Meanwhile on the plateau up the hill a strange
thing occurred.   This last conversation had drawn the eyes
of all to the animals feeding there, large herds of long-
legged, long-snouted swine, black and piebald, some two
thousand in all, with their herdsmen standing among them.
They had been grazing contented since sunrise, enjoying
the fresh grass, made richer by the morning dew.   Suddenly,
unaccountably, all became restless.   They stopped their
feeding ; they lifted up their heads and tossed themselves
to and fro as if they were in pain.   They began to rush here
and there, regardless of the blows of their masters ; they
seemed to have all gone mad.   Presently the glitter of the
lake beneath them caught their eyes, flashing back the
morning sun from below the steep hill on which they
grazed.   As a candle draws a moth the shining of the
water drew them ; one would have said they had all been
seized with parching thirst, and were prepared to risk their
lives to quench it.   They began to move pell-mell to the
edge of the hill, and would not be hindered by anyone.
Over the steep side they went, as if they were blinded,
those behind pressing on those in front ; in the space of a

few minutes a very torrent of swine-flesh tumbled down the
hill into the lake. There they struggled, one with another,
one above another, even as they had fallen, till the din
was gradually stifled in the water.

The herdsmen were paralysed. In the early morning,
from their higher ground, they had watched the little boat
hugging the shore, and then putting in at the beach. They
had seen the men land, obviously Jewish fishermen from
Galilee, no doubt come across for purposes of trade, or
perhaps prevented by the storm of the night before from
reaching their own home. Lazily they had followed them
with their eyes as they made their way up the valley ; on
a sudden their interest had been roused by the sight of the
demoniac. They knew the creature well, only too well ; if
these strangers did not take care he would give them trouble.
And yet the opposite had happened. They had been
prepared, if need be, to run down the hill to the assistance
of these strangers, but suddenly the man had changed his
manner. He was behaving differently from anything they
had seen in him before. In the group of strangers was one
who seemed to have cast a spell over him ; he was crouching
at that man's feet like a beaten cur.

But then, even while they were looking, this strange
thing had happened about them. They stood there,
unable to do anything. They ran to the cliff and peered
over ; they could scarcely believe their own eyes. And yet
the empty plain behind them, with not a hog left upon it,
convinced them only too surely that what they saw was true,
and that their day's work was done. Fear began to come
upon them. The demoniac quiet, their swine at the same
instant gone mad,—they began to link the two together.
There was something uncanny about it all ; this was no
place for them ; in a panic they fled from the spot and
made for home.

Thus in a very short time the news spread through the
fields and hamlets, and the little town up the hill.

The people hurried to the spot. In much less than an
hour from the time of the strange happenings a large crowd
had gathered. They were for the most part not Jews, and
the Jews were of as little account to them as they were to
the Jews. They traded with them ; they treated them as
neighbours ; but that was all. Some rumours had reached
them of wonderful things that had been taking place along

the opposite shore ; but these were Jewish matters with which they were not concerned. It had never occurred to them that the Wonder-worker of whom they were told would ever visit their shores. Now He had actually come into their little valley ; they must see Him for themselves.

They came ; and what did they see ? In the land below the tombs a Man, quiet, peaceful, self-possessed, whose self-possession commanded respect akin to awe. Behind Him was a group of other men, evidently His followers, who stood in readiness to obey His word, talking much among themselves, interested, eager. At His feet, most wonderful of all, the poor demoniac, the terror of the neighbourhood, whom for years they had been wont to dread and shun, lay at His feet completely quiet and subdued. At this Stranger's feet he lay upon the ground, as if at last he had found the one place of rest he had sought for all these years. He was no longer wild and naked ; a covering had been found for him, and he was dressed as any other. There was peace and understanding in his eyes, joy and satisfaction on his face ; though he was still unkempt, it was clear to every-one who looked on him that he was in his right mind.

It was indeed wonderful ; they were in admiration, yes, but they were also not unnaturally afraid. A new power had been manifested among them, a power that was beyond them, and they feared it. In groups they discussed the affair among themselves, enquired and enquired again of those who had been eyewitnesses of it all, the subduing of the madman, the declaration of the devils, their expulsion, the destruction of the swine. It was terrible enough to have devils in their neighbourhood, but an unknown power that could conquer devils was more terrible still. He had destroyed their swine ; what else might He not do ? True, He had done a wonderful thing ; He had healed their demoniac, but at what a price ! To say the least it was disconcerting. Such a power in their midst would disturb the quiet routine of their valley ; moreover, if they were to pay so dearly for benefits done it might go hard with them. They shook their heads. They wished this Man no harm, but they would rather that He went elsewhere ; on the whole they would rather have their devils and their swine than Jesus Christ and His favours.

Soon they found themselves more or less unanimous. Some leaders were chosen, magnates in their little village, to speak to this Stranger for the rest. They came nearer ; they were respectful, being oriental that was an easy matter ; but they were quite decided. Of course they had heard long ago of the great Man He was, and of the great things He had said and done in Galilee. They congratulated Him, they honoured Him ; they had great respect for their Jewish friends and neighbours, and therefore for Him still more. They were very much impressed by what He had done for their country-side that morning. They were indebted to Him ; they were impressed by His unique powers ; they said nothing about the swine. Truly, considering they were not Jews, they felt deeply honoured by His visit, and by all He had done. They would like to repay Him but they could not ; they did not even know how to treat Him. They were not Jews ; they did not know the Jewish laws and customs. They were only country farmers, unused to such surprises as these. They were sure their valley was no place for Him ; they were not the people for His company. His presence among them would be a waste of His time ; He would win more followers elsewhere. Here He would only provoke trouble, both for Himself and for them ; it would be much better if He went to some other place. They were not acting in a hurry ; they had thought the matter over, and knew what they were saying. They did not wish to hurt Him ; they did not wish to appear ungrateful ; but they had made up their minds, and had come to request Him to go away, and not to disturb the quiet of their little corner. And so on.

Jesus listened to them. He was not offended ; He did not blame them ; He did not even give them an answer. They knew no better ; they knew not what they did. His Father would forgive them ; perhaps some other day, when they had thought more over the event of that morning, some of them would long for Him and that alone would be gain. He bowed to them politely ; as politely as they had bowed to Him. He turned about and made for the boat lying by the shore. As He went His disciples turned and followed, silent, wondering, a little disappointed with this abrupt termination of what had promised to be an exciting day.

But there was one on that coast who was by no means so easily to be dismissed. So long as Jesus had stood quiet, so long had the poor healed man remained quiet too and

happy, and caring for nothing at all ; sitting at His feet
on the ground in the lane, taking no heed of the curious
crowd that stared at him, a picture of complete contentment.
But now Jesus began to move. He had heard the appeal
of this people, and without a word had accepted His
dismissal. He had turned towards the shore, and made as
if to depart. What then was to become of him ? Would
Jesus, his Benefactor, leave him ? He rose from the ground ;
he went down on his knees ; suppliantly he begged that
he should not so suddenly be left alone. Let him only be
taken along with the others, and he would follow Him
anywhere. He would give no trouble ; he would be no
hindrance. He would serve them all ; he would do anything they wished, if only they would let him stay. He had
' found Him whom his soul loved and would not let Him go '.

> ' Now the man
> Out of whom the devils were departed
> Began to beseech him
> That he might be with him.'

Such a prayer but recently Jesus had accepted from a
woman.

> ' Mary Magdalen
> Out of whom seven devils had been cast,'

had been permitted to join those who went with Him and
served Him ; the Twelve waited, thinking that to this man
too He might grant the same. But Jesus had other designs
for him. Here on this side of the lake the people were still
unprepared ; soon, in a few short months, He would come
again into the country and give it another opportunity.
He would use this man as His forerunner ; He would send
him forth to proclaim Him and the wonder He had worked.
The man cured, whom all had known in his state of bondage,
would be an eloquent witness to Himself. Once more we have
a singular instance of the trust of Jesus in weak men ; this
healed demoniac is appointed the first apostle to the Gentiles.

> ' And he admitted him not
> But sent him away saying
> Return to thy house
> To thy friends
> And tell them
> How great things the Lord hath done to thee
> And hath had mercy on thee.'

There was strength in the command which could not be resisted ; but there was also gentleness, and sympathy, and understanding, and friendship, and trust, and encouragement, and the man submitted. He followed them to the shore, the centre of a pressing crowd, but heeding them not at all. He watched them go on board and push off. As the ship turned northwards and was taken away, he followed it with his eyes. One by one the multitudes dispersed to their labour, relieved that the Worker of strange things was gone. But he stood there, rooted to the ground, his eyes fixed upon the vessel ; not until it was out of sight, and it was now clear that he must remain alone, did he turn about and go slowly up the valley. He passed the place of tombs, his miserable home for so many miserable years. He trembled to think of all that had been, and wept with joy and thanksgiving at that morning's transformation. He came into the city, clothed now and sane ; and men gathered round him and stared, some in suspicion, some as friends, many asking questions, one or two, with others following their lead, taunting him with the horrors of the past. And he received them all, and answered them, and told them

> ' How great things the Lord had done for him
> And had had mercy on him.'

' The Lord ! ' For must not this Man be ' the Lord ' ? Yes, indeed, whatever the word might mean He was ' the Lord ' ; as ' the Lord ' he would proclaim Him. There across the water was really ' the Lord '. He knew no more than this ; but what he knew he would confess. He would go from town to town, through all that half-pagan country, that all might hear it.

> ' And he went his way
> Through the whole city
> And began to publish in Decapolis
> How great things Jesus had done for him
> And all men wondered.'

45. The Woman with the Issue of Blood

Meanwhile the disciples rowed away across the water. It was not the first time their anticipated rest had been interrupted, nor would it be the last. Still they had received much in compensation. As they passed the middle of the lake, now with scarce a ripple on its surface, they looked up at the green valley to the north, and the mountains on either side, and recalled their adventure of the night before, and wondered again at Him, seated in the stern, who so easily had saved them with a word. They saw Him with His eyes turned backward towards the valley of the Gerasenes, whence He had been so summarily dismissed, and wondered the more at His quiet endurance of the ways of men. They thought of the miracle of that morning. It was nothing very new; it was only of a piece with other things He had done; but what had followed, when they reflected on it, made them for a third time wonder. Over in Galilee some whom He had healed He had bidden not to proclaim abroad what He had done; this man He had told to spread the news of his healing everywhere. Did they realize the reason? That the Galilæans had already begun to look for these miracles for their own sakes, to make them the object of their coming to Him, in them and because of them to forget Him whom they were intended to proclaim; while as for these poor pagans on the other side, the more they heard of the deed that had been done the more would they wonder at, and enquire about, and long to know the Doer, even though now they had sent Him away.

It was in the afternoon that the little boat put in again at Capharnaum, 'his own city', as S. Matthew here characteristically and affectionately calls it. Long before they reached the landing-place they had been sighted from the shore. The boat was well known; some had seen Him go away in it the evening before; they had noticed the storm in the night and naturally had wondered how they had fared. The crowd of yesterday was still there, gathered as it had been from distant places; the news of His coming spread quickly up the town, and many were on the quay waiting for Him. He landed, but could scarcely move further; with the multitude loudly pressing on Him, He gave Himself up to them by the seashore.

'And it came to pass
That when Jesus entering into the boat
Had passed again over the water to the other side
And came again into his own city
A great multitude assembled together unto him
And received him
For they were all waiting for him
And he was nigh unto the sea.'

Among those who were looking for His return that day was one man in particular. The synagogue of Capharnaum, like all others, had its governing body ; among the chiefs of this body was one named Jairus. Jairus had an only daughter, a child not yet twelve years old, the apple of his eye. She had fallen ill ; during the night before, when the storm had been howling down the valley, she had grown worse. All this morning the onlookers had felt that the child might die at any moment, and nothing more could be done to save her.

In his anxiety Jairus was beside himself. The physicians could do nothing, he himself was helpless. In the midst of his distress the news reached him that Jesus was again in the town ; and at once his thoughts turned to Him who had already done so much. He had healed so many, merely for the asking, surely if he were asked He would heal one more. He had shown special favour to two magnates in the town, even though they had both been pagans ; surely to a Jew, to one of His own kith and kin so to speak, He would be no less favourable. When He was yet in Cana He had healed the son of the civil magistrate in Capharnaum ; later He had cured the servant of the military authority without so much as visiting him ; surely He would do no less for a minister of religion. Of every-thing connected with the synagogue Jesus had been particularly observant. At the door of the synagogue He had worked His first miracle in the city ; surely He would listen to one of its official rulers.

It was true there might be some doubt. The Pharisees and Scribes, the priests and other masters of the synagogue in general, had not been very gracious to Jesus ; only yesterday there had been no small disturbance because of a deliberate insult that had been offered to Him. Still he hoped this would be overlooked ; Jesus had done the like before. Though He had hard words for the Pharisees as a body, He had never singled out any one for accusation. He had treated individuals as they had treated Him ; He had even dined with Pharisees. Jairus himself had little sym-pathy with others of his party, and therefore hoped he might succeed. In any case the matter was urgent ; he must run the risk of a rebuke ; a sense of despair drove him to make any venture.

When, then, the news reached him that Jesus had

returned, his mind was quickly made up ; the very timeli-
ness of His arrival gave him new hope, and banished all his
hesitation. He rose at once from the dying child's bedside ;
he hurried down the street to the shore. Being a ruler of
the synagogue, a passage through the crowd was easily
made ; more easily, be it noticed, than had been made for
the Mother of Jesus through much the same crowd the day
before. As soon as he had reached the spot where Jesus
stood he put aside all formality. He ignored his dignity ;
he was deaf to the criticisms of his friends, the priests and
the Pharisees. If any one of them had had a dying daughter
of his own, would he have let her die rather than ask
the help of Jesus ? He looked into the Master's face and
saw that he was welcome ; that alone was enough. Humbly
he went on his knee ; he bent his head in adoration ;
encouraged by the way he had been received he came at
once to his request :

> ' My daughter is at the point of death
> (Perhaps) is even now dead
> But come
> Lay thy hand upon her
> That she may be safe
> And live.'

He could not be asking for too much. It was less than
the magistrate or the military officer had asked for. And
even if his child had died while he was coming down the
road, might he not still have hope ? If out of pity for a
widow woman, across the valley at Naim, He had raised
her dead boy to life, might he not hope for no less for himself
here in Capharnaum ? Thus in this man, as in every other
case, even as he yielded to the urging of faith within him,
the faith itself within him continued to grow.

And again, as always, to the measure of that faith Jesus
responded. He made no answer ; He just moved forward
to go. This ruler of the synagogue should be treated as one
who had a right to ask and to be obeyed. Once more a
passage was made through the crowd. Excitedly, busily,
Jairus led the way ; Jesus came peacefully behind him.
The Twelve, who by this time had made their ship secure,
followed in their wake. Around them, in front and behind
and crushed against the walls of the houses in the narrow
streets, the noisy crowd pressed in, excited as usual, more

excited now that they had heard the request of the rule of the synagogue, and there was a hope of witnessing yet another miracle.

But before they reached the house something else occurred, so remarkable that all the three synoptists have thought fit to mention it ; two of them, Mark and Luke, the two most influenced by sympathy, at considerable length. Three things have struck the Evangelists as making this event different from anything that has gone before ; first the nature of the disease, secondly the extraordinary manner of the miracle, last the revelation that followed after. As for the first, hitherto we have heard only of such diseases and defects as were manifest to all ; lameness, blindness, deafness, dumbness, leprosy, demoniacal possession, fever, paralysis, even death itself, were patent matters for everyone to see, of which the sufferers need not or could not be ashamed, or which they could not hope to conceal. But pitiable human nature has diseases and ailments in vast number which it scarcely cares to own to itself, much less reveal them to others ; sometimes it will rather die than make them known. Among the sufferers whom Jesus healed there must have been many who carried such burthens, and whose healing is known only to themselves. Here we have a case in point ; from it we may conclude to others.

Again, with people so afflicted, inevitably it must have been more difficult to come to Jesus. Shame would prevent them from speaking, either to others or even to Jesus Himself ; often enough the disease would have been of such a kind as to seem outside the range of miracles. Such sufferers would shun the eye of the crowd. When the time of miracles came they would hide away. If they had the courage to make their trouble known to Him it would have been done in private ; if a cure were granted, from the nature of the case the person healed would have said little about it. Here we have an instance of subtle ingenuity, built upon faith in Him, and wonderfully rewarded.

Then, as we have said, there was the manner of the miracle. Jesus hitherto has worked miracles of many kinds, and in many different ways. By a word He has turned one thing into another ; by a word He has healed the sick, He has cast out devils, He has cast out sin, He has raised the dead, He has calmed the winds and the sea. He has healed by the touch of His hand ; strangest, perhaps, of all, He has cured those who were far away, whose condition He knew, men thought, by hearsay and no more. Still hitherto, in every case, at least He had known what was being done ; each single miracle had been a deliberate, a chosen act of His own free will. That the power of working miracles should be independent of His actual, specific choice, should, as it were, belong to Him, as naturally as the act of breathing, should exude from Him as blood from a wound, was a thing that could never have been thought. Nevertheless here was a case. Apparently at least it was a miracle that flowed from His very nature, not strictly depending on His will. He almost spoke of it as something which had happened in spite of Himself, which as it were had been taken from Him.

And there was another discovery, a sequel to this last. Jesus worked miracles in plenty, lavishly, on all who sought Him. Yet from this event it seems reasonable to gather that in some way each cost Him something, each took something out of Him ; that for every miracle He worked He had to pay some price in His human nature. As an athlete is exhausted by his feats of strength, as a student is worn with study, so this revelation seemed to show that by His miracles He was, sometimes at least, similarly affected. It was the first confession of the kind that had been drawn from Him ; later there followed other hints which might appear to confirm the discovery.

With these preliminary remarks the narrative that follows tells its own tale, and needs little amplification. The noisy crowd pressed up the narrow street, carelessly jostling one another, jostling Him who was in their midst, more especially at the street corners. At one of these corners a woman, elderly, but seeming more haggard than her years warranted, stands hidden and defended by the bend of the wall from being carried away by the rush of the multitude. Alone and regardless of others she is eagerly waiting. Her eyes are strained to catch a glimpse of Him who, she knows, is the centre of all this hubbub. She is muttering to herself ; she is passed by unnoticed ; as the throng grows thicker, and shouting men as they pass continually look back at One behind them, she knows that He is near. Crouching against the wall she ventures as near to the corner as she dare. Presently He comes. Where she stands there is scarcely room for two camels to pass one another, scarcely room for five men to stand together in a row. He will therefore be so near when He passes that by stretching out her arm between His companions she will be able at least to put a finger on His garment. At the bend of the road there is a block ; the crowd and Jesus are compelled to stand still. Quickly through the press she reaches out her hand ; she actually has her fingers on His robe ; she draws it back and shrinks further along the wall. The crowd that comes round the bend of the road envelops her, and her little drama, so she thinks, is over.

Who was this woman ? What had she done ? What had happened ? Let the Evangelists tell the rest.

> ' And behold there was a certain woman
> Who was troubled with an issue of blood
> Twelve years
> And had suffered many things from many physicians
> And had bestowed all her substance on physicians
> And could not be healed by any
> Was nothing better
> But rather worse
> When she had heard of Jesus
> She came in the crowd behind him
> And touched the hem of his garment
> For she said
> If I touch but his garment
> I shall be healed
> And forthwith
> The fountain of her blood was dried up
> And she felt in her body
> That she was cured of the evil.'

Gladly would the poor woman have slipped away again through the crowd unnoticed, keeping her happy secret to herself. But this was not to be. At the bend of the street, as soon as she had touched His robe, Jesus deliberately stood still, and the crowd was compelled to halt with Him. In His face was a change ; a look of effort in His eyes, an earnestness upon His forehead, a firmness on His lips, as if some serious thought had suddenly caught Him. He stood still ; He seemed to have lost something ; He searched about among the faces of those about Him as if to find it. Presently He said, loud enough for all close beside Him to hear :

' Who is it that hath touched my garment ? '

This was indeed a strange demand. Under the circumstances, what could it mean? Ever since He had left the shore with the multitude of people about Him, particularly since He had entered the narrow street up which the cortège was now moving, how many times had His garments not been touched? They were being touched all the time. Was He not their Jesus of Nazareth? And were they not proud of Him, familiarly proud, being as He was one of themselves, one of the common folk of Galilee, and therefore to be treated in their easy, familiar way? Was He beginning to resent their well-meant, if rough, familiarity? Did He wish to object to the pushing, and the thronging, and the noise, and the patronizing, and the boasting, and the want of respect shown to Him? Of course if He did it was quite intelligible. Another who had done what He had done, and won for himself such repute, would have long since insisted on more honour and respect being shown to him. Imagine a Pharisee being hustled in a crowd as at that very moment Jesus was being hustled!

And yet somehow so to insist was unlike Jesus. Only yesterday the hustling had been even worse and He had said nothing. On the contrary, His friends had declared that He was so submissive to the mob as to have become quite mad, and had had to interfere. They had gone out and rescued Him merely that He might have a little food. What then could He mean? He looked serious; had someone carelessly hurt Him? Had some ill-minded person struck Him, or in some other way done Him wrong? Simon, who was next to Him, who on such occasions was a master of the ceremonies, and was proud to assume to himself the care of Jesus, felt that in some way his own honour was affected. He looked about him, he enquired, first of one, and then of another. Though, of course, many owned that they had touched Him, still there was no one who would own that he had done more than knock up against Him as men will in a crowd; and to knock up against Him, what was that?

They began to resent His question. If He did not wish for their familiarity, if He wished to be treated as one aloof, He Himself should act differently. When He was so familiar, how could they be otherwise? Even Simon felt that the query was out of place. He must remonstrate. As Jesus had had to be saved from His own extravagance the day before, so to-day He must be shown that what He was asking was equally extravagant. So he took courage and replied :

> ' Master
> Thou seest the multitudes
> Thronging and pressing thee
> And dost thou say
> Who hath touched me ? '

And what he said was immediately approved by all around. It was quite unreasonable, quite absurd ; what could Jesus mean by asking such a question ?

But Jesus was not so easily to be set aside. He still stood where He was ; He paid no heed to their obviously reasonable remark. He looked only a little more serious, He was a little more insistent, as He said with emphasis :

> ' Somebody hath touched me
> For I know
> That virtue is gone out from me ' ;

and immediately again He began to search about Him, as if He would yet find something He had lost.

Meanwhile, close behind the inmost circle of the crowd, the poor woman had been hemmed in. The check in the procession had only packed it the more closely, the semblance of a quarrel had only made everyone try to come nearer. The remark of Jesus had made the people round Him stand back a little, so that in front of Him a small space was free ; but all around the crowd was dense. Crushed in the midst of this assembly the poor woman heard all that was said. She had scarcely drawn back her hand, she had scarcely felt the flow of vital strength soothing and binding the body within her, she had scarcely realized the peace of it and all the joy, when suddenly she became aware that something had gone wrong. He had stood still, almost as if offended ; the crowd had halted with Him ; she had been unable to move any way. An enquiring silence had followed. He had spoken ; when she heard what He said a cold shiver went through her. She stood there paralysed, holding her breath, catching every word that followed ; perhaps some other member of the crowd would own that he, too, had touched Him, had treated Him more roughly than was becoming. She strained to hear anything at all that would remove her dreadful suspicion that perhaps He alluded to her. But no ; not a soul would confess to anything ; on the contrary, they resented the enquiry. Even Simon, the great man who looked to everything, even he complained in the name of all the rest.

Had she, then, done something wrong ? Was He angry with her ? Did He take her act as a kind of theft ? His last words seemed to imply it.

'Virtue is gone out of me ',

He had said ; as if it had been taken from Him without His knowledge and against His will. What was she to do ? He still continued to stand there, quiet and enquiring, until she confessed He would not be satisfied. There was no escape ; she must confess, whatever be the shame ; He who had done so much for her must not go away discontented. Besides, she owed Him some kind of thanks, some kind of repayment ; perhaps this was what He was seeking, and she was wishing to escape without a word. It was true to confess would be dreadful ; the very thing she had hoped to avoid. And to have to tell it before this crowd, before this noisy, vulgar crowd, who would make only ribald jest of her story ! Could she do it ? She must ; for His sake she must, for her own sake she must. If she had done wrong this was the only amends ; if she had not, then would her confession show to everyone how right He was in asking, how glorious in giving, how truly wonderful. In her shame would be His glory, and that would be reward enough. Thus again with her, as we have already seen with others before her, even as she pondered, faith, and love, and devotedness grew to more and more.

Her actions now became impetuous. Around her the resentment was growing ; some were annoyed and even sullen. Why this unwarrantable delay ? Did He not remember that a child's life was at stake ? But she heeded nothing. She pushed her way through the wall of men about Him ; they might try to hold her back, but she would not be held. While the crowd still stood mystified and wondering, suddenly it became aware of a woman at His feet in the little space before Him.

'But the woman
Fearing and trembling
Knowing what was done in her
Seeing that she was not hid

Came and fell down before his feet
And told him all the truth
And declared before all the people
For what cause she had touched him
And how she was immediately cured
But he said to her
Daughter
Thy faith hath made thee whole
Go thy way in peace
And be thou whole of thy disease
And the woman was healed from that hour.'

There was affection and pity in both His look and His words, but far more affection than pity ; there was gratitude for one who had so believed in Him, and who had dared so much for His sake. She went away a happy woman. The shame was all gone. Out of her shame, like Mary of Magdala, she had gained an abiding friend.

46. The Daughter of Jairus

All this time Jairus had been standing there, anxious to lead the procession to his house, in his anxiety taking little notice of the wonderful thing that had been done before his eyes. There was still some distance to go across the town ; even now it might be too late. For if the child were really to die, could He or would He do anything ? Alas ! Even while he waited there the fatal message came. While Jesus yet was standing, refusing to move on, while the intruding woman at His feet was pouring out her tale, a tale which to Jairus seemed as if it would never end, messengers were picking their way down the street, squeezing through the crowd that went in front. The message they brought it was easy to guess. They wanted the ruler of the synagogue ; a passage was therefore made for them ; just as Jesus was ending His words to the woman, and was sending her away contented, they came into the middle of the group.

It was only too true ; the girl was dead ; there was nothing more to be done. Jairus had better come away. His wife, the unhappy mother of the child, was wailing in the house, looking to him for comfort ; already the mourners had been hired, and the entrance hall was filling. As for Jesus, the Master, it was of no use to trouble Him any more. Had He really wished to save the child, He could have reached the spot in time ; as it was He had deliberately

loitered on the way. Even now He was delaying, evidently
more interested in a chance woman's case than in that of
Jairus and his daughter. Yet He must have known that the
latter was more urgent ; the woman could have been healed
at any time. It would be better now to leave Him alone.
Had He meant to work the miracle, and had failed through
this uncalled-for delay, to leave Him would teach Him a
lesson for the future. In any case the matter was now
hopeless ; the child was dead and that was the end.

> ' While he was yet speaking
> Some come from the ruler of the synagogue's house
> To the ruler of the synagogue saying
> Thy daughter is dead
> Why dost thou trouble the master any farther ?
> Trouble him not.'

So this was the end of all his anxieties. His worst fears
had been realized. Jesus had not done for him what He
had done for unbelievers, for men like the civil and military
authorities. Even if He had not wished to come to the
house, He might at least have saved the child from where
He was, as He had saved the others. What was he to think ?
There still remained the story of Naim, but could he venture
to expect so much ? Jairus was in one of those dilemmas
when faith is most tried, when difficulty is akin to doubt,
when prayer is near despair. It was the dark night of his
soul ; but the sunrise was nearer than he thought.

For Jesus knew. He had overheard the message that was
brought. There had been faith at the beginning, therefore
Jairus should be helped. He was a ruler of the synagogue,
and yet had come to Him ; therefore all the more
should he be helped. He was the father of the child,
and was in distress ; therefore again out of pure sympathy
he should be helped. He looked at the man in his distress,
his anxiety leading to despair, his despair to trembling of
faith ; the bruised reed must not be broken, the smoking
flax must not be extinguished. He turned to Jairus where
he stood ; He had deep compassion on him. While the
crowd continued to make its noisy din around them, He
leaned over to him and whispered :

> ' Fear not
> Only believe
> And she shall live.'

Jairus heard the words. What they implied he scarcely dared to think ; but the 'Fear not' had its effect as it had everywhere. Somehow he knew all would yet be well ; and not fearing he believed the more. To the surprise of his companions he did not break down in grief ; he became only the more eager to bring Jesus into his home.

The house of Jairus, like all of his degree, stood in its own 'compound' in the suburb of the city. An enclosure surrounded it ; a gate opened on the road. The procession came to the gate ; here Jesus once again put on that authority which had always to be obeyed. The crowd made as if to enter with Him ; to enter a house of mourning and join in the lamentation was a common custom. But He would have none of it. He held up His hand to forbid them, and they could only submit. He would have none to enter, not even the disciples ; when the father had passed in, then He chose only three to come with Him, Simon, and James, and John the brother of the latter. It was the first occasion that these three were set apart from the Twelve ; henceforth they were destined to be nearer to Him than all the rest, in His joys, in His sorrows, and in His glory.

They came together to the door of the house. Already from across the compound they had heard the din that was going on inside. The entrance hall within, the verandah without, were crowded with seemingly distracted mourners. Instruments of music were playing a weird tune, that tore the heart with lamentation and mourning ; taken apart it would have been pronounced a soothing tune, in its surroundings it was sheer agony. All around, seated or crouching on the floor, was a plethora of women. They were clad in deepest mourning ; their hair hung about them dishevelled, their eyes had a look of loss and despair, except when from time to time curiosity stirred them to take notice of any new-comer. They shrieked, they wailed, they uttered cries of agony, they groaned, they chanted lamentations ; from time to time a word of deep affection would break from one in the background. Some in their seeming distress would tear their clothes apart, and beat their naked breasts with their hands. For this was a special death. The daughter of a ruler of the synagogue was something to mourn for, and a daughter of twelve years old, just on the verge of womanhood, was worth all their best efforts. There is nothing more impressive, more dramatic, more piercing, more contemptibly hollow, than the professional mourning of the East.

Jesus saw all this.   He stood in the path that led up to the steps at the entrance and took in all the scene.

> ' And he seeth a tumult
> Minstrels and the multitude making a rout
> People weeping and wailing much
> Who mourned for her.'

He saw it all and disliked it.   Mourning of such a kind was unreal ; it was far too demonstrative to be true.   Already in the Sermon on the Mount He had spoken His mind on such things ; though He had not mentioned death and its accompaniments, He had said what He wished on fasting and prayer and almsgiving.   This people was given too much to externals.   External show had corrupted its understanding of the Law ; because of its judgement by externals He Himself was even now coming very near to being rejected.   He would not openly condemn them ; that they would not understand ; but He would leave them in no doubt of His contempt for all this hollow pageantry. The weeping of the childless widow at Naim was one thing ; this kind of weeping was quite another.   The weeping of Jairus and his wife called for His compassion, not the weeping of these professionals.

For a moment He stood at the entrance ; then He walked up the steps, into the midst of this wailing company.   They knew very well who He was, but they did not move.   They looked at Him ;   the expression on His face made them silent ;   but they made no way for Him.   There was a feeling that in some manner He was rebuking them, they waited to see what this strange Man would do.   These professional mourners, with their livelihood at stake, were not altogether friends of Jesus.

His words soon confirmed their suspicion.   He looked round about Him, with a glance not unlike that with which He had once cleansed the Temple court of its tradesmen. Then came a word of command :

> ' Give place
> Why make you this ado
> And weep ?
> The damsel is not dead
> But sleepeth.'

He spoke to them in their own language, the language of the East ; had they chosen to understand they could have done so. For the Eastern is figurative ; with the dry exactness of the West he has little sympathy. Definitions make no appeal to him. He prefers to speak in symbols ; he will blend into one different ideas ; he will say what strictly is not, that he may the better express what is ; he will speak ultimate truth in terms that in the present seem unsound. So does Jesus here.

But so to understand Him did not suit the mourners in the house of Jairus ; it would have robbed them of their wages and their hire. They knew the girl was dead ; with their own eyes they had seen the corpse, and were experts in this kind of business. He had not seen her ; how then could He know ? He was talking only nonsense ; He had committed Himself to something absurd ; whoever or whatever He was reputed to be, for once He had made a vast mistake. The wailing ceased, the mourning was silenced ; professional mourning could stop whenever it would. Instead, a wave of ridicule and laughter went round the group. First one, more daring than the others, led the way ; a loud, a brazen laugh. The rest took it up :

' They laughed him to scorn.'

We may pause to think what this implies. Here in Capharnaum, after all these months, after all these wonders, in spite of the devotion of the multitude, here was a large gathering of people who with so little provocation could openly laugh Jesus Christ to scorn ! It is a revelation indeed. We have heard of the Pharisees and Scribes, we have heard of the Herodians, and their hatred at least we can understand ; yet not till they had Him nailed to a cross hand and foot did they venture to ' laugh him to scorn '. It is a revelation. In spite of the multitudes that followed Him, there were those in Capharnaum who did not believe in Him, who made nothing of all He had said and done.

Jesus took little notice of their laughter. The spirit to command was upon Him, and that was enough ; as He had with a look driven the traffickers from the Temple, so He commanded these mocking men and women, who but now were wailing as if their hearts were utterly broken. He pointed to the steps, and to the gate beyond. There was no mistaking what He meant. The ruler of the synagogue, the master of the house, stood beside Him and made no objection. Gradually the group began to move. The crowd in the road beyond made way for them, and they disappeared. But the air was filled, no longer with their cries of lamentation, but with yet more weird cries against Him who had so betrayed His folly and His falsehood, and had robbed them of their rightful place ; cries which were the harbingers of others that would, in a little more than a year from that day, howl around Him till He died.

Not until they were gone did He move. There remained about Him but a few ; the father and mother of the child, Simon and James and John, some members of the household whose mourning was true, servants moving to and fro or looking on in awe. In a room at the side of the hall, whose door was open, lay the body of the child. It had already been laid out, on a mattress raised above the ground, wrapped in white, with flowers strewn upon it, the hands lying one upon another above the coverlet, the head slightly raised on a pillow. Jesus called to Him the father and mother. He beckoned to the three to follow. He entered the room, and ordered the door to be closed. He walked up to the corpse and stood over it ; the five in silent wonder stood around. For a moment He surveyed the body ; His eyes were then riveted on the face, as if they saw through it and beyond.

Then another movement. While He gazed into the face, His hand sought the hands of the maiden. It separated one from the other. It raised it, the stiffened arm at once relaxed and yielded. Then gently calling her, as it were awakening her from sleep, yet with a firmness which death itself could not but obey, He said :

> ' Talitha cumi
> Damsel
> I say to thee
> Arise.'

The effect was wonderful ; it was almost terrible. The five onlookers stood around Him, fixed to the spot, unable to speak or move. For as He spoke the maiden on the couch opened her eyes. She looked up from where she lay and met His gaze. Immediately the pallor of her face was gone, conquered by an inflowing red. The stillness of death rippled into a child's unconscious joy. From head to foot the little limbs quivered into life. With her little hand resting inside His she sat up. Childlike she could not remain there ; she rose altogether on her feet. She looked at Him ; she knew Him ; like every other child she saw in Him One whom she could trust. From her mattress she reached up to Him and loved Him ; it was a happy moment for them both.

And as a child He treated her. Pleasantly He played with her ; gladly He humoured her. The little one had been ill and now was well ; she had been dead and had come to life again. For long she had eaten nothing, and now was hungry. Hungry little children liked to eat, yes, and little children even when they were not hungry. Therefore let something be given to her ; now she was well anything would serve.

> ' And he commanded
> That something should be given to her to eat
> And they were astonished
> With a great astonishment
> And he charged them strictly
> That no man should know what was done.'

Jesus took it all as something very ordinary and natural. As with the boy at Naim, so here with the little girl at Capharnaum, what He had done had been wholly of His own accord. Other miracles men had come to ask of Him as they would ask for the help of any ordinary physician ; that He would raise the dead they did not ask, not even His friends at the end. It was a miracle that at once put Him on another plane, put Him beyond the reach of human comprehension. As the child moved about the room, as she passed from Him to her mother and her father, these did not know what they should think or do. They were beside themselves ; they looked at their daughter and they looked at Him. Love of the child was not lessened, but it was swallowed up, intensified, in their gratitude to Him. Jairus in particular, who had been hurt, who for a moment had been near to doubt, now saw how much more had been done for him than had been done for the ruler or the soldier. Precisely because he had been more tried, his reward had been greater :

> ' Only believe
> And she shall be safe.'

Henceforth, though the world were to tumble down about him, his faith in this Jesus would never fail. What he meant he could not say ; he could not say anything ; he could only stand there, struck dumb with astonishment. But the heart of Jesus read what the heart of Jairus felt, and that was enough. Such is perfect prayer, believing, loving, trusting, adoring, unable to express itself in words, and Jesus understands the silence.

But the scene could not end there. In the street outside the crowd was still gathered, curious to know what was going on within. We can hear the conversations that went on. There were those who resented this arbitrary action of Jesus, who had so abruptly dismissed the mourners and cut short the recognized formalities. There were others who discussed His seeming carelessness in coming to the spot too late ; had He cared He could have arrived in time. Some were prepared for a new excitement ; they reminded one another that Jesus never failed. A few believed and loved, and were content to trust ; many spoke of Him and His miracles, but more of His miracles than of Himself. Already long ago He had begun to warn them of this danger ; they sought Him as the Wonder-worker, the consequences they ignored. Yesterday, when He began to teach in parables, He had told them with yet greater emphasis to what this blindness would lead ; to-day, with this still greater wonder wrought in their very midst, it was essential that they should see what it implied. For this reason He had raised the child in the presence of a chosen few, the five most likely to see and understand ; but for the rest, thoughtless, self-seeking, He knew there would be danger. They would be enthusiastic ; they might call Him ' a great prophet ' ; but there it would end. It was better for them that they should not know. Before He left the house, He turned to these five and bade them not to speak of what had been done. It was a miracle for them, a reward of their faith and trust and an encouragement ; the world at large would make nothing of it.

But, of course, it could not be hid. The child was known to have been dead, and now was up and about, and men met her in the streets. Of necessity she was the talk of all the country-side, of all her kindred and her class. Some looked on and sneered ; had not Jesus Himself declared that the child was not dead but merely asleep ? Others ignored the whole affair ; such things did not happen, dead men did not rise again, and to enquire further was futile. Others again were annoyed, and criticized the evidence, and asked countless qcustions, and came to no conclusion ; the matter was not proven.   Others were superior ; they said it was no concern of theirs and passed it by.   Yet others turned on Jesus, and hated Him ; they said that by so doing He disturbed the country-side.   Though in spite of His warning

> ' The fame thereof
> Went abroad into the whole country ',

yet was it evident enough that the warning was justified. The shadow of the end was already upon Him.

15

47. The Second Rejection at Nazareth

IT was now some three months since Jesus had last been seen at Nazareth. During that time He had toured Galilee, but the little town in the valley beyond Cana He had carefully avoided. Alone of all the Galilæans its people, and not only its Scribes and Pharisees, had rejected Him and sought His life ; the kindest thing He could do to them was to leave them alone for a time. While He was away reports of Him would reach them. They would hear of His teaching, of His miracles, of the way others believed in Him and followed Him ; perhaps in time their own hearts would be softened and they would relent. For that He would wait and would endure very much.

That Jesus loved Nazareth with a special love we have evidence to this day. While in Galilee every other town of His time is gone, Nazareth remains. There is Mohammedan Tiberias on the lake, succeeding the city of the Romans ; but we have no record that Jesus was ever there. In other parts of the country are a few dilapidated dwellings, along streets that hardly bear the name, to record the memory of a city. Here and there we gaze upon unearthed foundations, and believe that we are on the site of this place or that. Or we look at the ruins of a chapel, and know that at least they record a tradition dating back to the Crusaders, and therefore probably to S. Helen. But in Nazareth alone has this memory remained alive ; and there it still flourishes, like the greensward of an oasis in a barren wilderness. In spite of its waywardness Jesus never lost His love for Nazareth. Though in the end He could only curse Corozain, and Bethsaida, and Capharnaum, yet Nazareth He would not condemn. Whatever it might say or do against Him, He could not forget all it had been to Him and to His Mother for more than thirty years. For her sake, if not for His own, He would love it, and bless it, and be patient with it, and wait for the day when the scene of the Incarnation would yet be a joy to all the world.

This must not be forgotten when we watch Him in His going in and coming out of Nazareth. As He had chosen for His Mother the lowliest yet the most beautiful maid in all creation, so He chose as the home of His sojourn the lowliest town in lowly Galilee, yet the most beautiful spot, we would say, in all the country of the Jews. It had the faults of its condition. It was narrow, it was stupid, it was dull; it was jealous, it was contemptuous of its betters; it was touchy, it was violent, it was resentful, it was prone to excess; it had the mind and soul of boorish country-folk, it could see no further than its own little valley. For all this, while naturally others contemned it, the heart of Jesus softened to it. For it, more than for His enemies, He prayed:

'Father, forgive them
For they know not what they do.'

In spite of all they did, He would never look upon the Nazarenes as enemies. 'Having loved his own that were in the world, he loved them to the end.'

The time was now fast approaching when His career in Galilee must close. During all these months He had given it His best. A little more He had yet to give it, and then to put it to the test. At the testing point it would fail Him, and He would have to go elsewhere; before that separation came He would make a final tour of the country. The last two days in and about Capharnaum had clearly marked the beginning of a change; this last miracle had made it prudent to leave the district for a time. As He had begun His career of preaching from Nazareth, so starting from Nazareth He would close it; and we next find Him, with His disciples, on His way 'to his native country', as the Evangelists are pleased to call it.

He came into Nazareth as He had done before, forgetting or ignoring the sad episode of His last visit. He went to His relatives for His resting-place; there He waited for the Sabbath. When the Sabbath day came He entered the synagogue, with the rest, and took His turn at the lectern. But here at once the difference was noticed. Before, men had wondered at Him; now they were overcome by the things He said. He spoke as one having authority; He uttered words that went to the soul ; His language was coloured by all the life of Nazareth about Him. He was Master of the Law ; He was versed in its interpretation ; over and above the learning and teaching of the Scribes He gave His own, as One who was more skilled than they.

The men of Nazareth heard and marvelled. At first they admired ; they were impelled to accept Him ; but a little more and they would have become His ardent followers. But soon a counter-argument crept in. They went their way from the synagogue. Round the lamps within their cottages, or squatting together at their cottage doors, they discussed His teaching ; from the teaching they went on to discuss the Man. And this was their undoing. For who was the Man ? They had known Him for these thirty years ; during all that time what had they seen in Him to fore-shadow such assumption ? What had there been in Him different from any other man ? They had known His father and His Mother before Him, and in both of them there had been nothing. They had known His kindred, many at that moment were living in the village with them. In them, too, there was nothing ; less than in many others of the town ; and even some of these had no faith in Him. His father had worked for years as their carpenter ; He Himself had been apprenticed to that trade. He had had the schooling of other boys in Nazareth. As a youth, it is true, He had lived His own life, very much apart ; about the family there had been a conspicuous reserve, but nothing more. On the whole He had been voted rather taciturn, and that, in a village life such as theirs, was not to His credit.

Clearly, then, He could not be what His language sug-gested. He had not even aspired to be a Scribe, or a Pharisee, or a lawyer. For this required special training ; it needed at the very least some course of study in Jerusalem. If a man had not followed that course, how could he be pronounced in any sense a scholar, or a master of the Law ? It would not do ; however grand His teaching there must be something wrong. They did not pretend to be able to discover it. They were only Nazarenes, poor country-folk, and could leave intricacies of learning to their betters. But they were very sure that the Pharisees and scribes, who were known to be against Him, had at least learning, and experience, and authority, and tradition on their side, and therefore must be right.

And as for the reports about the miracles He worked, well, that too need not be conclusive. Was it certain that they were miracles after all ? Could they not be explained in some other way ? What was this that was being said about His acting under the influence of Beelzebub ? In any case what did miracles prove ? No, it would not serve. The evidence was doubtful ; what He said was doubtful ; and there remained the overwhelming fact of His insignificant father, His still more insignificant Mother, His insignificant relations, His utterly colourless and insignificant self. Let Him parade Himself as He liked ; let others proclaim Him as they liked ; those Nazarenes knew He was only a Nazarene after all, no more than any of themselves, and they would take good care that no Nazarene assumed airs, or lifted himself above others of his kind.

' So that they wondered, saying
How came this man by all these things ?
And what wisdom is this that is given to him ?
And such miracles that are wrought by his hands ?
Is not this the carpenter ?
The carpenter's son ?
Is not his mother called Mary ?
And his brethren James and Joseph
And Simon and Jude ?
And his sisters also, are they not all with us ?
Whence therefore hath he all these things ?
And they were scandalized in regard of him.'

So did the boorish mind of Nazareth gradually, nay quickly, talk itself out of the light that, for the second time, had been bestowed upon it. It was and it is a common line of argument ; we call it poisoning the wells ; when before a man can speak his character is taken from him, or when, after he has spoken, and no other argument will serve, he himself is demeaned before his judges. But in this case we have more. He cannot Himself be assailed ; all that can be said of Him is that He had debased Himself to be even as one of themselves. Then shall His relatives be flung at Him. There they were in the streets about them, no better than other Nazarenes ; it is hinted that they were rather worse ; and among them are mentioned not only three Apostles, but even His own Mother. Of her, after thirty years, in tiny Nazareth where everyone is known to every other, so little is there known, so insignificant is she, that all they can say of her is to call her by her name.

' Is not his mother called Mary ? '

The sentence alone sets us pondering over the monotony of those thirty years.

It was soon manifest in the little town what attitude its citizens were taking towards Him. They would not treat Him with the violence with which they had treated Him before. On that occasion they had learnt their lesson, and did not care to repeat the humbling experience. Besides, He had now friends about Him, who might easily rescue Him from their hands. Still, even that event had only tended to embitter them the more against Him ; a worsted enemy is not easily convinced that he is wrong. They would try another and more effective course. They would ignore Him ; they would contemn Him ; they would stand altogether aloof, treating Him as if He were not. They would sneer at others who took notice of Him ; gradually they would freeze Him out of Nazareth. As the days passed by the power of His words, spoken in the synagogue on the Sabbath day, was forgotten. Men were ashamed to own Him ; He was not the vogue ; He was better left alone.

Jesus saw all this. He was prepared for it. Long ago He had warned them of what they would do. Then He had quoted a well-known proverb ; now, in their streets, where they sat by their doors and refused to gather to hear Him, their whole attitude one of insolent contempt, He repeated to them this same proverb. It was a little more drawn out, because now more than ever He felt the wound of this second rejection.

' But Jesus said to them
A prophet is not without honour
Save in his own country
And in his own house
And among his own kindred.'

In the last phrase there was a further warning, which later we shall see was sorely needed. It was another foreshadowing of bitterness to come.

Still would Jesus not condemn His beloved Nazareth. He hung about the place for a time. If the people as a whole would have none of Him, nevertheless there were a few here and there among the poorest, crippled beggars and the like, who would receive Him according to their lights. His tongue had been silenced, yet He could do something ; if not to whole streets filled with sufferers as at Capharnaum, at least to one or two here and there. And to these He went ; in these He found what consolation He was able. There is something particularly pathetic in the words of the Evangelist. With special gentleness He treated them ; with His own hands He touched them ; grateful to them for this little recognition, while He was saddened by the obstinate, foolish unbelief of the rest.

> ' And he could not do any miracles there
> Only that he cured a few that were sick
> Laying his hands upon them
> And he wondered
> Because of their unbelief.'

48. Another Tour of Galilee

Again He had given Nazareth its opportunity, and again Nazareth had failed Him. He went away ; the like would never be given to it any more. He set out on a further tour ; in other parts of Galilee He would be better received. Though even there the country-folk would fail to understand, still they would listen, they would come to Him and let Him do them good. For the rest, dull and ignorant as they were, much could be excused them ; misguided as they were, how could they be expected to discover Him ? It was His last expedition on any great scale in these parts. The time was short ; with one great sweep of generosity and love He would overwhelm the land.

Such at least is the impression one receives from the simple description given in the Gospels.

> ' And Jesus went about
> All the cities and towns and villages
> Teaching in their synagogues
> And preaching the gospel of the kingdom
> And healing every disease
> And every infirmity
> And seeing the multitudes
> He had compassion on them
> Because they were distressed

And lying like sheep that have no shepherd
Then he saith to his disciples
The harvest indeed is great
But the labourers are few
Pray ye therefore the lord of the harvest
That he send forth labourers
Into his harvest.'

The picture speaks for itself. He had been rejected at Nazareth, but that did not alter His plan. Jesus was ever hopeful ; failure, as we have seen already and shall see increasingly more, never made Him falter ; through the blackest cloud He would see the sun that shone behind. There were in Galilee other ' cities and towns and villages ', which knew Him less and therefore would receive Him better ; on whom the reports of His works and His words had made a deeper impression. Nazareth might laugh at their credulity, but what was Nazareth ? They were too hungry and thirsty for the truth to mind what the Nazarenes might say ; too long had they lived on dead, dry bones to fear even their Scribes and Pharisees ; too much had they craved for they knew not what, not to welcome this hope of living water and of living bread.

For this, they felt, was the spirit of the Man who walked among them ; everlasting hope, eternal certainty, come at last, focused to a point, after all the centuries of waiting. From Sabbath to Sabbath, from village to village, from synagogue to synagogue, the routine was the same. Mercilessly He spared not Himself, and His disciples were compelled to imitate Him ; ceaselessly He poured Himself out on all, and the very torrent overwhelmed them. The fascinating words that He uttered welled up from an obviously eager heart, telling them of the Kingdom that was theirs, of the true Fatherhood of God, of the new life that was alone worth the name ; and all was theirs if only they would know Him, and believe in Him, and trust Him, and accept His love and try to give Him love in return. All this flowed out upon them, through lips that quivered with affection, more tender than that of any woman, more understanding than that of the largest-minded man ; giving the good news in their own language, in language they all understood, yet with a depth of inner meaning that not the noblest language could convey.

So He would speak to them, and they were spell-bound. He opened to them a vision of another world, and they knew that the one in which they lived was, in the light of that other, unreal. He ceased, and they returned to themselves, and they gazed at Him in silence, these naturally noisy, and turbulent, and effusive Galilæans. Only when He had passed out from their synagogue, and here at the door with a touch of His hand healed a ragged cripple, or there down the lane lifted up a sufferer, stretched on a mattress at his village gate, would the spell be broken and the cry of welcome recognition break forth. It was glorious, it was enthusiastic, it was surely convincing. Simon and the rest of the disciples watched it all, and saw in it the sign of the Kingdom at last at hand ; the crowds gathering along the country-side, escorting Him from town to town, the gatherings in the synagogues straining to catch every word, the lavish healing, as if the Master could never do enough ; surely at last the conquest of the world was near!

But Jesus was not deceived. ' He knew what was in man ' ; He gauged without mistake the value and depth of all this devotion. They had been so long in darkness that now they were dazzled by a little light. So long had they been lost, wandering like sheep without a shepherd on their Galilæan hills, that the prospect of an open sheepfold made them rush to it for shelter ; the sight of One who would lead them to new pastures, and would keep them there secure, filled them with delight, and made them leap and cry for very joy. Poor things ! Shallow as was their fervour, yet was it all well meant ; weak as was their service, yet it was the best they had to give. The fruit was still but small, but the soil was good ; if it were well tended there would be a goodly harvest in season. It was a lesson He must teach His Twelve. The time might come when they would complain that the field of their labours was barren ; rather let them look to it that labourers in the field were not wanting. The people were there, and always would be there,

> ' Distressed
> Lying down
> Like sheep that have no shepherd ',

ready to be called and led to green pastures, if only there were shepherds to lead them.

49. The Mission of the Twelve

Thus in matter of fact we discover the chief purpose of this last expedition. It was an object-lesson to His Twelve. He would have them see, with His eyes more than with their own, the 'sheep without a shepherd', 'the fields white for the harvest', and not merely an annoying crowd of ignorant and erring people. He would have them feel with His heart, to have compassion on them all, the erring, the troublesome, the turbulent, and not merely treat them with indignation and contempt. He would have them long, with His soul, to go forth and help them, and bring others to do the same, and not lie down before a task that seemed to them hopeless. He would have this sacrificing spirit enter into their lives, even as it had entered into His own, into their prayers as it was part of His ; that living with His life they should pray with His prayer, and give with His giving, and crave with His craving to give yet more themselves, and to draw others to give along with them.

And now at once, having taught them the lesson, He would follow up His words with deeds. The Twelve were still in their training. Since the choice had been made of them on the mountain-side above Capharnaum they had learnt much ; now He would test them. In the Sermon on the mountain He had shown them what they were to say and how they were to say it. Since then, before their eyes for their instruction, He had poured out compassion and affection on a very varied multitude. Once already He had taken them with Him through Galilee ; before all the people He had declared His special love for them ; on the lake He had proved to them apart how specially He had them under His protection. He had taught them plainly, He had taught them in parables, to them alone He had given the key to what He had said. Now, on this last formal expedition He would put their instruction to the test. He would send them forth in His name, and let them try for themselves what they could do.

But, for the purpose, with how lavish a hand He endowed them ! These feeble, half-trained men who had never yet been tried, surely must be put under some obligation before they could be wholly trusted ? Not so. From the first He would give them His full confidence. They should be

endowed with powers akin to His own ; at the beginning
He had promised it, now He would fulfil His promise.
Before He returned to Capharnaum He called the Twelve
to Him.   With solemn emphasis He gave them their
commission.   He set them in pairs, first Simon and Andrew,
then James and John, Philip and Bartholomew, Thomas
and Matthew, James the son of Alpheus and Thaddeus,
Simon the Cananæan and Judas Iscariot ; one sees in the
arrangement due consideration for natural affinities and
character.   Then He gave them His own powers to work
miracles ; nothing on His part should be wanting to ensure
their success.   One is appalled at His trusting generosity ;
the Twelve when they heard His words could have been no
less struck.

> ' And having called his twelve apostles together
> He gave them power and authority
> Over all devils
> To cast them out
> And to heal all manner of diseases
> And all manner of infirmities
> And he began to send them
> Two and two
> To preach the kingdom of God
> And to cure the sick.'

At this point, after his custom, S. Matthew introduces a
long address delivered to the Twelve before they set out on
their journeys.   That this address was not delivered exactly
as it is here presented to us is only to be expected ; the
Evangelist, as in so many places elsewhere, has collected
into one instruction many that were given on different
occasions.   This is here confirmed by many evidences.
The instructions contain allusions which can have had
little or no meaning to the Twelve at this stage of their
career ; they were not, then at least, to be scourged or
persecuted, to be set before kings or thrown into prison.
Again, here more than elsewhere, much more than in the
Sermon on the Mount, the parallel passages found in the
other Evangelists are scattered far apart.   Many of them,
and these the most striking, are found in their Gospels
towards the end, when Jesus is preparing His Twelve to
face a cruel world after He is gone.

For a perfect harmony, therefore, it might be more

accurate to break up the address given by S. Matthew and distribute its parts according to the guidance of S. Mark and S. Luke. But this would be a difficult and, at best, a somewhat fruitless task ; the failures of scholars in work of this kind, not in regard to Scripture only, warn us against the tearing up of texts into rags to suit our own subjective judgement. Much easier, much safer, and in the end much more profitable is it to combine texts rather than to divide them ; and if S. Matthew has found it best to bring together the various instructions, regardless of the time or the place where they were spoken, we may be sure that we shall do best by following his example. Such a method gives us a kind of textbook for the guidance of apostles composed by Jesus Himself ; and though the varying shades in so pliant a character may for the moment thereby be lost, nevertheless the words so brought together reflect on one another and result in a consistent whole.

Therefore, instead of dissecting and dispersing the discourse of S. Matthew, let us do here what we have done in the Sermon on the Mount. S. Matthew's text shall be taken as a background, combined with the parallels in S. Luke ; on these two shall be grafted other passages which are evidently also parallel. By so doing we may hope to see more clearly the unified teaching of the Master.

That there was a day of solemn inauguration seems clear ; all three synoptists mention it, each with his own peculiarity of style. Sometime during this last tour in Galilee Jesus, as we have seen, called His Twelve apart. For some it was the fifth time of calling, now at last they were to go forth and fulfil their office of ' fishers of men ', of ' apostles ', of ' witnesses '. He was about to trust them utterly, as only Jesus could trust ; His own reputation and life's work were to be placed in their hands. For the mistakes they might make, and they would inevitably be many, He would bear the consequences ; for any bad example they might give, He would take the blame. As they sat about Him in the little cottage that morning, and heard their names assorted two and two, and were told in what direction they must go, and how they must act now for themselves, and must forgather again before the paschal season at Capharnaum, bringing Him reports on their adventures,—as they listened to all these commissions their Galilæan hearts

beat high. In response to such trust they would do such
things, that they would. They would preach so fervently ;
they would win the world to Him ; they would go through
fire and water for His sake. Though they knew their own
weakness, and limitations, and inexperience, and need of
support, and chances of failure, still they would be brave,
and according to their powers would be worthy of this
trust. For the trust implied love. They were not hired
servants, they were not merely officials. They were friends,
chosen friends of Jesus Christ, and they had already learnt
that the gift of this friendship was reward enough for
anything. That day when they were appointed was indeed
a happy day, an enthusiastic day, a day on which it was
good to be alive ; it contained a joy, the uplifting joy of
self-surrender, which has its equal in no other joy in this
world.

So enthusiastic, even if fearful, were those happy men ;
therefore at first they were in need rather of warning than
of encouragement. Let them be careful ; let them not
make foolish mistakes, especially mistakes of over-confidence ;
on this note does the instruction begin.

'These twelve Jesus sent, commanding them, saying :
Go ye not into the ways of the Gentiles, and into the cities
of the Samaritans enter ye not ; but go ye rather to the
lost sheep of the house of Israel. And going preach, saying :
The kingdom of heaven is at hand. Heal the sick ; raise
the dead ; cleanse the lepers ; cast out devils. Freely have
you received, freely give. And he commanded them,
saying : Do not possess gold nor silver nor money in your
purses, nor scrip for your journey, nor bread, nor two coats,
nor shoes, nor a staff. For the workman is worthy of his
meat ; but to be shod with sandals. And he said to them :
Into whatsoever city or town you shall enter, enquire who
in it is worthy. And whatsoever house you shall enter into,
there abide till you shall depart from that place. And
when you come into the house, salute it, saying : Peace
be to this house. And if that house be worthy, your peace
shall come upon it, if the son of peace be there your peace
shall rest upon him. But if it be unworthy, your peace
shall return to you. And whosoever shall not receive you,
whatsoever place shall not receive you, going forth out of
that house or city, shake even the dust from your feet for
a testimony against them. Amen I say to you, it shall be

more tolerable for the land of Sodom and Gomorrah in the day of judgement than for that city.

'Go ; behold I send you as sheep in the midst of wolves. Be ye therefore wise as serpents and simple as doves. And beware of men ; look to yourselves. For they will lay their hands on you and persecute you, and they shall deliver you up to councils and into prisons, and they will'scourge you in their synagogues, and you shall be brought before governors and before kings for my name's sake. And it shall happen to you for a testimony unto them, and to the Gentiles, and unto all nations the gospel must first be preached. And when they shall bring you into the synagogues and to magistrates and powers, and shall deliver you up, be not thoughtful beforehand ; lay it up in your hearts not to meditate before, how or what you shall answer, or what you shall say. But whatsoever shall be given you in that hour, that speak ye ; for the Holy Ghost will teach you in that same hour what you must say. For I will give you a mouth and wisdom which all your adversaries will not be able to resist and gainsay. For it is not you that speak, but the Holy Ghost, the spirit of your Father, that speaketh in you.

'The brother shall deliver up the brother to death, and the father the son, and the children shall rise up against their parents and shall put them to death ; and you shall be hated by all men for my name's sake ; and he that shall persevere unto the end, he shall be saved. And when they shall persecute you in this city, flee into another ; amen I say to you, you shall not finish all the cities of Israel till the Son of Man come.

'The disciple is not above the master, nor the servant above his lord ; it is enough for the disciple that he be as his master, and the servant as his lord. If they have called the good man of the house Beelzebub, how much more them of his household ! Therefore fear them not. For nothing is covered that shall not be revealed, nor hid that shall not be known. That which I tell you in the dark speak ye in the light ; and that which you hear in the ear preach ye upon the house-tops. For whatsoever things you have spoken in darkness shall be published in the light, and that which you have spoken in the ear in the chambers shall be preached on the house-tops.

'And I say to you, my friends : be not afraid of them who

kill the body and are not able to kill the soul ; and after that have no more that they can do ; but I will shew you whom you shall fear : rather fear ye him who after he hath killed hath power to cast both soul and body into hell. Yea I say to you, fear him. Are not two sparrows sold for a farthing —are not five sparrows sold for two farthings—and not one of them is forgotten before God ? Not one of them shall fall on the ground without your Father. Yea, but the very hairs of your head are all numbered. Fear not therefore ; you are of more value than many sparrows.

'And J say to you : Whosoever shall confess me before men, him shall the Son of Man also confess before the angels of God ; I will also confess him before my Father who is in heaven. But he that shall deny me before men shall be denied before the angels of God ; I will also deny him before my Father who is in heaven. He that shall be ashamed of me and of my words in this adulterous and sinful generation, the Son of Man also will be ashamed of him when he shall come in the glory of his Father with the holy angels.

'Think ye that I am come to give peace on earth? I tell you, no, but separation. Do not think that I came to send peace on earth ; I came not to send peace but the sword. For there shall be from henceforth five in one house, divided three against two and two against three. For I came to set the father against the son and the son against the father ; the mother against the daughter and the daughter against the mother ; the mother-in-law against the daughter-in-law and the daughter-in-law against her mother-in-law ; and the enemies of a man shall be those of his own household. If any man come to me and hate not his father and mother and wife and children and brethren and sisters, yea, and his own life also, he cannot be my disciple. He that loveth father or mother more than me is not worthy of me ; and he that loveth son or daughter more than me is not worthy of me. And he that taketh not up his cross and followeth me is not worthy of me—cannot be my disciple. For whosoever shall seek to save his life shall lose it ; and whosoever shall lose his life for my sake and the gospel shall find it.

'He that heareth you heareth me, and he that despiseth me despiseth him that sent me. He that receiveth you receiveth me, and he that receiveth me receiveth him that sent me. He that receiveth a prophet in the name of a prophet shall receive the reward of a prophet ; and he that receiveth a just man in the name of a just man shall receive the reward of a just man. For whosoever shall give you to drink a cup of water in my name because you belong to Christ, amen I say to you, he shall not lose his reward. And whosoever shall give to drink to one of these little ones a cup of cold water only in the name of a disciple, he shall not lose his reward.'

To anyone who has followed the words and actions of Jesus to this point it must be evident that much that is contained in this address comes with a jar. It is utterly opposite to the tone of the Sermon on the Mount ; for though in that Sermon there are notes of warning, still they are warnings of consequences and little more. The Sermon on the Mount opens with blessings, continues with encouragement, ends with fear of failure ; the Sermon to the Twelve begins with a tone of command, continues with its eyes ever on the enemy, ends with blessing indeed, but no longer for poverty, and meekness, and mourning ; it blesses what man shall do for Him and for His own.

And yet it is not difficult to detect the same spirit speaking through them both. In the second discourse it speaks only on a higher plane. To the men on the mountain-side it had pronounced a blessing because of the sufferings and sorrows that were part of their lives ; here, to Apostles, there were other sorrows and other sufferings, but with them other and greater blessings if they would but persevere. To the first He gave courage in that they were children of the Father ; here the courage is made yet more bold by the assurance that they were the Father's chosen men. The former He freed from the burthen of the Law ; these men were to be the champions of a New Law, and to suffer in that cause was to be their glory. In His first address He countered sin, and made innocence of life and generosity of hand an ideal ; now He goes beyond, raises the ideal to total surrender of that life, with a generosity that shall know no limit to its giving. To the men whose life was surrounded by the things of earth, perfection is found in likeness to God the Father ; to these men perfection is not mentioned, it is found in the losing of life and all that it contains for His sake, and for the sake of His name. The first He taught to pray, asking for their daily bread, asking for forgiveness of their sins ; to the Apostles He says almost nothing about prayer, prayer for them is sacrifice, even of their daily bread, and suffering, and the joy of having nothing. In the first He denounces hypocrisy ; in the second He lifts His own to that which is more positive, the bold confession of Himself before all men whatsoever. In the first He encourages to blind trust in God ; in the second He repeats His lesson, but with greater warmth, for even should they die there shall be glory for them before the Father and all the angels. In the Sermon on the Mount justice is made perfect when tempered with mercy and equality ; in the Sermon to the Apostles it is almost lost in the ideal of service, giving, and giving again, and asking in return but the reward of a prophet. The first Sermon closes with the simile of the house on a rock which stands, and the house on sand which falls ; the second dwells on the reward that shall be to those who shall give His houseless wanderers only a cup of cold water.

The Preacher is the same, but His audience is different. On that mountain-side He had selected these Twelve, and then it had been enough to interpret this life in the terms of God and Father. During these weeks He had kept them with Him and trained them ; He had given them to see what others could not see, visions in which this life dwindled to a plaything. Now He sends them forth transformed, their visions reinterpreted, to preach to others the Sermon on the Mount, but for themselves to aim at that which corresponded to their special calling.

In consequence of this there appears from beginning to end a sterner note. Love is no longer only tender ; it is heroic. With His own that sterner note is seldom silent ; from this moment onwards we shall hear it more and more. The vivid everyday imagery of the former occasion is gone ; instead the same all-seeing eye looks into the future, and pictures that which one day shall be. He looks across the country, to Samaria southward, and the land of the Gentiles in the north, and then comes back to the land of Israel. He paints the portrait of the Apostle as He sees it, with neither gold nor silver in his purse, nor bread in his wallet, a single coat upon his back, sandals only on his feet. He watches him as he enters town or village or dwelling-place, and describes the meeting which awaits him. He goes beyond this to the nations ; to councils and synagogues, and governors and kings, experiences as yet beyond the dreams of these countrymen of Galilee. He sees them put there on their trial, foreshadows their sentence, and the turmoil and battle that must follow. Let them not be mistaken ; the Kingdom is one of conquest ; it is not peace but the sword, making for a greater peace which the world cannot give. Yes, even if the eye has wandered far, the spirit that sees is the same.

Again, as before His words were instilled with a deep understanding of the men to whom He spoke, so was it here. He caught their present enthusiasm, and stirred it the more by all the splendid powers He bestowed upon them. He had watched them in their service of Himself ; He now spread it out to the service of all the world. He knew all would not go according to their liking ; He anticipated disappointment by showing that even persecution was foreseen, all was according to His plan. They would be maligned, but so was He, persecuted, and so was He ; in all this we have foreshadowed that yet more intimate address He would deliver to them before He died. It is not impossible that S. Matthew here incorporates the record of the Last Supper itself. They would come to fear ; they would be made to go through death itself ; when He recalls this, then does His understanding sympathy break through the general sternness. His voice softens ; His vehemence grows more gentle ; He is very near to them indeed when He says :

> ' I say to you
> My friends.'

Undoubtedly it was the same Jesus who spoke, however different the sermon. At the same time here, as we have said, more manifestly than in the Sermon on the Mount, it seems evident that the address was not all spoken at this time. These Apostles were still but novices. Their work, as yet, was to be confined to Galilee ; the conquest of the nations would begin only when He had left them. At present, for their own sake, and for their encouragement, their preaching must meet with success ; persecution and failure would come in good time, when the Holy Ghost had come down and strengthened them. Here and now it would be enough to prepare them for possible rejection, from some one village, from some one household.

' And it came to pass
When Jesus had made an end
Of commanding his twelve disciples
He passed from them
To teach and preach in the cities.'

In this very formal way S. Matthew concludes the scene. Evidently to him it was another momentous step in the career of the Twelve. It was a week or two before the Pasch ; it was while He was in the midst of His missionary tour through Galilee. Many were beginning their preparations for their annual journey to Jerusalem ; the name of Jesus and His wonderful works were in the mouths of everyone. If His envoys would only be faithful, if they would not flinch, they would succeed. As for Himself, He would make His way back to Capharnaum. As He passed from town to town He preached ; but He was chiefly anxious to reach His resting-place. There He would wait till His beloved returned, praying for them in the meantime ; when they returned, then would be another and a yet greater beginning.

' And they going forth
Went about through the towns
Preaching the gospel
And that men should do penance
And they cast out many devils
And anointed with oil many that were sick
And healed them everywhere.'

They went forth two and two, these confident, uncultured, inexperienced men, not yet even half trained, knowing very little. These fishermen of Galilee, these labourers of Nazareth, these publicans and tradesmen of Capharnaum went forth and men heard them

' Speak in their own tongues
The wonderful works of God.'

Can we not see them as they go ? Some had learnt long ago from the Baptist by the Jordan. By the Jordan they had received further lessons from their new Master. Since that time they had been with Him, and He had grown upon them ; and they had believed, and again had seen more and believed, so that their first belief had dwindled into nothing. So it had grown and grown, till now they believed they knew not what, except that it was He. And with their belief had grown devotedness ; and they had gone to Him, and they had followed Him, and they had remained with Him, and when He went away they longed for Him, and when He came again their hearts were glad, and they forgot themselves, they forgot all else, because of Him. When He called them to Him they went, when He chose them apart they put all else aside ; so devoted were they, so lost to Him, and the devotedness was the abandonment of love, and they did not know it. It was He ; He was theirs, they were His ; what more was there to say ? They were not given to analysis ; they knew nothing of definition ; they lived, and their life was the life of love.

With such certainty of faith as its foundation, with such devotedness of love as its inspiration, how complete was the trust of these men in their Master ! They knew in whom they believed. It was not so much His words, it was not His miracles, it was Himself that held them. Had He worked no wonders, still would He have been Himself ; had He spoken never a word, still in His silence they were sure they would have known Him. These other things had helped to reveal Him ; they had opened ever new vistas into His immeasurable soul. From that first day when He converted water into wine, till the day when, just for them, He calmed the waters and the wind, they had seen what He could do, and had wondered, and believed, and trusted all the more. But underneath they knew that it was not because of these things that they trusted Him ; it was because of the utter truth of the Man Himself. So likewise was it with what He had said. He had spoken as one having authority ; He had uttered things hidden from the beginning of the world ; never had man spoken as He had spoken. Yet it was not because of His words that they trusted Him, rather it was because of Him that they trusted His words. It was He ; He had won them. He was now sending them forth ; because He sent them, the work He gave them, from a thing impossible, became a joy, and they were as children, delighted to run their race at His bidding.

> ' And they going forth
> Went about through the towns.'

Off they went that happy morning in their various directions, nodding to each other a light-hearted farewell, discussing with their partners what they should do, and what they should say, and how they should obey His instructions. Off they went, and came to the first town in their way. They stood in its streets, they proclaimed their message. The Kingdom had come ; they, even they, were its heralds. Let men listen, let men prepare, let men do penance by way of preparation. Men and women came to their cottage doors and listened. They had heard of Jesus of Nazareth ; many had seen Him. These preachers they recognized as some of His companions ; this was their first recommendation. They used His very words ; this was the second. And some believed and listened more ; and some were superior and smiled ; and some were indifferent, having other things to do ; and some despised these fishermen and labourers ; and yet others hated them for their intrusion. The messengers passed down the street. On their way was a sick man lying at his door. With a little oil they anointed him ; the man sat up well. The people about were struck with wonder ; the messengers themselves trembled to discover that such power was indeed in their hands.

They passed through the village. On the outskirts, crouching at a corner of the lane, was a man possessed. They hesitated ; they encouraged one another. He had said they could do it, and because He had said it they would try. They took their courage in both hands. They went nearer ; they commanded the unclean spirit. There was a howl, a leap into the air, a moment's terror, and the spirit was gone. It was wonderful ! And they went on and preached all the more, and worked miracles all the more, lost to all else in their conquests for the Master. They had yet much to learn. But for the present this was enough.

16

50. The Death of John the Baptist

NOW there comes upon the scene another character, whose name provokes only contempt ; except for this, that with such an ancestry, and with such an upbringing, contempt is softened into pity. Herod Antipas, the son of the Great Herod who had rebuilt the Temple in Jerusalem, and had massacred the Innocents in Bethlehem, and had died of a foul disease while his hands were still steeped in blood, had been reigning tetrarch of Galilee for these thirty years and more. The Romans had put him there when, on his father's death, they had found it convenient for themselves to partition the country. Their soldiers kept him there, at once a watch upon him and a guard to overawe the people. Their officials ruled the district for him, including Galilee and all Peræa, with such Jewish assistance as was needed for their purpose. As for himself, so long as he gave no trouble, he could do very much as he liked.

And he did as he liked. The reaction from the cruel treatment of his boyhood had been great. Bred of a stock of mingled Eastern and Western blood, born of a merciless father, brought up in constant and imminent fear, with the blood of his brethren and relations continually flowing about him, an atheist of atheists with not a noble ideal in his soul, he had made up his mind, once he was secure, to compensate at any cost for the misery of his early life. What a time during these last years he had had ! Convention scattered to the winds ; an Eastern monarch was beyond convention and criticism, and the blood of the Eastern monarch was in him. Safe from the prying eyes of his people he had fortified himself in his palace of Machærus, aloft in the mountains overlooking the Dead Sea. There he had lived, with pleasure only as his object, growing more callous and cruel as he indulged himself the more, gathering about him such courtiers as would encourage him in his revels, petty magnates, local rulers, rich men who affected Magdala, women who were ready to sell themselves for a share in his orgies. For thirty years it had gone on, from bad to worse ; for just those thirty years during which Jesus, his subject, was hidden away at Nazareth.

Then had appeared that interfering John. In the midst of his revels, for a single crime committed, one man had dared to denounce him to his face. He had put him in prison ; for security he had taken him far away from his favourite Jordan. He had locked him up in the dungeon of his own castle ; and though all the world had resented it, yet not a man subject to him had dared to raise a hand in protest. To the Romans, moreover, John was of no concern. The Jews with their religion were a dangerous thing to handle ; so long as Herod did not go beyond their law he could do with his own zealots what he liked. Indeed the more he embroiled himself with them the more his Roman overlords would like it. With John in prison Herod knew he had nothing to fear.

But unfortunately the trouble had not ended there. Herod had visited John in prison. He was always curious about religious revivalists, always on the look-out for a fresh excitement and distraction, and such men as John were a diversion. Moreover, as is common with his kind, he was superstitious, and John had for him an irresistible fascination. But these visits had strangely affected him. John in prison began to gain a hold on Herod. His anger had waned, and had gradually changed to awe, his awe to fear, fear to respect, and Herod had of late become less gay, less reckless, more thoughtful and moody. This had affected his courtiers. Their master of the revels was turning gloomy, morose, capricious, ill-tempered, unman-ageable, uninterested ; if they were not careful, now that age and unceasing self-indulgence were beginning to tell upon him, he might develop like his father and turn on them. It was all because of John ; somehow John must be got out of the way. The women in particular would not be thwarted by such vermin. At Machærus John lingered in his prison, surrounded by more enemies thirsting for his blood than his keeper Herod.

Among these women was one who had long made up her mind that he would be her victim. Herodias had been the wife of Philip, the brother of Herod, not the then ruling

tetrarch of Iturea and the country to the north, but an
elder brother of that name. But he had been much too
meek and quiet for Herodias, and his court was all too
mild. Through Philip she had come to know his brother
Herod ; he and his way of living were much more suited
to her taste. In spite of Philip she had angled for him ;
after all Philip had not cared. She had captured him ; she
had gone away with him to Machærus, and there she had
reigned as its queen.

Then had come this John from the Jordan with his
unwarranted interference. She had had this serpent
scotched ; she had prevailed on Herod to close his mouth
and clap him in prison, no matter what the despicable
rabble might say. But she had not been able to do more.
None of her further hints had been taken ; none of her
caresses had prevailed anything. On the contrary ; of late
Herod had grown annoyed at the mention of the name of
John, and she had found it prudent to desist. Still there
was war declared between that woman in the palace and
that man in prison, war to the death, war for the soul of
Herod, war for her own throne ; if she failed she was cast
out from her world of revelry, she and her daughter with
her. But she would not fail. She would bide her time ;
like a tigress she would watch her opportunity, and, when
the occasion came, like a tigress she would spring.

At last the occasion did come. John had now been in
prison some four months. The Pasch was drawing near ;
within a week or a fortnight pilgrims would be coming
down the Jordan valley through Peræa to go up to Jerusalem. They would miss John at the ford ; they would
certainly talk about him. That he was known to be alive
over at Machærus might stir trouble ; and trouble at
paschal time was liable to be hard to control. Herodias
was more on the alert than ever. But before the Pasch
there was held every year at Machærus a much more
solemn festival. About that time was Herod's birthday ;
more important still, it was the anniversary of Herod's
coming to the crown, and Herod always celebrated this
event with more than customary revelry.

This year, both Herod and Herodias took care that the
ceremony and feasting should be more than usually brilliant.
To him the year had not been a very great success. Both
his marriage and this business with John had, he suspected,

put him out of favour, even with his boon companions. He must live the matter down; he must brazen it out; he must be more lavish than usual. Such people easily forgave a brave fellow, who affected not to care, who defied God and man, and whose wealth and luxuries were at their service. As for Herodias, she had her own plans. Herod must be roused from this moroseness that was growing upon him; he was beginning to show signs of a conscience, and that must at once be killed. He was given to excess. When roused his passions would make him dare anything; when in a bragging mood there was nothing he might not say. Who knew what might not happen? To the fullest of her powers she would humour him, flatter him, capture him, even if she had to use her own daughter as a bait.

So it came about that in that year the celebration of Herod's birthday was an unusually grand affair. Invitations had gone out, with special inducements and attractions, though experience had long since taught many that they would have a good time. Caravans had come in, round the north of the Dead Sea, bringing petty chiefs from all about, and heads of the army, and magnates from Galilee and Peræa, Jews and Gentiles, Romans and Asiatics,—round the loaded table of Herod they sank their differences; as for religion, though at home they said it was the breath of their nostrils, for the time being it was left outside. Religion of any kind did not go well with Herod's banquets; it was best forgotten for the moment. When the revelry was over, and some of them would need to make their way from Machærus to Jerusalem for the Pasch, they could pick it up again along the road.

They settled down to table, stretched out on their couches; what happened then does not concern us. The more solid eating was done; the guests were feeling satisfied with themselves and with their host; Herod was on this account in better humour. Then came other amusements. There was music, stirring every nerve; dancing, stirring every passion; of that, too, we need not say more. Only at a special moment, well-timed, a single dancing girl flashed in, and from the moment that her delicate foot touched the floor she had conquered every eye that glared at her. For glare at her they did; in their sodden state they would have glared at every dancing girl; had they been sober, a creature such as this would have caught them.

She danced and danced, and the jewels upon her danced with her. Like a snake she curved her lithe body, and the spell entered into every soul that was there. Her dark eyes of fire fascinated, her laughing lips invited, her whole figure drew. She addressed herself to all ; at times, in the ecstasy of movement, she seemed to address herself to none ; but all the while, with the subtlety of infinite guile, her meshes were all thrown in one direction. Herod ! Cost what it might that man must be conquered. Her mother had impressed it on her, before she entered that room ; she herself knew she was playing for a great stake.

And Herod responded. He knew her who she was, though many at the moment did not know. He was proud of her ; he was won by her ; she was a credit to his family and his court. He would reward her for this, though for the moment his heated brain could not tell him how. What would please the girl ? She should choose for herself. Whatever she might ask, what did it matter ?

The dancing ceased. With all the simplicity of a delicate maiden the damsel made her curtsey and smiled. The guests applauded, everyone applauded. In spite of their much experience these men had not seen dancing like this before ; for once they were aroused. Who was the girl ? Whence did she come ? And the word went round that she was the daughter of Herodias, the former wife of Philip, the present wife of their host, Herod. They turned their congratulations on him. This was indeed a crowning feat to such a sumptuous banquet ; it did Herod honour. How proud he must be of such an addition to his household ! And so on, and so on. In the world's subtle way they let him know that if he was in need of their forgiveness for his act of indiscretion, he was forgiven.

And Herod's heart was turned. He succumbed to their flattery. Filled with red wine, he cared not now what he said or did. The girl had danced his misery away ; she had danced him back into the favour of his flatterers. She should be rewarded ; in a right royal way he would reward her. When the applause had ceased, and the talk had sunk again into a murmur, at last he spoke. Loud and boasting and full of low passion he cried out :

' Ask of me what thou wilt
And I will give it thee.'

The girl stood still. She knew well the part she had to play. She affected to be frightened ; she hesitated ; in her heart what she sought was some assurance that her wily uncle would abide by his word. He saw her hesitation, the questioning look in her eyes ; he was sober enough for that. He saw the guests gazing at him, gazing from him to her, astonished at his boldness, with their eyes almost challenging him to stand by what he said. He would not go back ; nay, he would go further ; these men should see what a daredevil he was. He leaned forward on the table towards the girl. He raised his arm as a pledge of his fidelity. He uttered a binding oath ; then added, huskily, aggressively :

'Whatsoever thou shalt ask
I will give thee
Though it be the half of my kingdom.'

It was enough. Having sworn such an oath before so many witnesses Herod could never draw back. But she must not delay ; he might yet repent ; the guests would soon depart, and she would lose the influence of their presence. She made her bow and hurried from the room to her mother. To her she told her story. These two knew one another, worthy daughter of such a mother ; they knew that their fates were inevitably interlaced. They must plot together ; in good and in evil they must take equal share.

'What shall I ask ? '

said the daughter, more than suspecting what the answer would be.

The mother did not hesitate. How she had waited for this moment ! We can see the hard face set, intent upon its prey ; the burning, hating eyes already glittering in their anticipated triumph ; the beauty of that Asiatic countenance frozen into something terrible, as without a moment's pause she hissed out :

'The head of John the Baptist.'

There was no waiting. The maiden tripped back into the banqueting hall ; merrily, gracefully, as if it were all only a child's prank and whim. This time, as she came in, there was dead silence in the room ; even the half-drunken men knew well that what she might ask might be momentous. Then in the silence the damsel grew stern. The child rose suddenly to a woman. Her face took on her mother's hard look, her eyes were fixed fast on Herod. With them she seemed to hold him to his promise, in some way to threaten him, even while with a graceful curtsey she said the words :

> ' I will
> That forthwith thou give me
> Here in a dish
> The head of John the Baptist.'

Such a request, on such an occasion, from such a creature ! Even those hardened worldlings were appalled. They had heard in their time brazen women say many hideous things, and had laughed at them ; angry women shriek out things which men would never dare to say, and had enjoyed it as a show. Romans among them had seen women, vestal virgins, in their amphitheatres, turn down their thumbs in heartless contempt, and so seal a gladiator's doom. But this was something wholly different. That slight dancing girl, asking for the life of that man ! Asking for his bleeding head as her plaything ! That man's life depending on the whim of such a creature ! Even they could scarcely hold their indignation, their disgust.

Yet had Herod sworn to please her ; he had sworn it in the presence of this crew. He could not draw back ; his coward heart could not face that humiliation. She was daring him to do what he had promised ; he must not be beaten. His face lost its colour ; he hung his head as if he wished to think. The silence grew more tense ; every eye was upon him, above all the cruel eyes of that unflinching dancing girl. There was no escape ; he must keep his promise. A negro guard of giant stature stood beside the curtain at the door. Herod gave him a sign. He had heard the girl's request ; let him see that it was granted to her. Let him go at once and bring back to him here on a dish the head of the prisoner, John the Baptist.

The guard saluted like an automaton, turned on his heel, lifted the curtain and disappeared ; it was now too late for Herod to recall his words. In that room there was now amazing silence. Now and then one or another tried to break the spell but it would not be broken ; they lifted the load that weighed on them, but it fell back again. These men, one and all, had seen men die before ; cruelty was a second nature to them. More than one had done a slave to death for a trifling annoyance ; a woman's death when she became inconvenient, was an ordinary thing to some amongst them; some had sanctioned death to satisfy a jealous wife. But this death, of this man, under these conditions, to please the whim of a laughing, smirking dancing girl,—the horror of it would not leave them. They looked at her where she stood on the floor in front of them, in all her finery and jewels, smiling as simply as if she were but toying with a trifle, yet with a set look in her eyes and a tightening of her lips which declared she would not be baulked of her prey. They admired, they hated, they were fascinated, they were repelled. They would not have missed this show for anything, yet they despised themselves for being there.

Presently there was heard a shuffling on the steps outside. The grip on those men grew more intense; their hearts stood still; like frozen corpses they lay around the table; in the midst, like a statue, stood the girl. The silken curtain at the entrance was drawn carefully aside; it must not be stained. From underneath, in all his richest armour and accoutrement, stepped the giant negro, swarthy, thick-muscled, carrying a silver dish. On the dish was something; was it what they longed, yet feared to see? There was long dark hair hanging wet over the edge; there was darkened ooze dripping down it. Presently that upon the dish appeared, blue-black and livid, eyes half-open but lustreless, nose pinched to terror, cheeks sunk and hollow, lips apart as if they were prepared to speak, blood trickling out from either end. It was a human head; it was *the* head; those who had known him in life recognized the head of John the Baptist.

The negro stood at the entrance with his trophy. He would present it to Herod; put it on the table before him with his wine and fruit; trophies were becoming ornaments to dining-tables. But Herod would have none of it; even the guests shrank from that. Hastily he pointed to the girl who still stood before him, triumph now getting the better of her, hatred becoming beyond control, eagerness to seize her prey passing all restraint. With due ceremony the negro turned to her; solemnly he bowed to her, as to one whom his master chose to honour. He held out the dish. He hoped it would not be too heavy for this delicate maiden. He hoped she would not tremble at the sight of blood and let it fall. A fall of such a thing upon the floor would be ill-omened.

But he need not fear. She did not tremble. Eagerly she

seized the dish resting it on both her delicate arms ; to her breast she pressed it for security. She now forgot her manners ; Herod and his party could for the moment be ignored. Glaring at her treasure she turned and rushed out of the room ; the servants shrank aside as she passed, lest blood should drip upon them.

> ' And he beheaded him in prison
> And his head was brought in a dish
> And it was given to the damsel
> And she brought it
> And gave it to her mother.'

There we may leave the two gloating over their victory ; when woman hates she ceases to be human. Let us close the story as the Evangelist closes it :

> ' Which his disciples hearing
> Came and took his body
> And buried it in a tomb
> And came and told Jesus.'

51. Herod and Jesus

But for Herod it was not to end there. The banquet was over. The guests went their different ways, some to their homes, others to Jerusalem to celebrate the Pasch ; Herod, with Herodias and his court, would follow soon. They parted good fellows. They thanked Herod for his hospitality; they congratulated him on the way he had played the game. After all, when one considered the matter coolly, it had been a fortunate ending of a very awkward nuisance. Sooner or later this John would have had to die, and if so the sooner the better. What had he been in life but a disturber of the peace, a sedition-monger ? On the whole the best thing had happened. They went their ways ; they told themselves it was no affair of theirs. They had given Herod what consolation they could ; the rest was his concern, and if harm came of it, let him look to it himself.

They went their ways, and Machærus took on again its ordinary routine. But there was gloom in the palace from that day. Herod and Herodias met, but one subject dared not be mentioned between them. Herod and the daughter met ; but the daughter soon saw that, for the present at least, it were better to avoid his company. The excitement of that night had soon passed, the moroseness had returned, blacker now than ever. There was a petulance about Herod, an irritation, a suspicion, a sudden looking round as if he felt someone behind him ; into the dungeon he would never go.

Then about this time a strange piece of news came up to him from Galilee. Scarcely had John been disposed of, than it was reported that another Man had appeared in Capharnaum, and was doing things uncanny. Like John He was winning the people ; more than John, He was said to have power to heal the sick, to give sight to the blind and hearing to the deaf, to cure lunatics ; the people even believed that He could raise the dead. The Pasch was drawing near ; round about the Lake of Tiberias there was great excitement. The Pharisees did not like it, his political supporters, the Herodians, were suspicious ; there was talk of this stranger, Jesus, being called a King. On the whole it had been thought well to let Herod be informed ; since he had disposed of John, he might think it well to dispose of Jesus also.

Herod heard the news, but his anxious and conscience-stricken soul read it very differently from that which his informers had expected. Herod had no faith, therefore he was superstitious ; he had blood upon his hands, therefore he fled from a pursuing Nemesis. He had sapped himself to cowardice, therefore he always stooped beneath an imagined hand ever uplifted to strike him down. Just at this moment this thing had happened ; just when John was dead, it was reported that another had appeared at Capharnaum. He put two and two together. It was only too evident. He would sit alone in his apartments overlooking the Dead Sea, that constant reminder of divine vengeance, and brood upon it. A servant coming in would stand and listen to him as he muttered to himself, careless who might hear :

'This is John the Baptist
He is risen from the dead
And therefore
Mighty works shew forth themselves in him.'

Through this channel of the servants what ailed Herod soon got abroad. Something must be done ; he must be given companionship, distraction, or he would go mad. At the same time he must not be contradicted. Herods

were not amenable to contradiction ; and with an idea
such as this obsessing him he could only be humoured.
So they came, now one, now another of his friends. They
talked the matter over ; they let him have his say ; solemnly
they pondered and affected to believe with him that possibly
this was indeed the risen John. Then others came and
modified their tone. Over there by the Jordan Elias had
gone to heaven in a chariot of fire. It was commonly
supposed that he would come again to earth ; was it
possible that this might be Elias ? Or indeed any of the
ancient prophets ? For that prophets might return again
was a common belief.

Thus they tried to play upon the tetrarch's superstition.
They dared not oppose it ; they dared not say his brain
was disordered ; he was in no mood for that. But the
more they tried to divert the miserable old man's fancy, so
much the more did he question, and in the end come back
to the first conclusion that haunted him. If he could only
gain an opportunity to see this Man, and to judge for himself
whether he were John or not, he would be more at ease.

> ' Which Herod hearing said
> John I have beheaded
> But who is this
> Of whom I hear such things ?
> John whom I beheaded
> He is risen from the dead
> And he sought to see him.'

In little more than a year from that day the opportunity
would come ; but the time was not yet.

52. The Feeding of the Five Thousand

The news of the death of John reached Jesus on His
return to Capharnaum. It marked yet another stage. Let
us look back. In the beginning John had stood alone, the
herald proclaiming the coming of the Kingdom and the
King ; one day the King had come and John had declared
Him. For a year or thereabouts John had gone on preaching ; Jesus meanwhile had just followed his example,
baptizing by the Jordan as he baptized, suffering men to
find Him if they would, never once superseding John or
suffering him to be put down. At length John had been
taken prisoner ; then it was that Jesus had begun His

public life in real earnest. He had gone at once into Galilee, and preached in the synagogues, and worked miracles, and taught everywhere that the Kingdom announced by John had come. Now John was put to death. It was close upon the Pasch. While this was being done, while one voice was silenced for ever, Jesus was sending out twelve other voices to proclaim Him. That same week was to see the climax of His popularity, the offer of the great test, the failure, the beginning of decline, the definite opening of warfare.

The news reached Him, it would seem, while the Twelve were still on their mission. If later He could weep for the loss of Lazarus, is it possible He did not weep for the loss of John? John alone among men had understood Him; John alone had known Him; though they had seldom met, though only once, perhaps, had they looked into each other's eyes, yet that once they had seen enough. The friendship, the love, the utter trust in each other had sufficed for the rest of their lives. Were they never to meet again it would matter not; and so far as we can learn they never met again. That day Jesus lost His dearest friend on earth, for His Mother was a soul apart; and He sat alone in Capharnaum and mourned for him, mourned, too, for all that his death implied.

But it could not be for long. The Twelve had now been away for their allotted time, and they would soon come to Him to report. They came; two and two they gathered round Him; one after another they went in to Him, and with the glee of happy children told Him all the wonderful things they had done. Simon came, all impetuous. How he had stirred the country-side! How many he had won to his Master! What a number of devils he had cast out! And John came, that youthful Son of Thunder. How he had preached to his villages, that they should do penance, and had moved them by his threats to great things, and had impressed upon them the wonders of the coming Kingdom! And Philip came, happy-souled, confiding, gentle Philip. He had preached in his quiet, shy, half-diffident way, agreeing it would seem with everybody; and though he had little enough to say for himself, yet Bartholomew could tell how he had won all hearts. And Matthew came, Matthew who always held himself the least of all, born as it were out of due time. He had preached the Kingdom ; he had reminded his countrymen of the prophets and their prophecies ; and he told his Master how they had listened. And Judas came, Judas of Carioth, shrewd, prudent, careful, business-like, reliable Judas ; and he told how he had saved his companion, Simon, surnamed the Zealot, from many indiscretions, how he had remembered his Master's warning not to trust men, how he had made quite sure that all was safe and well. Certainly the report of Judas was the wisest of them all.

And Jesus received them. Gladly He welcomed them each in turn. While they poured out their separate stories He listened to them. There was no need to question them, no need to draw them out. He was Jesus, and they could say anything to Him. And He encouraged them ; He had a kind word for them ; even though each received His guidance, His correction, His warning, yet there was none but went away an intensely happy man. 'Well done, Simon, but do not be too sure !' 'John, threats are good, but love is better.' 'Philip, yes, remain always simple as a dove ; but do not forget what I said about prudence.' 'Thomas, why this little despondency ? In my service even failure is success.' 'James, yes, get men to do great things ; but remember it must be for me.' 'Judas, thou hast been faithful over a few things ; but seek first the Kingdom of God and His justice, and all other things shall be added unto thee.'

At last the interviews were over, and Jesus came to them in the outer room. They were happy men. He had trusted them, and they had been faithful to their trust. They had worked for Him, and He in His own inimitable way had thanked them for it. He came in to them ; He was pleased with them, and they responded. They would do for Him anything He asked. But just now He would ask nothing more. They were tired with their labours, much more tired than they knew. He must give them rest ; He must have a care of His own. There was welcome on His face, deep affection in His eyes, as He looked upon them all and said :

> ' Come apart
> Into a desert place
> And rest a little.'

What an added joy was this ! They had looked for yet more labour, and instead He would give them peaceful

hours with Himself. Here in Capharnaum it had now come
to pass that there was no longer peace for them anywhere.
Whenever He appeared in the streets, invariably the people
thronged about Him ; when He retired into a house they
gathered round the door. In and out, in and out, visitors
never left Him to Himself ; honest enquirers, criticizing
doctors of the Law, would-be followers who still could not
decide, humble folks with their sick, others who were only
curious, who wished but to see this much-discussed Man,
and to be able to say they had spoken to Him. He received
them every one ; He seemed unable to refuse. He forgot
His meals, He forgot His sleep, He forgot Himself ; He had
need to be protected.

> ' For there were many coming and going
> And they had not so much as time to eat.'

Glad were they, therefore, that He had suggested this ;
for His sake as much as for their own. This time they must
make their holiday a success. The last had not been
successful, not at least as a holiday ; that day when they
had gone to Gerasa, and the Gerasenes had asked them to
go home again. This time they would take Him higher
up the coast. They knew a spot with the hills around it,
a grassy sward with a few brooklets running through, just
beyond the Jordan in Philip's territory, where they could
sit and rest all the day undisturbed. So they hurried their
preparations. It was still early morning, and as yet the
streets were quiet ; if they wished to get away undisturbed
they must waste no time. The ship was drawn down to the
water ; they went on board with Him. As the sun rose
over the mountains in front of them they set out, first into
the open, then to the north-east corner of the lake, beyond
where the Jordan flows in, behind which the mountains
rise high, shutting off the east wind from across the desert,

> ' And going up into a ship
> They retired into a desert place apart
> Which belonged to Bethsaida
> Over the sea of Galilee
> Which is that of Tiberias.'

But they were not to escape so easily. Jesus had been
absent from Capharnaum for now a long time, and the
crowds were glad to have Him back. Since He had
returned, while waiting for the Twelve, He had done little ;

now that they had come it was to be hoped He would begin again and give Himself to them. That He should go away at once, and that across the lake, was not according to their liking. When, then, in the early morning the few loiterers by the shore saw what the Twelve were doing, still more when Jesus was seen to step into the boat, they ran into the town and reported. Crowds soon gathered on the water's edge. They saw the little vessel, with its sails set, already beyond their reach. They watched its direction. This time they were making northwards, not to the south, and any point in the north could easily be reached on foot from Capharnaum. As the vessel slipped away the excitement grew. At last someone in the crowd gave it momentum. Let them go round the lake, and keep the sail in sight, and meet Him wherever He landed.

> ' And they saw him going away
> And many knew
> And a great multitude followed him
> And they ran flocking thither on foot
> From all the cities
> Because they saw the miracles that he did
> On them that were diseased
> And were there before them.'

S. John is careful to tell us that the event here described took place on a day immediately before the Pasch. (We accept the text as authentic.) This he may have done for two reasons, though if there were no reason it is quite in keeping with his ordinary method. First, perhaps, he would explain how it came about that so great a multitude, chiefly of men, was gathered together on this occasion. Secondly, he would emphasize the significance of the miracle that here was about to be performed.

> ' Now the Pasch
> The festival day of the Jews
> Was near at hand.'

For it may well be asked how so great a number, five thousand men and more, not to mention women and children, could have come together at that point, at so short a notice, in a deserted place, and for the most part not from the villages in the neighbourhood. The answer would seem to be this. First, there were the remnants at least of those crowds of whom we have already heard

mention ; of people from Judæa and Peræa in the south
and south-east, and from Tyre and Sidon in the west, who
had come long since to Capharnaum that they might be
with Jesus and hear Him. Next, there were the multitudes
that had gathered at this centre, that they might go up
together by Peræa for the Pasch, but who, because He
delayed, had also waited with Him. Thirdly, there were
the inhabitants of the towns and villages from Bethsaida to
the Jordan river, not only along the shore, but perched up
on the hill-side in the background. For these the paschal
time was also a time of holiday. The ripening corn for the
present did not need them ; as the noisy procession came
up from Capharnaum they would naturally have joined it.

The distance from the synagogue at Capharnaum to the
spot where the Jordan flows into the Lake of Galilee is a
walk of exactly an hour. Until one comes out on the open
plain to the north, it is at the present day very rough walking,
over successive spurs of hills, with here and there a rivulet
trickling down, the whole surface covered with boulders and
broken stones. Smoothed and weather-beaten as these
boulders are, one nevertheless has reason to suspect that at
one time almost all this coast-line was inhabited. It is not
impossible that these stones, running at times in remarkably
straight lines as if indicative of streets, are the remains of
ancient ruins ; now they are smoothed beyond recognition
by two thousand years of rain, and storm, and sun.

Crossing the Jordan, which even as it enters the lake
scarcely reaches to the knees, another hour at most brings
us to the range of hills on the opposite side of the valley ;
though the distance to be traversed is less, a number of
brooks to be crossed makes walking more difficult. At the
foot of the hills, sloping towards us as we approach them,
is a green plain ; even in October, when all around is
brown and withered, this well-watered space keeps its
verdure. Here, according to common consent, the miracle
took place of the feeding of the five thousand.

A vessel sailing from Capharnaum to the north of the
lake could easily be followed from the shore. We have seen
how the crowd gathered, how it made its way along the
bank ; if the wind were light or contrary, it would easily
reach the spot before the ship. At the north-east corner the
little boat put in. From the deck out at sea the disciples
had not noticed the excitement on the land ; they were

with Him, absorbed in Him, serving Him, and that was
enough. When then they turned their course towards the
landing-place, what was their surprise to find, already lined
up along the beach, an almost countless multitude ! Men
were gesticulating, calling to them, signing to them where
to land, talking much to one another, while no one heeded
what another said, delighted only to be noisy, officiously
preparing to receive the boat and its occupants, laughing
at their cleverness in thus forestalling and recapturing their
fugitive Jesus. Whence had they come ? The disciples
were not long left in ignorance. Soon they recognized
many of their friends from Capharnaum, and understood.

But what was next to be done ? They looked at their
Master in dismay. He had brought them to a desert place
for a day of rest with Him alone, and this had happened.
Would He dismiss these people, or would He yield to them
and deprive His Twelve of their holiday ? Alas ! They
knew how it would be. They saw Him rise from His place
in the stern ; He looked across the ship to the crowd
waiting for Him on the shore. They had come all this way,
just for Him, to be with Him, because they believed in Him
thus far. He was pleased, He was gratified, He must show
His gratitude ; He loved them, He pitied them, He must
go to them as they had come to Him. The Apostles read
it in His face before He spoke ; when at length He murmured
something about

'Sheep having no shepherd',

they knew the day was lost. Submissively they put in to
the shore and let Him land.

'And Jesus coming forth
Saw a great multitude
And he received them
And had compassion on them
Because they were as sheep not having a shepherd
And he began to teach them many things
Of the kingdom of God
And healed them who had need of healing.'

He came ashore among them. Proudly they received
Him, effusively they made way for Him. They would
welcome Him, they would do Him honour ; that they
tried Him with their demonstration did not occur to or
concern them ; He was Jesus, and He must submit. And

He did. He received their attentions ; they might pull Him to and fro as they chose ; they knew no better and they never would. But they were not wholly to blame. They ought to have been guided, and their guides had failed them ; worse than that, of late these guides had made great efforts to lead them astray. While He could He would be with them. He would help them, He would teach them anything He could, but chiefly of the Kingdom of God. He passed up the passage through the crowd that had been made for Him. Here and there, as He went along, a cripple boy was seen, a beggar with some sore. He paused at each, He stooped down and put His hand on each ; He looked into the sufferer's face and he was healed. He led the way across the green plain beneath the hill ; the crowd closed in and followed. As for the Twelve, they could wait ; before evening was come they would not be sorry they had sacrificed their day of rest.

Through the long hours they sat together, Jesus and the common multitude, on that green plain below the hill above the water's edge. Men came and went ; and He spoke to them all, and rested at intervals, and some came around Him and they just talked together. Time passed away unnoticed ; the sun began to bend over the western Galilæan hills. Almost suddenly it dawned upon the Twelve that unless they were careful the day might end in trouble. Their Master, good Man, was again forgetting ; so lost was He in His work that He did not notice how the time was fleeting. The sun would soon be down and the darkness be upon them. They were all far from home, two hours at least from Capharnaum, and all were in need of food and rest. They held a consultation together ; He must be reminded. They made bold, as they had often done before, and came to Him. They interrupted His discourse with the warning :

> ' This is a desert place
> And the hour is now past
> Send away the multitudes
> That going into the towns and villages round about
> They may lodge
> And buy themselves victuals.'

He seemed not to mind what they said. He seemed to be in one of His careless moods, when love got the better of Him and He was unreasonable. What other impression could they receive from His reply?

> ' They have no need to go
> Give you them to eat.'

This, surely, was too much. He knew very well that they had nothing with them ; in any case to expect them to find food for five thousand people and more was an extravagance. Had He again ' gone mad ' ? But perhaps He meant that they should go and buy what was needed. How much money had they ? Judas looked into the purse ; at most there were two hundred pence. It was the best they could do ; they could spend the money on bread and see how far it would go. So

> ' They said to him
> Let us go and buy bread
> For two hundred pence
> And we will give them to eat.'

Meanwhile Jesus had risen from where He sat and was moving to a spot higher up the mountain-side. Here again He sat down, and turned His eyes on the crowd gathered in the plain below. At first the sight seemed to surprise Him ; He seemed as if He were doubtful of being able to feed such a number. Philip was by His side, gentle, accommodating Philip.

> ' When Jesus therefore had lifted up his eyes
> And seen
> That a very great multitude cometh to him,
> He said to Philip
> Whence shall we buy bread
> That these may eat ?
> And this he said to try him
> For he himself knew what he would do.'

To the meaning of this, as he thought he understood it, Philip agreed. Two hundred pence ! For five thousand men and more ! The food supply of more than one village would be needed.

> ' Philip answered him
> Two hundred pennyworth of bread
> Is not sufficient for them
> That everyone may eat a little.'

Did Philip guess something at least of that which was about to happen ? Did it occur to him that He who had turned water into wine might, if He so chose, turn stones into bread? Did he remember how the Master had but lately said that should they ever be in need their heavenly Father would feed them? Did he recall the Manna in the desert, and how bread had been sent down from heaven, merely, as it were, to humour the people of God? From his words one suspects it; from other things we know of his simple faith we believe it. He seems to say, as he seems to hint elsewhere, that he believes more than he is able to express, even to himself.

Jesus looked at Philip no more. He fell back into one of those inspiring moods when He instilled peace around Him, and certainty, and trust; when men of goodwill obeyed Him, though He might command what seemed impossible or absurd. So it had been at the marriage feast at Cana; so with the ruler and his son; so in these last days when He had sent out His Twelve to preach, and in the strength of His command they had succeeded. Such a mood was on Him now. He seemed to live outside the world around Him; and Philip, here as elsewhere, was the first to catch the spirit that was on Him. To the rest Jesus turned, and quietly, almost carelessly, asked them:

'How many loaves have you?'

To them, then, it seemed that He was still living on false hopes. Loaves they had none among themselves; they had a little money, that was all. Surely He knew, for He had seen the hurry with which they had started from Capharnaum that morning; He had seen they had nothing with them when they came ashore. But He must be humoured. They moved about among those who were near. They found a little boy with a basket; in it were five loaves of common barley and two tiny fishes, more than he could need for himself. No doubt he was willing to sell them; probably he had brought them for that purpose. Evidently a native of that part of the coast; a boy from Capharnaum would never have brought such a burden. He was all the Twelve could find; they came to report their failure.

> 'And when they knew
> One of his disciples
> Andrew the brother of Simon Peter
> Saith to him
> There is a boy here

> That hath five barley loaves
> And two fishes
> But what are these among so many ? '

No ; there was nothing else to be done. They would
be compelled to go into the town, and buy what they could
with the money they possessed.

> ' Unless perhaps we should go and buy victuals
> For all this multitude ' ;

and Andrew looked around in dismay at the five thousand
men and more gathered on the plain beneath them.

All this time had Jesus waited. Deliberately He had
waited, that quite clearly beforehand the exact facts might
be made known to all. There were so many men ; there
was just this amount of food and no more. Even what was
to follow must be done in strict order, so that from first
to last there should be no room for mistake or misinterpreta-
tion. Never before or after was Jesus more careful or
exacting in the working of a miracle. On this occasion,
more than on any other, He acted like a king, and would
be obeyed, down to the smallest detail.

> ' And he said to his disciples
> Make the men sit down
> By fifties in a company
> Upon the green grass.'

It was so done. The Twelve stepped down from the
higher place to which Jesus had called them. They went
round among the crowd and set them in order. The
people were docile. They had come a long way that
morning ; they had listened through the day to One who
had brought solace to the hearts of them all ; there was
peace and contentment reigning in their hearts, and therefore they were glad to do His bidding. A submissive crowd
is as tractable as an adverse crowd is difficult to control.
Besides, by this time they were hungry, and hunger had
increased their weariness ; now they were told that if they
would but arrange themselves in order, food would be
distributed among them. So they easily submitted. They
were collected into groups of fifty, and the fifties were
united into hundreds. There were fifty such groups
gathered and seated on the green grass that evening before
the Pasch. Jesus had taken good care that the number
should be known for ever.

Meanwhile He sat there on the mountain-side with the little boy and his basket beside Him. He watched the scene beneath Him and approved. There was peace in His whole bearing, peace and assurance ; as they arranged themselves the people looked up to Him, and knew that somehow all would be well. He waited till all had been done as He directed ; not until the Twelve had come back to Him did He begin.

Then when all was ready, with the Twelve standing about Him, and all the people looking towards Him from below, slowly and carefully He took the little boy's five loaves and two fishes on His knee. He held them in His hands and looked up to heaven ; for a moment He was lost to earth. He placed a hand upon the bread and fishes and blessed them ; there was an uttered prayer of thanksgiving to the Father who would give to His children their daily, their supersubstantial bread. He broke the loaves in parts, then the tiny fishes. With the broken pieces on His knee, He called His Twelve yet nearer. To each He gave a part ; five loaves and two fishes divided amongst twelve men, scarcely a meal for themselves, let alone for the multitude below. But it was not for them ; they were to take what He gave them to others. So He bade them, and they could only obey.

The Twelve did as they were told. They came to their respective groups. With their fingers, as He had done, they broke their portions into smaller pieces. These they handed out ; they put their hands into their wallets for more ; there was something always over. Again they broke, again they gave, again they found something in the wallet. At first it may be they did not notice, but soon the truth grew upon them. They gave more freely and abundantly, so abundantly that some had more than they could eat ; and still their wallets never emptied. They passed down all the lines, they came to the end ; each of the Twelve had served the groups allotted to him. There was not a man there who was not satisfied, and still there were portions left.

> ' And when he had taken the five loaves
> And the two fishes
> Looking up to heaven
> He blessed and broke the loaves

> And when he had given thanks
> He gave the loaves to his disciples
> To set before them
> And the disciples to the multitudes
> That were sat down
> In like manner also the two fishes
> He divided among them
> As much as they would
> And they did all eat
> And were filled.'

But Jesus had not finished yet. He had given them the gift of bread,

> ' Full measure and pressed down ' ;

but before He had done it must be

> ' Flowing over.'

All the time the meal was proceeding He had sat there and watched them. With His eyes He had followed the Twelve ; with His face of content He responded to the contentment of the crowd ; in His whole body, strong, sure, yet utterly quiet, He spoke His own soul within. Now it was over. The Twelve had come back to Him speechless ; in truth they did not know what they should say or do. The people, too, sat in their places before Him, careless of the oncoming darkness, careless of the night. There was a stillness over them all, the stillness of contentment ; it was an army drawn up, contented with its Leader.

Then He broke the silence with another order. He turned to the Twelve. As if ignoring the miracle He had worked, as if bread were to Him an anxious matter, as if in spite of all this it were possible yet to starve, He said to them in earnest :

> ' Gather up the fragments that remain
> Lest they be lost.'

We have here again a striking instance of that strange combination in Jesus of which we have already spoken ; that combination of the strongest and the weakest, the greatest and the least ; that baffling contrast in one Man, which, nevertheless, was the secret of His intercourse with men ; why they could honour Him as no man was honoured, and yet could treat Him with a familiarity, sometimes even a contempt, which they would scarcely have shown towards a common servant. This Jesus Christ, who had just fed five thousand people with five loaves, was now anxious about the crusts and crumbs ! And His second command, that the fragments should be collected, came to the Twelve, not as something paltry after all that had happened, but as something quite natural, coming as it did from Him. They heard it and at once obeyed. They went to their new task, each with a basket ; they returned with the baskets full : they brought Him back, in remnants, more than they had taken away whole at the beginning.

In the later years, when the Twelve were left alone in the world to preach the Gospel, and to interpret Jesus to mankind, it is probable that they took this Feeding of the Five Thousand as the greatest, or at least as the most significant, of all the miracles that Jesus wrought. It is the only one which all the four Evangelists have described to us ; for once even S. John has thought fit to go again over the ground trod by the others. But he also gives us the reason. It is one of those miracles, indeed the most striking among them all, which were more than miracles. It was a parable in action, containing a definite instruction, not only con-firming all that had been already said, but foreshadowing the greatest doctrine of all that was yet to come, the doctrine of the true Bread from Heaven.

This may in part explain the otherwise astonishing comment of S. Mark upon this scene. When the day was over, when he had described the walking of Jesus on the waters which closed it, on a sudden, wholly unexpectedly, he reverts to the event of that afternoon, with the words :

' For they (the disciples) understood not
Concerning the loaves
For their heart was blinded.'

This expressly of the Twelve ! That they could have failed to see the miracle done before their eyes and through their own hands seems impossible ; even the crowds who were fed upon the plain saw it, and they could have seen no less. But it was the meaning they did not see, the application of the parable ; the sign of the bread, the use of themselves which their Master had made, multiplying the bread in their hands, not His own, distributing it through them ; the complete satisfaction that it gave, the fragments remaining, more than at the beginning, showing that the Bread which He would give would never be exhausted ; the care of Jesus throughout, both before and after, telling of the reverence that would one day be paid to the Living Bread which He would give. This as yet they did not understand. Even with them the dream of the Kingdom upon earth still prevailed, and therefore

' Their heart was blinded.'

Even with them Jesus still needed to be patient. But He could wait. The dawn of sight was now very near ; another mighty act of faith, and the rest would follow. He would protect them meanwhile and bide their time.

53. The Walking on the Waters

MEANWHILE the truth of what had been done dawned upon the men upon the plain. They had sat down and waited ; they had eaten their fill and were satisfied. They had noticed how the Twelve had gone among them, feeding them all, yet never had they needed to return to the Master to refill their wallets. At the end, when the remnants were collected, there was more over and above than there had been at the beginning. It was a miracle, a miracle of a wholly new kind ; a miracle done, not this time on the sick and diseased, but on healthy men and sound ; a miracle of bread.

And was not the miracle of bread the great sign of the prophet that was to come ? Melchisedech was one of the great foreshadowings of the Messias ; and Melchisedech was unlike others in this, that he sacrificed in bread and wine. Moses was a type ; and Moses brought down bread from heaven. The loaves of proposition were kept in the tabernacle, for a sign. David in his hour of need had been fed upon those loaves of proposition ; and David was a type. Elias in his day of trial had been nourished again with bread from heaven ; in the strength of that bread he had walked for forty days. Elias himself had multiplied the flour for the woman who had fed him ; and Elias was a special type. On these things they had been brought up. Other signs there were ; His other miracles had meant much ; but the miracle of bread was of all most convincing. When at Naim He had raised the widow's son to life they had cried out :

'A great prophet
Hath risen up among us
And God hath visited his people.'

Now they went much further. The word of discovery began to pass from mouth to mouth amongst them. The excitement grew ; soon it threatened to become beyond control. He was not only ' a great prophet ' ; the evidence before them proved that He was more. The cry began to rise from all that multitude :

> ' This is of a truth the prophet
> That is come into the world.'

But if He was ' the prophet ', then He was something besides. The Prophet that was to come was also to be King. This was the meaning of David and of Solomon ; on their throne He was to reign. On this hope their fathers had lived ; they had looked forward to the day when the kingdom should be restored to Israel. The Galilæans in particular had cherished the dream ; some of them had given their lives for it. And now they came to think of it, how often had He hinted it to them ! From the beginning the Kingdom had ever been upon His lips. It was all clear. The day had come at last. From that spot the movement should begin. They had only to proclaim Him, to follow Him, and the rest would be done. He would lead them to victory ; they would drive the Romans into the sea, as their fathers had driven the Philistines, and to Israel the kingdom would be restored for ever.

So the turmoil grew among this little people, whose horizon was confined within their Galilæan valleys. And Jesus looked down on them and knew their thoughts. Again the great mistake was being made. These poor, blinded men were again turning Him and His works to their own ends ; Himself, who He was, they would not see. Would they never learn ? But for them He was less anxious ; already He had accepted their failure as inevitable. He was more solicitous for His Twelve. For with all their devotedness, in spite of all He had taught them, in spite of all they had themselves discovered, they too were not yet freed from idle dreams about the Kingdom that was to come. If the people moved, in this hour of excitement, the Twelve might be tempted to join them and take the lead. That mistake must not be permitted ; He must save them from the danger. As the murmur among the crowd began to grow, as the enthusiasm developed to disorder, Jesus stood up in all His grandeur and authority. He pointed to the single boat lying by the shore, in which they had come across that morning. Sternly He turned to the

Twelve ; He could not be resisted. Let them go at once on board ; without delay let them push off and get home to Bethsaida. As for the crowd, He would look to it ; as for Himself, they need not trouble.

> ' Jesus therefore when he knew
> That they would come to take him by force
> And make him king
> Immediately obliged his disciples
> To go up into the ship
> That they might go before him
> Over the water to Bethsaida
> Whilst he dismissed the people.'

Reluctantly the Twelve obeyed. They looked at Him ; the spirit was upon Him and He could not be gainsaid. They turned and went down the hill-side towards the beach, with no hurried steps, ever and anon looking back at Him, looking at the excited crowd before Him. They wondered what it would do with Him when they were gone, what He would do with it. It had been a wonderful day, and they were loth to miss its issue ; they were eager to take their part in it, whatever it might be. They reached the boat and unmoored it ; they climbed on board. Even as they put out, the darkness was coming over them. There might be trouble in the night, but for the moment they did not think of that. They could only think of Him whom they were leaving behind at the mercy of that excited crowd ; and they would not be there to help Him !

And yet as they sailed away one thing struck them. They had expected the noise and clamour to increase ; once Jesus was alone and undefended, these people would rush up the hill-side and possess themselves of Him. But no ; while they were yet within easy hearing the shouting seemed to cease ; the excitement settled down ; all was comparatively quiet. They understood. When they had left the Master the spirit of command was upon Him. With that same spirit He had turned and faced the people. He had held out His hand and they had been silenced ; He had spoken to them and everyone had heard. He had inculcated peace ; He had bade them remember that the night was upon them ; He had told them to disperse for shelter, in the villages, on the open plain ; and they like submissive sheep had listened and obeyed. Meekly they gathered up their little belongings ; they found their respective friends, their wives, their children ; they began to melt away seeking shelter where they could. And Jesus, when He saw what was being done, quietly, quickly, slipped round a corner of the hill where He stood, and vanished from their sight.

> ' And when he had dismissed them
> He fled again into the mountain
> Himself alone
> To pray
> And when it was late
> The ship was in the midst of the sea
> And himself was there on the land
> Alone.'

The Evangelists dwell lingeringly on this particular night of prayer of Jesus. It is to be classed with that night before the day on which He chose the Twelve and delivered the Sermon on the Mount ; when

> ' He spent the night
> In the prayer of God.'

And indeed we do not wonder, for that night was to precede the greatest of the sermons of His career ; that night was to precede another choosing of the Twelve, another testing, in which one would begin to triumph and another would begin to fail. He had been with the people all that day. They meant well ; at least they knew no better. They were as sheep without a shepherd. He had been their shepherd ; He had fed them. Now He would offer them other food. Would they receive it ? Not all ; perhaps not many. Yet could He no longer delay ; the clouds were fast gathering, the hour had come. They must be given their choice ; and His heart went up to His Father for their sakes.

But even more did He pray for His beloved Twelve. Already they had gone far ; though there was yet much for them to learn, much in which they would need to be altered, still now they could be trusted. This at least they had learnt ; to believe in His word for His own sake, to believe in His word because He said it, however little they might understand. When He had begun to preach in parables, they had not understood but had believed. Of late He had done much for them apart from all the rest. He had separated them from the others ; He had kept them always with Him ; He had made them partners with Himself ; He had given them special instructions which they in their turn were to teach in His name ; He had worked special miracles for them, deepening their faith, revealing the fathomless abyss of His affection, inspiring them with confidence and trust which no storm could disturb. To-night He would give them more. With a last manifestation He would strengthen them, then they too should be tried ; and He prayed that when the moment of trial came they would not fail, so that in due season they might go forth to all the world and confirm the brethren.

Thus He prayed alone in the silence of that mountain-side. Meanwhile out upon the lake things were going ill with His Twelve. They were making their way, west by south, to Capharnaum and Bethsaida ; but this time He was not with them and they missed Him. As it had been before, so now again the wind had got up with the coming on of night ; a contrary wind, therefore coming from the south. The waves were high, it was very dark, they had to make their way as best they could. From the mountain as He prayed for them His thoughts went out towards them. He saw them where they laboured ; He loved them, He would try them, in His own way He would give them both fear and joy. He would turn their fear into joy, He would seize another occasion to deepen their faith, their trust, their love.

It was about the fourth watch of the night, in other words well into the morning. They had gone some five-and-twenty furlongs ; had they been able to steer a straight course, this would have been considerably more than half their journey. But, as the place of their landing later shows, they had been compelled to face the storm and to steer more southward. Suddenly, on their right, towards the north, a strange light appeared on the water. It was not the light of the moon, for the moon was new and had gone down long ago. It came nearer towards them ; it assumed a shape ; it had the figure of a man ; without a doubt it was a human form walking on the surface of the lake. But a human being could not walk on water ; then it was a spirit. Doubly now they feared, but this second fear terrified them more. In their terror they cried out, panic-stricken.

Meanwhile the figure drew nearer towards them ; its course was close by the ship, but it had made as if it would pass them by, looking towards Capharnaum. Only when the cry of terror was raised did it stop and look in their direction. It stood upon a crest of a wave ; when the wave sank the figure went down with it. Again it rose, and again it sank, yet the feet pressed the water as if they were on solid ground. At the same time they, too, in their little ship, rose, and sank, and rolled from side to side. Sometimes the vision was clear before them, sometimes it was hidden from their sight. In the darkness, with trouble all about them, they could not distinguish more than the outline of a man.

But Jesus could not and would not hold them long in suspense. They had cried in terror ; through the gale the cry had reached Him. He did not at once calm the storm, as He had done a few weeks before, almost on this very spot ; they were older now, had learnt much more, and therefore He would further try their faith and trust. Then, when the storm had been tamed, they had believed ; now He would test them whether they would believe even when the storm continued. Steadily, encouragingly, but in that voice they knew so well, the words came across the water to them :

> ' Be of good heart
> It is I
> Fear not.'

' Be of good heart, Son ! ' They were the words He had used on that wonderful day when He had released from his sins the palsied man at Capharnaum. Many times since He had used them ; they were words by which He might well be recognized.

' It is I ! ' That was yet more. After all, then, it was not a ghost, it was Jesus and nothing more. It was not an apparition, it was only the Son of God ; they had no cause to fear.

The men listened and were silent. They looked again, and they recognized Him. Yes, it was He ; and in their gladness they forgot their danger, they forgot their panic ; almost they forgot the wonderful thing that was happening before their eyes. It was He; He had come to them, He was with them, and, storm or calm, that was enough.

Still Jesus stood where He was on the water. He made no effort now to move onward to Capharnaum; but neither did He come nearer to the vessel. Simon looked at Him and longed for Him. He could endure it no longer; if Jesus would not come to them, he would go to Jesus. He who once, probably on this very ship, had fallen at His feet and cried:

> 'Depart from me
> For I am a sinful man
> O Lord',

now could not resist the fascination. Whatever we may think of Simon at this point, however many more faults he may have committed than all the other Apostles together, however many more he may yet commit, nevertheless in one thing he excelled them all. He saw deeper than any of the rest into the real nature of Jesus of Nazareth, and his own generosity of character carried him further in devotedness. His love was tempered only by his knowledge of himself; his desires went further than his deeds. In spite of his shortcomings and excesses he was a man wholly lovable; he was the one man among the Twelve in whom Jesus saw from the beginning the greatest possibilities. His very faults betrayed the greatness of his soul.

Nowhere does all this appear more in combination than in the scene before us. Simon in the ship, Jesus on the water; Simon longing for Him, Jesus as it were tempting him to dare; Simon at length asking to do that which in another would be mere presumption; Simon running risks which no other on that ship would have dared to run; Simon trebly believing, in the fact of Jesus, in the power of Jesus, in the voice of Jesus which had said:

> 'Be of good heart
> It is I
> Fear not.'

In that faith he forgot all else. He threw human prudence to the winds; as his heart prompted him he spoke. He paid no heed to those who might justly have reproved his arrogance; he forgot himself and the danger. If three

were faults in all this, they were the faults of one born to
rule, and to rule by the depth of his love.

> ' And Peter making answer said
> Lord
> If it be thou
> Bid me come to thee upon the waters
> And he said
> Come.'

It was indeed an astonishing request, but the answer was
still more astonishing. Once on a time Satan had tempted
Jesus Himself to do a thing akin to this, to walk upon the
air, and He had only answered :

> ' Thou shalt not tempt the Lord thy God.'

Now Simon asks that he may walk upon the water. His
companions are shocked ; of course he will receive some
rebuke as he had often to receive them. But no ; across
the water, distinctly heard, rings the single, inviting word :

> ' Come.'

For indeed Jesus understood. A few weeks before He had
said to these very men :

> ' Why are ye fearful
> Ye of little faith ? '

And here was Simon's effort at an answer. He would not
be accused of that again. He would be accused of too much
trust rather than too little ; and Jesus on His side would let
the world know which of the two He most approved.

The permission was given, and that welcome call was
enough for Simon. His companions might try to hold him
back, but he would not be hindered. He stood up by the
side of the boat ; it lifted and rolled, now high above the
water, now going down in the valley of the waves. At one
point the gunwale was almost level with the surface ; Simon
seized the moment and stepped out. The boat rose up
behind him ; he was left to himself ; the water held
beneath his feet. He was standing on the wave, rising and
falling with it ; he was able to walk upon it, up its steep
inclines, down into its hollows, in the direction of Him who
rose and fell with the rising and falling surface a few paces
beyond.

But then came a change. It is much to have the courage
to understand a superhuman task ; to continue in it needs

more. Most men will begin well ; not all will persevere to
the end. Some will even dare to step upon the water ; but
when they have done it, and when in addition they feel the
storm threatening their balance, then they will fear. So
was it with Simon. The water held him up ; but once he
was free from the shelter of the ship the strong wind beating
up the lake threatened to throw him off his feet. He could
scarcely stand straight ; he might fall ; what would happen
then ? He began to be anxious ; as he did so, instantly the
water began to give way beneath him. In fear he tried to
hurry forward ; the rising waters hindered him. They
rose to his knees ; clearly he was sinking ; with a frantic
bound he leapt towards Jesus as best he could and cried :

> ' Lord
> Save me.'

Instantly all was well. He felt his hand caught by the
hand of the Master ; he felt himself being lifted up ; once
more the water was firm. Grateful, almost triumphant, he
looked into the Master's face ; at once his triumph was
changed into shame. For that face had a cloud upon it.
It was not the danger, clearly, that troubled Him ; not the
water, nor the wind, nor the boat with the men in it. As
they stood together, rising and falling with every roll, Jesus
looked back into the face of Simon. Affectionately, a little
sadly, encouraging him to be yet more bold in confidence,
He said to him :

> ' O thou of little faith
> Why didst thou doubt ? '

Such is the way of Jesus Christ. In the way of faith, and
of confidence in Him as proof of that faith, He is never, He
never will be, satisfied. A few weeks before these men had
proved their faith in Him by begging Him to save them
from shipwreck. He had saved them ; because they asked
Him He had commanded the waves and the sea ; yet had
He added :

> ' Why are you fearful
> O ye of little faith ? '

Now Simon had gone further. He had walked upon water
at His bidding ; yet had Jesus found reason to repeat His
complaint :

> ' O thou of little faith
> Why didst thou doubt ? '

It would be the same to the end. He would always complain that men did not trust Him enough, did not ask of Him enough. In the last week of His life we shall still find Him stirring them to more by saying :

> ' Therefore I say unto you
> All things
> Whatsoever you ask when you pray
> Believe that you shall receive
> And they shall come unto you ' ;

and on the last day of all :

> ' Whatsoever you shall ask the Father
> In my name
> That will I do
> That the Father may be glorified in the Son
> If you shall ask me anything
> In my name
> That will I do
> Hitherto
> You have not asked anything
> In my name
> Ask and you shall receive
> That your joy may be full.'

Yet how much had they asked ! How much had Simon asked that night ! And still to Jesus it was nothing ; nothing to that which His heart longed to give.

Hand in hand these two, Simon and Jesus, walked down the dales and up the hills of the still tossing water towards the boat. By this time the men in it were satisfied. The evidence of Jesus alone on the waves had failed entirely to convince them, the evidence of Simon was convincing. The same concurrence of evidence would occur again, notably on that day when they would confirm each other's faith by crying :

> ' The Lord hath risen indeed
> And hath appeared to Simon.'

The two came to the ship's side as it rose and fell. They waited by it ; when again the swell had brought the deck on a level with the water they stepped in. No sooner had they done so than the wind fell ; the waves were quieted ; the ship answered the rudder ; they were out of danger.

> ' And they that were in the boat
> Were far more astonished
> Within themselves
> For they understood not
> Concerning the loaves
> For their heart was blinded
> And they came and adored him saying
> Indeed thou art the Son of God.'

They took him on board, wondering and wondering more. Again He had done a thing for them, and for them only. The miracle of the loaves had been done for all ; had they understood that aright they would have known. But not yet did they understand ; not yet did they fully understand the significance of that which had just been done before their eyes. Nevertheless something they did understand. They saw that this was a sequel to that which had been done for them on these waters before. Then they had asked themselves :

> ' Who is this ?
> For the winds and the sea obey Him ' ;

now they answered their own question, though still they knew not what they said. When at last they had recovered from their stupor,

> ' They came and adored him saying
> Indeed thou art the Son of God.'

54. A Morning of Miracles

> ' And presently the ship was at the land
> To which they were going.'

Scarcely had they settled once more to their work than the grey dawn began to appear over the hills of Gerasa. In its light, to their surprise, they found they were near to the shore. But not at Capharnaum or Bethsaida ; owing to the storm they had been compelled, as we have seen, to steer their course southward, and now they were opposite the coast south of Magdala and the plain of Genesareth, north of the city of Tiberias. If they chose they could return north by boat ; they saw that He preferred to land and go on foot. With no hindrances, they might reach Bethsaida in an hour or more, for the road bent inland ; to the centre of Capharnaum would be half an hour further.

On the way before them through the plain were several villages, some of them large enough to be called towns ; the first on the route was Magdala.

Accordingly at daybreak they came ashore ; a little below the site of Magdala there is still a little fishing-stake where they might well have landed. For a while they took their morning meal and rested. The day had been tiring, the night had been yet more, and had been sleepless ; a strange sequel indeed to that invitation of twenty-four hours before :

> ' Come with me into a desert place apart
>   And rest awhile.'

Still in the light of all that had happened they were well content. Somehow with Him they had found sufficient rest ; despite the crowd they had found a refreshing desert in their union with Him. The saints of prayer know well what this refreshment means.

But the morning quiet was not to be enjoyed for long. Soon He showed that He wished that day to reach Capharnaum. Now nowhere was Jesus better known than along that little strip of coast. He had often passed that way, going to and coming from Capharnaum ; He had stayed more than once in Magdala, in the villages on the plain He had often preached. When, then, they saw that He had landed below their valley, quickly the people of the neighbourhood began to gather. Instantly the word was passed along ; messengers were sent from village to village. In the course of the morning Jesus of Nazareth would be passing that way ; if they had any sick, now would be their opportunity.

> ' And running through all that country
>   They sent
> And began to carry about to him in beds
>   All that were sick.'

It was indeed a busy scene. For a long time now Jesus had not been that way ; only of late had the full advantage of His coming grown upon them. On former occasions sufferers had met Him and had been cured as He passed ; now they knew that if only men would come to Him, and would make use of Him, there was no limit to His healing power. This time there should be no stinting ; they would

take advantage of His presence to the full ; they would run
any risks. Not only should the villages and towns that lay
upon His route benefit ; but all the surrounding hamlets,
as many as could bring down their sick to line the road.
It mattered not what was their condition ; bedridden or
not, let them be brought along. There was much going
to and fro, much excitement, much carrying of beds down
into the valley ; there never had been such stir in the plain
of Genesareth before.

Then Jesus came. It was a triumphal procession, greater
than any that had been witnessed hitherto, the like of which
would not be seen again. He passed through village after
village. They were studded thick along the road through
that fertile plain, from Magdala to Bethsaida, and Bethsaida
touched upon Capharnaum. Along the way, in single rows,
the sick of all the country-side were arranged ; fever cases,
cases of dropsy, of diseases hidden and apparent, all were
lying on their mats, with the men standing over them who
had brought them there ; they had been given time to
gather and they had used it well. And they were sure of
their healing. He had never yet refused anyone ; of late
He had been more lavish than ever. Rumour even said
that the men who were always with Him had been taught
His secret. But most of all had they been impressed by the
tale of the good woman in Capharnaum who had touched
but the hem of His garment and had been healed of her
hidden disease. What He had done for her He would do
again for them. Even if He were too occupied, even if He
wished to move on quickly to Capharnaum and could not
delay at each and every bedside, they had but to touch His
garment as He passed and it would be well.

And it was so. He who yesterday had fed five thousand
men with five loaves, He who last night had walked upon
the surface of the lake, to-day, if possible more than ever,
lets loose the whole force of His healing power. With His
own hand, as He goes along, He touches many and heals
them ; while He is doing this, bending down over special
cases, others reach out their arms and touch His flowing
robe, seizing it when they are able, pressing it to their lips ;
and they too are healed no less than the others. There is
no restriction ; there is joy left all along the road as soon
as He has passed. Before, the plain of Genesareth had
looked like a hospital in the open air ; when He has

gone through it has all the joy and festivity of a country fair.

For that day the heart of Jesus was very full, full even to breaking, and must needs pour itself out ; before the day was over it would be struck to the quick and He foresaw it. Carefully from the first this people had been trained and prepared to receive the better thing He had to give them ; dearly all the time they had been loved and cherished. Now had come the hour for testing ; and He knew they would fail. Still He could delay no longer. The allotted time in Galilee was at an end ; in another year from that day, on the very next Pasch, He must lay down His life in Jerusalem. In the meantime other places must be visited ; the way must be prepared for those who were afterwards to spread His name throughout the world. But though He knew this people would fail Him, yet would He not fail them. He would give them all He could ; He would win them by His lavish favours ; He would conquer them to utter confidence ; He would spare nothing that might draw them to look beyond, and see Him who He was, and believe in Him, and accept His word whatever it might mean. On His side at least there should be nothing wanting that would give them faith in Himself.

But alas, their eyes were blinded, and they would see only that which was of profit to themselves ! They would see only the worker of wonders. Their ears were deafened, and they would hear only what it pleased themselves to accept. Their hearts were hardened, and they would take only that which meant no loss. They might say they were devoted, but within a few hours more that devotedness would snap. Jesus knew all this ; yet the knowledge of it did not stay His hand. His lavish generosity remained, His sympathy with this shallow, and thoughtless, and self-centred people. He poured out upon them His joy, such as no other could give ; but the least joyful heart on the plain of Genesareth that day was His own, and before nightfall He would reveal it.

55. The Bread of Life

Meanwhile, on the green plain beyond the Jordan to the north, where Jesus had fed the multitude, many had spent the night wrapped up in their blankets, protected as best they could arrange from the wind that blew off the lake.

In the morning they awoke and looked about them ; the wind had dropped suddenly in the early hours, and the day was bright. They thought of Him who had been so much to them the day before, and again searched for Him. He must be somewhere near ; the night before there had been only one boat on the coast, and His disciples had sailed away in it alone. He Himself had stayed with them ; when darkness came they had seen Him seek a place of rest on the hill-side. Therefore of a certainty He must be still in their neighbourhood. Up the hill they went in search of Him, as more than once before they had done at Capharnaum. But this time He was not to be found. They examined dips and crannies, such places as those in which they had found Him before ; they made careful enquiries one of another ; but all in vain. By the time the sun appeared over the hills of Decapolis it was clear that somehow in the night He had slipped away. The day before they had come to this spot to prevent Him from leaving them, and in spite of all they had lost Him. There was nothing left for them to do but to make their way back home again to Capharnaum. After all it was still possible that somehow He had returned before them. Certainly the Twelve had made in that direction, and nowadays He was seldom separated from them for long.

Accordingly they began to make their preparations to return. They looked at the spot where the wonderful event of yesterday had taken place. They discussed it among themselves ; they discussed, too, their own conclusions, that He who had done this thing must be the Prophet that was to come, and therefore must be the King. They wondered why He had rejected this last title ; He who had so often spoken to them of the Kingdom He had come to found. They commented on His sudden disappearance from their midst, and were the more suspicious ; they went back upon the miracle of the feeding, and were less enthusiastic. Perhaps, after all, they had been mistaken ; perhaps they had made too much of what had happened. For the moment they had been carried off their feet ; when they looked at it soberly and reasonably, was it so much after all ? Was what He had done as great as that which had been done by His predecessor, Moses ? For Moses had fed the people in the desert with bread brought down from heaven, and that for day after day ;

Jesus had fed them but once, and that merely by multiplying common barley loaves. Certainly when next they met Him there would be questions to be asked, explanations to be given ; until they did meet again it would be well to modify their enthusiasm, to suspend their judgement.

They had scarcely left the spot

> ' Where they had eaten the bread
> The Lord giving thanks ',

when a little fleet of boats was seen making in their direction. They were vessels from Tiberias, therefore not fishing boats, but merchants and carriers. They brought a cargo for that part of the coast, and for Cæsarea Philippi beyond ; they would soon discharge their burden, and would make for home again without delay. To put in at Capharnaum on the way would cost them little ; indeed they would probably call there for trade. Easily, then, it was agreed to take on board those of the people who came from Capharnaum or Bethsaida.

It would have been past midday before these boats from Tiberias landed their passengers on the Capharnaum quay. During the morning Jesus and the Twelve had been making their way up through the plain of Genesareth in the way that we have seen ; owing to the crowds, and the numbers to be healed, a journey of two hours had been lengthened, perhaps, into four. About the same time, therefore, the two parties would have come into the town, Jesus and His followers from the south through Bethsaida, the crowd from the landing-place just below the synagogue ; they might well have come together in the open square on its southern side.

There, as soon as they saw Him before them, one thought was naturally uppermost in the people's minds. That He should be in Capharnaum scarcely surprised them ; at the same time they could not but wonder how He had got there before them. Moreover it appeared that He had not come into the town from the north, which He must have done had He walked. Instead, from the first dawn He had been discovered far to the south in the direction of Tiberias, and in the company of the Twelve whom He had certainly sent on over the lake before Him. There was a mystery about it all and they must ask Him ; in their interest over this new wonder they forgot for the moment the great

event of yesterday. They came about Him; characteristically once more they dropped back into their old
familiarity. Yesterday He was 'the Prophet', fit to be
their King; to-day He is just Jesus, to be addressed
and questioned like any other labourer in that market-
square.

> ' And when they had found him
> On the other side of the sea
> They said to him
> Rabbi
> When camest thou hither ? '

But Jesus gave them no answer. How He had come was
the secret of the Twelve; it did not at that moment
concern the merely curious multitude. What did concern
them was the great thing He had done for them the day
before, and that they should rightly understand it. Already
for a long time He had prepared them, and had given them
sufficient warning. On the very spot where they had just
landed, a month or so ago He had begun to warn them by
preaching to them in parables. He had told them that
seeing they would not see, and hearing they would not hear
or understand. He had later pointed out to them that the
more He did for them the more they looked upon Him
merely as a material benefactor, and would not consider the
greater thing that must lie behind. They would make Him
their King to lead them to conquest and wealth; they
would not look to that other life, that other Kingdom, that
other personality which was His. He would make one last
effort. He would try to shame them into a greater act of
faith. Before that afternoon was over they were to receive
their final test; He had prepared them for it yesterday by
the feeding in the desert, now He would begin by provoking
them, as it were, into a corresponding belief.

Therefore, as if rebuking them, as if contemning the
curiosity they showed, He brushed their question aside.
That mattered nothing; what mattered more was the
miracle of yesterday, and the spirit in which they had come
to Him. He loved them, these ' sheep having no shepherd ',
but He would affect to blame them. He had so much
more to give them, but He must first stir them to ask for
it. He stood in their midst still as one of themselves, but
He must again assure them that He was more, and see

whether, in the light of all they now knew, they would accept Him and with Him the message He declared.

> ' Jesus answered them and said
> Amen, amen I say to you
> You seek me
> Not because you have seen miracles
> But because you did eat of the loaves
> And were filled
> Labour not for the meat which perisheth
> But for that which endureth
> Unto life everlasting
> Which the Son of Man will give you
> For him hath God the Father sealed.'

The very attitude of Jesus as He spoke was a sudden check. Again it was clear that He was in one of those moments when ' He spoke as one having power '. His first words proved it ; the rebuke in His second confirmed it ; instead of being gratified by their enthusiasm of yesterday, He seemed to have forgotten it. He had fed them and they had shown their gratitude after their own manner. Now He spoke of another food, of another life that came of it. He made light of their daily labour, and of their daily bread its reward. Instead He drew them on to Himself, the true goal of labour, the giver of a better reward, hinting to them what He would have them acknowledge once for all, before He applied it in detail.

But the suggestion these poor men ignored. They would go thus far, as far as their material minds would let them, but no further. God they would accept, the God of their Old Testament ; the Son of Man who stood before them was still a son of man and no more.

> ' They said therefore unto him
> What shall we do
> That we may work the works of God ? '

For after all these Galilæans were what nowadays men call practical. They would believe in a religion that had bread in it ; a religion that cured diseases and led to empires and thrones ; a religion that worked, in their own understanding of that word. Dogma had for them no attraction ; more especially such dogma as made this Jesus of Nazareth more than that which their own eyes saw before them. 'Son of Man?' Well, if He chose, let Him give Himself that title; it could be made to mean what they wished. 'Him hath God the Father chosen?' That too might pass; it might mean anything, to them for the moment it meant nothing. If He wished to instruct them, let Him leave those things alone and come down to earth; let Him teach them something about work.

But Jesus was not to be turned aside from His burthen of that day. He had reached the crucial moment of His mission upon earth; whether He were to be accepted or not He would answer them plainly. In their own words He would answer them. He took them into the synagogue close by; there they should have their answer. There when they had gathered around Him,

> 'Jesus answered and said to them
> This is the work of God
> That you believe in him
> Whom he hath sent.'

They were momentous words. Works, yes, as much as men would; but the first and greatest of all works was faith in Himself. Indeed without that work all others mattered little. More and more in the long years after, when the old man John reflected on his Master, he saw, as he had not seen at the time, how He had insisted on this fundamental faith as the beginning of all else. He saw, too, how in the intervening years, men had tended to ignore it. Men wished to see things done; men would always wish to see things done. In that craving they would fail to see the greater thing, which was life itself. And as he looked and pondered, and at times grew wellnigh despondent over the short-sightedness of men, instinctively he emphasized the more his Master's warning. It is a refrain running through all the teaching of S. John.

> 'This is the work of God
> That you believe in him
> Whom he hath sent.'
> 'This is eternal life
> That they may know thee
> The only true God
> And Jesus Christ
> Whom thou hast sent.'
> 'These are written that you may believe

That Jesus is the Christ
The Son of God
And that believing
You may have life in his name.'
' This is his commandment
That we should believe in the name of his Son
Jesus Christ
And love one another
As he hath given commandment unto us.'

In this last sentence the aged Apostle gives the key to all
the rest. The life of all good works is love, and only love ;
and the love that is most living flows through the veins
of man from the heart of Jesus Christ, which is its
source.

The men of Capharnaum gathered in the synagogue
listened. They were in a dilemma. They would be sorry
to part with Jesus. He was their benefactor ; He was their
friend ; He had done many good works among them.
They loved Him in their way ; they put Him above all
others in their esteem ; only yesterday they had hailed Him
as ' the Prophet ', and had been willing to proclaim Him
their King. But He wanted something more. He spoke of
giving food for life everlasting ; He said God the Father
had sealed Him ; He said God had sent Him ; He said
they were to believe in Him on this account alone. This
was much to ask. Why was He not content with the
homage they were willing to pay Him ? But if He did ask
for more, where was the justification ? Other prophets had
worked miracles ; they had even raised the dead to life ;
yet they had never asked for so much as this. The feeding
of yesterday ? Yes, at the moment they had been impressed ; but now on reflexion it was not so great a miracle
as that of Moses in the desert. If they would be safe they
must be cautious. They must not believe more than the
evidence He gave them warranted. They had no wish to
offend Him who was their friend, much less to lose so great
a benefactor. Still must they look to themselves and their
saving common sense, their human reason. Therefore, they
would not contradict Him. They would only wait ; they
would ask no further proof ; they would suggest to Him
their difficulty ; they would let Him see that at least they
were men of goodwill and open-minded.

' They said therefore to him
What sign therefore dost thou shew
That we may see
And may believe thee ?
What dost thou work ?
Our fathers did eat manna in the desert
As it is written
He gave them bread from heaven to eat.'
' And Moses said
This is the bread
Which the Lord hath given you to eat.'

Exodus xvi, 15.

' And he had commanded the clouds from above
And had opened the doors of heaven
And had rained down manna upon them to eat
And had given them bread from heaven
Men ate the bread of angels
He sent them provisions in abundance.'

Psalm lxxvii, 23–25.

' Thou didst feed thy people with the food of angels
And gavest them bread from heaven
Prepared without labour
Having in it all that is delicious
And the sweetness of every taste
For thy sustenance shewed thy sweetness to thy children
And serving every man's will
It was turned to what every man liked.'

Wisdom xvi, 20, 21.

The references to these passages could not be mistaken. It was an open challenge, coming this time not from His enemies, the Scribes and Pharisees, but from those who professed to be His friends. He had done for them a wonder in bread, but He had not brought down bread from heaven ; if He claimed to be greater than Moses, then let Him give a sign greater than that which Moses gave.

And Jesus accepted the challenge. He had prepared for it ; He had led up to it ; the miracle He had worked the day before had been intended to provoke it. But His answer should be given to them by degrees ; they should be led on step by step and gently. He would show them how, in these ways at least, the prophecy was fulfilled, but the greatest fulfilment was the last ; and to acceptance of that He must draw them. He would begin with that which was more easy for them, and which they would accept without demur ; it was little more than an applied definition.

> ' Then Jesus said to them
> Amen, amen I say to you
> Moses gave you not bread from heaven
> But my Father giveth you
> The true bread from heaven
> For the bread of God
> Is that which cometh down from heaven
> And giveth life to the world.'

Such a statement, in their minds, could not be questioned. For that which sustained life was bread, and that which sustained the life of all the world was the bread given to it by God, in whatever form it came. That bread, it was true, Moses did not give ; his bread sustained the bodies only of the wanderers in the desert. That He called God his Father did not trouble these men of Galilee. They had heard Him make this claim before, and had passed it over as a phrase of dignity ; only in Jerusalem had it been taken seriously, and was later to be taken more seriously still. Thus far, then, they could agree with Him. Evidently He spoke of truth divine ; they would show Him that they welcomed His words.

> ' They said therefore unto him
> Lord
> Give us always this bread.'

Now, on this acceptance, He must take them further ; He must give them that truth which they had just declared beforehand they would receive. It was not new ; in one way or another, by implication, by assumption, by parable, He had said something like it often enough before. Every time they had passed it by. They had ignored it as beyond their understanding ; they had looked on it as some figure of speech which it suited Him to use, and which they needed not to fathom. But this time He would let them see that it was no figure ; He would be taken literally as He spoke. It was a deliberate application to Himself of that which they had just accepted. The life was nourished by bread ; the bread that gave the life came directly from God the Father. He was that Bread ; He had come directly from the Father; to accept Him was itself to accept the life. This was, and had been all the time, His one message, and this they had so far failed to grasp. There was warning in His words as He spoke, but still more with the warning was the most plaintive appeal.

'And Jesus said to them
I am the bread of life
He that cometh to me shall not hunger
And he that believeth in me shall never thirst
But I said unto you
That you also have seen me
And you believe not
All that the Father giveth to me
Shall come to me
And him that cometh to me
I will not cast out
Because I came down from heaven
Not to do my own will
But the will of him that sent me
Now this is the will of the Father
Who sent me
That of all that he hath given me
I shall lose nothing
But should raise it up again
In the last day
And this is the will of my Father
That sent me
That everyone that seeth the Son
And believeth in him
May have life everlasting
And I will raise him up
In the last day.'

Was it a mere coincidence, or was it of set purpose, that the words of Jesus Christ on this occasion seemed to be a comment on one of the most beautiful passages in the Old Testament? In the twenty-fourth chapter of the Book of Ecclesiasticus Wisdom stands up and sings her own praises; and that with such beauty that much of her song is applied in the liturgy to Our Lady.

'In me is all grace of the way and of the truth; in me is all hope of life and of virtue. Come over to me, all ye that desire me, and be filled with my fruits; for my spirit is sweet above honey, and my inheritance above honey and the honeycomb. My memory is unto everlasting generations. They that eat me shall yet hunger, and they that drink me shall yet thirst. He that hearkeneth to me shall not be confounded, and they that work by me shall not sin. They that explain me shall have life everlasting. All these things are the book of life, and the covenant of the Most High, and the knowledge of truth.'

Ecclesiasticus xxiv, 25–32.

Let us pause here to link together other words of Jesus Christ, that we may understand the better the heart of Him who spoke on this wonderful occasion. Often, it would seem, the imagery of the passage just quoted was in His mind, and came spontaneously to His mouth ; but never more than on this day, when, if ever, He would win men to accept Him wholeheartedly and the special gift He had to give.

' I am the way, the truth and the life
Come to me
All you that labour and are burthened
And I will refresh you
Learn of me
Because I am meek and humble of heart
My yoke is sweet
And my burthen light
He that cometh to me shall not hunger
And he that believeth in me shall never thirst
Him that cometh to me
I will not cast out
That every one who seeth the Son
And believeth in him
May have life everlasting
And I will raise him up
In the last day
This is eternal life
That they should know thee
The only true God
And Jesus Christ
Whom thou hast sent.'

But the men of Galilee who heard Him on that day were in no mood to accept this open application of the words of Wisdom to Himself.

'The bread of God
Is that which cometh down from heaven
And giveth life to the world.'
'I am the bread of life
I came down from heaven
That every one who seeth the Son
And believeth in him
May have life everlasting.'

This time at least the statement was unmistakable and could not be avoided. He claimed, explicitly, to be the Bread of Life ; He claimed to have come down from heaven ; He claimed that belief in Him gave life everlasting. But how could this be ? With the best will in the world, how could this be literally accepted ? With all His supernatural powers, if indeed they were supernatural, was He not still only Jesus of Nazareth ? And were not His father and mother quite ordinary people, known to everybody ? In this way at last was it manifest that the arguments of Nazareth had trickled into Capharnaum. The familiarity of Nazareth which had led to contempt was being renewed here ; for the third time His antecedents were cast up at Him, His lowliness made an insuperable objection to His greatness. And so it has been through all time ; Jesus cannot be what He claimed to be, because He was what He was.

'The Jews therefore murmured at him
Because he had said
I am the living bread
Which came down from heaven
And they said
Is not this Jesus
The son of Joseph
Whose father and mother we know ?
How then saith he
I came down from heaven ? '

Jesus heard their murmuring, but He made no effort to correct them. Deliberately from the beginning He had taken up this place in human life, and He would abide by its consequences ; had He not done so, where would have been the humiliation ? He had hidden Himself beneath this human flesh ; He had intended that the work of men should be to discover Him beneath it. If they would seek they would find ; if they would not, He would remain to them always but Jesus of Nazareth and no more. He would give them the means to find Him, evidence in His deeds, evidence in His words, but above all evidence in Himself and in His own utter truth. To them who sought light would be given, and more light, and yet more light, until at last they would see what to human understanding was impossible. In the meantime He would wait, and endure, and, if He could, would find excuse for their ignorance.

> ' Forgive them
> For they know not what they do.'

Such was His story from the beginning ; such it would be to the end of time ; such was the story of this day. These men murmured because they did not see ; so long as they persisted in judging by human standards they would never see. Still, though the fault were their own, yet seventy times seven times would He endure them, in the hope that at last they might accept the light.

> ' Jesus therefore answered and said to them
> Murmur not among yourselves
> No man can come to me
> Except the Father who hath sent me draw him
> And I will raise him up
> In the last day
> It is written in the prophets
> And they shall all be taught of God
> Everyone that hath heard of the Father
> And hath learned
> Cometh to me
> Not that any man hath seen the Father
> But he who is of God
> He hath seen the Father
> Amen, amen I say to you
> He that believeth in me
> Hath everlasting life.'

It was the last warning before the great final teaching was given. He knew that teaching would, by the majority that then heard it, be rejected ; therefore would He prepare Himself for the disappointment by making what defence of them He could. He would not look at the present rejection ; He would look forward to the day when His doctrine would be grasped, and would be made a thing of life, and all the world would rejoice, and find in it its real peace. Again He looked back to Isaias, and in him found words of consolation and support. What He was then about to say would for the moment be rejected, but it would be accepted hereafter ; and then He would be able to bless.

'O poor little one, tossed with tempest, without all comfort, behold I will lay thy stones in order, and will lay thy foundations with sapphires, and I will make thy bulwarks with jasper, and thy gates of graven stones, and all thy borders of desirable stones. All thy children shall be taught of the Lord, and great shall be the peace of thy children, and thou shalt be founded in justice' (Isaias liv, 11–14).

Let us here add one thing more. After quoting this prophecy of Isaias, S. John makes Jesus revert to the fact that no man hath seen the Father. Now in one place S. Matthew plays upon the same idea, and he follows it with that wonderful invitation which is fixed for ever in the heart of every Christian. Nowhere else, one would say, are S. Matthew and S. John so close akin. Is it possible, as some have surmised, that this invitation was given here ? If so, a more perfect preparation for Holy Communion could not be imagined ; and it is a preparation given to us by our Lord Himself.

'Everyone that hath heard of the Father
And hath learned
Cometh to me
Not that any man hath seen the Father
But he who is of God
He hath seen the Father.'
'All things are delivered to me by my Father
And no one knoweth the Son
But the Father
Neither doth anyone know the Father
But the Son
And he to whom it shall please the Son to reveal him
Come to me
All you that labour and are burthened
And I will refresh you
Take up my yoke upon you

> And learn of me
> Because I am meek
> And humble of heart
> And you shall find rest to your souls
> For my yoke is sweet
> And my burthen light.'
> ' Amen, amen I say to you
> He that believeth in me
> Hath everlasting life.'

Whether or not these words find their right place here, it is certain that they rightly express the mind of Jesus at this moment. Never before had He been so lavish of His favours as He had been in these last four-and-twenty hours. In return He had had His lowly origin and upbringing cast in His teeth. Humble of heart He had accepted it ; meekly He had said nothing. Instead He had asked them gently not to murmur ; yet more warmly He had invited them to come. If they would come, and would believe what He was about to say to them, they would receive—Oh ! what would they not receive ?—He can only sum it up in the words :

> ' Everlasting life.'

But they would fail ; He knew they would fail. They would not come ; He knew they would not come. When He said

> ' You shall find rest for your souls ',

the warning words of another prophet were being echoed :

> ' Thus saith the Lord
> Stand ye on the ways
> And see
> And ask for the old paths
> Which is the good way
> And walk ye in it
> And you shall find refreshment for your souls
> And they said
> We will not walk.'

Jeremias vi, 16.

Still He would wait no longer. Let them accept it or reject it, the truth should be given to them. It was the Pasch ; on the next Pasch the promise would be fulfilled. They had been prepared enough, both in the long months preceding and during all that day. They had said they would believe, they had asked for the bread He had to give them ; carefully He had led them on, from the barley loaves to the bread unto life everlasting, to faith in Him, the Messenger from the Father, to faith in Him, the Bread that came from heaven. He had only one thing more to do. In plain terms He would say it, so plain, that by no possibility could the plain man mistake it ; to give His words another meaning would need the perverse ingenuity of one who must begin by saying : ' I will not believe '. Carefully He chose His words ; step by step He picked up what He had already said, driving each point further home. As was His wont He recapitulated, and in the recapitulation added something more ; the Bread of Life, the Manna of Moses, the Bread this time truly from heaven, the Living Bread, Himself, Himself in His very body, in His living body, His life thus passing into everyone who would eat Him.

Thus He went on :

' I am the bread of life
Your fathers did eat manna in the desert
And are dead
This is the bread that cometh down from heaven
That if any man eat of it
He may not die
I am the living bread
Which came down from heaven
If any man eat of this bread
He shall live for ever
And the bread that I will give
Is my flesh
For the life of the world.'

The last words were firm and emphatic ; to all, believers and unbelievers alike, they came with a shock. Their full meaning was not understood ; it was not intended that they should be understood ; in themselves, taken literally, they contained what to nature was impossible, but precisely in that came the test. Impossible or not, He had said it ; if men believed they would hear Him, knowing that somehow what He said would be found to be true ; if they did not, it would remain to them impossible and they would part. Still there were many in Capharnaum who were loth to do so. They would gladly keep Jesus if they could.

Not only had He done much for them, but even as a Man of God He was worthy of a following ; if they could find an interpretation of His words that would suit their ideas all might yet be well. They turned to one another ; they asked each other questions ; they made suggestions. None would hold ; the plain statement was there, and it must be taken as it stood or not at all.

'The Jews therefore strove among themselves
Saying
How can this man
Give us his flesh
To eat ? '

It is to be noticed that these men of Capharnaum added something to that which Jesus had said. He had thus far only told them :

'The bread which I will give
Is my flesh
For the life of the world.'

They asked :

' How can this man
Give us his flesh
To eat ? '

The addition is significant ; only too well had they understood Him. Every other interpretation but one was excluded ; had they not said it, then either a mystical meaning might have been found, or at least it might have been said that the ' flesh for the life of the world ' was given once for all on Calvary.

But crude Galilæan minds saw no such interpretation. To them His flesh was to be the Bread of Life, and as such was to be eaten ; if they were wrong then the Author of all truth was bound to correct them, as He had often done before. He did no such thing. Though He had not yet spoken so explicitly, still since they had so understood Him He would not draw back. Yes, they were right ; He meant exactly that ; He would drive the doctrine further home. Eat His flesh they must ; if they would not, so much would they lose ; if they would, then life everlasting would be theirs. Yes, His flesh was food ; His living flesh was living food ; let them eat His living flesh and they would eat His very life ; in this very eating of the real substance of Himself they fulfilled the sign contained in the manna in the desert. If before He had been emphatic, and had used words which no man of unprejudiced reason could interpret in any but one way, now He put what He had promised beyond a shadow of doubt. Men could take it or not ; its meaning in full they could not hope to fathom ; but in taking it or rejecting it they took or rejected Him, for by their faith in Him alone could they hope to believe in such a mystery.

This, then, was the tenor of His answer. More firmly now than ever, more exactingly, even to a threat, He spoke to them. He had hitherto used the method of appeal ; now He used that of authority. If before His hearers had been

'In admiration at his doctrine ',

now, had they so chosen, they might have been no less convinced.

' Then Jesus said to them
Amen, amen I say unto you
Except you eat the flesh of the Son of Man
And drink his blood
You shall not have life in you
He that eateth my flesh
And drinketh my blood
Hath everlasting life
And I will raise him up
In the last day
For my flesh is meat indeed
And my blood is drink indeed
He that eateth my flesh
And drinketh my blood
Abideth in me
And I in him
As the living Father hath sent me
And I live by the Father
So he that eateth me
The same also shall live by me
This is the bread that came down from heaven
Not as your fathers did eat manna
And are dead
He that eateth this bread
Shall live for ever.'

When he has written this the Evangelist knows that he has written something very momentous ; the most

momentous demand on faith that Jesus ever made of His
followers.   He must therefore let his readers know that he
is stating only the truth.   He has already told us the time
and occasion of these words, he must now add the place.
There must be no suspicion that he is only adding, as he
may seem to do elsewhere, some development of his own.
Hence he concludes :

> ' These things he said
> Teaching in the synagogue
> In Capharnaum.'

It was not only many of the common multitude that were
mystified by what they had heard that day.   There were
others who till now had been proud to call themselves His
friends, His followers, His disciples.   They had seen and
had known all that He had done, and had thought they
had learnt Him ;   and yet to-day their faith and understanding had a check.   To believe in Him, yes ;   to accept
what He said, provided it were consonant with their reason,
yes ;   but to be told that His flesh was to be eaten and His
blood to be drunk,—this was a test too severe.

> ' Many therefore of his disciples
> Hearing it said
> This saying is hard
> And who shall hear it ? '

And yet even to such as these Jesus will not yield ;   He
only, just a little, changes His tone.   If they will not believe
Him and trust Him when He Himself says this, what will
they believe when He is gone ?   It is well to believe what
their eyes have seen, but what of the meaning, the spirit,
of that evidence ?   From all this could they not infer
something more concerning Him who stood before them ?
And inferring something more, could they not be sure that
now He is not deceiving them, that He never could deceive
them ?   But alas ! for many it was useless to represent ;
in their hearts, in the last resort, they did not and would not
believe.   They wondered at Him ;   they enjoyed Him in
their midst ;   but that He could be more than man they
would not admit.

> ' But Jesus knowing in himself
> That his disciples murmured at this
> Said to them
> Doth this scandalize you ?

If then you see the Son of Man
Ascend up where he was before
It is the spirit that quickeneth
The flesh profiteth nothing
The words that I have spoken to you
Are spirit and life
But there are some of you that believe not.'

S. John concludes this memorable scene with his characteristic lament. Again mankind had failed.

' He was in the world
And the world was made by him
And the world knew him not
He came unto his own
And his own received him not.'

Here the lament is so expressed :

' For Jesus knew from the beginning
Who they were that did not believe
And who he was that would betray him
And he said
Therefore did I say to you
That no man can come to me
Unless it be given him by my Father
After this
Many of his disciples went back
And walked no more with him.'

It was a definite parting of the ways ; one may say it was the beginning of heresy ; and the Evangelist implies that the first arch-heretic, even at that moment, was one of the Twelve.

Gradually the crowd that had gathered in the synagogue began to melt away. In regular succession groups broke off and passed out of the door into the market square beyond,

' One to his farm
Another to his merchandise ' ;

angry faces, irritated faces, thoughtful, resentful, contemptuous faces, but upon them all the same look of disappointment ; and those outside who saw them knew that, for the first time, something within that synagogue had gone amiss. For the first time, it would seem, Jesus of Nazareth had overreached Himself and had tested His followers too far. Among those who saw the change were the ever-watchful Pharisees. At last their opportunity had come ; with a people so alienated they might now hope to have a hearing. They would redouble their efforts, they would criticize yet more ; now that His prestige as a teacher was shaken, they would even venture to set their teaching against His own.

Jesus stood in the synagogue with His Twelve around Him, and watched the crowd dwindle down before His eyes. Thus far He had led them ; thus far He had won them ; to this point they had followed Him in ever-increasing numbers. Yesterday they had proclaimed Him ' the Prophet ', and had wished to make Him their king ; to-day they had no further use for Him, and would ' walk with Him no more '. He had foreseen it from the beginning ; He had known that for the most part they had never really believed. He had worked for them, He had prayed for them, He had annihilated Himself on their account, and it had come to this. His very self-humiliation had been taken as proof that He was not what He claimed to be ; His very miracles had come in the way of the greater gift He had offered them. He had warned them of what they would do, He had appealed to them, He had threatened them, He had almost bribed them that they might be led to take the great leap of faith, and He had failed ; and He knew that this same failure would pursue Him and His followers till the end of time.

Still He would not relax His efforts. These same men who now rejected Him should not yet themselves be rejected. The great mind of Jesus of Nazareth saw beyond a present insult ; it would always pity rather than resent, forgive rather than condemn, persevere rather than despair, see cause for sympathy rather than for abuse, for love rather than for hate. Now as on Calvary the cry came from His heart,

> ' Father, forgive them
> They know not what they do.'

Already He had uttered that appeal. He had ' had compassion on them because they were as sheep having no shepherd '. To the last minute He had drawn them to Him ; during all the time He had been speaking to them He had defended their blindness ; He had ended on this last note. There was no anger, there was no indignation, there was only sadness because this grandest offer of love that even He, the God-Man, could devise, had been rejected. And it had been rejected just because it was so great ; just because puny little man, with his narrow understanding, did not think it possible. There was about Him the sense of loneliness because of this desertion, the craving for companionship, the bitterness of love un-requited, lost and wasted, seeking its object and finding none, crying in the air like a wandering ghost, wounded and bleeding from ' the hand of them that loved it '. Truly that day the heart of Jesus was smitten ; it was a strange return for the gift He had offered to all the world.

Proof of all this we have in a single sentence. In His loneliness He looked about for one who would relieve Him. There were the Twelve standing by ; they had not yet gone. He would put them to the test. In the whole story of Jesus Christ is there anywhere a more intensely human quiver than that which we find here, when His appealing eyes turned to them, and His trembling lips said to them :

' Will you also go away ? '

Such an appeal, in the midst of such a scene, was too much for Simon. What His Master had said that day he had not in the least understood ; but that did not trouble him. With his whole soul he believed in Jesus, and that was enough ; with his whole heart he loved Him, and that was more. He had already heard things he had not understood and they had later become clear ; he knew that of these words, too, in the proper time and place, the explanation would come. Meanwhile the Master must be comforted. He must be made to feel He had companions who cared, who believed, who trusted, who were faithful, who were willing to accept everything He said, whatever it might be. In his spontaneous outpouring Simon scarcely knew the glorious words he uttered :

' Lord
To whom shall we go ?
Thou hast the words of eternal life
And we have believed
And have known
That thou art the Christ
The Son of God.'

It was a wonderful confession ; in words at least there was little more to add. True, they were not much more than the words used on that first day by the Jordan river, but how much more they meant now than then ! Last night on the ship they had called Him ' Son of God ' ; but in these last hours how much had the mind of Simon grown ! Now he had come to this, that he knew not what he meant ; but he was willing to take all the consequences of his act of faith. But a little more and the grace of God would make it perfect ; and in one man at least the heart of Jesus would be satisfied.

The remainder of the Twelve stood about and rejoiced that once again Simon had spoken for them all. They too had stood there and listened. Less than Simon had they understood what the Master had said ; still they too had known that to understand all was not necessary. They had accepted ; for the meaning they were content to wait ; when He returned to them and asked them whether they would go or stay, they were almost hurt. Yet they could not say anything. They were tempted to protest, but that was out of place ; to promise allegiance, but that seemed too weak ; when Simon spoke, in his enthusiastic, heartfelt way, they were relieved and glad. Even Judas was relieved that the strain had been removed and the right word said ; even Judas, though on that very day, and in that very hour, his reasoning mind had received a shock, and the beginning of the end had set in.

And this too Jesus knew. Simon spoke for all and He was glad ; but Simon did not know that not all fully responded to his words. Therefore Jesus could not be wholly glad ; if one failure in a hundred could make Him go searching for that one, how much more the failure of one in twelve ! And such a Twelve ! That many of the multitude should leave Him was hard, but it was intelligible ; for them some excuse could be found. That one of His chosen Twelve should fail was far harder, because for him He could find none. His joy was marred, and He could not but show it ; His answer was also a warning to the only one who could have interpreted it aright.

' Jesus answered them
Have not I chosen you twelve ?
And one of you is a devil.'

To this John adds the significant explanation, repeated more than once later, as if the whole body of the Twelve were tarnished for ever with the shame of it :

' Now he meant Judas Iscariot
The son of Simon
For this same was about to betray him
Whereas he was one of the twelve.'

CHAPTER

18

56. The Pharisees and Unwashed Hands

THE eventful day was over ; the paschal season came and went ; the pilgrims from Jerusalem returned, and preparations began for the harvest season. It would seem that for this Pasch Jesus did not go up to the Holy City ; His hour was not yet come. But the news concerning Him had poured in, and had been still more spread abroad by the caravans that had come from Galilee and the north. That news was disturbing ; if before it had seemed worth while to send down Scribes and Pharisees to counteract His influence, it was far more necessary now. It was not so much the miracles they feared. These could be ignored ; by means of them He had violated the Sabbath ; it could be said that they were worked by diabolic aid. At least these objections could not be refuted, and therefore they could be renewed ; the miracles did not much concern the authorities in Jerusalem.

What concerned them much more was the attitude of the people of Galilee. They had begun by following Him in crowds. They hung upon His lips, drinking in every word He said. They contrasted, with very plain insinuations, the character of His teaching with that of their own. Wherever He went the synagogues were always open to Him ; when they or their fellow-Pharisees made objection to Him and His ways, the people seemed ever ready to take His side. Of late fresh alarms had been raised. At Naim they had hailed Him as ' a great Prophet ' ; now during this last paschal season they had proclaimed Him ' the Prophet ', and even King. They, too, were looking for a king and a prophet, but this Man was not the kind they had in mind. They looked for another David, another Samson, another Machabeus, who would shake off this hated Roman domination and roll it into the sea. If they could not have that, then they would rather have none at all ; for, all things considered, they were content enough with the Cæsars.

Accordingly soon after the Pasch a fresh detachment of Pharisees from Jerusalem made its appearance in Capharnaum. They came with no little anxiety, expecting no warm reception ; when they arrived what was their surprise to find a distinct change in the atmosphere about them ! Though there was still some enthusiasm, nevertheless the temper of the people of Capharnaum was different ; above all they noted how the more respectable classes, and the better instructed, no longer cared to have much to do with the Nazarene. Something had clearly gone awry ; what it was mattered not at all ; with this new spirit of distrust in the air they might hope to stir up enmity enough to force Jesus out of the way.

With these new allies the Pharisees could afford to expand their frontal attack ; and, since respectability was beginning to object to Him, they could find fault with His contempt of the formalities. This would now be easy, though before it would not have been worth while ; for though the Capharnaites were observant Jews, and kept the Law and traditions according to their state, still Capharnaum was a far-away provincial town, and Bethsaida with its fishing population was close by ; and there were some trades and pursuits which all but made a man dispense with some of the customs. For example there was the custom of continuous washings. Of course the respectable folk observed it ; indeed its strict observance was a hall-mark of respectability. But for the rest, their fishermen, their tax-gatherers, their field labourers, if they washed their hands when they came from the market or their labour it might be thought enough.

But this new state of things was a very different story. Here was a Carpenter from Nazareth who was passing as a Rabbi, a teacher of the people ; here were some common men, fishermen and labourers, who called themselves His followers, and in His name presumed to teach and to command. So long as they had remained in their proper place, in the rank in which they had been born, their behaviour mattered little to the rest. They were of the common sort, let them then be vulgar ; refinement would not be expected in men of their degree. But now that they had assumed this new rôle, things were different ; at least they must conform to those customs which every self-respecting Jew observed. These men had been seen before this, eating and drinking in their common way, and nothing had been said ; now they could be watched, and exception could be taken to their manners, and complaints could be made, far more personal and piercing than the old one of breaking the Sabbath.

Hence one day after the Pasch, when the Pharisees and Scribes from Jerusalem had organized . their forces and begun their new campaign, these men gathered around the house where Jesus and His Twelve were abiding, ostensibly, as usual, to hear Him and learn. It was the hour for a meal. They saw the Twelve come in and sit down at table. There was no ceremony, except that ' the Lord gave thanks '. The pots and pans were not cleaned more carefully ; the rough men were not too troubled with the con- dition of their hands. They settled down to eat ; by this time they had become used to the staring of the people while they ate, and though on this occasion it was chiefly scribes and Pharisees who watched them they were not disturbed.

Scarcely had they begun than something was seen to be wrong. These men who stood by and observed them put on a look of surprise ; surprise grew to contempt, they affected even disgust. They looked and whispered one to another ; they turned away their eyes, as if the sight before them shocked them. Some made as if they would leave the place, muttering to themselves, but so that others might hear them, that what they had just seen was alone enough to condemn this upstart and His following. The Twelve became uneasy, but their Master took no notice ; with His own hands He broke the bread and gave it to them, encouraging them to eat on.

At last the disgust of the onlookers broke out. Since He paid no heed to their mutterings, since He did not even seem to know what became a man of His status, they would teach Him.

> ' And the Pharisees and scribes asked him
> Why do not thy disciples walk
> According to the traditions of the ancients ?
> For they wash not their hands
> When they eat bread
> They eat bread with common hands.'

Jesus had waited for this moment. In His former contests with the Pharisees He had met them on religious grounds. In Judæa they had challenged His claim to set Himself up as a teacher ; in Jerusalem and Galilee they had blamed Him because He broke the Sabbath laws ; here in Capharnaum, in the early days, they had been shocked because He had dared to forgive a man his sins, because He had made common fellowship with publicans and sinners, even with a well-known sinful woman, lowering thus the whole tone of public decency. As to His miracles, since no other explanation could be found, they had openly declared that they proved Him to be no more than the devil's tool. They had said these things, and every time Jesus had answered them. For the most part He had answered with forbearance, enduring them, pitying them ; only on the last occasion, when they had openly blasphemed the Father who had sent Him, had His indignation roused Him to condemn.

Now the charge was made upon quite another plane, the plane of common life. In comparison with those that had been made before, the charge might indeed be called a trifle, but precisely on that account did it the more reveal the determined opposition. ' The traditions of the ancients ' ! It was no longer a question of authority, of Sabbath observance, of forgiveness of sins ; it was a question of external form substituted for internal truth, of external for internal cleanness. It was a renewal of the age-long struggle, between the prophets of old and the people of their day, between men who would hide the blackness of their hearts beneath the cloak of external ceremonial, would give to God and man clean hands, but would keep their souls to themselves ; and men who denounced this black shadow of religion had perished because of their denunciation.

Therefore at first Jesus did not trouble to reply to their carping question. Instead He struck deeper ; He struck at that which the question implied. Again He went back to His favourite prophet Isaias. He referred them to a passage which they could not but know, at once a condemnation of them and a prophecy of Himself. Let us quote it as a whole ; from beginning to end it is instinct with the spirit of the prophet, his wrath and his gentleness ; it paints exactly the Pharisaic spirit, its preference of form for inward truth ; what Jesus has to say against these men is little more than what Isaias had said in like cases before Him. In few, if any, passages of prophecy are the wrath of Jesus, combined with His fundamental gentleness and abiding hope, more vividly foreshadowed.

'Woe to Ariel, to Ariel, the city which David took ! Year is added to year, the solemnities are at an end. And I will make a trench about Ariel, and it shall be in sorrow and mourning, and it shall be as Ariel. And I will make a circle round about thee, and will cast up a rampart against thee, and raise up bulwarks to besiege thee. Thou shalt be brought down, thou shalt speak out of the earth, and thy speech shall be heard out of the ground ; and thy voice shall be from the earth like that of the python, and out of the ground thy speech shall mutter. And the multitude of them that fan thee shall be like small dust, and as ashes passing away the multitude of them that have prevailed against thee. And it shall be at an instant suddenly, a visitation shall come from the Lord of hosts in thunder and with earthquake and with a great noise of whirlwind and tempest, and with the flame of devouring fire. And the multitude of all nations that have fought against Ariel shall be as the dream of a vision by night. And all that have fought and besieged and prevailed against it. And as he that is hungry dreameth and eateth, but when he is awake his soul is empty ; and as he that is thirsty dreameth and drinketh, and after he is awake is yet faint with thirst, and his soul is empty ; so shall be the multitude of all the Gentiles that have fought against Mount Sion. Be astonished and wonder, waver and stagger ; be drunk not with wine, stagger and not with drunkenness ; for the Lord hath mingled for you the spirit of a deep sleep. He will shut up your eyes ; he will cover your prophets and princes that see visions, and the vision of all shall be unto you as the words of a book that is sealed, which when they shall deliver to one that is learned, they shall say : Read this : And he shall answer : I cannot, for it is sealed. And the book shall be given to one that knoweth no letters, and it shall be said to him : Read. And he shall answer : I know no letters. And the Lord said : Forasmuch as this people draw near me with their mouth and with their lips glorify me, but their heart is far from me, and they have feared me with the commandment and doctrines of men ; therefore behold I will proceed to cause an admiration in this people by a great and wonderful miracle. For wisdom shall perish from their wise men, and the understanding of their prudent men shall be hid. Woe to you that are deep of heart, to hide your counsel from the

Lord ; and their works are in the dark, and they say : Who seeth us, and who knoweth us ? This thought of yours is perverse ; as if the clay should think against the potter, and the work should say to the maker thereof : Thou madest me not ; or the thing framed should say to him that fashioned it : Thou understandest not. Is it not yet a very little while, and Libanus shall be turned into charmel and charmel shall be esteemed as a forest ? And in that day the deaf shall hear the words of the book, and out of darkness and obscurity the eyes of the blind shall see, and the meek shall increase their joy in the Lord, and the poor men shall rejoice in the Holy One of Israel. For he that did prevail hath failed ; the scorner is consumed ; and they are all cut off that watched for iniquity, that made men sin by word and supplanted him that reproved them in the gate, and declined in vain from the just. Therefore thus saith the Lord to the house of Jacob—he that redeemeth Abraham ; Jacob shall not now be confounded, neither shall his countenance now be ashamed ; but when he shall see his children, the work of my hands in the midst of him, sanctifying my name ; and they shall sanctify the Holy One of Jacob and shall glorify the God of Israel, and they that erred in spirit shall know understanding ; and they that murmured shall learn the law ' (Isaias xxix, 1–24). ' But he answering said to them : Well did Isaias prophesy of you hypocrites, As it is written : This people honoureth me with their lips, but their heart is far from me. And in vain do they worship me, teaching doctrines and precepts of men. For leaving the commandment of God you hold the tradition of men, the washing of pots and of cups, and many other things you do like to these. And he said to them : Well do you make void the commandment of God that you may keep your tradition ; for Moses had said : Honour thy father and thy mother ; and he that shall curse his father or mother dying let him die. But you say : If a man shall say to his father or mother : Corban (which is a gift), whatsoever proceedeth from me shall profit thee ; and further you suffer him not to do anything for his father or mother ; making void the commandment of God by your own tradition which you have given forth.'

This was indeed a turning of the tables. Hitherto, in dealing with the Pharisees, He had been mainly content to defend, now He proceeded to attack. He quoted the prophet who long since had denounced the substitution of formality for truth ; He applied this to a fundamental point, known to everyone in that audience ; a point in which not only the law of God but a most elementary law of nature had been violated. It could not be gainsaid ; it struck deeper than their criticism ; after exposure such as this, how could they now talk of pots, and pans, and soiled fingers ?

But He would not stop there. The Pharisees had of late tampered with the people, and the people themselves had wavered ; He would seize this occasion to warn them, and to put them again on the right path. He rose from the table ; He strode out of the door as He had done on like occasions ; He beckoned to the crowd to gather round Him. They had heard what the Pharisees had said, and had been impressed ; for the Pharisees were their legal guides, and were understood to know what was right and what was wrong. They had heard His reply and that, too, had impressed them ; still their fear of His rivals was great, and they hesitated. Therefore must He drive His words home. Though He were to maintain His new manner of speaking to the multitude in parables, still in some things He must be explicit. He would make them feel and know, not only that He stood by what He said, not only that formalities and customs were no substitute for the laws of God and man, but that there were other principles of right and wrong than those of mere ceremonial washings.

' And having called together again the multitudes unto him
He said to them
Hear ye me all and understand
There is nothing from without a man
That entering into him can defile him
There is nothing going into the mouth
Can defile a man
But the things which come from a man
What cometh out of the mouth
These are they that defile a man
If any man have ears to ear
Let him hear.'

He said no more. Since the time when He had begun to speak in parables His addresses to the people in Capharnaum had tended to be abrupt. He had now other work to do. On the one hand His enemies were more on the

alert, and He would not ' cast pearls before swine ' ; on
the other He was concentrating more and more on those
who were to succeed Him. So He dismissed the people ;
by action more than by word He bade the Pharisees be
gone ; He turned again into the house and the Twelve
gathered round Him. But they were not a little troubled.
Now that opposition had definitely set in, now that the
triumph of a week or two before had begun to change into
conflict, they were less easy, less assured, than in the old
days of successes. While they had dealt with the people
only all had been well ; now the enemy had appeared in
all his force, and it would be needful to be cautious. The
Pharisees were all-powerful ; they had authority still over
the people. If they could be won to favour Jesus, success was
assured ; if they could not, what trouble might not follow ?

Surely Jesus saw this for Himself as well as they. And
yet what had He just done ? They had found fault as they
had done before, and, as before, He had answered them ;
but this time He had done more, He had openly abused
their teaching. They had gone away offended ; more than
offended, they had taken scandal ; to their very faces He
had flouted the inviolable traditions of Israel. They must
warn Him ; they must counsel Him to be more prudent ;
as they had been compelled to do before, when He would
not give Himself so much as time to eat, so now they must
protect Him from Himself.

They came around Him and waited. At length one of
them took courage and suggested :

' Dost thou know
That the Pharisees when they heard the word
Were scandalized ? '

Jesus knew, only too well, what this hesitating question
implied. Long since, it is true, the Twelve had learnt to
prefer the leadership and teaching of the Master to that of
the Pharisees and Scribes. Still, until lately, active opposition had been little. But now it was growing fast. Already
He had been compelled to leave Capharnaum for a time ;
since that day He had seldom been able to stay there for
long together.

There was clearly danger in the air, and these, His
Twelve, were beginning to be afraid. They feared this
powerful rival ; they were dreaming of compromise ; they

were asking themselves whether it were not wiser to practise more conciliatory methods. With all their rejection of the Pharisees, they still held them in awe ; in their presence they forgot the authority of Him who, for them in particular, had quelled the storm, and scattered the clouds, and had walked dryshod to them on the waters.

He must guard them against this growing danger. The lesson would take time ; again and again He would have to repeat the warning, driving it ever deeper home. From now to the end there is nothing more vehemently repeated, more explicitly exposed, than the charge against this particular enemy; yet at the end of all He has to encourage them still not to fear. Not till after He has gone, and the Holy Ghost Himself has come to strengthen them, are they able altogether to lay their anxiety aside. Is it too much to say that to this day, and throughout all time, there is no enemy more dreaded by prudent and good men than the scandalized Pharisee, above all the Pharisee who has the authority of religion on his side ? This at least is true ; that of all adversaries there is none with whom, to human eyes, conflict seems more hopeless, more certain to end in disaster.

But the method of defence was His own. The force of the enemy against Him He refused to measure ; they were wholly in the wrong, and that was enough. The Father was greater than all enemies. Moreover error could only lead to error, no matter what support and show of righteousness it might muster on its side ; and error, in the face of truth, must always perish in the end. Let His own learn betimes to ignore that which was not true, be it ever so powerful ; error left alone would destroy itself.

> ' But he answering said
> Every plant which my Father hath not planted
> Shall be rooted up
> Let them alone
> They are blind
> And leaders of the blind
> And if the blind lead the blind
> Both fall into the pit.'

With this He ended. Later He would have much more to say, but for the moment that was enough. Meanwhile the less timid Simon was not so anxious as the rest. He was more concerned with that which the Master had said, more eager to understand the parable which He had used. In the silence that followed he turned the conversation.

'And Peter answering said
Expound to us the parable.'

The reply appals us with its plain speaking, though it would have much less appalled the far more homely Asiatic mind. At the same time, because of its very plainness, it contains the most explicit distinction in all the teaching of Jesus between physical and moral evil. In its vigorous way it gives the distinction between the pagan ideal and His own. It is at the root of all the moral teaching of S. Paul, it anticipates S. Augustine, both of whom had need of this sharply drawn line in the face of the enemy with whom they had specially to contend.

'And he saith to them : Are you also yet without understanding ? Understand you not that everything from without entering into a man cannot defile him ? Do you not understand that whatsoever entereth into the mouth entereth not into his heart, but goeth into the belly, and goeth out into the privy, purging all meats ? But he said : The things which proceed out of the mouth come forth from the heart, and those things defile a man. For from within, out of the heart of men, come forth evil thoughts, adulteries, fornications, murders, thefts, covetousness, wickedness, deceit, lasciviousness, blasphemies, pride, foolishness : all these evil things proceed from within and defile a man. But to eat with unwashed hands doth not defile a man.'

57. The Syro-Phœnician Woman

The Pasch was now well over ; the crops were ripe and the harvest had begun. Galilee had received its message, and to a certain point only had accepted it ; the reaction had set in, and Jesus knew the old order could never be restored. The Pharisees had now gained a sure footing among the people, and would spare nothing in their efforts to counteract His influence. With all the excitement and enthusiasm, except for a few here and there, the Galilæan ministry had failed. Moreover there was now increasing danger. He no longer could count on the protection of the multitude ; the enemy was confident and aggressive, on

one side the Pharisees, justifying any violence in defence of
their sacred traditions, the Herodians on the other, aware
by now that Herod was troubled about Him. He could do
no more in Capharnaum; it was time for Him to go
elsewhere; without a miracle He could not be protected,
and He would not use that means.

Thus it is that we next find Him, driven from Judæa,
driven from Galilee, a wanderer upon the earth, making
His way across the north-western border of the country to
the coast-line of Syria. Here was the city of Tyre, once the
most famous city along all that coast and still a great
emporium, where shipping was abundant and where many
from the land of Israel found employment. North of Tyre
was Sidon, a city still more decayed, yet with a great and
warlike history hanging about its ruined walls. The people
of these parts were a placid people; they had seen better
days, and the memory of their past had softened them.
Jews from the south found among them a contented home;
Jesus Himself, when He came there, was well received, even
if little notice was taken of Him. Here at least He could
retire and rest awhile, safe from the annoyance of His
enemies.

He found a house that gave Him shelter; He expressed
a desire that He should be left alone. His mission did not
reach to Syria; the day for Tyre and Sidon would come
later; for the present He would sanctify it by His presence
and prepare it by His prayer. But it was of no avail. No
sooner was His coming made known,—and with the Twelve
about Him it could not be concealed,—than many began
to come together. Long ago Jews from Tyre and Sidon had
been to Him in Capharnaum, and there had shown themselves among His most devoted followers. They had come
back to their friends along the coast with wonderful stories
of this Man, and of what He said, and of the miracles He
wrought. Their accounts had been consistent, one had
confirmed another, in all there was the ring of truth. Even
their non-Jewish neighbours, who knew little of the Messias
and cared less, had been impressed by what they had
heard, and were at least curious to see Him.

Among these last was one poor woman upon whom
misfortune lay heavy. True, she was only a Gentile. She
was only what a Jew, proud of his own ancestry, would call
a contemptible Canaänite; what a Roman would call a

Syro-Phœnician, a more or less degenerate Greek. She lived in her cottage by the coast, little known to anyone, uncared for by anyone ; one of those whom one finds in the East living apart in their single-roomed huts, and who make one wonder who they are, and whence they come, and what they do, and how they live. More than this, she was burthened with a daughter, now growing up but quite mad ; mad, and violent, and in other ways distressing, possessed by an unclean spirit. For this child's sake the mother was compelled to live more than ever apart from her neighbours ; shame compelled her, her mother's love compelled her, for in spite of the burthen this mother loved, and pitied, and lived for her child.

Still, while she spent her days apart with her sorrow, the poor woman had her friends ; and among them were some of the labouring Jews living along that coast. When these folk passed her door they would give her a kindly greeting. They would see her child, sometimes cowering morosely in a corner, sometimes in a state of wild frenzy, occasionally quiet and at peace, revealing what might be if only she could be released from the bondage that enslaved her. They would tell the mother of the wonderful Man over in Capharnaum, and in particular of His control of devils. They would discuss the possibility of their meeting, of her going over to Him, of her taking her child ; if only she could be brought to Him, something would certainly be done. And the woman had listened and believed ; despair of other help had made her believe all the more. She had listened and dreamed and hoped that her dream might yet come true ; that somehow she might be able to go to this Worker of Wonders and ask Him for His help.

Suddenly in the midst of her dreams she hears that actually He has come into the country. Her neighbours tell her ; the excitement among her Jewish friends confirms the news. She must see Him ; she must meet Him ; she must watch Him and judge whether He will be likely to look at one such as herself. She must not delay ; He may not be staying long in the district. Shall she take her child with her ? It would be almost impossible ; alone she could not do it. But was it necessary ? She had heard that He healed sufferers at a distance, and one who cast out devils was not bound by space limitations. No ; she would go alone. There were friends about who would care for the child in her absence ; all the world over the poor will always help the poor. Her Jewish neighbours in particular would be only too glad to give her this relief.

Her arrangements were soon made ; they were not many. She was told where He had gone ; she hurried after Him ; she found the house where He was staying. Without more ado she went straight into the room ; as we have seen before, in such cases people did not stand on ceremony, and access was easy. She looked into His face, and it was enough ; she knew. Boldly she went forward to Him and fell down at His feet.

> ' And behold a woman of Canaan
> Who came out of those coasts
> Whose daughter had an unclean spirit
> As soon as she heard of him
> Came in
> And fell down at his feet.'

But what now should she say ? How should she address Him ? There came into her mind all she had heard her Jewish neighbours saying when they had talked among themselves. They were earnest people, these Jewish friends of hers. They discussed Him and called Him ' the Lord ' ; they spoke of Him as the coming ' Son of David ', whatever that might mean ; they were intent upon a coming kingdom, to be restored by a descendant of David, and some said that this was He. She looked again at Him ; He was true, He was a Master, He was gentle, He was enduring, He was hopeful ; He encouraged, He was safe, He would not take offence ; every second that she spent at His feet made her brave to dare the more. At last her heart found words. For those around her she cared nothing ; with a cry that pierced she put up her petition.

> ' And she besought him
> And crying out said to him
> O Lord
> Thou Son of David
> My daughter is grievously troubled
> By a devil.'

Jesus looked at her. He did not seem to be displeased ; yet He answered nothing. Evidently He sympathized, evidently He wished to be kind ; yet He answered nothing. He even turned away as if the sight of this poor woman hurt Him, and He would gladly put her from His thoughts. Nay more ; He rose from where He sat and walked away. This time at least He would not help ; perhaps it was because He could not. So at least the Twelve, who looked on the scene and followed Him, were inclined to interpret His behaviour. After all the woman was not a Jew ; she was only a Canaanite, only a Syro-Phœnician, and Jesus was not for Gentiles like her.

But the woman was not to be so easily discouraged. She had seen something in His eyes and she knew He was not one who could be happy in refusal ; till He actually dismissed her she would persist in her prayer. They went out of the house and she followed. They ignored her but she still appealed ; she followed them, pleading, up the street. They turned and bade her go away, but she pleaded only the more. At last the Twelve grew impatient. He had clearly shown that He did not mean to help her, and that should be enough. They would ask Him to send her away ; with her repeated crying she was a trouble to them, she was an annoyance, the whole disturbance was unseemly.

> ' And his disciples came
> And besought him saying
> Send her away
> For she crieth after us.'

Jesus stood still. The appeal of the Twelve seemed to recall Him to the poor woman who followed Him. He turned to her and looked down at her. He made as if He approved what had just been said.

> ' I was not sent ', he told her
> ' But to the lost sheep
> Of the house of Israel.'

It was almost a rebuke, almost a declaration that He could not even if He would ; and yet there was something in His manner that told her it was nothing of the kind. On the contrary, she now knew, just because He had not dismissed her, that she had only to persevere and she would win the day. He had not said He could not, therefore He could ; He had not said He would not, He had but offered an objection ; she had only to live down that objection and all would yet be well. He had at last taken notice of her, and it had been with sympathy ; He had spoken to her, and therefore to Him she was not an outcast.

More feelingly than any of the twelve men about Him He had addressed her ; therefore she could leave them alone. When He stood still she pushed through them and came forward ; once more she was at His feet ; with more appeal in them than ever, her eyes looked up to His :

    ' She came and adored him saying
           Lord
          Help me.'

The heart of Jesus was glad. Anything quite like this He had not had before. He would carry it further ; He would try her a little more, that in return He might bestow upon her blessing flowing over for her fidelity. So again He affected to hesitate. She had seen that He could do what she asked ; she had seen that He would ; now He objected on the ground of preference. As the Twelve were thinking, so He pretended to think.

    ' Who answering said
    Suffer first the children to be filled
      For it is not good
    To take bread from the children
    And to cast it to the dogs.'

This was indeed a victory. Step by step the woman knew she was beating down His opposition. He had begun by pretending to ignore her ; she had persevered, and at last He had taken notice. She had urged again, and again He had yielded. How her ready wit, sharpened by her earnestness, seized on the words He had spoken and made her appeal irresistible. ' The bread of the children ' not to be ' cast to the dogs ' ? What was the fact to be seen every day, in the houses alike of rich and poor ?

    ' But she answered and said
        Yea, Lord
    For under the table
    The whelps also eat
    Of the crumbs of the children
    That fall from the table of their masters.'

Could the retort be resisted ? It was a humble prayer ; the woman was only as a little puppy pleading for a crumb. It was faithful ; perseveringly it relied on Him, in the teeth of all opposition. It was a prayer of love ; she asked for another, nothing for herself. It was hopeful for it never ceased. What had He Himself declared ? True, He had once said :

' Give not that which is holy to dogs ' ;

but immediately after He had added :

' Ask, and it shall be given to you
Seek and you shall find
Knock and it shall be opened to you
For everyone that asketh receiveth
And he that seeketh findeth
And to him that knocketh it shall be opened
Cr what man is there among you
Of whom if his son shall ask for bread
Will he reach him a stone ? '

He had said this, and He must keep His promise, even to this poor Canaanite. Besides He must teach His Twelve a lesson. The gift of God was not to be confined ; there was no man or woman on this earth, Jew or Gentile, who might not have it if he or she would. His heart expanded ; with one of those outbursts of affection which we have now seen several times, and ever apparently increasing, from the day when He blessed the ruler of Capharnaum, and again the Roman soldier, to that other day when He made a friend of the sinner of Magdala, and again to the day when the woman was healed who would touch but the hem of His garment.

' Jesus answering said to her
O woman
Great is thy faith
Let it be done as thou wilt
For this saying go thy way
The devil is gone out of thy daughter.'

It was a victory for the Gentile world, and the faith of that woman had won it. She needed to hear no more ; she could trust His word. The joy in her face as she looked up at Him was thanksgiving enough ; they parted and never met again. She hurried back to her cottage by the sea, knowing well what she would find. And it was so. There lying on her mattress was her daughter, sound now and well, with not a shadow of madness about her. And never again did it recur. In the years that followed mother and daughter recalled the tale again and again to one another. In a year after He was dead ; did the story of it reach them from Jerusalem ? A few years later and the followers of Jesus made their way along the high road that

ran along that coast to Tyre ; did they find there the
Syro-Phœnician and her daughter ? This much at least is
certain. Somewhere in heaven is a saint whom even the
Twelve pushed aside, but whose canonization is fixed by
the words :

> ' O woman
> Great is thy faith ' ;

words very different from those of a few weeks before :

> ' Why do you doubt
> O ye of little faith ? '

It was indeed a lesson for the Twelve. It was the one
lesson which, from now to the end, He was never tired of
repeating ; the one lesson which we all need to learn, hard,
it may be, in the learning, but when we have learned it we
wonder at its ease.

58. The Deaf Mute and others in Decapolis

> ' And again going out of the coasts of Tyre
> He came by Sidon
> Nigh to the sea of Galilee
> In the midst of the coast of Decapolis.'

Nowhere in the life of Jesus do we find more explicit
statement of the route He traversed in His journeys than
we have in this place. From Capharnaum, after His
formal condemnation of the Pharisees, He had walked
across Galilee westward to the coast land of Syria. Now
He strikes north, from Tyre through Sareptha, famous for
the visit of Elias, with the sea on His left and the mountains
on His right, crowned in those days with the woods of
Lebanon. He goes as far as the promontory on which
Sidon is built ; here He turns again eastward, over the hill
country in the direction of Damascus. Before He reaches
that city, again He turns south by way of Cæsarea Philippi
through Gaulanitis, till He comes once more to the sea of
Galilee, but away on its eastern side. All this time He has
carefully avoided the country where He is best known. He
has gone into pagan districts ; He has returned through
districts that were half, or more than half, pagan ; finally
we find Him resting in Decapolis where Judaism is not
strong. Here

> ' Going up into a mountain
> He sat there.'

In this meek way, and to this extent, Jesus avoids for a time the onset of His enemies. He has still other work to do ; when He has done it, then we shall see Him face them and fight them even unto death. But first He must teach His own yet other lessons. The day will come when they must go forth to teach all nations ; He would give them this example of a missionary tour. There was still to be won from them the great confession of faith on which all the future was to be built. By drawing them away from their surroundings, by keeping them with Himself, by showing them that faith was to be found even in so-called unbelievers, He would open out their minds and their souls to the work that lay before them.

But there was also something yet more immediate to be done. These Twelve had already gone far in their discovery of Him ; He must now purify their understanding till they saw Him as He was. The Messias, the Son of David, the King of Israel, the Prophet, the Son of God,—they must see the meaning of these names until at last, free from all qualifications, the title should ring out in all its golden purity from the mouth of one among them. This now was His goal. While He worked towards it He would keep them apart, uninfluenced by fear of Pharisees or scribes, undisturbed by false popular estimates. The crowds He would now attract about Him would have a different spirit from those He had drawn before ; less Jewish it might be, less versed in the prophets and the signs, but more human, more spontaneous, and to that extent more sincere. Such an influence would expand the vision of His Twelve ; by no other means could He more completely break down the narrow walls in which they were imprisoned.

He came into Decapolis beyond the lake. Twice at least we have evidence that He had been in this neighbourhood before. One apostle He had sent into that country, and he had done his work well ; the poor demoniac whom He had healed and made His lasting friend in the land of the Gerasenes.

> ' And he went his way
> Through the whole city
> And began to publish through Decapolis
> How great things Jesus had done for him
> And all men wondered.'

The result was manifest. Before when He had come

into this neighbourhood a single miracle had frightened the inhabitants, and they had asked Him to leave their coasts. Now all was different. They had seen for themselves what a wonderful thing had been done among them and had reflected on it. They had learnt from Capharnaum how much more had been witnessed there. The story of the progress through the plain of Genesareth in the week before the Pasch had reached them. Now that He was here in their midst again, and seemed inclined to stay and rest awhile, they hoped that they too might have a share in His beneficence. They watched Him where He settled down upon the mountain-side, choosing a desert place apart from men, apparently willing to be left there alone, not anxious to impose Himself on anyone, not even seeking to teach, and His very spirit of seclusion gave them courage. Gradually the group of visitors about His little camp increased. The word went round to other towns and villages, and soon there were large crowds assembled. These talked among themselves. They would bring their sick and their defectives to Him and see what He would do. To ask Him outright they scarcely dared. It might be, as some said, that His favours were reserved for the strict Jews living across the water. Still they could try. So they brought up their sick ; they laid them where He might see them ; and the rest they left to Him.

They were not disappointed. One day He came down from His place of prayer and passed among them all. He said little or nothing ; we have no record of a single address given, of a single word spoken. He just moved about the bedsides, placed in rows upon the ground. He had an eye for all, even for these who were not of the fold ; He had a living sympathy for each. When He had done' they were all healed.

> ' And there came to him great multitudes
> Having with them the dumb
> The blind, the lame, the maimed
> And many others
> And they cast them down at his feet
> And he healed them.'

It was indeed wonderful. They were drawn to this Man, who seemed to have nothing to gain from His coming among folks like them ; who here at least showed no desire to preach; who just gave what He had to give, asking for nothing in return; who allowed His quiet hours on the hill-side to be broken by this constant going and coming of strangers; who was never ruffled, never showed Himself superior; who in spite of His powers, in spite of the attentions of His little band of followers, was always mysteriously an equal with them all; who could be approached by all, treated familiarly by all, made each one that came to Him feel and know that from the first moment of meeting He was an understanding friend. The influence grew, the victory was complete. It was a new kind of conquest, very different from that which had swept over Galilee. Silently He left His personal impress on Decapolis; of His preaching there we have no record whatsoever.

The crowds of blind and maimed had been cured and had been joyfully led away. The work of healing was over, and He had again retired to His place of rest. Suddenly it was found that one case had been passed over; a particularly pitiful case, of a boy deaf and dumb, and they would gladly see him healed like the others. They brought him up the hill; they laid him at the feet of Jesus; by this time they had courage to speak, and they besought Him that He would do for this one remaining sufferer what He had done for so many.

> ' And they bring to him one deaf and dumb
> And they besought him
> That he would lay his hand upon him.'

Jesus turned and looked at the petitioners and at the deaf and dumb boy before Him. He seemed to hesitate. Here once more we are brought up against the mystery that lies behind the miracles of Jesus. We have seen how in one place the Evangelists describe Him as having the spirit to heal upon Him, as if that spirit were not always with Him. At Nazareth we are told that He ' could not ' work many miracles, because of the people's unbelief. In the streets of Capharnaum He was conscious of the woman's secret cure because, as He said, He had felt on the instant ' virtue go out of ' Him. Now we find another case; what it signifies, who shall say? For some reason it would seem that there was difficulty in healing this boy; it ' could not ' be done in the ordinary way. It had to be done apart; a ceremony had to be performed; it cost Him a groaning prayer, then a word of stern command ; when it was over it is described almost as if it were the happy ending of a hard task. Thus much alone we can say ; for the rest we can do no more than look on, waiting till Jesus Himself gives us to understand.

He said nothing. He took the boy aside, apart from the expectant and enthusiastic multitude ; entirely alone He could scarcely have been on that hill-side, probably the Twelve were witnesses. As soon as they were apart Jesus stood the boy in front of Him. Then, first, He put a finger into each of his ears ; next, putting a finger into His own mouth, He moistened it with His own spittle. Last, opening the boy's mouth, with His moistened finger He touched his tongue. With this the ceremony was complete, but so far no effect seemed to follow. Jesus left the boy alone ; His eyes looked up to heaven ; He seemed to struggle in prayer ; He uttered a groan, as if the effort that He made was great. At last, turning to the boy, He said with stern command :

'Ephpheta.'
'And taking him from the multitude apart
He put his fingers into his ears
And spitting
He touched his tongue
And looking up to heaven
He groaned and said to him
Ephpheta
Which is Be thou opened.'

The effect of the word was instantaneous. The boy looked about him, to this side and that, his eyes wide open with amazement, almost with alarm. Sounds were beating on his ears and it was strange. His tongue, too, was loosened, and he made effort to speak ; it was no longer the weird cry of the deaf mute that came from his mouth. He was healed, without a doubt he was healed. He knew it himself, soon the onlookers knew also. The news spread among the crowd hard by, and down the hill. They had witnessed what Jesus had already done, but this single case brought their enthusiasm to a head.

'So that the multitudes marvelled
Seeing the dumb speak
The lame walk
The blind see.'

But Jesus took no heed of their display of fervour. If in Galilee, in spite of their better preparation and enlightenment, He had need to warn the people against making too much of His miracles, it was still more necessary here. For these people were more ignorant ; they expected little ; they had not before them the inspiring dream of the Messias ; miracles to them might be more easily misread. Therefore He came down to them. He endeavoured to quiet them ; He warned them not to make too much of that which He had done, not to speak too much about it. He had done it ; let that be enough. Let them thank God for what they had received, and prepare themselves to open their hearts to the message He would one day send them.

They listened, but they did not obey ; was it to be expected that they would ? Were these ' charges ' intended to be more than warnings, seeing how impossible it would be for a multitude such as this, on such an occasion, to keep silence ? The story could only be repeated, its repetition only roused them the more. His fame spread among them ; and not His fame only but the glory of the God of Israel ; so far as the Evangelists tell us the effect, here at least, was only good.

> ' And he charged them
> That they should tell no man
> But the more he charged them
> So much the more a great deal
> Did they publish it
> And so much the more did they wonder
> Saying, He hath done all things well
> He hath made both the deaf to hear
> And the dumb to speak
> And they glorified the God of Israel.'

' They glorified the God of Israel.' This at least this half-pagan people learnt ; they glorified the God of the Jews. It was a beginning.

> ' This is eternal life
> That they should know thee
> The only true God
> And him whom thou hast sent
> Jesus Christ.'

CHAPTER

19

59. The Feeding of the Four Thousand

JESUS lingered for some days in that neighbourhood. The crowds came and went; in these parts, not as hitherto in Galilee, He did not go to them, they came to Him. Around His hill-side many settled down, content, it would seem, to remain with Him so long as He chose to remain with them. It was a new kind of fidelity. These people who knew less than their neighbours across the water, were caught by the personality of Jesus only; and, though their aspirations were less high, still they were more faithful to Himself. It was a new consolation; a relief from the turmoil of Galilee, and from the molestations of the enemy; in spite of the multitudes that gathered about Him it was another happy pause in His life.

Now we come to one of those strange and significant repetitions of miracle which cannot have been either performed or recorded without a purpose. In the season before the Pasch, on the plain to the north of the lake of Galilee, the day before He had announced the promise of His body as the food from heaven, Jesus had fed five thousand men with five loaves; and then, as always since, the feeding was taken as a parable and a prophecy of that which was the next day defined. Now in Decapolis, a month or more later, the miracle is repeated; and that with circumstances, or at least with phrases, so similar, that a superficial reader might suppose the one to be only another version of the other. But a little observation will show that the differences are more than the resemblances; that these differences have been carefully inserted by the writers with set purpose; that the resemblances are rather in the words used than in any matter of fact.

Moreover it is clear that both Jesus and the Evangelists have carefully guarded against any such misconception. S. Matthew records them in succeeding chapters of his Gospel, S. Mark in the sixth and eighth; surely so near together that the two seem to challenge the interpretation that the two are one. Almost immediately after, when the disciples are again on their journey, both S. Matthew and S. Mark give the reference of our Lord Himself to the two events, contrasting the one with the other.

See Jesus, then, on this occasion, settled for a time on this mountain-side, whose western slope falls into the Sea of Galilee. Beneath Him is the plain shut in eastward by the hills, westward by the water of the lake. Multitudes have gathered there, as in the East multitudes will gather, disregarding time and convenience, contented to remain under the warm summer sun so long as He is willing to keep them. They are there in thousands. The news of Him has spread north, and east, and south throughout Decapolis, and from all sides the villagers have come in. The harvest has long been over, and their time is free. They have brought with them their little supply of food, but it has long since been used up ; nevertheless, carelessly, giving little thought to the morrow, they have lingered on about the spot. For three days together many have been there, and only now, when hunger threatens, does it occur to them that they must leave Him and make their way home. They are a quiet and peaceful multitude, unlike the more demonstrative crowds we have seen in Galilee ; their lot in life, their homes in lonely places, have taught them silent endurance. Call it fatalism, call it apathy, call it what you will, the mind of the Asiatic peasant everywhere is marked by this meek submission to what may come ; it is the will of God.

Jesus looks down upon this patient gathering. On the other side of the lake He has spoken unceasingly of faith, asked for it, upbraided the effusive people for their lack of it ; here He says nothing about it. There He preached His Kingdom ; here He has before Him plain humanity, for which the Kingdom as He taught it is not yet ; humanity ignorant, unenlightened, but which of itself, if it is not prevented, will come to Him and find in Him its satisfaction ; a lovable thing, but because of its condition love shows itself chiefly in pity. So is it with Him now. These people have been with Him all these days ; He loves them for it. Because of Him they have forgotten their own needs ; He loves them for it. He must make them some return ; remote as they yet are from true faith and understanding, He must give them the best He has to give. He calls the Twelve about Him. He points to the crowd ; His face relaxes into tenderness. Then He speaks :

> ' I have compassion on the multitude
> For behold
> They have now been with me three days
> And have not what to eat
> And if I shall send them away
> Fasting to their homes
> They will faint in the way.'

Surely there are not in the Gospels words which more reveal the human nature of Jesus than these. He sees these poor country-folk before Him ; He knows why they are there. Specially He lingers on the cause that has drawn them : ' They have been with me '. With His fond eyes He has discovered their need : ' They have not what to eat '. Those same eyes look into the future and see that if He does not provide they must suffer on His account. He has compassion on them, that is, He suffers with them ; and His compassion stirs Him. Because of what they have done for Him, because of their present condition, because of suffering they are prepared to undergo on His account, He has compassion and will help them.

Thus much at once the disciples understand. In this respect by this time they have come to know Him ; when His heart is won there is nothing He will not do. And yet what it will be they do not know. True, a few weeks before, up there on the plain almost within sight, on a like occasion He had fed five thousand people with five loaves. But then they were Galilæans, ' lost sheep of the house of Israel ', for whom He had said He had been sent. These were from the cities of Decapolis ; they were of all beliefs ; to such as these they had themselves been forbidden to preach ; He had Himself but lately said :

> ' It is not good
> To take the bread from the children
> And cast it unto dogs.'

In Tyre some days before He had cured a Canaanite woman's daughter ; but He had shown what an exception that had been to His rule. Here He had cured many blind, and lame, and deaf, and dumb ; but a single case had proved that it had cost Him something. No, this time they must not expect anything unwonted. The feeding of the former multitude was a thing unique, and could not be repeated here.

Still He 'had compassion', and that meant beyond a doubt that He would do something. What would He ask? That they should distribute their own provisions? They would do it gladly, but of what use would that be? Besides, here where they were, far away from any town, it was not as it had been on the Jordan plain. There they would have gone into the towns to purchase food; here it was not possible. They could only tell Him the plain truth; in His over-generosity He must be warned against making a mistake.

> ' And his disciples answering him
> Whence then
> Can anyone have so many loaves
> In the desert
> As to fill so great a multitude? '

Jesus heard what they said, but was not disturbed. He only asked them :

> ' How many loaves have you? '

They could tell Him at once. Judas was there and knew.

> ' But they said
> Seven
> And a few little fishes.'

He seemed satisfied. At once they saw coming over Him that spirit of command which they knew so well, never more than upon that day when He had fed the men on the northern plain. They recognized it, rightly interpreted it ; in spite of their surmises, even for these Gentiles, He was about to do again what He had done then ! This time there was less formality than there had been before ; He said nothing about fifties and hundreds ; He stood up where He was, beckoned to the people that they should be still, bade them sit down where they were.

> ' And he commanded the people
> To sit down upon the ground.'

They obeyed ; it was easy for them to obey. They looked up to Him where He stood ; perhaps at last He would speak to them. But no ; when they had sat down He did likewise. He called for the loaves and fishes and took them on His knee. Then the Twelve beheld the same little ceremony that they had seen before ; they knew now what He was doing, and what He would do. He looked up to heaven ; He poured out prayer of thanksgiving and petition. He took the flat loaves and broke them into pieces ; He distributed the pieces to the Twelve. They took them in the folds of their garments ; what they were to do with them they did not need to be told.

> ' And taking the seven loaves
> And the fishes
> And giving thanks
> He broke
> And gave to his disciples
> And the disciples gave to the people.'

Confidently they went down the hill-side. Again they gave and gave ; they came to the end and their store was not exhausted. Then, without the word of command, they knew what next it would please Him that they should do. They secured baskets from the crowd ; they poured in the remnants they still possessed ; they wandered back through the seated multitudes, picking up what fragments they could find ; when they had reached the place where He sat they had filled seven baskets with the pieces that were over. Seven loaves at the beginning ; seven baskets of bread at the end ; they had again come back richer than when they had gone away.

This time we do not read that there was any great emotion displayed. Before, from the sign of bread, the men of Galilee had discerned the Messias and had cried :

> ' This is of a truth the prophet
> That is come into the world ',

and on the strength of their discovery had wished to pro- claim Him their king. Here there was no such discovery. These people saw what He had done ; they could not have failed to see it ; but to them it conveyed no further meaning. In some way they were scarcely surprised. A day or two before they had summed up their judgement of Him when they had cried :

'He hath done all things well
He hath made the deaf to hear
And the dumb to speak.'

That He should add this to the rest of His well-doing was not strange.

And He was content.   For the present it was enough that these people should

'Glorify the God of Israel';

the rest would follow in good time.   He had their number counted; for the sake of the future that would be important. There were present

'About four thousand men
Besides children and women.'

While they counted them the Twelve could not but recall the fact that these, for the most part, were not their own people, but men from the Greek cities.   And yet for them this wonder had been done.   Therefore the bread, the Living Bread, was not to be for the chosen people only; it was to be for all the world.   If at the moment they did not understand they would know it later; they would know why Jesus wrought this wonder twice, and they would carefully record it.

The conclusion of the scene was very different from the scene on the plain by Bethsaida Julias.   There was no confusion; gratitude was shown by that almost passive trust, common among the Asiatic poor.   They had now been fed; they could make their long journeys home without danger of fainting on the way.   Let them go, and remember what great things 'the God of Israel' had done for them.   Quietly they obeyed; Jesus waited till they had gone, and then with His Twelve came down to the shore of the lake.   A boat was there.   It was hired.   They embarked, and He directed them, not to Capharnaum as they had expected, for they had been a long time from home, but further south to the point where the Jordan renews its course to the Dead Sea.

60. The Request for a Sign

'And having dismissed the multitude
Immediately going up into a ship
With his disciples
He came into the coasts of Magedan
Into the parts of Dalmanutha.'

Jesus still delayed to return to Galilee, though He had now been months away. The break with the northern province had been definitely made, and its meaning must be brought home to the Twelve ; later, when the Holy Ghost enlightened them, they would understand. While they grew, and their horizon widened, He was content to wait, content to do apparently nothing, content to waste precious days and weeks : the hidden life of Jesus did not end when He left Nazareth for the Jordan.

The little party sailed down the lake to the plain that stretches southward from its southern bank. Here, as we have already seen, the main road between Judæa and the north recrossed the Jordan, running north and south along its eastern bank through Peræa. Not far from this crossing John the Baptist, in his last days, had preached and baptized ; here, probably, He had been taken and carried off to prison. It was a busy thoroughfare, where many traders and pilgrims of all kinds gathered, on their way to and from Jerusalem. Hence when Jesus came into the district the news would soon get abroad. It would quickly reach the ears of the Pharisees, especially of those who had been sent into Galilee from Judæa to oppose Him and counteract His influence.

It was some weeks, perhaps even months, since He had slipped away from them into Syria ; and that just at a moment when it would seem that His power over the people had begun to wane. Since that time He had disappeared ; He had certainly not been in their neighbourhood ; if any rumours of His whereabouts had reached them it seemed that He was doing very little. In the meantime this respite had enabled them to formulate more definitely their method of campaign. Two things they had done. We have seen how on a former occasion they joined forces with their political enemies, the Herodians ; thus they hoped to win the power of Herod to their side, and the death of John the Baptist had made this hope the stronger. Now they allied themselves with their no less hated rivals in religion, the Sadducees. These men despised their worship of religion as futile ; they had no faith in another world ; but in that they were Jews they could meet the Pharisees on common ground. They had faith in a Messias to come and in signs that would mark Him ; when they discussed these signs together a new plan was suggested to them. In future they would come to Jesus as enquirers. They would renew their request for His credentials. Miracles, they would say, to them meant nothing ; personal influence meant nothing ; if He were what He claimed to be, He must give some unmistakable sign from heaven, some sign which they would be compelled to recognize from prophecy. And this, they felt sure, He could not do ; for there was no sign possible which could not be questioned and explained away.

Armed with these precautions they sallied forth to meet Him. They came down from Galilee to the Jordan ford ; they found Him there still resting, close by the shore of the lake. This time they came in no suspicious or aggressive manner ; they affected simplicity and a desire to learn even as the country-folk had done. They had been thinking matters over in His absence ; before they went further and decided to support Him, they would be grateful if He would give them some clear evidence of His claim. For after all He would remember that they were something more than the common herd. They were the leaders of the people ; they were responsible for their guidance ; the Sadducees in particular were select. They were above mere sentiment and emotion ; miracle and excitement might serve to draw the vulgar, but for them something more solid was needed. If He wished to win them, and He might, they must ask Him for some more direct and more convincing proof than had yet been given.

> ' And there came forth to him
> The Pharisees and Sadducees
> And began to question him
> And they asked him
> To shew them a sign from heaven
> Tempting him.'

The heart of Jesus was weary. He knew these men ; how could He fail to know them ? They asked for a sign, but if a sign were to be given them they would not recognize it ; they would ask and ask again for more convincing proof. Had they not already had signs enough ? There was the sign of John the Baptist, the ' voice crying in the wilderness '. He had proclaimed him to be

> ' The Lamb of God ',

and in the power of that sign many had followed Him ;

but as for them, the sign had only made them question the authority of John himself.

> ' And they asked him and said to him
> Why then dost thou baptize
> If thou be not Christ
> Nor Elias
> Nor the prophet ? '

There was the sign of Himself, of His unique personality. That from the first had been enough for such men of goodwill as Simon and Andrew, James and John, Philip and Nathanael ; in that alone they had recognized

> ' The Messias
> Him of whom the prophets spoke
> The Son of God
> The King of Israel.'

As for them, they had only persisted the more on this account in their phrase of contempt :

> ' This man.'

There were the signs in Jerusalem ; the signs which had brought Nicodemus to his feet by night saying :

> ' Rabbi
> We know that thou art come
> A teacher from God
> For no man can do these signs which thou dost
> Unless God be with him.'

As for them they had only persisted in their demand :

> ' What sign dost thou shew us
> Seeing thou dost these things ? '

There was the sign of His lordship of the Sabbath ; they had seen in it only a breaking of the Law. There was the sign of His forgiving sins ; they had taken it only as a proof that He was

> ' A blasphemer.'

There was the sign of His miracles, of His raising of the dead, of His command of devils. These had sufficed for the still hesitating followers of John ; they had driven the people to proclaim Him, first

> ' A great prophet '

and then,

'The prophet
That is to come into the world.'

As for the Pharisees, they had only said :

'This man
Casteth out devils by Beelzebub
The prince of devils.'

There was the sign of His words and His teaching, which had made others say that

'His speech was with power
And not as the Scribes and Pharisees ' ;

as for them, it had only enraged them the more against Him. Lastly there was the general sign, going on daily before their eyes, the time full of expectation, the age when prophecy should be fulfilled, the fulfilment of the prophets if they would but read them rightly. But they would not see ; they were cased in and blinded by their false traditions, and by their frankly confessed will not to believe.

Yes, there were signs enough for those who had the goodwill to see them. Even some of their own had not been wholly blind, Nicodemus, and Simon of Magdala, and Jairus of Capharnaum among them ; and surely these men had not kept their conclusions to themselves. But more than that ; He had already answered their question, that day when He had cleansed the Temple before their eyes, and they had asked Him for a sign, and He had said :

'Destroy this temple
And in three days I will rebuild it.'

On that occasion, as later it would be confessed, they had more than suspected what He meant. Did they then again ask Him for a sign ? He would repeat to them now what He had said then ; they should have that sign and no other.

'And sighing deeply in spirit
He answered and said to them
When it is evening you say
It will be fair weather
For the sky is red
And in the morning
There will be a storm
For the sky is red and lowering
You know then
How to discern the face of the sky
And can you not know

The signs of the times ?
Why doth this generation ask a sign ?
Amen I say to you
A wicked and adulterous generation
Asketh for a sign
And a sign shall not be given it
But the sign of Jonas the prophet.'

He would say no more ; by His manner He would let them see that He knew the value of their question. Abruptly He turned away from them, as He had done the last time He had met them before He forsook Capharnaum. The ship in which He had come was still lying close beside the shore. He went up into it and His disciples followed. He gave orders to put out to the middle of the lake, perhaps that none might know where He would land. Not till they had reached Bethsaida Julias, fifteen miles away on the northern shore, where before the Pasch He had fed the five thousand, did He set foot on earth again.

And as He sailed away the Pharisees and Sadducees looked on and hated Him the more. They recalled His severe condemnation in Jerusalem when they had first put this question to Him, and they knew in their hearts that only by His blood could they be avenged.

' I know you
That you have not the love of God in you
I am come in the name of my Father
And you receive me not
If another shall come in his own name
Him you will receive
How can you believe
Who receive glory from one another
And the glory which is from God alone
You do not seek?
Think not that I will accuse you to the Father
There is one that accuseth you
Moses
In whom you trust
For if you did believe Moses
You would perhaps believe me also
For he wrote of me
But if you do not believe his writings
How will you believe my words ? '

Signs ? There were already signs enough. But to one who is unwilling to believe no sign is convincing. And for them, as for so many, at all costs they must remain always unconvinced.

61. The Leaven of the Pharisees

The little party sailed due north up the lake, keeping all the way along the eastern shore. It was a distance of some fifteen miles, perhaps a matter of four hours. On the right they would pass the hill-side where the day before He had fed the four thousand ; higher up, the valley of the Gerasenes, and the plateau where the devils had entered the herd of swine. Away to the left, in the distance, first the turrets of Tiberias appeared, then Magdala, with its villas gleaming white on the slope of the hill. Higher up again might just be seen Bethsaida and Capharnaum, with, behind them, the mountain running high on which they, the Twelve, had themselves been chosen, and the great sermon had been preached. As they sailed along every corner of the lake seemed to speak to them of their Master, His preaching, His lavish generosity, His constant per-severance, His self-sacrifice, His longing, His love for men, and yet His strange sense of disappointment which in these last months had been manifestly on the increase. Even as they sailed, they knew they were flying from a dangerous enemy. The suddenness with which He had left the southern shore, after He had barely landed there, as if this unexpected meeting with the Pharisees and Sadducees had made Him alter His plans, had given them a surprise. It was further clear that He was avoiding Capharnaum and Galilee, keeping them well on the left. Frankly they were uneasy ; not without reason had they warned Him of the determined opposition of the men in power.

But soon a new anxiety drove out all these reflexions. They had not gone far up the lake when it was time for their midday meal ; and then they remembered that in the hurry of departure they had forgotten to take in provisions. For once even the careful Judas had failed them. They searched about and found they had only one loaf among them, and one loaf among thirteen would not go far. They had no barley, they could not make more. They talked their trouble over among themselves, to Him they did not care to mention it. Maybe He would not notice their mistake before they reached their destination, and then all would be well.

While they were soothing themselves with this hope, suddenly He intervened in their conversation. They were talking about bread ; He turned to them and interrupted :

> ' Take heed and beware
> Of the leaven of the Pharisees and Sadducees
> And of the leaven of Herod.'

It was a strange intrusion. Evidently He had overheard ; and He had seized the occasion, so it seemed, to warn them against certain kinds of bread which He wished them in future not to eat. The Pharisees and Sadducees, and the Herodians, were notoriously fastidious and rich-living people ; perhaps He meant that they should beware of growing fastidious like them. If that was His meaning, then it was a further addition to what He had said when He sent them out to preach. For their minds were still dull and drab, material still in their outlook. To them a spade was a spade, and bread was simply bread. We have seen their slowness of understanding, at the time of the preaching of the parables and elsewhere, but seldom so vividly as we see it here. We may judge what patience was needed to endure them, what long-suffering to continue to work on for their enlightenment.

For indeed it would seem to have required little understanding to interpret what the Master meant. Already He had warned them with vigour in Capharnaum to be in no way afraid of the hatred of these men. He had rebuked them before the world ; He had spoken scathingly about them ; He had turned His back upon them, and meekly the Twelve had followed Him. But now He would go further. It was not so much their opposition that He feared for His own, it was their subtlety. Before, the Pharisees had blamed Him, for His miracles, for His other good deeds ; He knew that this would not take His friends away from Him. Now this morning they had come, with an affected simplicity, a show of desire to know the truth, an appeal to the prophets, a zeal for tradition, a respect for law and order, and obedience to the powers that be ; and all this, He knew, would be likely to affect His own more than any open enmity. Like leaven, unless they were careful, it would spread unconsciously among them. Therefore against this also they must be warned betimes ; He would have them rightly understand the encounter of that morning. These poor men, how easily they were misled ! In their fancied sagacity, how very shallow were they after all !

Jesus saw that they did not understand. They were preoccupied with the thought of bread ; they could think of nothing else. In spite of all that had happened, especially in these last days, they could get no further ; we now see why S. Mark had already said :

> ' They understood not concerning the loaves
> For their heart was blinded.'

He must begin at the beginning. He must go through it all with them, teaching them their lesson step by step, like little children in a school. To stir them to attend He must let Himself be troubled with their dulness ; He must a little scold them. They sat there in the boat looking at Him, afraid, anxious, like boys that knew they had done what they should not, yet not certain what it was. He looked down upon them, a little more flushed than usual, as if He were disappointed with their want of progress. Then He broke out, love in His words but troubled love, patience but a complaining patience ; a lesson taught, but not without rebuke that it had not been learnt long before.

> ' But they thought
> And reasoned among themselves
> Because we have taken no bread
> And Jesus knowing it said
> Why do you think
> And reason within yourselves
> O ye of little faith
> For that you have no bread ?
> Do you not yet know nor understand ?
> Have you still your heart blinded ?
> Having eyes see you not ?
> And having ears hear you not ?
> Neither do you remember.
> When I brake the loaves among five thousand
> How many baskets full of fragments took you up ?
> And they say to him, Twelve
> When also the seven loaves among four thousand
> How many baskets full of fragments took you up ?

> And they say to him, Seven
> And he said to them
> How do ye not yet understand
> That it was not concerning the bread that I said to you
> Beware of the leaven of the Pharisees and Sadducees ? '

' O ye of little faith ! ' This was the third time, upon these same waters, that He made this complaint. Now their trouble had been chiefly out of concern for Him ; yet once more did He seem to blame them. It was always the same story ; with faith He would never be contented until it became one act of complete and blind surrender. The more He received, the more He would stimulate and urge, until at last He had all without reserve. The people on shore He had left to themselves. He loved them, for them He ' did all things well ' ; but on their implicit faith He did not rely. With His Twelve it was different. On the depth of their faith all the future of the world would depend ; therefore must He have it pure, and understanding, and deepened ever more and more. In the early days, when they knew but little, He had been gentle with them, He had sweetly drawn them on ; now the days were closing in, and they had far yet to go, and the going would be rough, and He would be compelled more than once to use the whip and the spur.

They heard what He said, and to a limited degree took home their lesson.

> ' Then they understood
> That he said not
> That they should beware of the leaven of bread
> But of the doctrine
> Of the Pharisees and Sadducees.'

It seemed but little fruit of so much labour. But it was another step in the training. Very soon now the summit would be reached, and though it were only one man among them that was at first to reach it, nevertheless that one would be reward enough. On him all the rest would be built.

62. The Blind Man at Bethsaida

In the course of that afternoon the vessel reached the northern shore, and put in at Bethsaida Julias. It was not

far from the spot where, a few months before, Jesus had fed
the five thousand. It was strange, it was disappointing,
that even as they came towards the place His chosen Twelve
should need to be reminded of what He had done there on
that momentous day. Not only had He fed the multitude,
but for the Twelve themselves He had provided, from what
was over and above, more than they had had at the beginning ; and yet to-day they were uneasy and were whispering
among themselves, because they had with them only one
loaf of bread ! They seemed incapable of learning ;
nothing seemed to enlighten them ; yet upon their learning
depended all the salvation of the world.

They landed at Bethsaida and went into the town. At
once the news was spread ; at once men began to tell
themselves that they must make use of His presence ; not,
it would seem, to learn from Him, not to show to Him any
special mark of honour, but to get from Him what healing
they might, as from some gifted physician. There was in
the town a blind man, who had so far missed being cured.
They had kept him in mind ; some day the Wonder-worker
might come again to their coasts ; now when He appeared,
forthwith they brought the blind man to Him. They
pleaded for him ; they asked the Master but to touch him ;
they were confident about the rest. Let it be remembered
that these people of Bethsaida beyond the Jordan were for
the most part not Jews. To them the Messias had little
meaning. They were men of the Decapolis class, like those
whom we have already met lower down the lake, willing
to proclaim Him as one who ' did all things well ', but
understanding little more.

> ' And they came to Bethsaida
> And they brought to him a blind man
> And they besought him
> That he would touch him.'

Jesus responded ; but again in that strange way which
seems to show that not always was His wonder-working
power free to act as it would. Though in Capharnaum a
Jewish woman had been healed by the mere touch of His
garment, yet in Syro-Phœnicia the Canaanite had won her
request only after long pleading. Though in Galilee He had
healed deaf mutes on the instant, sometimes of His own
accord, yet in Decapolis a single case had required a long

ceremony and deep groaning. Though in Genesareth He had healed all as He passed up the lane between the fields, yet here in Bethsaida Julias this one blind man seemed to require great effort. Behind the mystery of miracles there lies another mystery which in this world we shall never fathom.

But Jesus was willing to make the effort. He responded, but not at once. He looked at the petitioners and answered nothing, as He had answered nothing to the like a few days before. Instead He took the blind man by the hand ; the touch did not heal him, as those who had brought him expected. He led him out of the town, as if in some way the very atmosphere of the place interfered with His power, as it had been at Nazareth. Outside the town He stopped ; and now began a ceremony even more elaborate than that which the mystified Twelve had witnessed lower down the coast a few days before.

First from His own mouth Jesus took a little spittle. This He spread over the blind man's eyes. He laid His hands upon his head. After a few seconds He asked him whether he yet saw anything. Yes, the man did ; from his answer it may be judged that he had not been always blind. He had seen men and trees before. He saw something ; yet it could scarcely be called seeing. He saw light ; he saw things in motion ; he knew that the things were men, but he could not distinguish them as such. All was yet a blur, a thick mist, and in the mist everything was magnified. The moving men about him appeared to him large as trees ; more than that he could not distinguish.

> ' And looking up he said
> I see men
> As it were trees
> Walking.'

Jesus showed no sign of disappointment or surprise ; on the contrary, He seemed to expect what the man had said. From His question it was clear that He did not expect a full cure ; He did not ask whether the man saw, He asked whether he saw anything. It is the only question of its kind in the whole record of New Testament miracles. Now slowly He went on with the ceremony. He took His hands from the man's head, and laid them on his eyes. Then He took them away and stood apart ; gradually, it would seem, not all at once as in other cases, sight came back to the sufferer :

'He began to see.'

The mist lifted ; the light came through it more clearly. The trees that seemed to walk diminished in size ; they grew more distinct in outline ; they became real men. Before many seconds were over the cure was complete.

'After that
Again he laid his hands upon his eyes
And he began to see
And was restored
So that he saw all things clearly.'

It is S. Mark alone that tells this strange story, differing as it does from every other miracle that Jesus wrought. Now S. Mark, as many think, is the spokesman of S. Peter, and S. Peter was present at this scene ; moreover it is very significant that the next event to be recorded is that of S. Peter's confession. Are the two linked together ? Has S. Mark thought it desirable to tell of this unique miracle because it has some bearing on that which follows ? And if so, may it not well be that this was a final test of the faith of the Twelve ? 'O ye of little faith !' Jesus has often said to them of late. He has had from them one grand response when in the synagogue Simon declared :

'Lord
To whom shall we go ?
Thou hast the words of eternal life.'

Now He is about to test them for the great response of all. But He prepares them ; with His usual forethought He prepares them against themselves. On the lake He has forewarned them to have faith, and yet more faith. Here He has given them a preliminary trial. His power has seemed to weaken ; He has appeared to be less able to work miracles than He was before. Twice of late He has done it with an effort ; let them ask themselves how far they still believe.

Be that as it may, we do not read that the miracle caused any great commotion. Jesus and His company did not return into the town ; their route lay up the valley, in the direction of Cæsarea Philippi and Mount Hermon. The man stood there healed, unable to speak, beside himself, not knowing what he should do, dazzled by the light so

suddenly poured into his eyes. He lived away from the
city ; Jesus bade him go home.

> ' And Jesus sent him into his house saying
> Go into thy house
> And if thou enter into the town
> Tell nobody.'

It was another of those commands which could not be
obeyed ; but again it showed the mind of Jesus, and the
misuse that men made of His wonder-working power.

63. The Confession of Peter.

We have now reached the climax of the life of Jesus.
That afternoon He left Bethsaida and the Lake of Galilee,
and made northwards up the valley along the Jordan bank,
past the Waters of Merom in the direction of Mount
Hermon, whose snow-capped summit stood up in front of
them. On a spur of Hermon running down into the
valley was Cæsarea Philippi, a modernized town, dear to
Philip the Tetrarch, the son of Herod. Here Jesus could
hope to be yet more hidden from men. For the Jews did
not come here, except for purposes of trade ; even the
pagan country-folk of lower Decapolis were different from
the people here. These had no interest in such things as
religious disturbances. If Tiberias in Galilee was too
Roman-worldly to give Him the least recognition or notice,
no less Greek-worldly was Cæsarea. Therefore He had not
come into these parts to labour ; He had come that for
a critical time He might be quite alone with His Twelve.
It is true He went from town to town in the neighbourhood,
but that, it would seem, was done that He might be the
more alone. There is no word of preaching, no word of
miracles ; nothing is said of His meeting with either friends,
or enemies, or strangers. All we are told of Him is that on
the way He was in prayer.

> ' And Jesus went out
> And his disciples
> Into the quarters and towns
> Of Cæsarea Philippi
> And it came to pass in the way
> As he was alone praying
> His disciples also were with him.'

Let us here emphasize again this special feature in the

character of Jesus; His propensity to prayer even at most unexpected moments and in most unlikely places. We saw Him first in prayer on the banks of the Jordan, after He had been baptized by John; this He followed up by forty days of prayer and fasting in the desert. He was indignant in the Temple because that place which should have been ' a house of prayer ' had been turned into ' a den of thieves '; so we first see Him in Jerusalem. When again He came into the city, and at the Probatic Pool healed the cripple beggar, He was next discovered in the Temple whither He had gone alone to pray. There followed the months of great activity in Galilee; nevertheless, during all that time, especially at the beginning, the days of silence are significant. More than once, in the early morning, He is found to have slipped away, to the mountain or to the water's edge, to pray. Then comes the great day, the day of the choosing of the Twelve and of the Sermon on the Mount; and before that day we are expressly told:

> ' He spent the night
> In the prayer of God.'

Before He fed the five thousand outside Bethsaida He lifted up His eyes in prayer; later when He fed the four thousand in Decapolis He did the same. The healing of the deaf mute in the latter place had cost Him groaning and prayer.

These are explicit instances, given in the busiest period of His life; each one is significant, not only in itself, but also as implying a formal and constant habit. Whatever else Jesus was, He was a Man of prayer; one who lived intimately with Him, were he asked to choose between the two, would have called Him a Man of prayer rather than a Man of action. Nowhere does this appear more than at this time. Since the Pasch He had almost seemed to have avoided work. He had left Galilee; He had moved quickly through the country about Tyre and Sidon, and there had endeavoured to be hid; He had come down into Decapolis, and had retired into a mountain; though the people had gathered about Him and had stayed with Him for days together, still He seems to have done little more than heal their sick and feed them; about Magedan He had been accosted by the Pharisees and Sadducees, and had deliberately turned His back upon them.

And now His attitude is still the same. He is on the road,

moving from one place to another ; yet ' in the way ' He is able to draw aside to pray ' alone '. When we compare this explicit occasion with that mentioned before by S. Luke, we cannot doubt the reason of it. Then He was about to choose the Twelve, now He is about to put them to their final test ; for both He would prepare them beforehand by the power of His own prayer.

On this occasion, then, in the early morning they gathered round Him. What He was doing was nothing new or strange ; they were accustomed to wait till His morning prayer was ended. At length He had done, and with the unconscious ease that was His custom He resumed His place among them. Then, as though He would at this point sum up the work He had accomplished, as though He would review the effect of His preaching, and His work, and His life upon the people, He turned to them and asked :

> ' Whom do men say
> That I am ?
> Whom do men say
> That the Son of Man is ? '

It was indeed a leading question ; in its answer would be contained all the fruit of all His labours. Yet how strange and meagre was the answer He received ! When He had first appeared by the Jordan a voice from heaven had proclaimed Him :

> ' This is my beloved Son
> In whom I am well pleased.'

In his turn John the Baptist had pointed to Him saying :

> ' Behold the Lamb of God
> Behold him who taketh away the sins of the world.'

In the strength of that witness He had been followed ; and those who had followed Him came away saying :

> ' We have found the Messias
> We have found him
> Of whom Moses in the law
> And the prophets did write
> The Son of God
> The King of Israel.'

Enthusiasm because of their discovery had made them accompany Him to Galilee. At Cana He had worked His first miracle, and there

'His disciples believed in him ',
more sure than ever that their first conclusion was right.
Months had followed, during which their former master
John had confirmed them in their belief.

'This is he of whom I said
After me cometh a man
Who is preferred before me
Because he was before me.'

Since that time things had moved so quickly that they had
scarcely been able to formulate their conclusions. They
had come up through Samaria, and a Samaritan woman
had made them marvel with her quick intuition :

'Is not this the Christ ? '

He had been with them on the lake, and had given them a
miraculous draught of fishes ; and the eyes of Simon had
been opened, and in fear he had cried :

'Depart from me
For I am a sinful man
O Lord.'

They had heard the very devils cry out :

'We know who thou art
The holy one of God.'

They had heard Him say :

'Be of good heart, son,
Thy sins are forgiven thee ' ;

so that onlookers had been compelled to confess among
themselves :

'We have seen wonderful things to-day
We never saw the like.'

They had heard Him claim to be Lord of the Sabbath ;
they had listened to Him while in His own name, and on
His own authority,

'I say to you ',

He had laid down His own law, till

'The people were in admiration of his doctrine
For he was teaching them as one having power
And not as the scribes and Pharisees.'

After this they had seen Him raise the dead to life, and
had heard the multitude cry in recognition :

> ' A great prophet
> Hath risen up amongst us
> And God hath visited his people.'

In the house of a Pharisee they had heard Him again forgive a poor sinner her sins, so that even the Pharisees had been compelled to ask themselves :

> ' Who is this
> That forgiveth sins also ? '

On the lake He had quelled the storm for them, and in awe they had said to one another :

> ' What manner of man is this
> Who is this, think you
> For he commandeth both the winds and the sea
> And they obey him ? '

And the very next day they had had their answer from the mouth of an evil spirit :

> ' Jesus
> The Son of the Most High God.'

They had seen Him work miracles in abundance, miracles at hand, miracles at a distance, miracles apparently without advertence ; more than this, He had given this same power to themselves. They had heard the people again say :

> ' Of a truth this is the prophet
> That is to come into the world ' ;

and because of this belief they had wished to make Him their king. In response He had said :

> ' I am the bread of life
> The bread which I will give is my flesh
> For the life of the world.'

On that occasion they themselves had gone far, hardly knowing what they said. The night before He had come to them walking on the waters :

> ' And they came and adored him saying
> Indeed thou art the Son of God.'

Then when the people had failed Him they had stood by Him. They had shut their eyes to consequences, and their spokesman Simon had said for them all :

> ' Lord
> To whom shall we go ?
> Thou hast the words of eternal life

And we have believed
And have known
That thou art the Christ
The Son of God.'

Since then, down in Decapolis, they had heard the very
Gentiles confess :

' He hath done all things well
He hath made both the deaf to hear
And the dumb to speak
And they glorified the God of Israel.'

All this and much more had they seen and heard ; yet
nothing of it all did it occur to them to mention. Much
more now were their minds coloured with other things ; the
recent desertions, the growing aggression of the Pharisees,
His own constant flying from His enemies, the restraint of
His power in these last days, the cavillings and criticisms
that of late had reached their ears. Whatever was proclaimed before His face, in the bazaars and in private
conclaves there had always been, and still were, different
conclusions. More than once His origin had been made
a permanent block of stumbling ; more than once He had
been harassed by the crowd and laughed to scorn ; more
than once men had affected to take scandal at His non-
observance of the Law. Alongside of all the praise there
had always been this other side ; and it had grown with
time and not diminished.

But apart from these extremes, there were the moderates ;
and these had, perhaps, the greatest following among the
people. What then did they think ? How did they talk ?
To what conclusions had they come ? Jesus had appeared
at the Jordan, on the very spot where Elias had gone up
in a chariot to heaven ; was He perhaps Elias come back
again to life ? John the Baptist had perished ; Herod was
anxious about the consequences ; was He John the Baptist
resurrected to haunt his murderers ? True, He was in the
country before the Baptist died ; but might not the spirit
of the latter have passed into Him ? Or what if one of the
ancient prophets had returned ? Jeremias, for example, or
any of the others ? The men in the bazaars discussed these
matters ; when the Twelve went among them they were closely
questioned. Whatever the multitudes in their moments of
enthusiasm might have said or done, this was the more

common talk ; no doubt this was what He wished to know.
Therefore

' They answered him saying
Some John the Baptist
And other some Elias
And others Jeremias
And others say that one of the former prophets
Is risen again.'

Jesus listened and for a moment was silent. What they
said did not seem to surprise Him ; it was nothing new.
He showed a little sadness ; still He passed it by as if it
were of little interest. Let the men in the bazaars think
what they liked. He had known from the beginning what
was in men, and He did not count upon them. They were
as sheep without a shepherd, and He would be their shepherd,
not their judge. If they would not take His lead, then He
would provide them with others. For that reason He had
chosen the Twelve. One by one He had called them to
Him ; He had kept them at His side, He had shown them
Himself in all His grand simplicity, He had hidden nothing
from them. To each one He had given special care, special
affection ; each one knew from tender experience that He
was a special friend. They had been with Him everywhere,
at home and abroad ; they had seen His miracles, they had
heard His words. Special miracles had been worked for
them alone, special instructions had been given to them ;
they had been told that to them He would explain mysteries
and parables which He would not explain to others. Last
of all He had trusted them beyond belief. He had framed
them into a group apart ; He had sent them to preach in
His name ; He had given them power to work miracles
even as Himself ; through their hands He had fed the
multitude ; when in return the people fell away from Him,
He had appealed to them at least to stand by Him, as if in
them He would find enough to compensate for all the rest.

All this and much more He had done for them. He had
always consistently borne with them. He had endured
their dulness, their familiarities, their blunders, their
worldly wise assumptions, their self-esteem, their negligence,
their pompous ways, their complaints, their ignorance, their
timidity, their fear of men, their littleness of outlook, their
want of understanding, their want of faith ; on the other
hand their officious interfering, their impatience with

Himself and with others, their lack of self-control. When men had complained of them and their ways He had always stood in their defence, even when He scorned to defend Himself. Of all men He valued most their company, He laboured for their progress, He asked for their affection ; of all men He wished that they should know Him. All this was written on His face as His appealing eyes looked into theirs. Let other men say what they would ; but them He seemed almost to compel to loyalty as He asked :

'But whom do you say
That I am?'

What were they to answer? That He was John the Baptist, that He was Elias, that He was Jeremias, that He was a prophet risen again, answers such as these were beneath them. That He was the Lamb of God, that He was the Messias, that He was the King of Israel, that He was the Holy One of God, these they knew were not what He wanted. The Son of God they had already called Him more than once, each succeeding time meaning something more than they had meant before ; they knew that in that was the answer. They hesitated ; they looked at one another ; it was not that they did not believe, but that they did not dare to speak.

Once more Simon solved their problem for them. With his spirit of spontaneous self-surrender he made the leap blindfolded. He had seen so much, he had himself received so much, there was only one conclusion. He could trust with an absolute trust ; he could love with a limitless love ; therefore would he believe with a faith that knew no limit. He had used before the words he would now use again ; others, too, had used them ; but thus far neither he nor they had fully understood all that they implied. Now he would be generous. The Master asked for all and he would give all. With a full heart, meaning everything the words could literally mean, he answered :

'Thou art the Christ
The Son of the living God.'

At once the heart of Jesus responded. All these months He had looked for this moment and it had come at last ; at last one man had been found who would own Him for what He was. It was indeed a confession greater than could have been expected from human nature ; man of himself could never have attained to such a vision. This Jesus of Nazareth; this Carpenter whom His fellow-villagers had known only too well; this 'sinner' by the Jordan whom even John the Baptist could not recognize; this Man tempted by the devil; this common citizen of Capharnaum, whom other citizens could pull about, and treat as one of themselves, and even while they did Him honour could nevertheless laugh to scorn; this human frame that could be weary with travel, could be in need of food and drink, could lie down on a ship's deck and immediately succumb to sleep; this Man who had so many enemies, who stirred hatred seemingly no less than love; who had to fly from His foes to avoid their machinations, who at this very moment was virtually an exile from the land He loved, wandering in a strange country where men knew Him not; this sensitive Man, who responded so quickly to every touch of sympathy or ingratitude, who could be depressed by failure, who could so easily be hurt, who hung so much upon the love of others, who could be so extravagant, so 'imprudent' in His love that His friends had to defend Him from Himself; this Man who so loved His own and His Mother most of all, even as an infant loves its mother; this Man who could never resist a woman's tears, witness Samaria, and Naim, and Magdala, and Capharnaum, and even Tyre in Syria; what power on earth of itself could have penetrated to that which lay beneath?

Yet had Simon done it. With all his faults, and impetuosities, and reactions, in faith Simon had never yet failed. Step by step as month succeeded month he had gone forward, and with each step he had been given further light. He had accepted the lead, from the day when he followed Andrew down the Jordan, and he had only once looked back; that day when on the deck of his own ship he had fallen at the Master's feet and cried:

> ' Depart from me
> For I am a sinful man
> O Lord.'

But that had not been cowardice. It had been only humility, it had been only recognition of Himself; and the Master had not blamed him, He had only loved him for it all the more. Now Jesus knew Simon could be trusted. True, he was still only Simon, human, over-zealous, imprudent, rash and then timid Simon. He would yet fail in many ways ; he would need all the grace that the prayer of Jesus Himself could gain for him ; yet was he faithful in his heart. He had seen, he had been captivated, he had loved, he had surrendered himself out of love, he had trusted to the uttermost, blindly he had believed all. Now, first of all men, he had defied all human limitations and had declared Him to be what He was. He had trusted Jesus utterly ; utterly, whatever the results, Jesus would trust him ; in generosity Jesus would not be outdone. The reward to Simon is overwhelming, so overwhelming that even to this day wise and prudent men will not credit it ; none the less, to one who understands even a little of the lavish outpouring of the heart of Jesus Christ, it is a reward that is only consistent with the gift of Bethlehem, the gift of the Cenacle, the gift of Calvary, the gift of Pentecost. When we hear Him blessing Simon in such full measure, pressed down and flowing over, we can only say : Behold, how He loved ! How like Jesus Christ ! And we know that the only way to be true to the revelation of Him is to accept every word of this blessing as literally true.

'And Jesus answering said to him
Blessed art thou
Simon Bar-Jona
Because flesh and blood hath not revealed it to thee
But my Father who is in heaven
And I say to thee
That thou art Peter
And upon this rock I will build my church
And the gates of hell shall not prevail against it
And I will give to thee
The keys of the kingdom of heaven
And whatsoever thou shalt bind upon earth
It shall be bound also in heaven
And whatsoever thou shalt loose upon earth
It shall be loosed also in heaven.'

A carpenter of Nazareth, hiding from the Law, in a pagan district which knew nothing of Him, at a time when His work seemed most to have failed, says this to a fisherman of Bethsaida, a man particularly prone to spoil good work begun, by his imprudence and impetuosity. Either that carpenter of Nazareth was a wild enthusiast, or He was what Simon had declared Him ; let history, not ourselves, decide which we must choose.

The Twelve listened, they dared not speak. Never before had they heard Him say anything so tremendous, or with such confident assurance. A few months before, down this same valley by the lake of Galilee, the people had cried :

> ' This is indeed the prophet
> That is to come into the world ',

and had wished to make Him their king ; but what was that in comparison with this overlordship of two worlds which they were hearing from His own mouth ? And He was speaking to one of themselves. That Simon should be chosen did not surprise them. There was one other whom they might have chosen as more safe, more human-prudent ; there were several who might have been thought more competent ; but there was none more according to their hearts, whatever might be his shortcomings. From the first all had recognized his transparent and spontaneous sincerity ; they ever looked to him to speak their minds ; when he spoke he seemed always to say that which, if they had dared, they would gladly have said themselves. Before this day Simon had been a recognized leader among them ; from to-day, in spite of many lapses and rebukes, he remained to them always Peter.

During these last months, during paschal time, Jesus as we have seen had done very little. He had kept away from Galilee ; He had preached seldom, if at all ; He had tried to be hidden. But now He seemed again to awake. They had acknowledged Him and He was contented ; He was among them as of old. Still from the rest of men He seemed desirous to remain concealed. They knew at last who He was, but for the present they must keep that knowledge to themselves. Others would not yet understand ; let them grow in wisdom till they were able to learn. Men whose faith would rise no higher than John the Baptist, or Elias, or Jeremias, or one of the prophets, would never accept the Son of the living God. They turned their steps southward, to their surprise ; as they went along,

> ' Then he strictly charging them
> Commanded his disciples
> That they should not tell any man of him
> That he was Jesus the Christ.'

A HARMONY OF THE GOSPELS

		MATTHEW	MARK	LUKE	JOHN
1	The Coming of John the Baptist	iii, 1–10	i, 1–6	iii, 1–14	
2	The Prophecy of the Messias	iii, 11–12	i, 7–8	iii, 15–18	
3	The Baptism of Jesus	iii, 13–17	i, 9–11	iii, 21–22	
4	The Temptations in the Desert	iv, 1–11	i, 12–13	iv, 1–13	
5	The Witness of John the Baptist				i, 19–34
6	The First Disciples				i, 35–43
7	The Feast at Cana				ii, 1–12
8	The First Cleansing of the Temple				ii, 13–25
9	Nicodemus				iii, 1–21
10	Further Witness of John the Baptist				iii, 22–36
11	Jesus goes to Galilee ⎫	(xiv, 3–5)	(vi, 17–20)		
12	John the Baptist in Prison ⎭	iv, 12, 17	i, 14, 15	iv, 14–15	iv, 1–3
13	The Woman of Samaria				iv, 4–42
14	The Second Miracle at Cana				iv, 43–54
15	The Beggar at the Probatic Pool				v, 1–47
16	The First Rejection at Nazareth			iv, 16–30	
17	Settlement at Capharnaum	iv, 13–16		iv, 31	
18	The Call of the Four	iv, 18–22	i, 16–20		
19	The Demoniac in the Temple		i, 21–28	iv, 31–37	
20	Simon's Mother-in-law	viii, 14–15	i, 29–31	iv, 38–39	
21	A First Evening of Miracles	viii, 16–17	i, 32–34	iv, 40–41	
22	The Beginning of His Tours	iv, 23	i, 35–39	iv, 42–44	
23	The Miracle in Simon's Boat			v, 1–11	
24	The Leper	viii, 1–4	i, 40–45	v, 12–16	
25	The First Forgiving of Sins	ix, 1–8	ii, 1–12	v, 17–26	
26	The Call of Levi ⎫	ix, 9–13	ii, 13–17	v, 27–32	
27	The Banquet at Levi's House ⎭				
28	The Disciples of John the Baptist	ix, 14–17	ii, 18–22	v, 33–39	
29	The Disciples and the Ears of Corn	xii, 1–8	ii, 23–28	vi, 1–5	
30	The Man with the Withered Hand	xii, 9–14	iii, 1–6	vi, 6–11	
31	Retirement from Capharnaum	xii, 15–21			
32	The Choice of the Twelve	x, 2–4, iv, 24–25	iii, 7–19	vi, 12–19	
33	The Sermon on the Mount	v, 1–vii, 29	(with parallel passages)		
34	The Centurion's Servant	viii, 1, 5–13		vii, 1–10	
35	The Widow's Son			vii, 11–17	
36	The Embassy from John the Baptist	xi, 2–19		vii, 18–35	
37	The Woman who was a Sinner			vii, 36–50	
38	A Tour of Galilee			viii, 1–3	
39	The Charge of Beelzebub	xii, 22–37	iii, 19–30 ⎰	xi, 17–23 ⎱ vi, 43–45	
40	The Coming of His Mother and Brethren	xii, 46–50	iii, 31–35	viii, 19–21	
41	The Beginning of Parables	xiii, 1–23	iv, 1–25	viii, 4–18	
42	Further Parables	xiii, 24–53	iv, 26–34	xiii, 18–21	

479

		MATTHEW	MARK	LUKE	JOHN
43	The Storm at Sea	viii, 18, 23–27	iv, 35–41	viii, 22–25	
44	The Demoniac at Gerasa	viii, 28–34	v, 1–20	viii, 26–39	
45	The Woman with the Issue of Blood				
46	The Daughter of Jairus	ix, 18–26	v, 21–43	viii, 40–56	
47	The Second Rejection at Nazareth	xiii, 54–58	vi, 1–5		
48	Another Tour of Galilee	ix, 35–38	vi, 6		
49	The Mission of the Twelve	vi, 7–13, x, 5–xi, 1	vi, 7–13	ix, 1–6	
50	The Death of John the Baptist	xiv, 6–12	vi, 21–29		
51	Herod and Jesus	xiv, 1–2	vi, 14–16	ix, 7–9	
52	The Feeding of the Five Thousand	xiv, 13–21	vi, 30–44	ix, 10–17	vi, 1–14
53	The Walking on the Waters	xix, 22–33	vi, 45–52		vi, 15–21
54	A Morning of Miracles	xiv, 34–36	vi, 53–56		
55	The Bread of Life				vi, 22–71
56	The Pharisees and Unwashed Hands	xv, 1–20	vii, 1–23		
57	The Syro-Phœnician Woman	xv, 21–28	vii, 24–30		
58	The Deaf Mute and others in Decapolis	xv, 29–31	vii, 31–37		
59	The Feeding of the Four Thousand	xv, 32–38	viii, 1–9		
60	The Request for a Sign	xv, 39–xvi, 4	viii, 10–12		
61	The Leaven of the Pharisees	xvi, 4–12	viii, 13–21		
62	The Blind Man at Bethsaida		viii, 22–26		
63	The Confession of Peter	xvi, 13–20	viii, 27–39	ix, 18–20	
64	The First Prophecy of the Passion	xvi, 21–28	viii, 30–ix, 1	ix, 21–27	
65	The Transfiguration	xvii, 1–13	ix, 2–13	ix, 28–36	
66	The Demoniac	xvii, 14–21	ix, 14–29	ix, 37–43	
67	Another Prophecy of the Passion	xvii, 22–23	ix, 30–32	ix, 43–45	
68	The Temple Tax	xvii, 24–27	ix, 33		
69	Lessons to the Twelve	xviii, 1–35	ix, 33–50	ix, 46–50 &c.	
70	The Feast of Tabernacles			ix, 51–56	vii, 1–10
71	The New Disciples	viii, 19–22		ix, 57–62	
72	At the Feast of Tabernacles				vii, 11–36
73	The Last Day of the Feast				vii, 37–53
74	The Woman taken in Adultery				vii, 53–viii, 11
75	The End of the Feast				viii, 12–59
76	The Man born blind				ix, 1–41
77	The Good Shepherd				x, 1–21
78	The Mission of the Seventy-two	xi, 20–24		x, 1–16	
79	The Return of the Seventy-two	xi, 25–30		x, 17–24	
80	The Parable of the Good Samaritan			x, 25–37	
81	At the House of Martha			x, 38–42	
82	In the House of the Judæan Pharisee			xi, 37–54	
83	With the Multitude in Judæa			xii, 1–59	
84	The Galilæans slain in the Temple			xiii, 1–9	
85	The Infirm Woman on the Sabbath			viii, 10–17	
86	The Feast of Dedication				x, 22–39
87	The Number of the Elect			xiii, 22–30	
88	The Threat of Herod			xiii, 31–35	
89	The Man with Dropsy			xiv, 1–24	
90	Discourses on the Road			xiv, 25–xvii, 10	

		MATTHEW	MARK	LUKE	JOHN
91	A Résumé				
92	The Raising of Lazarus				xi, 1–46
93	The Hiding in Ephraim				xi, 47–54
94	The Last Tour	xix, 1–2	x, 1	xvii, 11	
95	The Ten Lepers			xvii, 12–19	
96	The Coming of the Kingdom	xxiv, 23–41	xiii, 21–23	xvii, 20–37	
97	Two Parables on Prayer			xviii, 1–14	
98	Jesus and the Children	xix, 3–5	x, 13–16	xviii, 15–17	
99	The Rich Young Man	xix, 16-xx, 16	x, 17–31	xviii, 18–30	
100	Third Prophecy of the Passion	xx, 17–19	x, 32–34	xviii, 31–34	
101	The Ambition of the Sons of Zebedee	xx, 20–28	x, 35–45		
102	The Blind Men at Jericho	xx, 29–34	x, 46–52	xviii, 35–43	
103	Zacchæus			xix, 1–10	
104	The Parable of the Talents	xxv, 14–30		xix, 11–28	
105	The Supper in Bethania	xxvi, 6–13	xiv, 3–9		xii, 1–11
106	The Procession of Palms	xxi, 1–11	xi, 1–11	xix, 29–44	xii, 12–19
107	The Cursing of the Fig-tree	xxi, 18–19	xi, 12–14		
108	Monday in the Temple	xxi, 2–17	xi, 15–19	xix, 45–48 xxi, 37–38	
109	The Fig-tree withered	xxi, 20–22	xi, 20–25		
110	The Last Day in the Temple	xxi, 23– xxiii, 39	xi, 27-xii, 40	xx, 1-xxi, 4	xii, 20–36
111	The Reflexion of John				xii, 37–50
112	Last Words outside the City	xxiv, xxv	xiii	xxi, 5–36	

Daughters of St. Paul

MASSACHUSETTS

50 St. Paul's Ave., Jamaica Plain, Boston, MA 02130 **617-522-8911.**

172 Tremont Street, Boston, MA 02111 **617-426-5464; 617-426-4230.**

NEW YORK

78 Fort Place, Staten Island, NY 10301 **718-447-5071; 718-447-5086.**

59 East 43rd Street, New York, NY 10017 **212-986-7580.**

625 East 187th Street, Bronx, NY 10458 **212-584-0440.**

525 Main Street, Buffalo, NY 14203 **716-847-6044.**

NEW JERSEY

Hudson Mall Route 440 and Communipaw Ave.,
Jersey City, NJ 07304 **201-433-7740.**

CONNECTICUT

202 Fairfield Ave., Bridgeport, CT 06604 **203-335-9913.**

OHIO

2105 Ontario Street (at Prospect Ave.), Cleveland, OH 44115 **216-621-9427.**

616 Walnut Street, Cincinnati, OH 45202 **513-421-5733.**

PENNSYLVANIA

1719 Chestnut Street, Philadelphia, PA 19103 **215-568-2638; 215-864-0991.**

VIRGINIA

1025 King Street, Alexandria, VA 22314 **703-549-3806.**

SOUTH CAROLINA

243 King Street, Charleston, SC 29401 **803-577-0175.**

FLORIDA

2700 Biscayne Blvd., Miami, FL 33137 **305-573-1618.**

LOUISIANA

4403 Veterans Memorial Blvd. Metairie, LA 70006 **504-887-7631; 504-887-0113.**

423 Main Street, Baton Rouge, LA 70802 **504-343-4057; 504-381-9485.**

MISSOURI

1001 Pine Street (at North 10th), St. Louis, MO 63101 **314-621-0346.**

ILLINOIS

172 North Michigan Ave., Chicago, IL 60601 **312-346-4228; 312-346-3240.**

TEXAS

114 Main Plaza, San Antonio, TX 78205 **512-224-8101.**

CALIFORNIA

1570 Fifth Ave. (at Cedar Street), San Diego, CA 92101 **619-232-1442.**

46 Geary Street, San Francisco, CA 94108 **415-781-5180.**

WASHINGTON

2301 Second Ave., Seattle, WA 98121 **206-441-3300.**

HAWAII

1143 Bishop Street, Honolulu, HI 96813 **808-521-2731.**

ALASKA

750 West 5th Ave., Anchorage, AK 99501 **907-272-8183.**

CANADA

3022 Dufferin Street, Toronto 395, Ontario, Canada.